Hattie

A Woman's Mission to Burma

Joan W. Swift

Half Meadow Press
San Geronimo, CA
2003

Half Meadow Press
PO Box 99
San Geronimo, CA 94963

This book is dedicated
to my grandfather, Herman K. Phinney,
family errand-runner, who so meticulously
preserved the Burma letters,
and to my mother, Louise P. Woodcock,
who saved and passed them on to me.

Table of Contents

Author's Prologue

When I was a child growing up in a New York City apartment, my grandparents' home in Rochester, New York, was always a place of fascination for me. This fascination was based in part on my mother's tales of her childhood in that house, and in part on the house itself and its contents.

To me, the only child of two career-centered parents, my mother's stories of growing up in Rochester in the late 1800s and early 1900s seemed to exemplify all the glamour of small town life in America: living in a single family house with an extended family, grandparents, parents and sibling, occasional visits from aunts, uncles and cousins, in a community of friends and neighbors of all ages, attending church socials, picnics by the river, Hallowe'en and the Fourth of July celebrations — these were familiar to me only in books or through my mother's reminiscences.

The house in Rochester held another kind of glamour as well. It was filled with curios from a romantic-sounding foreign place, Burma. These "curiosities" had been sent home by my grandfather's brother and sister who were missionaries in Burma. There were colorful lacquerware boxes on the corner whatnot, brightly colored fans on the wall, two tall, elaborately decorated vases standing in the hallway entrance to the parlor, and several images of Gautama Buddha arranged on the bookshelves. Two larger Gautama figures surveyed the living room from their places on the floor as door-stops, their lowly positions ensuring that this devout Baptist family could not be accused of worshiping heathen idols. These curios and the stories I heard about my great-aunt and uncle seemed reflections of a true-life Kipling story; the Road to Mandalay with its flying fishes, pagodas, and Burmese maidens seemed to embody all the mystery and excitement of the East.

When the time came to close up the family home in Rochester and sort through the accumulated relics of three generations of family living, I became the custodian not only of those long-coveted Burma curiosities, but also of a legacy of considerably greater significance: the "Burma letters." These letters, saved faithfully by my grandfather throughout his lifetime, covered the period from 1882 to 1938, and consisted of weekly letters from my great-uncle Frank Phinney, who served as Superintendent of the American Baptist Mission Press in Rangoon for 40 years (1882-1922), and from my great-aunt Harriet, or Hattie, Phinney, who served as a teacher and missionary in Burma for over 52 years (1886-1938). Also included were the weekly letters to Frank and Hattie from the members of the Rochester household covering the first nine years of the correspondence (1882-1891). These had been saved by Frank and returned to the family archives on a visit home. In all, the collection included several thousand individual letters from family members, most handwritten although many, from later years, were typed. Accompanying the letters were literally dozens, if not hundreds, of photographs, clippings, and various other enclosures.

Just as the Rochester household held special meaning for me as a child, I found that the letters had an equally compelling meaning to me as an adult. The two facets of the Rochester household that had attracted me as a child, I found reflected in their contents. The early letters provide an intimate view of daily life in late nineteenth century middle class America; the later letters provide a similarly intimate view of daily life in a foreign land, against a background of jungles, Buddhist temples, and the might of the British Raj.

To the family, Frank Phinney was always the hero of the Burma story and his accomplishments were related at length and with great pride. As I read the letters, however, I found Hattie's story the more significant one. Frank's life in Burma was, in many respects, the same that he would have lived had he remained in America: a respected businessman, active in his church and community affairs.

Hattie's life was much more one of her own making. She actively rejected the life that would have been typical of a young woman growing up in her social and economic circumstances. She was determined to find a role that would allow her life "to mean something," as she expressed it. Her search for such a role, her determination in preparing for it, and the particular form that it took, I found to be the more interesting story — one with particular relevance to the women's movement of her day and to the contemporary interest in women's studies in our own.

The decision to make Hattie's story available to a wider audience than the immediate family was based on two attributes of the material: its relevance to an important period in women's history and the firsthand nature of the material itself.

Harriet Phinney might, at first glance, seem an unlikely candidate for biographical attention. Biographies most commonly depict the lives of men or women of historical importance whose leadership, originality, great works of art, literature, or scientific discovery have brought them to the attention of the world. In these terms, Harriet Phinney cannot qualify.

The value of Hattie's life story lies less in her specific accomplishments or her importance as an individual, than in the light her story sheds on a significant time in women's history and in the extent to which her life exemplifies those of many single women of the late nineteenth century who sought to make a life of their own outside the usual domestic role prescribed for them. These women represented an important faction of the women's movement of their day, extending its influence beyond American shores to women around the world.

Students of women's history have decried the paucity of material concerning the role women have played in the major historical events of our society. Equally scarce has been material on the effect of these events on the lives of the women themselves. This lack has been used to explain not only the one-sided nature of historical reporting, but also the failure of society to recognize and address the legitimate political and social concerns of women. As contemporary historians attempt to construct a more accurate picture of the roles women have played, as individuals and as a class, they have come to recognize the invaluable resource represented by the firsthand accounts of women's lives to be found in their personal documents. The answer to the proverbial question "What *do* women want?" is found not only in the demands of political activists but in the study of individual women's lives as revealed in their own words in letters, diaries, and journals.

Hattie's letters provide such a resource — a picture of the life of one woman, her activities, hopes, and concerns on an almost daily basis over a period of 56 years, from late adolescence to her final illness at the age of 77. They offer a close-up, firsthand view of the times in which she lived and the events in which she participated.

The format in which I have elected to present Hattie's story was chosen with these considerations in mind. For readers' convenience, abbreviations have been filled in and spelling and punctuation modernized, but insofar as possible, I have let Hattie tell her story in her own words as she wrote them in her letters home or, as in the early letters, to her brother Frank in Burma.

Acknowledgments

I would like to express my appreciation to the American Baptist Historical Society and to the Baptist Convention in Rangoon for their assistance in providing valuable information about the Burma mission and other materials relevant to Hattie's story. I would like to thank U Tha Din, director of the Myanmar Theological Institute, for his hospitality.

I would also like to express my appreciation to my daughter Barbara, who not only served in her professional capacity as editor, but whose interest and enthusiasm for the project made it more enjoyable. Also to my son-in-law, Laurence Brauer, in his role as typesetter and publisher, and to my husband Hewson, as photographic adviser, who made this project a family affair

The family circa 1867: Hattie, Elizabeth, Frank, Lincoln (1865-1867), Smith Hollister, and Herman Phinney.

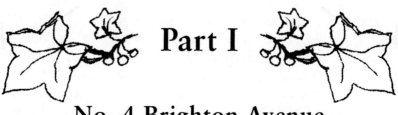

Part I

No. 4 Brighton Avenue

The correspondence upon which this life of Hattie Phinney is based began in January 1882, when her older brother Frank left home to assume a position at the American Baptist Mission Press in Rangoon, Burma. The family's weekly letters to Frank provide an intimate picture of the Phinneys and the household in which Hattie grew up and lived as a young woman.

In 1882, Harriet ("Hattie") Elizabeth Phinney, at 20, was a quiet, demure looking young woman, still girlish in her enthusiasms and interests. Her life was typical of many young women of her day and social class, centered around home and family, church and friends. As the youngest and the only girl, her role in the family was relatively undemanding.

Her father, Smith Hollister Phinney, was a skilled cabinetmaker and carpenter who worked as an independent contractor on a wide variety of jobs. While he enjoyed working with his hands (as the many examples of intricate inlaid furniture among the household furnishings attested), carpentry had not been his first choice of vocation. As a young man, he had aspired to a career with the church, but lack of money for the necessary education had made this impossible. He had had to be content with involvement as a layman in local church affairs, serving as a deacon and participating as fully as he could in the support of foreign and home mission work.

Smith Hollister's awareness of the importance of an education was reflected in the academic achievements of his two sons. Despite what must have been a serious economic burden on the family, both attended college and went on to complete Master of Arts degrees at the University of Rochester. Their sister, by contrast, received only a high school education.

Hattie's oldest brother, Herman Kent Phinney ("HK" to the family), was 25 years old in 1882 and employed at the University of Rochester Library. He lived at home, helping to support the family with his earnings and serving as errand-runner and escort to the ladies of the family. A quiet, gentle, and self-effacing person, Herman was a Greek and Latin scholar, and held a degree in Library Science. He, too, was an active member of the Baptist church, serving in a variety of roles in church activities.

Frank Dennison Phinney, a year younger, was the more outgoing, opinionated, and adventurous of the two brothers. Well-educated, well-read, and intellectually keen, Frank was also a hands-on practical person, whose skill with machinery of any kind was fully utilized in his vocation as printer. He was, in addition, an excellent business man. During and after college, Frank had operated a small printing business.

Their mother, neé Elizabeth Caroline Sill, was homemaker and church member, actively involved in the Woman's Home Mission Society. She was a strong, independent character, and, it seems, the decision maker of the family. She emerges from the letters as the central figure in the family constellation, the person to whom the children related most closely, whose opinion they relied on, whose approval they sought, and over whom they expressed the greatest concern. Where "Papa" was optimistic and accepting (except in matters of church doctrine or politics), "Mama" was a worrier, pessimistic and often critical, her letters filled with admonitions and complaints.

The family lived in a neat two-story frame house located at 4 Brighton Avenue, on a tree-shaded street not far from the university and center of the city. Built by Smith Hollister Phinney in 1862, it would remain the family home until Herman Phinncy's death in 1939. Painted grey with white trim, it was a modest house, both out of economic necessity and moral principle. Downstairs the front hall opened to the parlor, appropriately furnished for formal visiting, and the sitting room, with comfortable chairs for reading, a center table for writing, an organ, a variety of bookcases, and pictures on the walls. A small room that served as the library, a small bedroom, and the kitchen opened off the sitting room. A back door from the kitchen led to the workshop where Smith Hollister kept his woodworking materials and tools, and Frank set up his printing press. A flight of stairs just inside the front door led up to four bedrooms on the second floor, each opening off the small central hall. In the backyard grew pear, apple, and cherry trees.

If not actually poor, the Phinneys were certainly not well off. Their principal income came from Smith Hollister's work as a cabinetmaker and carpenter. He was not salaried, however, and the demand for his services fluctuated widely. Herman's salary at the university and from extra small jobs he undertook contributed to the support of the family, but the amount was modest. Frank, once settled in Burma, also took it on himself to contribute to the family's support. There was always enough to eat, one can assume, but not always enough for a needed new winter coat or assistance with the housework. Attendance at out-of-town church meetings, family trips, new clothes, or needed household items were always subject to the family's financial situation at the time.

As devout members of the Baptist church attended by students and faculty of the Theological Seminary, the Phinneys numbered many of the latter among their family friends. The seminary graduates supplied numerous mission stations, and the Phinneys took an active interest in their work. Charts kept by Smith Hollister tracked missionaries' comings and goings between Rochester and foreign stations.

Frank's assignment to the Mission Press was an excellent opportunity for a young man of his skills and business acumen. The Burma Mission, headquartered in Rangoon at that time, was well established. The press played a central role in the work of the mission, providing religious tracts for evangelical use as well as texts and pamphlets for the mission schools.

Frank Phinney sailed from New York on the *City of Berlin* on January 26, 1882. Reaching London on February 7, he boarded the *India* for Calcutta on the 23rd, and finally arrived on the *Chinsura* at Rangoon, Burma, on April 18th. His departure began a correspondence between Rochester and Burma that would continue for the next 57 years.

Harriet Elizabeth Phinney (June 1881).

1

Hattie at Home

1882

The letters sent to Frank from 4 Brighton Avenue each week were a family project in those early years, each member writing his or her contribution to the joint letter, often commenting on the others' remarks. As her portions of the letters reveal, Hattie's relationship with Frank was particularly close and affectionate. While his letters were addressed in a general way to the whole family — "Dear Folks at Home" — Hattie's were intimate and personal (calling herself "Your Old Woman" and him "My Old Man," "Bohunkus," etc.), filled with references to family jokes and activities they had shared. With their myriad details, the letters offer a view of Hattie, and her life and interests at that time.

Hattie's social life revolved around the small group of friends with whom she had grown up, members of the church and Sunday school she attended. The Manvels next door, Livia, Mary, and Emily; Julia Perry, Nellie and Mamie Phillips and others figured regularly in her letters. While young men were mentioned in her accounts of Sunday school or Young People's Mission Society meetings, they played little part in her everyday social life, primarily made up of visits to friends' homes or short excursions to nearby attractions.

Frank had been an important and popular member of the social group to which they belonged, and Hattie had enjoyed a measure of reflected glory as his sister. In his big brother role, he had been escort, advisor, and confidante. In Frank's absence, Herman was available for escort service when needed, but his attentions were usually engaged elsewhere, as escort to Miss Hopkins, whom he later married; Hattie was often obliged to attend major social events as a third party. Not surprisingly, Hattie felt Frank's absence keenly.

Attendance at church and Sunday school on Sunday, and prayer and mission society meetings during the week provided a consistent structure around which life's more temporal activities — visiting, household chores, shopping — were ordered. Hattie was expected to help her mother with domestic chores, but these do not appear to have interfered with her hobby of painting, her enjoyment of reading, trips downtown, or visits with friends. Although considered "weakly," Hattie's letters report a wide variety of projects undertaken and completed.

Hattie's strongest interest and particular skill was painting, which she used in a variety of projects designed to brighten up the house. A major project over several months was that of decorating a complete china tea set for the family. Each week's activities were duly noted in Hattie's letters.

Apr. 9, '82

Beloved Beeswax,

I've been on the go four nights out of six this week, besides going downtown twice. Thursday evening was the Young People's Mission Society at the Williams on Rowley St. It rained as it has the last three times, so that only about 40 came out. We had a review Geography lesson by Mr. Burton; I read a short history of the year; Joe Gilmore gave a treasurer's report. The collections have amounted to $32.60; $6.00 went to pay freight on the goods sent to Mr. Cohenour (Joe read a letter from him and Dr. Morehouse), the mounting of the map of Burma was paid out of it, and $7.00 each was sent to the Home and Foreign Mission Societies, leaving a little over $8.00 in the Treasury. Maggie Townsen read a letter from Mr. and Mrs. Waterbury and then, as before arranged by the committee, Joe moved that Mr. Burton appoint a committee of nomination. He appointed Joe, Mr. Williams, Miss Osborn. They soon returned and gave the list the committee had decided upon, viz. — Mr. Barss, Mr. Ellison, C. Caldwell, Jennie Knowles, Lillie Whiting, Carrie Arnold, who were unanimously elected.

Wednesday Julia Perry and I went calling on the Arnolds who sit before us in church and on Mrs. Lewis and Mrs. Thomas. Livia had been at me to call on the Arnolds and said if I would she would make some candy to sweeten me up, so last night she sent for me (and Herman) and they made molasses and white sugar candy — partly coconut — chocolate and nut. It was all very nice. I wished you were there. Herman came in there after Library.

This week I painted a tile for Mary Manvel's birthday, the background dark-green-clouded and pink cyclamen in the white leaf [sketches]. Miss Alling gave me two little holly plates, a shoe and fan to be painted in watercolor for a friend of hers. As there was to be some gilt on them I got some gold powder and liquid to put it on with, at Barnard's, I painted them yesterday thereby earning $1.00. I haven't given any lessons this week.

I have read lately two volumes of essays by Matthews. I've also been busy getting up watercolor patterns for china paint-ing to use if I should ever have pupils. I painted an Easter panel (grey) with yellow, purple, and white crocuses growing out of snow and the motto "Behold I am alive forever more." It stands on the bracket over the organ. I don't take lessons on that yet, but play considerable.

I hope you are well and have lots of bananas and not too much work. Give my regards to all the folks that are good to you!
> Your forlorn old woman,
> HP

Mar. 26, '82

Dear Old Boy,

I suppose you remember the pieces of birch-bark that you sent me from Michigan; I've just got around to paint on them, putting a young man waving a handkerchief on one and a girl throwing a kiss on the other, both in quaint costumes.

Monday I went to see Miss Towsey [of the Deaf-Mute Institute]. I also saw Mr. Sutherland but Mr. and Mrs. Westervelt are in New York. I took the views you sent from London and Miss Towsey showed them to her pupils and explained. One of them had asked the day before where Mr. Phinney was. As she talked one boy asked where Mrs. Phinney was and thought that I was Mrs. Phinney. When she said that I was your sister he inquired if I was her sister.

Tuesday I gave a lesson to Miss Marshall and positively the last one to Mrs. Coats.

Frank Dennison Phinney (August 1881).

We have three odd tea plates like the others but no cups or saucers. One is painted with a spray of blackberry blossoms across the plate, which is tinted brown-green one side of spray, the other is tinted light brown with a band left white and across this is a brown branch with scarlet berries on it. I have also been making watercolor patterns for any pupils I may have.

Thursday we had Miss Coats and Julia Perry to tea and Friday Mamie came and stayed to tea; both times we used china. Under the impression the photos were directed to me, I took them down and had them mounted. We all enjoy them, whoever they were sent to. Last night Mama and I took the "Tomus Tertius" [the third volume of the log Frank kept on his voyage from America to Burma] to the Manvels. Nellie and Mrs. Dickson were there; they all enjoyed it very much, but not more than we have. I'm sorry you had such a rough voyage; you didn't say how the [Thomssen] baby stood it.

The Coats have got to move this week but don't know yet where they can go!

As ever,
Your Old Woman

May 7, '82

Dear Bohunkus,

Monday, having come to the conclusion that I needed a new dress as a "go-between" Mama said if I could get one up for $4.00 or less I might have one, so Monday afternoon I went downtown and bought the material, black serge and small round yellow (gilt) buttons — two dozen. The rest of the week till Thursday afternoon was spent in making it. It cost the immense sum of $2.50! but it is quite pretty and satisfactory. I also bought an embroidered turn down collar, 50 cents.

Monday evening I heard Dr. Jameson's lecture on Burma at Seminary Chapel, and Thursday evening I went to the Young People's Mission Society at the Campbells. Mr. Barss presided and did very nicely. The subject was China. Mr. Burton led in prayer, remembering you and the Waterburys. Then a short geography lesson on Africa by Mr. Barss, a short article by Mr. Ellison on the religious observances of Chinese in connection with small pox; a very good essay on Confucius by Mr. Simonson; a duet by Misses Barrett and Weed; an interesting essay on the condition of women in China by Fanny Heath. It was a very good meeting and attended by 60 or 70.

Papa has paid for a pickle dish to go with our tea set and I shall probably paint it this week. It is the last article of the set. The whole is worth between $60 and $70.

Today I taught Mrs. Coats' class, she being at Auburn; she wants me to take it for the summer as they are going to spend the summer at Auburn, Mr. Coats continuing to preach there; perhaps I shall.

That's all.
Ye Old Woman.

May 28, '82

Dear Old Beeswax,

All the painting I've done this week is a watercolor sketch of a branch of firebush, but the frames for my oil painting came Monday and they have been hung — the scarecrow in the sitting room and the other one each side of the heliotype on the parlor; they serve to fill up blank space very well.

I made me a black lace and silk collar to wear with my black dress and wore it to the sociable at Miss Bannings. The sociables are rather stupid and some of the young gentlemen (?) ill behaved. I've made a commode cloth and bureau cloth of white linen with knotted fringe and drawn work for my room and a bureau cloth like mine for Mama.

I received a letter from Miss Coats, she is teaching a country school of 15, on her father's farm. I have also, at last, heard from Lucy. She says your visit was the pleasantest thing that had happened since they went to India. They were at Rose Cottage, Ercand, and had been there four days — April 5-9 and felt 10% better already.

Friday afternoon Nellie Phillips had a half day off and she and Mamie came up here. They said they were dead beat but were bound to go <u>somewhere</u> anyway, and wanted me to go too and Julia if she would; so we four took the street cars and went to the lower falls; we didn't take a boat; the river is very high and the current rapid. Mama had given us a nice lunch to which Julia contributed a cake and Nellie four oranges. We had a pleasant time and came back with our hands full of apple blossoms.

Tom Phillips with two others sailed for Europe yesterday on the *Australian Monarch*. Mr. Bing sailed on the same steamer.

I guess that is all. If you've got any bananas to spare send 'em round and oblige,

Yours,

Old Woman

June 4, '82

The great event of the week was the Young People's Mission Society meeting, which was held here Thursday evening; and the most we have done was to get ready for it and straighten up after it. The whole house looked bright and pleasant and as good as anybody's and the society wasn't stiff at all. The subject was home missions: a letter from Mr. Hoppel was read by Julia Perry, letters from Albert McGill and the matron (at Columbia) of Benedict Institute, and a composition by one of the pupils there, were read by Nellie Phillips, an essay by B. Fay and an article by Miss Thomas. After the exercises the society voted to give $50 to support the pupil, before mentioned, next year at the Benedict Institute as Mr. McGill requested in his letter; $20, which was in the treasury, was appropriated toward it; $18.50 was subscribed at once, to be paid in a month — the rest will doubtless be raised soon.

Monday evening Julia took me to an entertainment given by the Young Woman's Temperance Union; it consisted of music and readings by Professor Thatcher.

Hattie's description of a visit from May Parker, a friend who lived in Philadelphia and whom she had not seen for some time, was an unusually lively one. May had returned to Rochester for a three-week visit and Hattie was able to reestablish their close relationship. Some of the "high jinks" reported seem to reflect an earlier period in their lives. Hattie clearly enjoyed the opportunity to regress a little.

Aug. 6, '82

May and I are sprawled over a section of the floor with various pillows, fans, books, and your lap-robe; having been here for four hours or more, we are in a somewhat crumpled condition (May says her crimps are all out, and she has wrinkled one waist

so much that she has put on No. 2 to wrinkle). It's awful hot!!!!
May came here last night and has spent the day with me; of
course we went to church, and since then we've talked!

Aug. 16, '82

This is a Wednesday morning but since we had some
high jinks yesterday it is thought best that I should chronicle
them at once for your edification. May, Eva, Julia, and Livia
were invited over yesterday for the afternoon and evening.
All came but Eva. Before tea we did fancy work, then we
five had tea early (as Papa comes rather late). We all did
justice to the supper; of course we used the china — Mamie
always chooses the pink set (Mama's). Then we adjourned
to the front steps and all sat in a row on your rug, but just
after tea we had all escorted Livia over home and back to
get a box of knitting samples, which we examined on the
steps. While Julia tried to show May some stitch, Livia and I
sang the "Vassar Song" to their great amusement. Then we
tried Livia's performance of slapping your knees and then
finding your nose and one ear; after much hilarity May and
Julia got so they could do it. While we were fooling Mary
and Emily came over and we all sat on the steps and told
stories. Livia asked, "Why kissing the girls was like eating
soup with a fork?" — "Because you never get enough!"

Just then Mama came to the door and invited us in. On the
extension table in the dining-kitchen room we beheld plates,
fruit knives, and napkins and watermelon! May jumped
straight up and down and the rest said "Oh!!!" Then we fell to,
everybody helped someone else and we had a jolly time over it;
Livia got a very thick piece the second time and said it was too
thick for her mouth. Mary said it wasn't and Julia seized the
hunk in one hand, held Livia's head with the other and so put
one corner in her mouth, when Livia immediately vanished
into the pantry to swallow it. May had to hop up and down to
settle hers. I had given Emily the caster chair and after a little
she tipped forward on two legs of it when it rolled from under
her, letting her gently flat onto the floor, much to her own and
our amusement.

Sept. 24, '82

Big chair, Parlor window

Here followeth the "weakly" chronicle. Monday evening
we five, viz. the Marshalls, Miss Stobum, Julia, and I, having
agreed to meet every Tuesday afternoon and have me read
while they worked — Julia and I went to the Professor's and
borrowed the *Undiscovered Country* by Howells; the Professor
also lent <u>me</u> *Gaddings with a Primitive People* (in the Tyrolese),
then we dropped in on the Manvels for a few minutes. Tuesday
morning Mrs. Manvel started alone for Massachusetts. The
afternoon I spent at Julia's reading to the girls the first five
chapters of the aforementioned book. Wednesday afternoon I
made calls on Mrs. Coats, Miss Knowles, and Miss Gaylord —
who wished to be remembered to you. She is tutoring some
pupils and helping Jessie through High School. On my way
home I fell in with Miss Hopkins who was coming to see us; so
Mama persuaded her to stay to tea. Thursday evening I went
to a candy-pull at Julia's, "we five," her brother Ed and his
wife, her cousin Maggie Mathews and another young lady
being the party. We sang the "Vassar Song," played "School"
and "Tub" and "Going to Jerusalem" and as some doubted the
possibility of a number of people lifting a person with their
forefingers, all holding their breath, I lay down and they lifted
me as high as their shoulders. Herman came for me while we
were all pulling candy, so we each had a little plateful to bring
home. Friday Eva Kratz called; she says May is to be married
in October.

Through letters, Hattie and the family were able to keep Frank
current with activities at home, and also to share, vicariously, in his
adventures. The first of his letters received at No. 4 Brighton Avenue consisted of Frank's account of his two-month voyage to
Burma recorded in a series of detailed logs, which the family proudly
shared with neighbors and friends, as Hattie reported.

Feb. 26, '82

Your Log-a-Rhythm [Frank's title] duly arrived. . . . Last
night Mama and I took Volume 1 over to the Manvels and I
read it aloud for their benefit; they enjoyed it as much as we.

Apr. 23, '82

In the afternoon Nellie Phillips came from school here to
read your logs (fourth and fifth) and Mary and Emily came to
hear the fourth so then Nellie went after Livia so that all might
hear the fifth.

June 11, '82

Thursday evening I read the last Log to the Manvels; they
gave me a vote of thanks for reading them all and sent their
best wishes and regards etc. etc. to you and said that if there
were no more Logs they would be thankful for Sticks or Chips.

Oct. 29, '82

Wednesday morning, as it was pleasant, I went to keep my
promise of reading to Mrs. Anderson some of your logs. I read
half of "A Tramp on the Tow-Path" log and then a caller came
so I withdrew. Mrs. Anderson said she enjoyed it very much
indeed and she wished to be remembered to you.

[Thursday] Mrs. Anderson came in a carriage and made a
call on us. Her errand was to borrow the log I had read from,
and others if we were willing, to read to the Doctor, as she was
very much interested and knew he would be. So she has the
second, fourth, and fifth Logs.

The arrival of a shipment of curios from Frank was greeted
with great excitement and enthusiasm.

Mar. 13, '83

We haven't done much of anything all this blessed week
but look at the things from over the seas, and show them to
others. Twenty persons have seen them so far, part of them
came in without knowing about them. Mrs. Ben Harris came
on an errand shortly after the goods arrived Monday, so she
was the first outsider to see them; then Julia dropped in in the
afternoon and we called in Hattie Perry as she was passing; we
gave Julia a napkin with your compliments, she was very much
obliged. The Hopkins were invited to come and see Tuesday
evening but before they arrived the three Manvels and Nellie
came over for a call, not knowing what had come, so while we
were showing them the things, the Hopkins came; they all

enjoyed the "show" very much. Mama has sent one of each kind of napkin to Miss Hopkins and she sent one large one to Mrs. Manvel and gave Mary and Emily each one of the smaller ones. Livia and Nellie were pleased with their parasols.

Thursday evening the Caldwells, Susie Webb, Joe Gilmore, Bert, and Mamie were invited and Livia to help us entertain the boys, all came but Bert and Mamie, tho the boys had another engagement and so didn't stay very long but examined everything while they did. Joe looks very well in the solar topee and you should hear Charles ring the Delhi bell as if he was a very enthusiastic scissor grinder.

Mrs. Perry came to see the things Thursday afternoon and yesterday just after dinner Mrs. Coats happened in and while she was looking at the goods, Lillie Whiting came on an errand and before they were through looking Mamie came, the last stayed to tea and went to church with me. While we were at supper Jessie Titus came, so I did nothing all afternoon but act as show-woman. I don't think I want to explain them all over <u>more</u> than four or five times in <u>one</u> afternoon.

We have put up one of each kind [of napkin] in the sitting room — under the plaques and over the machine under the picture, the Manvels have put theirs up in the parlor and so has Mrs. Caldwell. I have put up three in my bedroom also; they show up beautifully on our white walls, and so does the scroll (which was a little mildewed); it hangs between the bedroom and closet door. Mamie and I got up quite a charming (?) concert yesterday with the Delhi and Burmese bells and the Chinese gong.

But what shall I say of the fans, slippers, and screen? Words fail me!! Of course the screen goes ahead of all else and is the pride of our hearts and the delight of our eyes, not to say the envy of our neighbors! It's handsomer than anything we've ever seen or expect to see, and the effect when it is stood open in the doorway between the parlor and sitting room is charming and so is the effect of the lamplight or sunlight shining through it. Everyone admires it intensely and some exclaim "Did <u>that</u> come too!!!!" But I'm not sure but that my slippers get quite as much admiration; they show off magnificently in the evening and are altogether the handsomest piece of embroidery seen around here. They are quite too utterly too-too. I'm afraid I can't "live up" to them!

The sandalwood fans are exquisite. I shall enjoy carrying
mine very much indeed. I think I shall come out next summer
under the green ribbed parasol. I consider it the prettiest, tho the
inside of the priest's umbrella is something surprising. Please
accept my most profound and elaborate acknowledgements and
thanks ad infinitum, for the slippers and fan, also the pleasure
received from all the collection.

Filled with descriptions of her many daily activities, Hattie's
portions of the weekly family letters reflected no discontent with
her life. In a private letter to Frank written during a visit away
from home, however, Hattie expressed a different sentiment.

Jan. 28, '83
   A year today since you sailed and a pretty long year it's
been, and certainly not over jolly or satisfactory. About the
pleasantest thing in it has been the friendship of Julia and the
four teachers I know at the Deaf Mute Institute, but I'm almost
entirely cut off from them now that the cars are stopped.
There has ceased to be much but an ordinary acquaintance
between Mamie Phillips and I — she has not visited me but
once since September (when May was visiting) and that was to
see your gifts. But I shall not cry so long as I have at least five
to take her place, each one of whom is more loveable than she
is now. Of course we have never quarreled but simply grown
apart. I presume outsiders think we are as great friends as ever.

By the end of the first year of Frank's absence, Hattie's role as
little sister and obedient helper to her mother was no longer enough
to fill her life. This letter foreshadows Hattie's increasing determination to find an adult role for herself to which she could apply
her varied and considerable skills. Her search would continue over
the coming months.

 2

Seeds of Change

1883 to 1884

In the year following Frank's departure, a number of changes had taken place among Hattie's friends and the young people of her acquaintance. Her close friend May Parker had moved away and was soon to be married; Julia Perry and Mamie Phillips had similar plans. Other young women were establishing themselves in careers. Helen McGill, Miss Ely, and Miss Towsey taught at the Deaf Mute Institute. Several others were also teachers.

> Sept. 17, '82
> Angie Oviatt teaches at No. 25 Public School, corner of
> Goodman and Bay Streets; Maggie Townsen teaches at No. 9,
> Nellie Phillips, Emily, and Livia Manvel are at their old places.

Hattie, with neither matrimonial plans nor training for a career, could not help but feel some lack in her life. Two events the following April served both to accentuate Hattie's situation and, each in its way, help move her closer to articulating a plan of her own.

The first of these was her brother Herman's marriage to Ada Hopkins, who joined the family in the 4 Brighton Avenue home. Eleven years Hattie's senior, Ada was a trained kindergarten teacher who had operated her own small private school in Rochester. She was a spirited and attractive young woman.

The marriage was precipitated by a sudden breakdown in Ada's health and the necessity for her to give up her school and the home she had shared with her parents. Ada thus entered the family as a semi-invalid, adding to the burden of the housekeeping rather than

Wedding photo of Herman K. Phinney and Ada Hopkins, April 1883.

providing assistance to Hattie and her mother. While Ada's health made it impossible for the couple to establish an independent household initially, it is probable that the financial situation of the family required Herman's income to meet expenses. There was no talk of Herman and Ada's setting up a home of their own at that time.

Mar. 25, '83

Dear Old Man,

Last Sunday I heard for the first time that HK intended to commit matrimony in the immediate future. Only three weeks or so before the time. When you get married if you don't let us know longer ahead I won't come to the wedding (perhaps) so there!

Thursday I went and bought me a new spring dress, which I needed anyway, and as I can't afford anything better it will serve to wear to the wedding. Mama has nothing suitable to wear there, in my opinion, and don't talk as if she intended to get anything; says she has ordinary dresses enough and can't afford a very nice one. Mine is olive green (rather light) cotton one way and wool the other, and has collar and cuffs of very dark velvet. It will have a sack to match. I wanted to hire Mary Manvel to work the button holes; she did work them and then wouldn't take any pay. Mama and I got the dress pretty well along.

Saturday Mama and I went downtown and ordered for HK a new carpet for the big room upstairs of the same tints as the one in my room (which I leave for them; HK will get one for the room I shall have by and by). Mama says she will give me $25 for my room; as far as preference goes I rather have the room than the money, but it is evident they can't be comfortable otherwise.

What do you think of having a new sister anyway? You can't call her <u>Your Old Woman.</u>

Apr. 15, '83

Dear Bubby,

It's orful hot and I'm <u>orful</u> tired. This having a wedding in the family is powerful hard work, <u>I tell you</u>! Monday I got some very pretty brass handles for the newly blacked hall table drawers. It's a very nobby table now. Tuesday I helped in the

work of settling etc. upstairs some, and blacked the old lounge
for Ada to have in the front room; it has on the red cushions
that were on the hall lounge and <u>that</u> is in the shop, and a hair
cloth tete-a-tete of Ada's is in its place. Wednesday morning I
went and got for HK an oilcloth to put under their stove,
which is a little one of Ada's.

In the afternoon I went to the wedding!!!!! Which was a
very quiet affair — Mrs. Converse, Pray, Robinson, Ballou,
Cogswell, Miss Florence, and Josie Kendrick (all better dressed
than Mama or I), Dr. Benedict, Will Witter, Ed Angell, and Mr.
Cogswell were about all that were there beside Dr. Kendrick
and the two families, i.e., we three and Mr. and Mrs. Hopkins.
Mrs. Ballou and I went in the carriage to the depot with them.

That night and the next morning early Mama and I finished putting down the hall carpet which had been up and
cleaned. The carman brought Ada's things over in two loads,
the tete-a-tete, bureau, spring bed and mattress, small stand
and table, and trunk; and the rest was all small articles, pictures, books (lots of 'em), boxes innumerable and bric-a-brac
by the bushel. I guess if Ada had been well enough to see to it,
alot of it wouldn't have come. It took Mama and I all day to
get it up to their rooms and "sorter" settled; they (the rooms)
are well-filled now I assure you and are <u>very</u> pleasant and
homelike.

Forlorn Old Woman. No beau left.

Not long after the wedding, the Phinneys received a visit from
Will Witter, a family relative and student at the Theological Seminary. Mr. Witter would be graduating from the Seminary in the
summer and planned to go into missionary work in Assam, India,
the following fall. Hattie's account of his visit is the first mention
of her personal hope to follow Frank to Burma.

Apr. 29, '83
The great happenstance was Mr. Witter's visit yesterday.
He came some after five and stayed to tea. I wonder what you
would have said if you could have heard him <u>go for</u> me in his
most hearty and emphatic way. He and his future bride, Mary
Potter, expect to sail in September and he does <u>so much</u> want
me to offer myself to the Woman's Mission Board to go as a

teacher to the Kemindine School and <u>sail with them.</u> "What <u>would</u> Frank say if you should turn up someday at Rangoon? Why, he <u>would just collapse!!!</u>"

He is <u>perfectly</u> certain that the Board would gladly accept me and pay me $500 a year for what work I could do and <u>he</u> knows I could do a fair amount, even if I am not strong. "There's Mr. Waterbury, whose health was so poor that many thought he was crazy to go, but he writes that his health is better than when here." Mr. Witter wants me to go on your account and because he knows I'd like to and because it would be so perfectly splendid to go together.

All this was "iterated and reiterated" with great earnestness. I remarked that I had been talking of taking up a collection to meet expenses so I could go to Rangoon and take care of my old man (of course he needs it and Mrs. Binney [Frank's housekeeper] can't live forever) and do missionary work besides. He instantly thrust his hand into his pocket and brought forth and offered me a handful of change saying that he would give me all he had. But as he is going on a mission I didn't take it.

Now if I was big and fat and hearty! But then I might also be stupid and want to stay at home. What you think? Hay? Got any place in the Press where I could be useful as well as ornamental. I'm neither here, but no knowing what I might develop into under favorable circumstances. Ain't it?

While Hattie's description of the visit might suggest a spontaneous interest in joining Frank in Rangoon, Hattie's private letter, sent two days later and separate from the weekly family letter, reveals the sincerity of her feelings.

May 1, '83

My Dear Brother,

This is a very much in earnest letter. I am disgusted with this kind of life, doing a little of everything and not much of anything and being dependent, and am <u>very much</u> averse to puttering away any more years as I have the last five. There must be two or three times as many girls here as there is occupation for, of any kind, and the most I have to look forward to, or hope for, is by some means, I don't know what, to earn something for my support. But my hopes are almost extinct even about this, for I've had it on my mind ever since I graduated and have never seen an opening yet. Even if I had some secular occupation right to my hand I shouldn't be contented for I do want my life to amount to something; I want to live for something higher than mere food and raiment.

I've long been thinking that if I were once at Rangoon, where there is more Christian work and fewer to do it, I certainly would find something to do that would be <u>worthwhile</u> and I shouldn't be, at least, entirely dependent on others. If I were there, couldn't I have some such position as Mrs. Sloan did; or could not I help Mrs. Binney, be her amanuensis, etc. etc. enough to pay for board and perhaps later we two could set up housekeeping; or couldn't I teach little children of missionaries; or in some school after I learned the language (you know I like to study) and as minor work — a class in Sunday School and taking care of your clothing?

I hope you won't take this as a romantic notion of a lazy girl. I don't expect any such easy time as I now have. I want good honest work that shall go toward evangelizing the heathen. Mother thinks if my mind and heart were in the work, and they would be, I could keep up in health as well as others.

As for applying to any Missionary Board, it would take forever and a day and if I was accepted I would be under them, obliged to go and come and work where they said and perhaps not be with you at all.

I don't just know where the funds will come from; how much did your fare cost? But you see how very nice it would be to travel with Mr. Witter and wife (to be); he is so jolly and she, I'm sure, is very lovely. Of course if you don't want your old woman and say you won't have her, why I 'spose she would have to settle down at home, but that would be a bitter pill.

If you should answer this by advising me to come (particularly if you could help) it would leave me over a month to get ready, and Mother and I think it could be done, as I shouldn't want any such outfit as you had and your constantly sending for goods makes it easy to supply any lack. There may never be a better opportunity to come again, and your being in the field already makes it much easier, pleasanter and safer for me to start out on missionary work, than for anybody else I know of.

You are used to thinking fast and acting promptly and I am in hopes you see a niche for me and will let me know at once (one way or the other).

Mother says if it is for my happiness or profit, I won't be hindered from going any more than you were. Mama would lend me her $200 that's in the Bank and I guess I could get the rest from HK and gradually, if I had a salary, I could pay back (and perhaps you would help). If you say "come," make what suggestions you can about bringing bedding etc. etc. I could find out about clothing here.

Hoping a favorable answer, I am,
Your affectionate
'Tother Half

[Postcard] May 5, '83

Dear Brother,

As only Mother knows of my letter about coming to Rangoon with Witter and wife you won't be surprised at its not being mentioned in coming letters, till I hear from you.

<u>Do say I can come.</u> Money will be forthcoming when wanted for passage etc. What would I need for <u>nice</u> dress? Would you meet me at Calcutta?

Hattie.

July 15, '83

I'm tired of waiting for an answer to my letter of May 1st. I find that three months is long to wait in suspense, as I haven't the least idea what your answer will be. I hope it will be favorable or that if you don't advise me to come this fall you will want me next year. Miss Van Meter expects to sail then; of course it would be pleasanter to go with the Witters and Miss Whitman — I think she will sail then and perhaps two more. . . If you say "come" I think you deserve a vacation long enough to come to Calcutta for me. I'm afraid your letter will be hindered by the cholera in Egypt.

The long-awaited reply arrived on August 4 and was clearly not the answer Hattie had hoped for. Frank's letter is not among those sent to the family and must have been directed to Hattie privately. The nature of his answer, however, is clear from Hattie's response.

Aug. 5, '83

Dear Bub,

Your letter in answer to mine came yesterday and quite settled the matter. I've no intention of going to Rangoon just for the fun of the thing, or to live with you with no occupation or income. I perceive there is about as much of an opening there as here, which is none at all. As for teaching at the Deaf-Mute Institute, if I had $100 training in a Kindergarten and some year or two of experience to back me, as Helen McGill had, and if there happened to be a vacancy, I might hope to get in, provided there weren't too many others trying for it. I might perhaps get a position there as attendant or nursery maid.

Your views on marriage are evidently sound; I hope you'll live up to them. I haven't any use for the good advice — my acquaintance among theological students being exceedingly limited (HK looks after me as well as his wife) — but I'll carefully preserve it for future reference. You can set your mind at rest.

I'm very much obliged for your promptness and clearness in answering.

If you ever do see an opening for me let me know. Mama thinks a Board wouldn't look at a girl not more than 22 years old.

As ever,
Hattie.

The Witters sailed for India in the fall, and there was no further mention of the Witter-inspired plan in Hattie's letters. It was to be almost a year before the subject of Hattie's leaving home surfaced again.

Meanwhile, faced with a return to "doing a little of everything and not much of anything," Hattie explored the few options for employment she could find.

Aug. 26, '83

Wednesday I wrote to S. A. Ellis asking if the position of drawing teacher was vacant at the Deaf-Mute Institute and to whom one should apply. He answered by suggesting that I apply to Mr. Westervelt in person, if he were home, or to write to him. I did the latter, as I couldn't go so far on a supposition, and now wait an answer.

Sept. 2, '83

I heard from Mr. Westervelt that they were not going to have any drawing teacher there, on account of lack of funds.

Over the previous year and a half, Hattie's painting had served both as a hobby and as a small source of pin money. She had given painting lessons to friends, decorated china pieces for birthday gifts, and undertaken lettering tasks for Church and Sunday School events upon request. The previous December, Mrs. Alling, the owner of a small commercial china decorating firm had approached Hattie about helping out on a number of occasions. In August of 1883, Hattie began work with the Allings on a more regular basis.

Aug. 19, '83

Friday and Saturday I painted at the Allings'. I don't like it as it is cheap store work on which I learn very little, and tho it is hard, wearing work I never can earn, at it, more than $1.20 or at most $1.40 a day ($.20 an hour). Mr. Alling expects to have a good deal of work for me, much of it decorating tobacco jars! Highly improving and important work!!(?)

Sept. 9, '83

Wednesday I painted and went to Prayer meeting which was a good one. Thursday I painted! Friday I painted! Saturday I painted!!! Most of this week's work has been on the fruit plates, tho the green (dinner plates) ones are not near done. The fruit plates have all sorts of fruits in natural colors, life size, outlined in black with gold background and edge. They will be the handsomest fruit plates I ever saw. I have painted the leaves and Miss Alling the fruit except that I have painted entirely two plates with thorn-apples. They have all got to be done next Saturday. Wish you could see them. The fruit plates must be done Tuesday for a breakfast to be given the Judge Advocate from England. Last night Mr. Alling paid me $14.65 for two week's work (lacking about two days).

The family home at No. 4 Brighton Avenue, Rochester, New York.

In addition to her work with the Allings, Hattie took on other job opportunities that came along.

Oct. 28, '83

Wednesday Andrew Phillips came and asked if I could come down to M. H. Briggs' office and help (with a lot of other girls) in directing envelopes for a few days. So Friday and Saturday I went; we work 7-1/2 hours for $1.25, paid daily; the work for me and also Mamie Phillips, Fannie Holyland, and Hattie Millard, so far, has been mostly putting posters and ballots into folded circulars and then into envelopes. After performing this highly interesting occupation rapidly for 3 or 4 hours it becomes "tejus" to say the least. Fannie gets nearly distracted. There are 15 to 17 girls and 8 or 9 young men, lawyer's clerks etc. working at this sending of circulars. "To the Electors of the 7th Judicial District" (I'll send you one). They are going to send out 50,000 of them "for a beginning" as M. H. Briggs said. I'm going Monday, also two sisters of "Nancy Hoyt" (at Wisners), two Lintweiler girls from East Avenue, Beezy Fay, and some I don't know are there.

While her efforts to find satisfying employment proved unsuccessful, Hattie continued to be an active participant in the mission society. The next year was one of increasing participation and leadership in society activities.

Nov. 11, '83

Monday I spent mostly in picking out bright cards for the Freedman's barrel, and mending what we had put in either barrel. My dark red calico dress and the dark grey flannel both went in the one for the South, i.e., Christiansburg, Virginia; the other barrel went to Indian Territory. Wednesday morning early I went to get part of the dress for the home missionary's wife (which was bought to put in the barrel) and brought the skirt trimming home and made it. As there wasn't enough to go round I went again Thursday morning and got another breadth and hemmed, pleated, etc.

Thursday after dinner I went to the Church and helped Mama pack the two barrels and take a list of the articles with their value. The Freedman's barrel we valued at $32 and the other $68.

Dec. 16, '83

Monday on my way home I spent $1.00 in 10 nice little Testaments, which will be sent to Florida. Four of my class responded to the invitation and brought here yesterday enough in the line of toys, Sunday School papers, etc. etc. to fill our old clothes basket full. I shall send my small doll with its outfit of clothing and some tracts, children's books, the 10 Testaments, and we'll put in 1 year of *The Christian Weekly*. Perhaps we'll send the things in the box the chutney came in.

Dec. 30, '83

Monday morning I trotted over to Reuter's and got a Babbets Soap box, good sized, and brought it home and we packed it full and HK went to the Express Office that morning, so that it was "come for" that afternoon. It was weighed,

47 lbs., and I paid the expressage, $5.00. I understand that
Live Oak is a "poverty struck" place, not much to buy and less
to buy with, so I think it pays to send. I have quite a pack of
Scripture cards which I'm going to mail tomorrow for New
Year's: they were overlooked.

Hattie's involvement in the mission society soon expanded
beyond the Rochester group, bringing her into contact with a wider
circle of women interested in missionary work. At the meeting in
Buffalo, New York, Hattie met Mrs. Cushing, the wife of Dr. Josiah
Cushing, an important member of the Baptist mission in Burma.
This meeting proved propitious in a number of ways. While Hattie
was acquainted with several Rochester families who had served as
missionaries in Burma at one time or another, Mrs. Cushing appears
to have been the first person with whom Hattie discussed her interest
in missionary work and who actively encouraged Hattie to prepare
herself for such work.

Apr. 20, '84

<u>This</u> has been a red-letter week, <u>I tell you!!</u>
   Wednesday morning Mama, Julia, and I started off in
Durand's coupé for the depot. We found there, also going,
Mrs. Rowley, Lewis, Reynolds, Woody of our church, and Mrs.
Baldwin and Andrews of the 1st Church, and Mrs. Barrett and
three of the Waytes and one other of Lake Avenue. Three
ladies of the 2nd Church came afterwards. So you see we were
ahead in the number of delegates. We had to take a hack from
the Buffalo depot to the Church and got in during the
secretary's report. You will see from the Programme what the
exercises were. It was all good, especially the talks of the
returned missionaries. Of these we met personally and had
talks with Mrs. Cushing, Mrs. Bixby, Miss Payne, also Mrs.
Kindley of the home at Newton Center. We liked each of them
very much; they all spoke of you.
   Mr. and Mrs. Potter were there and from them we learned
that the Witters and Rivenburgs were together at Sibsangur, as
there was trouble among the hill tribes, and it wasn't safe for
the Rivenburgs to go into Molong.
   We were entertained at Mrs. Wade's, a young married
woman, the mistress of a very pretty and elegantly furnished

house and the mother of three children of 12, 9, and 7 years.
She was very pleasant and entertained us as nicely as anyone
could. We were glad we had black silks to wear and looked as
nice as anyone. We stayed over the second night in order to
hear Dr. Clough. We returned on the St. Louis Express at 9:15
A.M., got here before 12 M., making no stops at all between
Buffalo and Rochester.

The Buffalo meeting also provided Hattie the inspiration and
impetus to undertake a new, more immediate venture in support of mission work: "show and tell" visits to Baptist circle
groups in communities outside Rochester. Hattie's enthusiasm
for the "curiosities" Frank continued to send from Burma provided the material.

May 4, '84
So the boxes [of curiosities] are started! My! won't we
think we're proud!! If I should get on all the things you are
sending and have sent me I should be too awfully stunning for
anything! Nobody could look at me twice! We'll have to buy
another lot and have an addition to the house built to keep the
curiosities in.
By the way, I found a way to utilize those we already have:
when Miss Payne was showing some she had to the children at
Buffalo I thought we had more and better than she had there and
they might be shown and explained to the "circles" and "bands"
in the country churches around here and serve to arouse interest
and increase general information, so spoke about it to Mrs.
Griffith of Fairport (Secretary of West New York) and she caught
at the idea at once and now has invited me to exhibit them to the
circle at Fairport next Wednesday afternoon. Then we'll see how
it takes there; of course I can't take all we have, but as many as I
can carry of the most interesting.

Like the meeting at Buffalo, the visits served to introduce Hattie
to a range of new experiences, such as traveling alone to unfamiliar communities, meeting new people, and speaking to groups of
strangers, many of whom were unfamiliar with mission work and
had little knowledge of Burma.

May 11, '84

The main event of this week to me was going to
Fairport. I took all of the things I could carry, three bundles,
or one basket and two bundles, one the size of the topee and
the other the size of the Burman book. It rained hard all the
time going, Mama went with me to the Depot, and a lady
met me there at Fairport and we were taken to the Church
in the public carriage of the town. There was a good sized
company for a rainy day and about an hour's meeting and
then I took a half hour to show and fully explain the
curiosities and the customs therewith connected. I took the
chatties Lucy sent and the Burmese clothes that belonged to
Miss Van Meter as well as the other things. The ladies and
children (quite a good many of the latter were present) were
very much interested and pleased and gave me a vote of
thanks. Tea was served afterward there and I went home to
Mrs. Griffith's and stayed till the 9 o'clock train. I sold
three of the photos that Papa had printed for sale.

June 8, '84

Thursday was also a red-letter day. I went alone to Greece,
rode in the 1st Church carryall, had hardly got into the vesti-
bule when Mrs. Cushing, whom we met a minute at Buffalo,
came up and spoke to me, and we went into the body of the
Church and had <u>such a good visit</u>. . . .

Mrs. Griffith brought up the subject of my visiting and the
ladies voted to engage me to visit the circles of Monroe County
and exhibit your curiosities (the new ones will come into play).
Mrs. Cushing gave a splendid talk in the afternoon and Miss
Wayte gave a good one as to why she goes as a missionary.

Friday I went to see Mrs. E. R. Andrews, as Secretary,
about the visiting; she made me stay all the afternoon and visit,
and invited me to remain to tea. I shall probably visit the
<u>country</u> churches, at least, with Mrs. Andrews using her horse
and buggy.

Mrs. Cushing had told me at Greece that she would speak
to the children of the 2nd Church and to come and see her. So
I went, and she came in the cars home as far as the Townsens
where she wanted to call on Mrs. Earnest Burton (of whom she

says "a nice little thing but not much to her"). There was no
one there so she came right home with me. And we had
another splendid visit of 1/2 hour; she enjoyed the things more
than most do. She pounded and laughed over the Burmese
gong, saying "That <u>does</u> sound good!" But she says "He's an
extravagant brother," and when I showed her the necklaces
and said you hadn't said which was for which she said at once,
taking the one I think the prettiest "You keep this and wear it
to the reception; your sister can have the other <u>but you keep
this</u>!" So I think I will (it's the one so [sketch]). I know I shall
care more than Ada for it, wear and enjoy it most. She told me
to wash the mottled piece and it would be right. There's
enough for a dress without it anyway.

Hattie's painting for the Allings had continued on a regular
basis throughout the year, but despite Hattie's increasing skill and
the recognition she received for her talent, the work was no more
satisfying than it had been initially. In the spring of 1884, Hattie
began again to address the issue of her future in earnest.

She turned to Dr. Henry Morehouse for information about
home mission work in the South. As Field Secretary for the American Baptist Home Mission Society at that time, Dr. Morehouse
was in a position to know the situation there as well as anyone. He
was also a family friend and former pastor to whom Hattie felt
comfortable addressing her requests for information and assistance.
Her confidence was justified. Dr. Morehouse was the first person,
besides Mrs. Cushing, to take Hattie's desire to prepare for mission work seriously and to offer both helpful advice and direct
assistance. She told Frank:

> May 4, '84
> Awhile ago I wrote to Dr. Morehouse, asking if they had
> more applications for positions in Freedmen's Schools than
> positions, and if a special examination was required etc. I
> received a very kind letter in return saying that "he thought an
> application from me would be favorably considered" and that
> my Regents and High School diploma would be sufficient. But
> after writing to him I found that Julia wanted to go to the
> Missionary Training School at Chicago if she had someone to

go with, and the more I thought about it the more I thought
that as I had no experience, it would be a grand good thing if I
could go and have a course of training (theological, medical,
industrial, normal, practical) then I would be as well fitted as
most anyone for either home or foreign work. The expenses
are about $250 (no tuition fees). Of course I would have to
borrow either of you or Mama, but as there would be little
doubt but what some of the numerous Societies would employ
me somewhere I could pay back what I borrow after a while.
Now will you lend me about that sum or shall I borrow out of
Mama's little inheritance? I have written to Miss Burdette,
Principal of the Training School, for full particulars.

May 11, '84

Wednesday morning I received from Chicago the list of
questions for applicants to answer, various leaflets and a letter
from the Corresponding Secretary, Mrs. Ehlers. We've no
settled pastor to give me a recommendation so I wrote and
asked Dr. Morehouse for one.

May 17, '84

Monday I received a letter from Dr. Morehouse (in answer
to mine, asking him for a recommendation to the Training
School) saying, in substance, that he thought a position as
teacher in one of their Institutions would be better for one of
my age, education, tastes, etc. and for such a position it would
be unnecessary to incur the expense of a course at the Training
School; but whatever I decided to let him know and he would
do anything he could for me. There are various other reasons
why it would be better to go South than to the Training
School, and if he can give me an appointment I think I better
accept. It remains to be seen if he can or not.

June 8, '84

Mrs. Cushing thinks teaching in the South will be just the
best possible preparation for foreign work, if the way should
be opened for that, as I hope it will in time. She spent three
years South herself.

June 22, '84

I had a call from Dr. Morehouse; he hopes to have all business, appointments, etc. etc., settled before July 7 — the next Board meeting — but they are not as yet.

Hattie's hopes for a position in the South or a year at the Training School in Chicago were part of a long range goal that Hattie was finally able to articulate — first to Frank in a private letter and later to her parents in a letter written while they were away from home on a family visit. Her goal to become a foreign missionary had clearly been in her mind a long time. It may be that Witter's suggestion the previous year (that she apply to the mission board for a position in Burma) had helped to give structure to what had been an undefined wish on her part. By this time, Hattie had both defined her goal and a plan for achieving it.

June 25, '84 [Private letter to Frank]

I want ultimately to be a Foreign Missionary, altogether aside from the question of making a home for you. They have no trouble in finding teachers for the Home Mission work, having very <u>many</u> more applicants than vacancies. (I think it doubtful about my being appointed on that account) but it's not easy to find those who wish to go abroad and it seems as if those who <u>are</u> willing, yes, anxious, ought to go. I would like to put my life work into the part of the field where there's most to do and fewest to do it. Besides, your being there makes it easier, pleasanter, and safer for me to go than for many other women. Mrs. Cushing expects her husband to come home next year, so even if you keep bachelor's hall with him, it won't be for very long.

I don't think there would be much trouble about being accepted by the Board, particularly if I first spend a year at the Training School or teaching; my health has been improving and I'm stronger and <u>older</u> than when you last saw me. Don't imagine me to be just the same girl I was 2-1/2 years ago. I told Mrs. Cushing just how my health was, and she didn't seem to think it was going to stand in the way. She remarked at the last "If the Lord wants you to go, He'll open the way — <u>if some-body has to die for it.</u>"

Mother is not at home and of course I've had no conversation on this point with her, but I'm very sure neither Papa or Mama would raise any objections to my going to make a home for you. I think Mother has made up her mind that I'll not be at home this coming year anyway.

I don't think it's for nothing that the Lord has put the desire to devote my life to His service into my heart (3 years ago I felt it) and kept it alive and made it grow till it has swallowed up all else, and nothing beside seems worth living for: do you? What do you think of the whole matter? I'm bound to be a missionary if I have to wait till I'm forty! providing of course the Lord don't stop me.

Hattie's letter a short time later revealed that events were moving rapidly and some of the decisions about which she had written Frank had been made by the time her next letter was mailed.

July 6, '84

Now for the <u>news</u>. I have just received the announcement from Miss Packard, Principal of the Spelman Seminary, Atlanta, Georgia, of my appointment as teacher in that school, by the Board of the Woman's Baptist Home Mission Society at Boston. This is the school where Mrs. Albert has and is going to teach, so I shall have nice company going and coming, and will be with someone I know. Mrs. Albert is very nice; in fact Miss Packard won't have any teachers under her who are not Christian ladies; she says who she wants and the Board approves. The school is for girls only, and is of a very marked religious character. Miss Packard and Miss Giles of Boston went down and started it in a wretched dark basement three years ago, with 11 pupils; now it occupies five of the Yankee Barracks buildings and numbers 500 pupils.

When Dr. Morehouse was here he said there were no vacancies in his schools so I asked about Spelman Seminary of which I had learned through Mrs. Albert; he said at once "That's just the place, and they are wanting teachers. You write to Miss Packard and I will, too, and you get acquainted with Mrs. Albert." So I did both, and obtained the appointment, tho there were a number of applications in before mine. There were 35 applications for the position Mrs. Albert took last year. You see there is no lack of those who are willing to work in the Home field, which is more than can be said of the Foreign.

As president of Spelman's Board of Trustees, Dr. Morehouse's recommendation was probably a crucial factor in Hattie's appointment to Spelman.

After the decision had been made to accept Miss Packard's offer of a position, Hattie wrote a letter to her parents concerning her determination to be a foreign missionary. The announcement of her intention through the medium of a letter rather than in person indicates some hesitancy on her part, whether to their possible reaction or uncertainty over her ability to state her position convincingly — or both — can only be surmised.

Rochester, N.Y. July 11, '84

Dear Father and Mother,

I want to tell you that it has become my firm conviction that it is to be my future duty and privilege to be a foreign missionary. I can't help but believe that the Lord put the wish into my heart (some years ago, before Frank went) to devote my life to His service, and has kept it and strengthened and developed it into a final consecration to the foreign work. This cannot be the wish of a simple <u>natural</u> heart since every impulse toward Christ and His work is from the Holy Spirit; and I feel assured that God is thus calling me to His service and He would not call if He was not going to give the strength to perform. I regard the work at the South to which He has opened the way, as <u>preparatory</u> to the other, because He has turned my heart to the Foreign, made it easier for me to go than for many and to many who will work at home He has not given the willingness to work abroad. It is not simply because Frank is there, for I shall want to go just as much if he marries or comes home.

Of course I don't know how soon the Lord will want me to go, whether after one or two years.

I wish this might make you as happy as it does me, which is saying a great deal.

Yours lovingly,
Hattie.

In a long, private letter to Frank, Mama expressed her ambivalence over her wish to keep Hattie at home and her recognition of Hattie's ability to "enlarge her field of usefulness." It articulates, too, the considerable pressures and expectations Hattie encountered in carrying through her ambition to be a missionary.

Aug. 13, '84 [ECP]

My dear son,

Hattie has gone to show and explain things from heathen lands; she will tell you about it in her next. What I want is to write about her leaving home. She seemed just as contented after you left as before and did not exhibit any more missionary spirit, wouldn't attend the ladies' circle, except union meetings where we had tea and one missionary service, though she did her share, perhaps more, in keeping up the Young People's Missionary Society, but that was about the state of things when Witter asked her to sail with them. I now think the sole object of Witter's was to get Rivenburg and her together, thinking that they make a match, for he said to her long before he asked her to sail with them, "I do wish you would marry Rivenburg, he is a good fellow, and I do hate to have him go off there all alone." I did not hear any expression of disappointment or regret at her not going after it was known that Rivenburg was to be married before they sailed.

She knows that I do not approve of her going, do not think her strong enough and that I need her at home, but I help her to get ready just as heartily and faithfully as I did you. She would like it better if folks did not say quite as much about her leaving her mother. Dr. Pattison said, "I think a missionary will have to be sent from the other side to help your mother and take care of her." Mrs. E. A. Andrews said to me, "I don't see how you can have her go." As I did not make an immediate reply, she said, "I suppose you submit as mothers do when their daughters make up their minds to leave home." When Hattie said, "Oh, she is helping me to get ready to go," Mrs. Andrews said, "I have no doubt of that."

Mrs. Banning was in a few days ago and said considerable. Among the rest she said, "If it was just your father and mother, it would not be so bad, but she has too much to do, and she is not at all strong." Hattie said, "Oh well, if the family is too large, Herman and Ada might keep house themselves." You just imagine the way Mrs. Banning said, "<u>She</u> keep house! She <u>ain't able</u> to take care of herself." I think she noticed that Hattie did not like so much being said, for when she went out she said to Hattie, "Oh well, if you think it's your duty to go, you go and if your mother gets sick I will get someone to take care of her. I am worth a good deal yet, if I have one cripple arm." After she had gone Hattie looked as if she might cry, but I think she did not shed any tears.

The next morning she said, "I am getting tired of all this talk. No one said a word against Mary Phillips going away but because I think I can do some good in the world, if I ain't married, everybody must talk about it," and she is about right there. I do not say a thing against her going but she knows what I think and how I feel. I don't want she should think herself a martyr nor do I want she should ever feel, if she should ever regret going, that she went because I encouraged her.

She will not need to go tired out as she has but little to do to be ready to go, all the sewing being a couple of dresses to make and one, the "seersucker gingham," is most done. She now sees the wisdom of my always keeping her a large supply of under-clothes made up, more than she thought was at all necessary.

I know just as well as she does that she is capable of more than to just stay at home and help me, but if she has not health for greater things I do not see as she is called to attempt more than in the best judgment of all her friends she is able to do. If she will only be wise and not try to do more than teach until she gets used to that much. She usually takes a nap every day after dinner, at least lies down for an hour or so. Today she took her rest before dinner as the Pittsford folks said a carriage would call for her at 1:30, and they were on time.

When I think how efficient she is compared with Ada, I think perhaps I am selfish not to want her to go away, enlarge her field of usefulness as some might say. She can keep house and cook quite as well as the ordinary girls of the period and is able to do all her sewing, with very little advice and assistance from me, dress and millinery, and her education ought to be good for she is studying something all the time now, constantly bringing a book and keeps HK hunting up and bringing a book for her.

I have often felt in the past year or more that I should feel better and she be just as well off, if she help me more and read less. When she had painting to do I did not expect her to help me, and now that she is soon going, she must have all the time she needs to read and study and get ready without getting tired out. She may break down as Ada has, and be worth as little when she is thirty.

While we were in Ohio we received a letter from Hattie, directed to me on the outside which I will send with this. Please return it when you write a private letter to me. I do not know as Papa has said anything to her about it and she does not seem willing to talk with me. In fact she has been very silent ever since I came home, will read by the hour and not a word and the same when sewing unless she wants my opinion or assistance. I think her talks with and letters from Mrs. Cushing and her going around to missionary meetings have a great deal to do with her feeling.

Do you remember how the neighbors used to ask if Hattie was going to be a teacher during the last years that she attended? and that I used to say, "Why no, I haven't but one girl and I will keep her at home." Well, she's been at home six years, and now expects to be a teacher after all that's said.

Frank's letter in response to Hattie's regarding the Training School in Chicago, once again, was not encouraging. Although he did arrange for money to cover her expenses, should she need it, he was depreciatory of her ability to carry through on her plans and critical of her visits to show the "curiosities." His paternalistic advice reveals an unwillingness to accept the idea that Hattie was capable of making sound decisions about her own life. Frank had not received Hattie's private letter about her ultimate plan of becoming a foreign missionary nor the later letter of her appointment to Spelman.

June 15, '84 [FDP]
Next I notice Hattie has turned "Showman" and has "taken the Road." All very well; but I think the first time would be the last, if carfare, or at least an extra collection for the Union, were not forthcoming.

Now for the last matter mentioned in the letter.

I expect to enclose a draft on Boston for $100, which with what I have sent before will, I think, put at least $250 in the bank, so that there will be money enough for Hattie on my account if it is needed. But as I look at matters I do not think Hattie should go to the Chicago Training School. I do not think it is what she needs to make herself useful in life. I see that Julia Perry would go if someone would go with her. Now I think that is not by any means the way to look at the matter. If Julia Perry or if Hattie Phinney is not strong enough, or has not force of character enough, or does not feel the call of duty enough, or is afraid or unable for any reason to go to Chicago and go through that School alone, the probabilities are every-thing to nothing that both will make failures of work, either home or foreign, after having had the training and entering upon the work. I have the more suspicion of the plan as proposed by two than I should have had, had either one started out alone to carry it through. If the failure of either one to go keeps the other one from going, I shall be sure that my posi-tion is correct.

On the other hand, I do not believe that Hattie ought to think of becoming a Home Mission school teacher. Let those who must teach for a living have these opportunities for doing good while they are doing what they must. Hattie can do a great deal more good in keeping the missionary spirit alive in the East Avenue Baptist Church and in sending things to different places, than she possibly can as a teacher of a few children in a large school. I think Hattie's idea of the relative value of work in a Home Mission School compared with what she may do in Rochester, coupled with her duties to her parents, is entirely at fault. I think that if Hattie goes from home now and stays for a year, she will repent it afterward, when it will be too late to change its effects. None of the Woman's Societies would take Hattie at her present age, and I do not believe she would stand more than one year's work as a school teacher away from home.

Now look at the expense you are proposing to incur. The sum of $250 is just half a year's salary for a single lady on the foreign field, and to repay it would take a long time, if you had no doctor's bills to pay, and even a short sickness here would spoil all you could save in one year. I do not think the Home Mission teachers lay up much money. It seems to me that unless Hattie is ready to accept the amount as a present, she had better not undertake this step.

Now for some volunteer advice. Hattie seems to be
groping around for some great and good work, she knows not,
and seems to care not, where. The preparation she seeks to
make is general also, or if special, has reference to something
of which she now knows but little. She is young yet, and her
health has not fully settled. She works with almost feverish
energy while she has something new to do, and then drops
back all tired out as soon as it is done. (Don't I know? Haven't
I seen it time and again? Don't her letters tell of just such a
course?) It seems to me that Hattie should give up all such
plans for the present, and while doing all the good at home
possible, should at the same time learn to work <u>steadily</u> and
without excitements and to rest without complaining when
there seems nothing to do. Then, I believe, Hattie should give
herself <u>two full years</u> in which to grow stronger and to settle
down into full strength. During this time she can look about,
make up her mind just what to do, and make such preparation
for the work as can be made at home. I do not believe in going
haphazard. Choose a work or a field and prepare for it. If at
the end of two years Hattie wants to be a foreign missionary or
home missionary, either alone or as the wife of some good
fellow, I shall have no opposition (unless it be to some special
field or especial form of work which I would not advise
anyone to take up).

I have thought over this matter a good deal since receiving
Mrs. Cushing's letter after her return from Buffalo, and what I
have hastily written is my decided opinion. I don't suppose Hattie
will like it any more than I do the medicine I am taking, but it
can't be helped. I only hope both are equally good and beneficial.
If Mrs. (Dr.) Anderson is in town I think she would do well to
take this part of the letter to her and talk it over. I do not think of
anyone else whose opinion would be worth more.

Frank

Hattie's response to this long and discouraging letter demonstrated clearly her growing independence of Frank's opinions and
her confidence in her own decision to find a constructive role for
herself in mission work. She was even able to poke back a little at
his self-importance.

Aug. 17, '84

Your letter in regard to my going to Training School is just arrived. I always heard that people were blue when their liver was in trouble.

I should have been glad to go to Chicago "<u>alone</u>" and should have endeavored to do so if I had not been appointed to Atlanta. Julia's going or not would not have affected my desire in the least, tho she suggested the idea and it was not in vain for I have read three and bought two valuable theological works, as a result. As to its fitting me for usefulness, I guess you don't know what the Training School is!

As to letting those who "<u>must</u> <u>teach</u>" go South — first: they <u>don't want</u> those who simply teach for a salary and besides I don't see but that I need to support myself, and I never can by painting.

As to keeping the missionary spirit alive in East Avenue Baptist Church I can do it in no more effectual way than by entering the work myself, and if I go those who, if I stay, will leave the responsibility to me, will be raised up to take my place.

As to my power of endurance, you forget that I've grown or changed a bit since you saw me. I might as well say that because you never had but three men under you here, therefore you were not capable of controlling 70 men now!

As to working "in feverish haste" and breaking down, I would like a better illustration of it than your worshipful highness! If I can stand the continuous and very trying painting I did last winter I can teach bright pupils about 4 hours a day — just wait and see!

No, the Home Mission teachers don't "lay up much money" but that don't happen to be my object in life, and as I'm not to go to Chicago, I shan't be very seriously in debt when I start.

As to staying at home two years more, I've tried this "little of everything and not much of anything" sort of life for six years and two years more would neither improve my health or materially add to my experience; it would just be the same thing over and over.

As to my exceeding youthfulness, I am just the same age that you were when you began to think of going to Burma, and my undertaking don't compare, in risk and difficulty, with yours.

You needn't worry about me; if the Lord didn't intend to carry me through the year at Atlanta, He wouldn't have let me be appointed.

I am very much obliged for your willingness to lend the money (which I shan't need). I'm very sorry that you have been sick. I should think you had tried the experiment of doing the work of three men with the strength of one about long enough.

Yours lovingly,
Hattie.

If Hattie at 20 had seemed young for her age, busy with her craft projects, her friends, and living in accordance with the sheltered expectations of her parents, at 23 she was well along in establishing her independence and determining her adult role.

The future Hattie had chosen was challenging and far more demanding than those of the other young women of her social group, yet one consistent with the values with which she had been raised. It might have been expected, then, that her family would be supportive of her goal.

Instead, her efforts to establish a career met with strong opposition on the part of the two people she had always looked to for advice and counsel. When neither Frank nor her mother provided the support or direction she sought, Hattie continued to search for those who could. In the end it was the support and direction of two outsiders, Dr. Morehouse and Mrs. Cushing, that helped Hattie define her goals and select the path to achieve them.

Hattie spent the summer of 1884 preparing for her year at Spelman, continuing her visits to local mission circles, attendance at social events, and participation in household chores. She completed her painting assignments without regret.

Aug. 10, '84

I've got to the end of china painting for the present, having completed and taken to be fired all my orders. At least I hope it is the last for awhile for the turpentine or something about it don't agree with me.

Papa and Mama went downtown and Mama bought me a little square trunk as the one I bought won't be big enough and Papa got me this stylographic pen and some nice paper and envelopes. Friday I got my winter shoes and rubbers and trimming for my flannel skirt and Saturday I had Mary Manvel help me make the skirt which is in a style she saw at New York!!!

Despite her reluctance to have Hattie go, her mother seems to have accepted her daughter's decision and to see some value in it.

Sept. 28, '84 [ECP]
Hattie will have a chance to see how she likes collard [sic] folk for schollars [sic] and get some used to "low down folks" before she starts as a missionary, either home or forreign [sic].

Hattie left home for her teaching appointment at Spelman Seminary in Atlanta on September 25, 1884. The departure was a family affair. Mama was up at 3 A.M. to bake bread for the two days' journey on the train; Herman saw to Hattie's trunk. The entire family went by carriage to the station to see Hattie off.

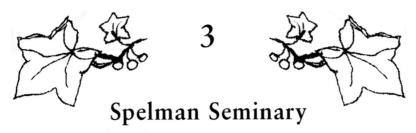

3

Spelman Seminary

September 1884 to June 1885

Spelman Seminary (Spelman College today) in Atlanta, Georgia, was founded in 1881 as the Atlanta Baptist Female Seminary by Sophia B. Packard and Harriet Giles, two women educators from Boston. Its mission was to meet the educational needs of African-American women, "freedwomen," for whom no educational resources existed at the time. A major emphasis in the curriculum was teaching the women such practical skills as sewing, cooking, and millinery, along with basic literacy skills. As a Baptist mission society institution, Bible study and religious services were also important aspects of the school's activities.

The school opened under the auspices of the Woman's American Baptist Mission Society in the basement of the Friendship Baptist Church, with 11 students. Following two years of greatly increasing enrollments, the school by 1884 had been relocated to property formerly used as barracks and drill grounds for federal troops after the Civil War, under an option taken by the society. Funds to pay off the remaining debt for the property were provided by John D. Rockefeller and the name of the institution was changed to Spelman Seminary, in honor of Mrs. Rockefeller's mother.

Virtually every aspect of Hattie's life at Spelman was different from what she had known at home. The living conditions, the climate, the nature of the work she was to do, and the requirements of institutional living were all new experiences for which nothing in her earlier life had entirely prepared her. Each represented a challenge to be faced and mastered.

The journey to Atlanta with Mrs. Albert was Hattie's first major trip away from home. To judge from her account of it, however, it might have been an everyday occurrence. Hattie was well aware that any sign of anxiety or lack of confidence would be a matter of concern to her family and a confirmation of their conviction that she was too young and too frail for the job she had undertaken.

Sept. 28, '84

The folks saw me to the Depot in a carriage, we met the Alberts, said goodby all around with a laugh and jokes and started at 6:45 P.M. We should have met a sleeper at Salamanca at 11:30 P.M. but it was delayed and we waited in a wretched little Depot from 11:20 to 1:20, but finally got to bed about 2 A.M. In the morning we got coffee where they stopped for breakfast, had a table put between the seats and ate in style, same at noon. We reached Cincinnati at 6 P.M. and had to wait there till 8:50 but in the most spacious and elegant Depot I ever saw. I took a nap in the waiting room, and slept well all night on the sleeper. But in the morning an idiotic conductor put us on another car instead of another train and so we missed connections at Chattanooga and had to wait there from about 8 A.M. to 2:55 P.M., making 9 hours of waiting during the journey. There had been no rain for 53 days and the ride from Chattanooga was the very dirtiest I ever took.

We arrived at 8:30 P.M., gave our checks to a baggage man ($.30 for two trunks), took a carriage ($.50) and came up here. We were welcomed by Misses Packard, Giles, Champney, Mallory, and Horton. (Miss Grover and two more new ones are to come — Misses Pratt and Johnson.)

Hattie's first night at Spelman was spent with one of the teachers already settled in, but by the next day she was established in her own quarters and at work preparing for the girls assigned to her house.

Sept. 28, '84

I am in my room now, which I expect to share with Miss Pratt. It is carpeted through the middle (three varieties), has a pretty bedroom set, two stands, a fireplace with a grate in it, green and gold baize curtains at the windows and before the recess used as a closet; when I get my ornaments up it will look very pleasant.

In the afternoon I helped fix the rooms for the girls in my house, and twelve of those who came were put in it. The evening devotions were held in my hall, and afterward I had to go to each room, open the beds and tell them plainly to make sure of their getting in <u>between</u> and not <u>on top</u> of the sheets, a thing the new ones would have been likely to do! Then we had a teachers' meeting (didn't amount to much) and I slept for the first time in my own room.

By the end of the first week all the teachers were on hand and preparations for the school year were underway. The days that followed were spent in getting the students settled and preparing for the official opening of school — attending teachers' meetings, classifying the students, and setting up the schedule.

Oct. 4, '84

There are ten resident teachers and Mrs. Mallory the matron, and two music teachers (Miss Hunter instrumental, Prof. Kruger vocal) who come, one daily and one weekly, (Mrs.) Dr. Hicks gives a weekly lecture also. Miss Mallory now has charge of the teachers' kitchen and Mrs. Mallory of the girls' kitchen. Miss Horton is now out of that work entirely and teaches Reading and sewing, Miss Mallory also has two classes in school.

Miss Packard is very much like Hanah Reynolds in feature and manners of speech, tho larger in figure. Miss Giles is very fine looking, calm, dignified and very pleasant and amiable. Miss Horton is a pretty good-looking jolly little piece. Miss Grover very refined, intellectual, and very well liked. Miss Champney has worked for the negroes 20 years and is a very self-sacrificing excellent lady. She is our missionary and Miss Grover our literary member.

Tuesday Miss Johnson arrived, a pretty slender young lady from North Adams, Massachusetts. A normal teacher about my age. Wednesday Miss Pratt came at noon, a plump lady of say 35 from Massachusetts; she is my roommate. I think we shall get along nicely; it would be too much for me to be alone and see to all the girls and oversee their rooms etc. etc., see that they use and not abuse their bedding, toilet arrangements, that they are neat, quiet, busy, and happy.

It is a rule that the teacher must take an inventory of each pupil's personal property, so if anything is lost or stolen we can know what belongs to who. So Friday afternoon we went from room to room and had the girls show all their possessions and we made lists. I made five and Miss Pratt eight and we now have two more in our house (15 in all) to take inventories of.

Miss Pratt and I are or <u>do</u> have and sell all the stationery and postage to the boarders; of course it is furnished to us by the Principals. Every letter written by the girls must be corrected and then mailed by a teacher. I corrected three Saturday and they <u>needed</u> it <u>tremendously</u>; we also sold a good deal of paper, etc.

Another teachers' meeting after dinner — talk five minutes on business and ten minutes on other general subjects, about the dispatch shown as in the ladies' business or missionary meetings at home.

After devotions in the evening I examined three girls, didn't amount to anything; we often have to do things that don't, just to keep the girls occupied. About 225 pupils registered Wednesday.

Wednesday at 9 A.M. we went to the Chapel to the opening of school. There was singing under the music teacher, Prof. Kruger, for one hour. Reading and prayer and talk by the Principals and talks by two colored preachers, one hour, registering of names, which took an hour or so and then dismissal.

Thursday the forenoon was spent in beginning classifying, a long tedious process not near completed yet.

We had a teachers' meeting from 3 P.M. to 5:25 and decided Monday's programme.

The first weeks of school were ones of some confusion, false starts and changing schedules as new students arrived, settled in, and were assigned to classes. By November things had settled down and a regular schedule was established.

Hattie was hired as a teacher, but within hours of her arrival at Spelman it was clear that teaching, in the academic sense, was only one of her responsibilities. She also served as housemother to the "girls" in her house, a role she shared with her roommate, Miss Pratt. With a total of 47 girls (by year's end), it was a demanding job.

Oct. 11, '84

Here are the things jotted down to talk to the girls about Tuesday evening: "Wash heads — keep closets clean — spreads ditto — baths once a week — getting in <u>between</u> sheets — letters coming and going are to pass through our hands — heads off the wall!!!"

All the letters written by pupils we have to read, correct, and mail, and also read or hear all they receive. I corrected two Tuesday which contained nice compliments for me. One of our girls forged a letter pretending her brother was dead and Miss Pratt was to give her money to go home. Miss Pratt received a letter from her father showing it to be all false. You see the good of inspecting letters.

Feb. 1, '85

I've said good night to all my girls and given out the usual number of doses of Jamaica ginger (I've used 1-1/2 bottles of it, mostly for the girls) and now it's bedtime. We keep a regular apothecary shop and nightly make doses of sage or thorough wort or Jamaica tea, or give salt peter for chilblains, or vaseline or suthin' or other. You've no idea of the cares and responsibilities of a family of 46 children!!!!!!!!

Feb. 8, '85

Monday after dinner I took nearly 80 girls to walk. They did very well, if I was all alone with them. Saturday afternoon Miss Pratt, Miss Champney, and I took about as many in another direction. We had a long pleasant walk, and saw the chain-gang at work.

Hattie maintained the family system of a weekly letter home. Her letters, mailed to Brighton Avenue, were then included in the family's and sent on to Frank in Rangoon. Hattie's letters home were deliberately upbeat and uncomplaining. In a private letter mailed separately to Frank, however, Hattie gives a more candid picture of her initial feelings about life at Spelman.

Nov. 18, '84 [Private letter to Frank]

Dear Old Man,

As my lessons are prepared for tomorrow and our family of 42 are studying in the hall at their evening study time, I'll begin a letter to you, can't say when I'll <u>finish</u> it.

This comes the nearest to perpetual motion of anything you ever saw. We get up and have breakfast at 7:30 A.M. and generally answer a few knocks at the door before that and if it is my day to be present at the girls' meals I have to go over to their 7 A.M. breakfast, then return to my own. After that, fix up our rooms, answer any number of knocks, see that the girls and that the house is in order, get ready, and go to school at a quarter before nine.

I have first (after the hour given to devotions) a class of 37 in the third reader; this week we use in place of our reader the "Temperance Catechism." Then a class of 50 in Practical and they stay to a recitation in Intellectual. Then a class in writing, followed by a 15 minute recess and lunch.

After recess I have a class in Geography of 60, then one in Geometry of two! We get back to our room somewhat after two and there is hardly five minutes until after 9 P.M. that there is not a knock at the door for something. The bell rings at 2:30 P.M. for half to go to sewing class and half to come to study hour in our hall when we must call the roll, see that all are present, and keep them in order and at work till four unless our dinner bell rings earlier than that.

<u>Nov. 19</u> There, another day is gone, and I've just finished looking over a quantity of examples, and Miss Pratt is showing a girl right side of me (we are sitting before our fire) how to work an example and the rest are in the hall studying (i.e., supposed to be).

As I was saying, after dinner we do all sorts of things till 5:30 P.M. when we all go to the chapel for evening devotions, which takes one hour, and the girls have to be settled to their study at once and kept settled (which is quite a job) till 9 P.M. when we have a song and prayer and go to bed. <u>Then</u> we have a little quiet and freedom from knocks, but we are too tired generally to enjoy it, or do anything but go to bed.

I have given three 1/2 hour lectures on the "Solar System" this week and am about done with that subject, I guess. I believe I said someone had given the Seminary a Helliotellus; also a nice Microscope, both of which I was called upon to put in working order.

I went to the Church for the third time Sunday last and heard Dr. Hawthorn. I teach a large class of the girls at the afternoon Sunday School. And last Monday Miss Pratt being away and Mrs. Albert very tired, I led (at the latter's request) the evening devotions (much like a prayer meeting) and that morning Miss Packard had called on me to lead the entire school in prayer; she never called on anyone except Miss Giles before; we are often called on to ask the blessing. Glad I was brought up to "speak in meeting"!

Miss Packard has the sharpest tongue <u>you</u> ever heard — is more peculiar, blunt, and plain spoken than Hanah Reynolds or Mrs. Banning and a <u>great deal</u> more "cantankerous" and hard to get along with. It takes lots of tact, and ability to hold your tongue, and a very thick-skin. She never spoils a story for relation's sake, and woe betide anybody who don't please her!! She will lash us most outrageously on the spur of the moment and in 24 hours declare she never said anything of the sort. I take care she don't have a chance to come down on me, and she has treated me remarkably well; there are one or two who are afraid of her and they have to take it!

Don't imagine she is all bad or always disagreeable; she is often very pleasant and she must be good or she could never have done the grand work here and elsewhere that she has. She was Dr. Lorimere's assistant in Boston for years. You ought to hear these Massachusetts and Boston folk pray on "the Hub"; it's too funny, sometimes we New Yorkers have to laugh. There are only three or four of us out of eleven or twelve.

The big scroll you sent, and various little things and one of the cummerbunds and three Japanese napkins help to decorate our room, and are much admired. One of the cashmere caps I wear almost constantly, back and forth to the Seminary.

Now I've given the girls a 15 minute exercise in calisthenics and got them to bed and I guess I'll eat an orange that was given me and go to bed.

Don't refer to what I've said about Miss Packard in your letters home. I don't mention such things — it would worry Mama and make Papa mad.

All the other teachers are as nice as can be. As for these girls being so very eager to learn — well, some few are but a large proportion of the new ones and young ones are as dull, stupid, indifferent, and hard to beat anything into as you can imagine. It seems almost impossible to teach them anything. This is "between us."

Hattie's initial feelings of strangeness and disappointment with the women and girls she had come to teach changed considerably as she became better acquainted with them, and in later letters home her reports were much more positive.

Jan. 10, '85

We have some of the dearest, nicest girls in our house. I wish you could know them, two in particular, Mary and Nora Gordon. I care as much for them as I ever did for any friend.

Now Papa's prayers as well as ours are answered, "Rejoice with me for I have found my sheep."

As Hattie outlined in her letter to Frank, she carried a demanding teaching schedule. Without training beyond her high school studies (completed six years earlier), Hattie was nevertheless called upon to teach a wide variety of subjects.

Oct. 11, '84

Someone has given the School two microscopes, a little child's microscope and a large nice one, nearly as large I think as Frank's. Misses Packard and Johnson tried to set it up one morning before school but couldn't and Miss Packard asked me to try my hand at it, so I spent some time over it this morning and succeeded in putting it together and left it all right to use, also the little one. Monday I'm to show a mosquito in the microscope, and give a little talk on it, so I've been hunting up the subject, and got one of my girls to catch me a mosquito; they are plenty but lively, and I have him now in the object box of the microscope.

Oct. 18, '84

Monday morning I gave a talk on the mosquito, drew one, two feet long on the board, and had one in the little microscope. The teachers all complimented me on it and said they enjoyed it. Don't know what I'll do next time.

Nov. 30, '84

My November report is as follows: Branches taught — Reading, Writing, Arithmetic, Grammar, Geography, Geometry. Days taught — 20; Hours daily — 5-1/4; Classes 7; Pupils in class 272; Prayer meetings 26; Bible reading 7; Bible classes taught 4.

Writing letters about the school to mission circles was another chore to be carried out by the teachers. Money for the everyday expenses of running the school and paying the teachers was an ongoing problem at Spelman at this time. While the Woman's American Baptist Mission Society provided a major portion of the teachers' salaries, the teachers themselves were called upon to assist in raising additional funds to supplement the monies from the Society.

Dec. 14, '84

Miss Packard received a note from Mrs. Pollard asking for "a sweet little note for Bands from Miss Phinney to be put into the *Watchman* and then published as a leaflet." So all odd minutes have been put into that and I finished and read it to Miss Packard last evening. It met with her approval.

I received a note from a lady in Taunton, Massachusetts asking for letters and saying that what they raised should go toward my salary. There is not enough money in the Treasury to pay all of our salaries (Miss Packard has supplied the lack of it out of her own pocket, but don't let this last fact out at all) so I must do what I can to raise my own salary. The letter to Mrs. Pollard will go for the Taunton Association for the first time.

Jan. 18, '85

I received a letter from Mrs. Pollard, thanking me for their letter, asking for more, and enclosing a letter from a lady in Worcester to me asking a lot of questions about the school. The band she has charge of sent $5.00 toward my salary. I suppose she saw my name in the *Monthly*. So I have the Taunton letter and one to Worcester to write, and I spent all day yesterday struggling over them, with a knock at the door every few minutes, and I couldn't finish them for all my efforts.

The school's acquisition of a printing press enabled Hattie to make an even greater contribution to the school's fund saving and fund-raising efforts. A printing office was set up to serve a variety of purposes: to provide students with skill in typesetting, to enable the school to print up its own "dodgers" and tickets for special occasions, and, most importantly, to initiate a publication — later to become the *Spelman Messenger* — about the school and its work. It can be assumed that Hattie had had some familiarity with Frank's printing press at home and that Miss Packard was aware of this special knowledge on Hattie's part. The printing office was a major responsibility that absorbed much of Hattie's time for the remainder of the year and demonstrated perhaps more than any other single activity Hattie's ability to assume responsibility for a task and carry it through with resourcefulness and practicality.

Nov. 18, '84

There has been a printing press purchased and Miss Packard expects considerable of me in connection therewith. We'll see!! I don't know enough to teach the art of typesetting. I'll let you know when I go into that work.

Dec. 6, '84

Miss Packard tried to get a lady to teach typesetting, but she charged $10 a week to come but three afternoons to teach!!!! There's southern extortion for you! I don't see but I'll have to try my hand at it. Of course it will be taught to but few; there is a chance for six to set type at a time. There is a Model Press 8 inches x 10 inches, I guess; three sizes of type, Small Pica, Pica, and Brevier; and two larger fonts, and I think all necessary accessories except an imposing stone and hand roller. We are going, if possible, to get out a paper from this school to send to the Exposition at New Orleans and elsewhere. I wish HK could send me a book or something on the subject of Printing, arranging pages etc. I guess with such a work I could get along and save the establishment a good deal.

If I do this I would be excused from other afternoon duties. I wouldn't have to be in the office every afternoon either.

Dec. 18, '84

Monday before school Miss Packard took me to town with her to see about getting what was needed in the Printing Office. The School is to give a Concert or Entertainment next Monday in Friendship Baptist Church (colored) and Miss Packard wanted the tickets and dodgers printed here. We went and she bought an imposing stone, tickets etc., and engaged a lady compositor from one of the big establishments to come three days a week to teach typesetting. Nothing could be done till the leads were cut and so after school I went again, got them cut, bought paper for bills, ink, etc. In the evening I wrote to Cincinnati for things not to be had in the city, composing sticks, etc.

Tuesday morning Miss Packard had a note from the woman who was to teach typesetting saying she could not come. So Miss Packard went for the other lady, Miss Hilton, who charged so much and I spent the time from school till dinner in the Office with three girls showing them about things in general.

Thursday I went downtown in regard to printing things again (nobody else knows the first thing about it) and wrote to Cincinnati for the remainder of things needed.

Friday I worked hard all the afternoon with the teacher in the office and found that the quads and spaces of two fonts had been omitted, so that we could not set up a decent ticket or dodger (there is not enough variety of type anyway) and that Miss Hilton knows <u>nothing</u> about the press and so is no good in <u>this</u> office. Guess she won't come but once more. So I had to write to Cincinnati for the quads etc. and Saturday morning take the tickets down to be printed. There is a man coming Monday to teach the girls about the press. We can do very well about the typesetting, particularly if HK sends that book on Printing, and save the School $5 a week that would be paid to Miss Hilton. Times is <u>fearfully</u> hard and money <u>very</u> scarce.

Feb. 2, '85

This has been a busy week as usual. I've spent four afternoons
in the office and intended to spend six but Miss Packard would
not allow it. And yet she is in a hurry for the paper, which as you
can imagine grows <u>very</u> slowly with only three or four slow
setters working but an hour and a half, three or four afternoons in
the week. I've written two or three short articles for it; the other
teachers also write. We have high stools to sit on to set type now.
The composing rules [made to order by Hattie's father, according
to her specifications] came and are just right, and are a great
convenience. <u>Very much obliged.</u>

The publication of the first *Spelman Messenger* was followed
immediately by the necessity of starting work on the next number.

May 3, '85

Wednesday I went into the office before breakfast and worked
there all day long except just while I taught four classes and ate
my meals. The paper had to be got out this week so as to be an
April Number. Thursday I finished making up the forms and took
a proof myself. Then Miss Mary Packard and I read it, and I
worked till after seven in the evening correcting the type. Miss
Packard had arranged to have the forms taken at 7 A.M. so I got
up and into the office at 5:45 A.M. and took another proof which
Miss Mary Packard read and I corrected and then I locked the
forms into the big chase! (sent up from town). It was awfully hard
work to get it all tight, some lines bothered, which accounts for
"here" being spelled "heer." The men were waiting and I had to
hurry so; however I got it off and went for my breakfast. They
were printed the same day. There are various mistakes I would
have corrected if I had had more time.

Now I must go right on with the May Number. We have over
three columns set left over from this so there's not so much to set.
I have to do much the girls might if I had more time.

Throughout the year at Spelman, Hattie entered into all the
duties and responsibilities given her with diligence and determination, but it was the missionary aspect of the work that she found
most rewarding. Before coming to Atlanta, it is unlikely that Hattie
had ever known people who could be considered "heathen" or

"sinners"; her interest in missionary work was not grounded in personal experience with the unconverted. At Spelman, there was a strong missionary component in all the school's activities, and conversion of the "sinners" was an ongoing concern.

Oct. 18, '84

Sunday evening last we had a very good prayer meeting, about 25 expressed a wish to be Christians, and remained for us teachers to talk with. I think some were converted; one, and I hope both of the two little girls, of our house, that I talked with, were. Lulu Washington (one of them) wrote a very good letter home regarding her conversion. One of the girls asked prayer for her Mother, in these words. "<u>Do</u> pray for her, she's not a Christian and she'll be lost, and <u>just imagine</u> for me to stand at the Judgement seat of Christ and say 'Amen' to my Mother's damnation!"

Oct. 25, '84

In the prayer meeting last Sunday evening one girl asked for prayers for a girl by her side in this way, "Pray for Mattie Warner. She's a hard-hearted sinner. I've talked and prayed but she's so hard. She wants to be a Christian, all pray for her." They frequently ask in this way, and anyone who wishes asks "All sinners to rise" and then exhorts them to repent. There were three conversions in Miss Grover's house Sunday evening after prayer meeting. Such crying and wailing and taking on I never heard before and their rejoicing afterward is equally painful. Miss Packard is down on all such noises. Glad we weren't any nearer to it.

Friday we had a good noon prayer meeting. The Home Mission Society is often prayed for by the older ones and they seldom omit prayer for the teachers. One petition was "May we not <u>talk</u> our religion but <u>walk</u> it." One of the married girls said with great earnestness and indignation, "Seems like you sinners don't want anything but to serve Satan and then go to him after death. We have to talk to the Lord so much about you, we've no time to talk to Him about the teachers or about building up this school." Friday evening we had a good time over the Sunday School lesson.

Nov. 15, '84

This has been a glorious week spiritually. There was a very solemn meeting Sunday evening and on Monday evening the entire time was occupied with confession, testimony, and prayers by the Christians. Tuesday evening one of Mrs. Albert's girls was converted and Wednesday morning one of ours; they both spoke Wednesday evening and very many asked for prayers. During the study hour I talked and prayed in our room with Lottie Williams, one of our girls, and she was converted before we left the room and at the same time another girl went to her room and gave her heart to Christ. They both told of it just before the girls went to bed (we always have a song and prayer then); as they started up the stairs someone started the song, "Good News from Heaven" and all joined in with a will. Thursday night another of our girls gave up the struggle and came out rejoicing in the morning, and before school Friday still another gave her heart to Christ and both told of it at the morning exercises in School. Then this morning (Saturday) we teachers had a little prayer meeting while Miss Packard and Miss Giles held an inquiry meeting and 2 more of our girls were converted and 1 of Mrs. Albert's before the meeting, making 7 in our house this week, and there are only 4 "sinners" left out of 41 girls in the house. I'm sorry to say 1 of the 2 I told of early in the term was mistaken, but the other holds fast. There has been no excitement, it is just the answer to prayer; there have been 14 conversions in all this term but there are scores unconverted among the day pupils.

Jan. 10, '85

Such a meeting as we have just had! Before the meeting I brought one of the new girls in and talked and prayed with her and she gave her heart to Christ at once. Then we went to the meeting which was made an inquiry meeting at once, and during it 3 more of our girls (one of them the <u>one</u> who has held out so long) gave up and "came through" <u>shouting</u>. And after returning the last one in our house yielded and <u>then</u> such a scene, singing, shouting, laughing, and crying, the whole 44 and we two just as happy as can be. Not a sinner left in the house! Alice Hunter (the hard sinner) in her rejoicing when she gave up knocked Miss

Packard down flat and gave Miss Pratt a hug that made her ache;
she was calmed a little before she came to me but I got a very
emphatic hug. Two from other houses were also converted, 7 in
all. Some only wait to be asked and others are hard as rocks.

Mar. 14, '85

Two of the day pupils have been converted this week. At
the Friday noon meeting one of the married women spoke as
follows: "I've been trying ever since I came to this school to
cast my burdens on the Lord and now I just put them down at
His feet and let him <u>tote</u> them just as it says in the Bible!" We
had very hard work to keep our faces straight, I assure you.

The Spelman academic year provided for no extended vacation at Christmas time. A welcome break came in April when Hattie
had an unexpected opportunity to see a little more of the world.

Leland University, New Orleans, Louisiana, Apr. 11, '85

Now I guess you are surprised for once!! But you can't be
much more so than I am. You see Miss Packard decided to
come to New Orleans with the Coles (who were at Spelman)
to get ideas about a new building and besides she needed the
change. And she wanted Miss Grover, who was run down, and
I to come the day after she did, so as not to have too many go
at once. I thought I couldn't afford time, money, or strength,
but she was afraid I would break before the term closed (as the
last two months are hardest). It was a chance to come cheap
and have a peep at the "Great World Expo," the "Cotton
Centennial," and a change if not a rest. She thought Mama
would want me to go, so as I didn't want to break down and
thought it was an opportunity of a lifetime, I'd better come.
My expenses, including what we've bought for the teachers
and to send home, and our board here (75 cts. a day) won't be
over $23.

We left Atlanta Thursday at 3 P.M. and came straight
through in a sleeper, arriving about 9 A.M. The journey was
delightful, especially the last end, where we saw the pines and
live oaks with the moss growing all over them, but I don't
think the latter is beautiful. It is "death's banner" sure enough.
The foliage down here is out and just lovely, the gardens are

full of wisteria, orange trees with fruit and flowers, and such a wealth of roses everywhere, in the yards and on the people, the air, just out of the city, is fairly rich with the perfume. This is five miles from the center. We come out by street car.

It is the prettiest, quaintest old city. I like it so much except the gutters. Just imagine <u>open sewers</u> along both sides of every street, full of slimy, stagnant water, mud, and refuse.

The first afternoon, yesterday, we went to the city and visited the French Quarter, the scene of Cabel's stories, and into the old, old French Cathedral. The square where they used to execute criminals is in front of it and on one side the old arch and palace, and on the other what was the Court House. On each side of the Square is a long row of red brick buildings owned by a French countess who lives in France and has her agent here. The Cathedral is full of altars, images, shrines, pictures, etc. etc.; the windows are square panes of most brilliant plain glass.

This morning we started out early and spent the entire day at the Exposition and of course didn't see one hundredth part of it. We were only in the Main and Government & 2 Buildings.

Don't say much about this trip, for some will say they can't afford to pay teachers to go visiting, forgetting that we are entitled to a vacation which we've not taken, and that they don't work as hard all year and do spend more for their vacations. I came from a sense of duty, but I've had a grand time so far. We expect to start home tomorrow evening at 8:20 P.M.

Sunday Mr. Woodsmall of Leland, took Miss Grover and I to the Coliseum Baptist Church where we heard a good gospel sermon, perhaps the best I've heard down here. Mr. Needham has been with Messrs Moody and Sankey.

Monday morning we spent in Leland University; they have not nearly as many [students] as we, only 260 enrolled instead of 612, and only 80 boarders in all instead of 200, but they have two nice large brick buildings (and the <u>malaria</u>).

We started home at 8:20 P.M. We didn't arrive here till 4:24 P.M. Tuesday. Of course we had a sleeper; Miss Packard and I below and Miss Grover above us. The girls were hilarious at our arrival. I felt tired for a day or two, but am feeling better now, think the trip did me good. It was very enjoyable anyway.

The year was winding down, but the last weeks of the school year brought little relief from Hattie's duties as housemother.

Apr. 24, '85

We've got our hands full. The girls are coming down or are down with "roseola," five in our house, and some in the other houses; two of ours are quite sick. It's likely it will go through the school. I hope to escape it.

Later. No, it's <u>measles</u> (spelt right?) and nine are down with it here, and one in Mrs. Albert's and one in Miss Grover's and one in the Seminary and one in Miss Johnson's house.

The doctor's been here and says the sickest one has pleurisy, and the others measles; some of the girls will have to sit up with her to give medicine and to keep her bag of water hot.

May 3, '85

Well, another week gone and we still exist! Our five have got almost through with the measles, but another seems to be coming down. The pleurisy case is also convalescent. I was up once or twice during Sunday and Monday nights, so Monday I was excused from two classes and came and fed the sick and then rested for a little time before going into the office.

Apr. 26, '85

I've just received a letter from Livia. She thinks there's not over much to being a teacher with <u>47</u> children, sick and ailing and grunting and fussing; school to teach, examinations to prepare for, two more papers to publish, a picnic and concert on foot, et cetera ad infinitum!!!

Hattie's printing office responsibilities also lasted till the very end of the school year.

May 31, '85

Miss Packard said this morning that we were all free to go tomorrow, our time was up, I could leave the paper, the girls could go and she would get someone to finish it or let it rest till next Fall!!!!!!!! It's a way she has of throwing the fat in the fire at the last minute after a body has worked like everything to accomplish anything and she happens to get discouraged or vexed or someone happens to look tired. Of course I shall finish the paper; it would be idiotic to drop it now and throw away a month's work. She knows well enough that I won't leave it. Nobody else could possibly take it now and put it in shape and she couldn't get anyone anyway.

Saturday I worked all day in the Printing Office. Mary Gordon and one other stayed to help me. I hope to get it printed Tuesday and we fully expect to leave here Wednesday, about 1 P.M., spend the night in Chattanooga, take a sleeper the next night (Thursday) from Cincinnati and so on home . . . Later: We have had a most delightfully restful Sunday. Miss Johnson starts home tomorrow and my printers also toward night. About 20 girls are here today but they are going shortly. The quiet that reigns is marvelous. Next time I have anything to say, I'll say it!!!! "Ain't got long to stay here."

Hattie traveled home to Rochester with Mrs. Albert and Belle Horton. It was a tiring and uncomfortable trip, complicated by errors in routing and a touch of dysentery.

June 14, '85

Such a time as we had getting home! We left Atlanta about 11 A.M. Wednesday, reaching Chattanooga about 6 P.M. We went back to the Hotel for the night, starting next morning for Cincinnati at 5 A.M. There was no sleeper to be had so we took a state room in a "Boudoir Car" and made ourselves as comfortable as we could considering that we were not very well and were very tired. The scenery through Kentucky and Tennessee was wild and beautiful.

We reached Cincinnati about 6 P.M. and discovered that instead of taking a sleeper through to Salamanca our tickets sent us by a different road 65 miles to Xenia, change cars and go 20 miles to Springfield where we must go another 2 miles to another depot and make connections if we could. It was well for the Agent who sold us those tickets that he wasn't around about that time!

We arrived in a hard rain storm at Springfield and found that we must wait there from 11:30 P.M. to 11 A.M., so we had to take a carriage to a Hotel and stay till the next day, when a bus took us (for 50 cts. apiece) to the other depot and we started for Salamanca, arriving at 9:45 P.M. Friday when we ought to have been at home. We could not make connections there and so went to a Hotel again, (where I was quite sick), and started for Rochester about 8 the next morning, reaching here at 1:30 P.M.

All the folks met us (except HK) with a "Kerridge" and took us home. They put me to bed, and I ornamented that or the lounge most of the time for two or three days, but "I'm quite tolerable now, thank you!"

The Spelman experience, with its heavy and varied teaching load, the printing office work, responsibility for writing "little articles" for fund-raising purposes, and her service as housemother to 47 women and girls of assorted ages and temperaments — often "sick and ailing and grunting and fussing" — had provided Hattie an opportunity to develop and utilize skills in a variety of areas, skills that would be built upon in other settings and other roles in the years to come. Despite the gloomy predictions of her mother and Frank, her health held up under a wearing schedule and she was able to complete the year with a sense of accomplishment.

The year at Spelman marked a turning point for Hattie. It justified her belief that her life could "amount to something," and that she was capable of carrying out a hard and demanding job. It demonstrated, too, her ability to adjust to and function effectively in unfamiliar surroundings. Most important of all was her feeling that she had "found her sheep." The satisfaction she experienced in the conversion of the "sinners" in the school and her part in the conversion of the girls in her house, confirmed and reinforced her decision to go into missionary work.

 **4**

Summer of Decision

June to November 1885

The quiet, relatively undemanding life at home to which Hattie returned was a sharp contrast to her life at Spelman. Visits with friends, a trip to relatives in Corning, New York, the annual group excursion to the lake, church meetings and events, shopping, and sewing once again made up her days. Yet few of these familiar activities were enjoyed with the enthusiasm that Hattie had felt in previous years. Many of her old friends had moved away and her own increasing maturity separated her from the younger members of her circle. More satisfying for Hattie were the opportunities she had to speak on behalf of Spelman Seminary to church or home mission groups.

> June 21, '85
>
> I'm that lazy that I don't "bring things to pass" with alarming frequency. We have had about 25 calls since I came home, but I haven't made any, except to the Manvels and Alberts.

> June 28, '85
>
> The event of the week was the picnic at Seabreeze, which was rather slow to me. The church folks seem to be either strangers or mere acquaintances, and I feel considerable like a cat in a strange garret. Mama and I got tired (I did not work any but she did) and came home on the 4 P.M. train.
>
> Saturday evening Mr. Morse, who visited Spelman during the YMCA Convention, called to invite me to speak at the 8th Ward Mission Sunday School of which he is Superintendent. So this afternoon I went and Papa escorted me. I spoke about 35 minutes, and considering how warm it

was, they paid good attention; the room was crowded. The collection taken was for Spelman Seminary, or rather for the new building.

Hattie had returned home looking forward to a quiet summer in which to rest up and prepare for another year at Spelman. To be a foreign missionary was still her ultimate goal but she was content to do the work at hand until the way should be opened for her. This opening came more quickly than expected.

Despite the difficulty and delay in communication between Rochester and Rangoon, Frank's opinion was still weighed in important family matters. His criticism of Hattie's original plan to take a position at Spelman had ceased once the decision was made, and during her year there his letters had included encouraging and appreciative comments.

Aug. 31, '84 [FDP]
I did not know how much spunk Hattie had in this matter. All I can say now is, "Go to it, Old Woman, and let me know when you get there!"

Nov. 30, '84 [FDP]
Hattie is getting along first rate. Don't be upset by any small thing in the way of a microscope, Old Lady!

June 7, '85 [FDP]
I think Hattie did just right to go to New Orleans.

It must have come as a surprise to Hattie, therefore, when at the end of what she felt had been a year of successful accomplishment, Frank once again expressed his disapproval of her teaching at Spelman.

May 12, '85 [FDP]
I quite agree with Mother that Hattie is working too hard. I thought Burma was a bad place for a "free horse," but it can't hold a candle to Spelman. One thing in Burma's favor, we are each more of our own masters than Hattie is in that Seminary. We <u>can</u> say, "I won't."

In a series of private letters to Hattie and her mother, Frank spelled out his disapproval of Hattie's plan to return to Spelman. Several of these are not among the family letters, but Hattie's replies provide the gist of the correspondence. Frank's initial and primary advice that Hattie remain at home for another indeterminate period, was summarily dismissed, as it had been the year before.

> July 27, '85
> You say "for my <u>own</u> sake" you would advise me to stay at home. I got tired of living for "my own sake" some time ago and found it very delightful and highly satisfactory to live for somebody else's sake. Neither do I wish to be a missionary because I have nothing else to do. Mama don't want me to come till I'm considerable older <u>unless I do come to you.</u> There seems to be a remarkable unanimity of opinion. I might as well run the risk of climate there as to be driven to death at Spelman; as to congenial companions, I got along quite well with an <u>entirely uncongenial</u> one for a roommate at Spelman.

Unable to persuade her to remain at home in Rochester, Frank modified his stand on Hattie's wish to come to Burma. Reiterating his concern over her return to Spelman, he suggested that if she was determined to go into foreign mission work, she should apply to the mission board in Boston regarding the possibility of an opening at Kemindine School in Rangoon, perhaps working on a part-time or limited basis while she became acclimatized and learned the language. Hattie lost no time in following through on this suggestion, writing to Mrs. Gates, the Foreign Mission Secretary of the Woman's Board.

> [July 27, '85, continued]
> Since the arrival of your private letters to Mama and me, I have been corresponding with Mrs. Gates. The Board has no idea of sending anyone to the Kemindine School, as other fields need a helper more. She quite agrees with your ideas, as I told her just what you said. In her last letter she says:

"Your brother's thought is a good one — for a young lady to spend a year or two in the study of the language and people before she enters on the hard work on the field. In your own case it would be a most fitting and happy thing for you to do so under the care of your brother. This question has come to me — would your brother give you a home for this preparatory season? I wrote you that our Board for various reasons would not send a young lady to Kemindine — not that it would not be a good place for her, but for prudential reasons. If you think it worthwhile to open negotiations with your brother on this point, do so and meantime I will confer with our Board and be able to write you officially of its views. Mr. Bushell of Maubin expects to come home for a stay of a year or two, and then will need a young lady to go with himself and family and have care of their 100 girls, a fine field. And the fields are always opening."

<u>What have you to say to that?</u> Of course I expect to spend one more year at Spelman, and would lay the matter on the table till next summer, were it not that I must know before the close of the coming school year whether or no I can go back. Miss Packard will want a definite answer. So if you will express your opinions on this point, it will greatly oblige, etc.

I've answered the questions to "Candidate" [on the application to the Board] and sent those to the "Pastor" to Dr. H. L. Morehouse. Mrs. Gates said I need not "create" a family physician for the sake of filling that out.

Yours lovingly,
Hattie

P. S. Of course your giving me a home would not include clothing. I shall be at Atlanta before your answer can reach here, I suppose. HP

With Mrs. Gates' assistance, Hattie's application to the board for appointment as a missionary to Burma proceeded rapidly. Hattie was invited by Mrs. Gates to meet the board in Boston in September. An invitation from Mrs. Cushing for Hattie to stay with her during her visit to Boston was gladly accepted.

Sept. 6, '85

I started for Boston last Sunday evening as I expected; had a pleasant journey for one on a sleeper, and reached Boston about 8:30 A.M. Mrs. Cushing met me and we went out to her home. Monday afternoon Mrs. Gates came to see me about meeting the Board Tuesday, etc., and Tuesday morning Mrs. Cushing took me into Boston early for some sightseeing.

At noon we went to the doctor's and she gave me a clean medical certificate, recommending me to the Board. She is very thorough and particular and has failed to recommend three or four who applied this past summer, so we were pleased when she did approve of me.

At 2 P.M. I met the Board. They asked but few questions after hearing what I had to say, and in a few minutes after I withdrew, Mrs. Gates came and said I was accepted by the Board as one of their missionaries and would be recommended to the Executive Committee in the Spring.

Mrs. Gates told me afterward that they would like to send me this Fall if I were not engaged. Miss Packard goes South this week and I don't see how I could ask to be released at this late day. But I do now intend to follow Mrs. Gates' suggestion that I resign and come home before the close of the year, giving me a chance to attend the Annual Meeting and get rested from my work. The idea of spending a year with you, learning the language, getting acclimated etc. seemed to please the Board, Mrs. Gates told me, and they thought it would be a good plan to send all the young ladies in a similar manner. Of course the salary that year would be little or nothing, if there were someone to give them a home; they would not be expected to engage in the work that year. She spoke of their wishing to send two ladies to Mrs. Thomas at Henzada, and one to the Bushells at Maubin and told me to ask what you thought of either of those places for me to go to after my year with you. She said they would like to send me to Miss Whitman in Japan if I hadn't a brother in Burma.

I spent the forenoon Tuesday sightseeing with Mrs. Cushing, went out to Cambridge, saw Harvard, went into Memorial Hall with its dining room and theater. Before going out we went into Philip Brook's Church which is certainly grand but I would not change it for ours. We saw

the Common, Public Gardens, Beacon Street, Bunker Hill
Monument, and Capitol dome from a distance, also went
into several of the grand stores.

Tuesday evening and Wednesday I spent at Mrs. Gates'.
Wednesday afternoon she got a carriage and took, or Mr.
Gates did, Miss Elwin and I out riding all around the
various Newtons, up on Institute Hill where we had a fine
view of Boston and the country between. In the evening I
went back to Mrs. Cushing's. Thursday morning Mrs.
Cushing went to the depot with me, Mrs. Gates was on the
train (she lives one station beyond Newton Center) and saw
me on the train at Boston for home. I reached here
Thursday at 10:25 P.M. after a pleasant journey.

So if all goes well I will probably sail a year from now.

The two month turn-around time for letters between Rangoon
and Rochester complicated attempts to coordinate Frank's sugges-
tions on the one hand with Mrs. Gates' planning on behalf of the
mission board on the other. Hattie's plan to return to Spelman for
one additional year before coming to Burma had not met with
Frank's approval. In an earlier letter he had implied that if she
were still determined to come to Burma, it would be better for her
to come immediately, rather than return to Spelman for the additional year.

Aug. 9, '85

Your letter came yesterday and was duly perused by the
family (except Ada) as your private letters always are, at least
those that come to me. As to its contents, without wishing to
be hypercritical, I must say it was not as lucid as one of my
dull comprehension might wish. You seem to think that if I'm
coming I better come this year and that in some way (unknown
to me) it might be easier, but I don't find any <u>reasons</u> for that
opinion in the letter.

You don't approve of my spending another year at
Spelman. My return is on the principle that if a little of a thing
is good, more is better. Though of course I was tired out, as all
were, at the close of school, yet on the whole my health is
better now than a year ago, and I hope it will be still better a
year from now. I don't intend to work next year as I did last,

and so not be as tired at the end. I told Miss Packard that I would go on with the care of the printing but that I could not attempt a <u>monthly</u> paper (which is what she wants). Moreover also I <u>won't</u> attempt it.

Yours as ever, Hattie Phinney.

A telegram and then a letter from Frank reiterated what his earlier letter had implied.

Sept. 20, '85 [FDP]

Hattie writes that she did not understand why I want her to come now if she is bound to come sometime. The reason is simply this. You all know what effect Ada's work had on her, and we have had <u>two</u> examples of ladies sent out in apparently perfect health who have shown in a few months that it was a mistake. Each had been doing years of hard work, had rested a few months and then come out, only to find that in a less bracing atmosphere they were not able to do the work put upon them.

It seems to me that Hattie might do two or three years work in Atlanta and think that she was doing it easily and without harm, only to find on trying a change that her constitution was too much weakened to bear the strain of such a complete change of life habits. Then by coming now she can have a year or more of comparative freedom from responsibility, and so get well settled into work by the time she has any responsibilities to bear.

Behind Frank's determination that Hattie should come to Burma "now" was another consideration. At this time, Frank was living at the Kemindine Girls School, roughly four miles out from the city of Rangoon. In July he had left the house he rented in Rangoon to board at Kemindine in order to be under the care of the director of the school, (Mrs.) Dr. Douglass, a doctor who ran a small hospital in connection with the school. It seems likely that the ease of living at Kemindine, with all matters of housekeeping taken care of by the school staff, and the social environment of the school itself, were factors both in Frank's original suggestion regarding Hattie's application to the mission board and in his continuing insistence that Hattie come as soon as practical.

Frank's strongly stated preference to have Hattie come to Burma at once instead of returning to Spelman, was duly related to Mrs. Gates.

Sept. 13, '85

As I wrote last week, I let Mrs. Gates know about your telegram and Monday morning I had a letter from her saying that as everything seemed to point to my going this fall except my engagement at Spelman she thought the thing for me to do was to see if I could be released from that, and if I could, to go forward the other way. The Board wanted to send me, you advised me to come now if ever, my health was sound and might not be after another year's work, and there were return-ing missionaries, Mr. and Mrs. Phillips, delightful people, with whom I could travel at least to Calcutta, where you could meet me. She offered to see Miss Packard before she left Boston if I wished.

So considering all things I decided to ask to be released. I telegraphed for her to see Miss Packard and I wrote to her, Miss Packard, Monday afternoon. I heard nothing decisive until Saturday morning when two letters arrived from Miss Packard written on her way south, one before and one after seeing Mrs. Gates who was on the same train going to see Miss Van Meter off. The letters were very cordial and affectionate, releasing me from my engagement and saying if the Lord had called me elsewhere He would fill my place there. So now I am free to sail this fall and feel satisfied that this is the right way. I hope you'll know by telegram that I'm coming long before this. I've written of my release to Mrs. Gates and expect she'll proceed to perfect the final arrangements.

Sept. 20, '85

I have had two cards from Mrs. Gates, one saying that the Board all approved my going this fall and the other that Mr. and Mrs. Phillips with whom I expect to travel as far as Calcutta, expect to go about the middle of November. So on the strength of that, HK wrote yesterday to Dr. Murdock to telegraph to you.

I wrote to Mrs. Gates that I should be satisfied if the Board provided for my outfit, passage, and native teacher, and that you would provide my board and lodging, that, of course, for one year only, this on the strength of your telegram. I presume little can be done till the next Board meeting, Oct. 1.

Only one more step was necessary to complete Hattie's official appointment as a missionary to Burma, a final trip to Boston to appear before the Executive Committee of the Mission.

Oct. 4, '85

I received a letter from Mrs. Gates, saying that the Board had voted my outfit $250, passage, personal teacher, and $100 incidentals to Oct. 1, 1886. She expected the Executive Committee would approve tomorrow (Monday) and then I could draw my $250.

Oct. 19, '85

I've been to the Hub again! I reached there Monday morning and was met by Mr. Gates as Mrs. Gates couldn't leave the Rooms. He took me to a Mrs. Goodwin's (one of the Board), to rest till Mrs. Gates came with Miss Bond.

We had our dinner at a restaurant and then went to the Rooms. After a while Mr. Lawson came and invited Mrs. Gates to bring her two young ladies in, so we went. They didn't keep us very long and after a time Mr. Lawson came out and told us that the Executive Committee very heartily approved the action of the Woman's Board and voted our outfits, etc. Miss Bond and I had to meet the Executive Committee before they voted the money because they have been criticized for not seeing the young ladies first and they could not be got together when we were in Boston before.

With the committee's decision, Hattie had achieved her wish; she was now an officially appointed foreign missionary, soon to be on her way to Burma. Once home, she and her mother quickly set about the necessary preparations.

Sept. 20, '85

Another busy week spent in sewing and fixing. I've got almost to the end of my underclothes making. Mama has made me some 3 sheets and is making the pillowcases. Miss Edmondson will come and help me about some light dresses, and Mary Manvel about some better ones. My outfit will be very medium size and won't kill me or anyone else in the making.

Mama and I have been shopping twice (got a set of tin boxes like yours for one thing) and that with the usual prayer meeting has been all my going this week.

Oct. 26, '85

This week has been divided between sewing and going. Monday I went downtown with HK and got my outfit money and bought a light woolen dress for steamer wear when my flannels grow too heavy. Tuesday, Wednesday, and Thursday Mary Manvel sewed for me and I sewed with her. We rejuvenated my black silk and made my new thinner silk and she cut the waist to the woolen dress. To finish this dress is all the sewing I have left to do.

By "going" Hattie referred to the round of social visits, farewell events, and appearances connected with her new role as missionary. While there had been no formal ceremony acknowledging Hattie's appointment during the Boston visit, the following weeks provided many opportunities for her new status to be recognized and celebrated.

Oct. 4, '85

I received a letter from (Mrs.) Dr. Robins asking me to speak for a few minutes at the Foreign Mission Meeting at the Association at Fairport next Wednesday to which I agreed, and one from Mrs. Elgin who wants Mama and I to come to North Parma next Friday (Oct. 9), let her send for some of our curiosities and she give me a parlor reception, inviting the church folks. We'll go if nothing prevents.

Oct. 11, '85

Wednesday morning Mama, Papa, and I went to the
Association at Fairport. The first thing was a Ladies Home
Mission Meeting. At 1:30 P.M. was a Foreign Mission meeting,
just an experience meeting. I spoke and then Mrs. Griffin, then
we returned to the Association and heard the various Societies
presented. In the evening Mr. Peeples preached a pretty good
sermon, then we came home.

Friday at 6:45 P.M. Mama and I started for N. Parma where
we arrived a little after 8 P.M. There was quite a houseful (they
have a nice large house) and Mrs. Elgin introduced us all
around and we had a little social and then she introduced me
to all and I spoke and explained the curios. (Mr. Elgin had
called for them Thursday) and talked and told where and how
and what for I was going. Some did not know where Burma
was or how I was to get there!!! Never saw a missionary and
don't know anything about missions anyway. Mrs. Elgin says
my visit and talk would help her a great deal in her efforts to
get them interested and at work.

Oct. 4, '85

Friday I trimmed Mama's fall bonnet and sewed and in the
evening in response to the President's invitation, I spoke to the
Judson Missionary Society at the chapel of Rockefeller Hall. Dr.
Pattison suggested it to Mr. Holt, the President. Mama went and
there were six or eight other ladies and Dr. Strong came in. I
talked 35 or 40 minutes and then they, the students, asked
questions for about 10 minutes more. They gave good attention
and it was quite as pleasant as speaking to any audience.

Nov. 2, '85

In the afternoon Mama and I went shopping and got all my
big things, mattress, chair, etc.

Tuesday I sewed all day and Wednesday ditto. I received a
card from Mrs. Gates saying that their Society were to have a
meeting Nov. 18-19 in Philadelphia and wanted to host a
farewell service the 17th and greatly desired me to be there. So
I 'spose I'll be there.

I received a letter from May Parker Albrecht expressing a
great desire to see me before I go, which desire will probably

be gratified and also one from Miss Keech of Brooklyn, saying
that she doesn't intend me to cut short my visit there, she has
spoken to a great many ladies of her church and they want to
meet me and have me speak at some meeting. She wants me to
come there next week, and stay till I sail. Of course I couldn't
do that for various reasons and because our church will give
me a farewell meeting Nov. 16, but Mama plans and everyone
seems to agree that I go Wednesday or Thursday this week and
stay one week, then return and go straight to Philadelphia
when the time comes. Shouldn't wonder if I did so.

For Hattie, the New York City visit was one more opportunity
to meet new people, see new sights, and enjoy her role as a celebrity.
Carrie Keech, a friend of Ada's who had visited in Rochester,
had many times urged Hattie to visit her home in Brooklyn.

Nov. 15, '85

I believe it is two weeks since I sat down and took my
pen in hand to write you a few words to let you know that I
was in good health and hoped you were enjoying the same
great blessing! So I'll begin back two weeks. Monday I
sewed, shopped, and made a bonnet. Tuesday in the
afternoon Papa, Mama and I packed my one big box.
Wednesday Mama and I packed my trunks and I went to
prayer meeting and at 11 P.M. I took a sleeper for New York,
which I reached at 11 A.M. Thursday.

Carrie Keech met me and I rested that afternoon and in the
evening attended an Entertainment at her Church given by the
young ladies, who, through Carrie, presented me with a ticket.
I met Dr. and Mrs. Kerfoot (the pastor and wife) and he
invited me to speak at their regular mission meeting the next
evening. I met a good many other nice people, a lady physician
from Vassar, etc.

Friday we went by Hamilton Ferry to New York, visited
the Produce Exchange building, Trinity Equitable Building, and
had a peek into the Custom House and Post Office, and came
back over the Bridge.

In the evening we went to Church and I spoke as agreed.
At the close of the meeting a great many came and spoke to
me — the older members of the Church, the toniest people

and the richest, as Carrie told me; she pretended to be very much set up by my receiving so much attention from the big bugs.

Sunday morning I went to the Tabernacle with Miss Ketchem and heard Talmage but didn't fancy him. In the afternoon went to Ada's old church, the Baptist Tabernacle, with the Misses Forrester and stayed a little while and then Mr. Grigg, a friend and boarder at the Keeches came for me and took me to the Song Service at the Five Points Mission.

Tuesday we spent in New York, visited Temple Court and saw Dr. H. L. Morehouse, then went to and through Stewart's, Macy's, Boutiliers', Stern's and then to Central Park, saw the animals and walked down Broadway to 1st St. taking in with our eyes the two Vanderbilts', Whitneys', and Stewarts' mansions and many others and then went into the Cathedral. After that we went through Tiffany's and to Parkinson's photo gallery and came back over the Bridge.

In the evening I led the Young People's prayer meeting by invitation of the one who has charge of them, Oscar Smith. Had a good meeting.

Wednesday I started home at 6 P.M. and reached here at 4 A.M. and waited in the depot till 5:30 and then walked home by electric, gas, and star light, and took a nap before breakfast.

To be continued from Liverpool or Glasgow.

This was Hattie's last letter before sailing, her subsequent activities reported by other family members. In the following letter to Frank, her father described his own feelings in regard to Hattie's departure.

11/15/85 [SHP]

It is a cold raw and gloomy day and I feel an unusual sadness in the thought that it is Hattie's last Sunday in beloved America, that is if the programme laid down is fully carried out. And yet I would not have it otherwise than as God directs. It is not all sadness and gloom, but as the sun is now shining brightly through the rifts in the clouds, so there is a joy in the midst of and mingled with our sadness that can be felt in no other way. Dr. Bond who has come into our Sunday School class has got hold of the matter in a sensible way. He spoke with me today about Hattie's going, as he thinks it is a great honour to have children go to the foreign fields and yet he realizes the pain it costs and sympathizes with us in the loss of the presence of our children. Others have a like view but some seem to think it a great calamity to have children go so far from home.

Hattie returned from her visit to New York on November 15, in time to attend the farewell ceremony at the family Church. Two days later she was on her way again, this time for the promised visit to May Albrecht and to attend the farewell ceremonies in Philadelphia and New York arranged by Mrs. Gates. Herman accompanied Hattie on this trip, which was to terminate with Hattie's departure on the S.S. *Devonia* from New York. Hattie's mother joined them in New York for some of the farewell festivities and to see Hattie sail. Herman reported in detail the final round of farewell activities as well as Hattie's departure the following day.

Nov. 22, '85 [HKP]

Hattie and I went by Broadway car to Madison Avenue Church, corner of 31st, where a ladies' missionary meeting was appointed. The exercises here were as follows: Singing; reading of scripture and prayer by Rev. Mr. Moon (Lexington Avenue Baptist Church); address of welcome to the missionaries present (all on the platform) and to the visiting ladies by Mrs. J. B. Colgate, who presided throughout. Address by Mrs. Bixby; singing address by Miss Barrows, and singing in Burmese by Mah Mya; address by Mrs. Hancock; prayer by Mrs. Van Dusen; collection; solo by Miss McCullom; addresses by the outgoing missionaries, Mr. and Mrs. Phillips, Miss Bond, Miss Mason, Hattie; farewell address by Mrs. Gates, who also gave to each lady a few special words with hand-clasp and kiss; prayer by Mrs. Whiting; letter from Mrs. Bainbridge, who had been invited but was at a missionary meeting in another part of the state; singing; address and benediction by Dr. Buckingham. Then much more standing about and visiting and the afternoon was about gone. "Dinner" at the Pyles' at 6:30 or 7 P.M.

In the evening Hattie and I started from dinner for Dr.
McArthur's new church, 57 Street near 6th Avenue, and
Mother and Mrs. Pyle came by next car. It was a regular prayer
meeting given up to a farewell missionary meeting. Hattie was
taken to the front with the other missionaries; Mother and
Mrs. Pyle sat well forward. I saw Dr. Morehouse at the back
and sat with him. After the usual opening exercises, Dr.
McArthur called Mr. Brigham to the platform, who made an
address and then introduced the missionaries who were
present, who spoke as follows: Mr. Phillips, Mrs. Phillips,
Hattie, Mrs. Hancock. Then Dr. McArthur called on Dr.
Burlingham, who spoke from the front, and Drs. Morehouse
and Bright, who spoke from their seats. After meeting, many
present were presented to the missionaries.

[The next day] at 1:20 P.M. a carriage came to take us to
the dock. A good many folks came to see the party off. Dr. and
Mrs. Morehouse, Dr. Burlingham, Dr. Judson, Mrs. McArthur,
Mr. Brigham, Mr. and Mrs. O. W. Gates, Mr. McGill, Carrie
Keech, and Miss Ketcham, Mr. and Mrs. Forrester, and two
daughters, the father and mother of Mr. Phillips, and so on. By
the way, we were all very favorably impressed with Mr.
Phillips, who was a DU in Madison. We think he has a sound
head and a sound heart, and are satisfied to have him purser
and conductor of the party. You know Mrs. Hancock and Miss
Rathbun better than we.

The usual basket of goodies and the steamer chairs were on
hand for each stateroom. At three o'clock good-byes began to
be said and in a few moments the bell rang and the cry came
"All visitors ashore." There was no such long delay as when
you sailed, and we watched the ship towed out and swung
downstream.

It had been over two and a half years since Hattie's letter to Frank
asking him to find a place for her in Rangoon, a request he had firmly
rejected. In the time that followed, she had received little encouragement — if not active discouragement — from both Frank and her
mother, the family members to whom she looked for support in her
search for a meaningful adult role. Marriage to a suitable man would
probably have met with their approval; Hattie's wish to make something of her life on her own, certainly did not.

It cannot have been easy for Hattie to defy these two key figures. Her lifelong role as adoring sister and obedient daughter had not prepared her for open defiance of their wishes; nor, it would seem, had it prepared them for the independence-seeking young woman that Hattie had become. In turning to others — notably Mrs. Cushing, Dr. Morehouse, and Mrs. Gates — for help in finding her way to an independent life, Hattie was able to find the support she needed to take the first step. It was her own unwavering determination, strength, and skills, however, that carried her successfully through the major challenges of the year at Spelman, and her application and successful election by the mission board.

Hattie was on her way to Burma at last.

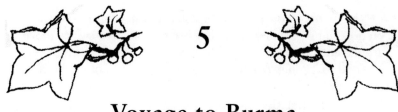

5

Voyage to Burma

November 1885 to January 1886

Hattie sailed from New York on November 21, 1885, on the S.S. *Devonia*, bound for Glasgow on the first of the long, multi-stage trip to Burma. The traveling party of eight consisted of Mr. and Mrs. Phillips, Miss Bond, and Miss Mason on their way to India; and Mrs. Hancock, Miss Rathbun, Mai Myit, and Hattie who would continue on to Burma.

Like Frank's "Log-a-Rhythms," Hattie's account of the trip was made up of a series of dated entries in single letters, mailed as the opportunity arose.

Nov. 22, '85

Dear Papa and all the other folks,

I'm writing in the "Music Saloon" with my feet braced against the organ stool, Mr. Phillips is lying on the settee near by (he is sick when he moves around), and all the rest are in bed, and have been so since before six. All have fed the fishes but myself. I have taken my meals as usual, except the 8 A.M. lunch — three meals a day is enough for me. I have lain in my berth a good deal but not because of sickness but weariness and a slight headache. The sea has been quite calm and only a little sprinkle this morning.

After sailing Saturday I put up my shoe bag and laid out my gown and slippers etc. then we all went on deck till dinner at five. The most of the evening we spent around the organ, talking, singing, etc.

Miss Bond and I played, Mrs. Hancock has a new copy of the Jubilee Volume and we tried a new song from it. While the rest went to 8 P.M. tea, I went on deck and watched the moonlight on the sea.

Today the whole party have rested a little while in our chairs on deck but mostly here or in our berths, some too sick to move around and all too tired. Mrs. Hancock and I went to lunch, we two and Mr. Phillips to dinner but they both left before the end.

Hattie used her time during the voyage to begin her projected year's study of the Burmese language.

Nov. 26, '85

I have settled down to a sort of a routine; reading the New Testament with notes after breakfast, studying Burmese from 10 to 11 A.M., reading *Life of Christ* and Mrs. Custer's *Boots and Saddles* and crocheting till lunch at 1 P.M. The same after lunch till dinner at 5 P.M. and writing and reading in the evening. Mrs. Hancock has produced a Burmese grammar which is helpful but not as good as a primer.

Nov. 29, '85

I did not write yesterday because it was too hard work. There are four sails up and great swells on the sea so that since sometime on Friday night the ship has rolled back and forth between this position to this and I know of <u>no work</u> so hard as the constant posturing, bracing up, and holding on with both hands, knees, and elbows, the doubling up like a jack knife and then undoubling if you are sitting up and the rolling back and forth if you are lying down with the expectation of rolling off, or out, if you let go or go to sleep. The first night of it I was afraid I would roll out of my berth (the upper) and there were no straps or anything to hold one in, so I got out and tried to rest on the settee and on the floor: but finally became so tired I climbed back, put one pillow in front of me and braced myself in till morning. Saturday night I packed myself in with robes folded up one each side and so slept more; an extra board has been put in to make the front higher. I think the swells are subsiding for we have now a few moments of comparative steadiness between rolls.

I wasn't to be "rolled" out of my study yesterday, however, and so for an hour morning and evening I braced up between a settee and a table and with Mai Myit curled up side of me I "did" my Burmese. I have learned the 33 consonants and 10 vowels with their heathenish sounds and jawbreaking names and have gone over it combining each consonant with each vowel. The others did not try to do much, even to read.

This morning I managed to play some on the organ, but the lively gymnastics required to stay on the stool, keep the pedals going and get hold of the right keys and stay in range of the book, would have done credit to that Burmese jumping jack.

Nov. 30, '85

We had "divine service" in the dining saloon last evening at 6:30 P.M. A colored missionary, bound for Africa, who is sent by the Presbyterian Board, preached a very good sermon. Miss Bond played, and two men; she and I sang by way of a choir! The preacher travels second class so we had not seen him before.

You would laugh to see the performance during the first hymn Sunday night. I tried to hold Miss Bond on the stool but in the midst of the first verse the ship gave such a lurch that I slid three feet away in spite of frantic efforts to hold on, and she was almost spilled off, but managed to keep on with music and song. I had to lose a few words while I straightened out my face. We were up in the music saloon and so out of sight of the congregation which was very fortunate.

On December 3 the *Devonia* reached Greenock, 13 days out of New York. The party was eager to rest up and contemplate the next phase. Details of each subsequent connection, from Liverpool to Bombay, from Bombay to Calcutta, and from Calcutta to Rangoon, were to be worked out as each portion was completed and the options for continuing travel considered.

Waverly Hotel, Glasgow, Dec. 6, '85

We reached Greenock Thursday at 11 A.M. The Custom House Officer came on board and our 17 trunks and 20 packages, bags etc. etc. were passed with not much inspection. Then we landed and the Company Agent gave each a ticket and we came by rail to Glasgow, reaching here about 1 P.M. We then came here with our baggage. We had been so long on the way that we wanted to get at our trunks and had them brought up and how the porters did sweat and groan over them. How good we did feel in the evening when we had a bath, got into clean clothes and into nice, easy, <u>stationary</u> beds.

It is decided that, as there is no steamship for Calcutta before the 26th, we will sail from Liverpool, December 12, on the *Persia* for Bombay — 28 days voyage — then go overland to Calcutta — 2-1/2 days — and we four take a Steamship there for Rangoon. This will save a month's time, and the extra expense of going part way by rail will not exceed the expense of our board here if we waited till the 26th; besides we will arrive in a better time of year. Shall probably reach Calcutta in a little over five weeks from now.

The stay in Glasgow was not particularly comfortable, but afforded Hattie the chance to observe a different environment and customs, and do a little sight-seeing. The group also attended local Baptist church services where they made the acquaintance of the local supporters of mission work and were accorded a measure of celebrity status.

[Dec. 6, '85, continued]
    This is the foggiest, smokiest, dirtiest, dingiest, <u>somberest</u> old city you can imagine. The buildings are all stone, black with smoke and coal dust. The streets are very nicely and smoothly paved and are very clean, but only lit by gas. It's been too foggy to do sightseeing since Saturday. Our hands and clothes are in a chronic state of smuttiness; we've had one washing done and will have another.
    The air was so thick all day yesterday that everything was invisible at the distance of half a block. We burned gas until about 11 A.M. and lit it at 4 P.M. This morning was but little better though it's lighter now, at 11:30 A.M. The air came in the little crack that the window was up last night so thick with the smoke that it woke us up and choked us. We'll all be glad to get away.
    The food is good, better than on the steamship but we often have to wait a long time for a meal to be served. Napkins are only furnished at dinner (1:30 P.M.) and the butter is very white and not salted at all; we do that as we eat it. There is no way of warming the hotel except by little open grates, so the rooms are seldom comfortable and we do as we did down South, fry on one side and freeze on the other. My gown, wool shoes, jersey flannel jacket, etc. all come into use, as well as the rest of my duds . . .

In the afternoon we all visited the Cathedral, built in 1181 or earlier. The windows were just superb, far ahead of anything I had ever seen. Many of the faces were beautiful and the colors of the dresses were richer than anything you can imagine. One part had subjects taken from the Old Testament and the rest from the New. Some of the handsomest windows were in the crypts below the Cathedral. The yard was paved with ancient tombstones.

Dec. 10, '85

Last evening we all went to the Adelade Place Baptist Church where Dr. McPherson formerly of Chicago is pastor. He was very cordial and so were all the folks. He called on each one to speak a few words, saying he wanted his people to see how American ladies could speak. His women-folks never speak in meeting. It was equal to another farewell meeting. The most striking feature was that when anything pleased the folks they cheered with their feet on the bare floor, which seemed out of place to us. They did it in their own meeting and when each of us went up to speak and when we ended. The meeting was in the session room downstairs, the walls were pretty and tasteful and there were red curtains at the windows, but the seats were uncushioned, the floor bare except matting in the aisles, and there were hooks all around the room for the men to hang their overcoats on, which looked odd. It was a large stone Church. We had a very pleasant time indeed and were invited to tea tonight at a Mr. Bowser's who gives his thousands to Foreign Missions every year.

The next stage of the journey began with the trip from Glasgow to Liverpool, not a particularly comfortable one.

Liverpool, Dec. 11, '85

We took the train at 10 A.M., having our 20 packages and 17 trunks and bundles in the luggage apartment back of us. We traveled 2nd class; being shut into a small apartment for nearly seven hours, with only a chance to rise up and sit down again in all that time was not nice.

We arrived at 4:40 P.M. (had our lunch with us) and were met by the company's agent and sent to his house as they take lodgers. It is a small place but we are comfortable. We go aboard at 12 M. tomorrow to sail before 1 P.M.

The voyage from Liverpool to Bombay took just a month, from December 12, 1885, to January 12, 1886. The only major delay encountered was a slow-down in passing through the Suez Canal. The steamship took three days to complete the passage, spending much time waiting for other ships to pass through.

S.S. *Persia*, Suez Canal, Dec. 28, '85

We reached Port Said at 4 P.M. yesterday, the 27th, and tied up for the night with the other ships. We arose about 6:30 A.M. to see when we entered the canal, but it was cold and raining and there was little to see. It has been so chilly we have hardly been able to keep warm all day.

There are four steamships ahead of us and two behind. Twice we stopped because a ship ahead was stuck in the mud. We never stop for a minute without being tied up to the bank so as not to drift around and get stuck. The town of Ismailia is on the right shore, 1-1/2 miles away.

Sometimes a half dozen little Arab boys in their long scant, blue or dirty white petticoats run along the bank shouting for "bucksheesh." Some threw sea biscuits to them which they grabbed up out of the sand and put in their mouths or under their arms and ran on. They could easily keep up with us by running, so you see how fast we go. Just before entering this lake where we are anchored, the banks are high and steep. The scenery consists of sand banks, with either desert or water of the same color as the sand beyond.

Dec. 31, '85

Today it has been <u>warm enough to sit on deck comfortably.</u> I shall soon shed winter clothes at this rate. Some have come out in cambric already, but it looks forced.

There are double awnings over the decks and single ones to be let down at the side which makes the decks very pleasant. The Red Sea is very much like the Mediterranean; don't see any red about except just at sunset!!!

Jan. 1, '86

The new year was rung in at 12 o'clock by the ship's bells and some of the young men who were up went around and

pounded and slammed on all the stateroom doors with racket
enough to wake the seven sleepers. They also had cake and
whiskey.

The punkas were put up in the dining saloon this morning
and are kept going while we are at meals. I can't say I like it,
too much like eating out of doors in the wind. They are made
of heavy cretonne pleated double onto a flat bar and swung by
a cord passing out of one of the port-holes.

Once through the canal and into the warmer waters of the Red
Sea, the Gulf of Aden, and the Indian Ocean, there were other new
sights to see.

Jan. 3, '86

The phosphorescence tonight is a milky wake back of the
ship, with brilliant sparkles in it, and now and then a big ball
of light.

We saw this morning some of the red seaweed which
sometimes covers the water making it red: this is where the
name Red Sea came from. This evening we passed a group of
twelve islands called "The Twelve Apostles."

A still calm day in the Gulf of Aden. We saw a great many
jellyfish today near the surface of the water which was very
smooth. They appeared about six inches in diameter and
consisted of a bright pink rosette with its center a delicate
white film around it. When they turned up sideways we could
see the tentacles underneath.

Jan. 11, '86

We were just now called up to see the phosphorescence,
which is different from any we have seen before. It is at the
bow and as if the crests of the waves made by the steamer were
burning intermittently with a pale blue flame — as if we set
fire to the sea as we passed. Sometimes the smaller waves at a
distance had the same appearance.

On the morning of January 12, 1886, land was sighted and by
2 P.M. the ship had reached the harbor at Bombay.

Great Western Hotel, Bombay, Jan. 13, '86

It took till about five to get the steamship into the dock, through six inches of mud, and get her tied up. Then the boat had to be got down and we taken ashore. We had to clamber over a native coal boat to land and then wait on the dock while our 17 trunks and innumerable parcels were loaded, with endless jabber, onto three two-wheeled bullock carts, of which the streets are full (just like the pictures Julia has of bullocks). Then we walked quite a distance through the strangest sights to the Custom House, a small affair, where Mr. Phillips told what we had and we were passed without any inspection and but a minute's delay. There our guide, who had "Cook's Tours" on his collar, put us into two carriages and we went at a good rate. Our driver wore a rig of white cotton and white dotted muslin over it! Imagine a Rochester driver in white figured muslin!!!

The street sights are indescribable, naked children — men hardly better off — some nicely dressed — women in bright silks — a few Europeans — open street car — tiny shops where the dealer sits in the middle and reaches all his goods — endless carts with their little patient, humpbacked bullocks — bright pretty black babies now and then, and so on ad infinitum. Having seen Julia's photos made it seem not so strange. I didn't feel shocked or distressed. Miss Mason thought it was well enough to <u>see</u> but didn't want to live in such a place — but I've learned to love black people before, so I like it all, or at least can stand it.

Their baggage not reaching the depot in time for them to take that day's train to Calcutta, the party spent the night at the Great Western Hotel in Bombay. The extra day gave them a chance to see a little of Bombay and prepare for the long trip to Calcutta.

[Jan. 13, '86, continued]

About 11 A.M. this morning we had carriages (the distances are immense) and went to a big market or bazaar to get fruit to take on the train, and to get hats. It took almost endless bargaining and fussing and hunting to find something to suit. The Assam party got small sized topees, and Mrs. Hancock and I got Terai hats — ventilated, silk lined, both hats bound and the inner one lined with white silk, broad brimmed and quite high crowns which we crush in — for R7, for which they first asked R12!!

We also got small chintz-covered pillows for 8 annas each, to use on the train as no bedding is furnished. Mr. Phillips got for us in Liverpool cheap blankets, 3s9d; I can dispose of mine in Rangoon if I don't want it.

Walters' Boarding House, Calcutta, Jan. 16, '86

The afternoon of that day we took gharries and went for a drive. The contrast between the immense and very beautiful Govt. buildings and the wretched thatch hovels of the natives is striking. The women wash their clothes, long straight strips of cloth, in big brass chalices and hang them on the eaves of their huts to dry. This is in the city, but in the country we saw them washing in the streams on a big stone, and drying the things by spreading them out on the mud or clay, stones being scarce.

After passing the Govt. buildings we drove up Malabar Hill, where the English live in high fenced compounds; but we went mainly to visit the Parsee "Towers of Silence." You know the followers of Zoroaster, not to defile earth, water, or fire, which they regard as sacred, expose the dead on a tower for the vultures to strip of flesh. There are five of these towers in a large compound, full of flowers and nicely kept, on Malabar Hill. They are solidly built of stone about 350 feet across, and are low — not above the treetops. A Parsee showed us around and showed us the model of the tower, and the description of it printed in English. The Parsees are the richest and most intelligent people we see. The women dress very prettily in clear bright colors; it is a relief to see a group of them, for the universal filth, nakedness, squalor, and manifest ignorance and degradation on every side is oppressive; and appalling when one thinks how little is being done to help it.

We got our baggage at the hotel and went on to the depot, and took the train at 6:30 P.M. for our 1430 mile journey of three nights and two days.

There was nothing furnished in the car but water in the wretched little bathroom. The settees were cane bottom and back and very hard and narrow. All the bedding we had couldn't make them comfortable, and if we drew up our knees they stuck over the edge. Miss Rathbun said she lapped over 6 inches all the time. It was also very hard to keep warm the last half of the night. We took second class because first class costs so much more, and we had to pay Rs.200 for our extra baggage; each passenger being allowed only 36 pounds.

For the first 85 miles the road ascends, in some places at the rate of 1 foot in 37 feet; there are numerous bridges and viaducts some 190 feet high. We sat up till 11 P.M. and watched the scenery by moonlight, as this ascent of the Gautes is the best part of the journey. The rest of the way is mostly fertile plains or jungles.

Thursday morning after an unrestful night we had "early tea" at Burhanipur at 6 A.M. Mr. Phillips got out and bought toast and eggs, and we had fruit with us.

Everything is dry and parched, the grass dead and shrubs very dusty. The mango trees are of a dark rich green, and shaped like an apple tree. Cactus hedges, either flat or round leafed are quite common: a wire fence extends both sides of the track, but the native fields are separated by low mud walls.

We got out and had a regular breakfast at Khandwa about 11:30 A.M. and dinner at Sohagpur at 4:35. We had excellent meals both days, better than on the steamship, I think: beef, mutton, fish and meat balls, rice and curry, pudding and fruit are served, and a half-hour allowed for breakfast and dinner.

We crossed a pretty river — the Burra Zowa (?) on a five-arch bridge 1147 feet long. There are pretty buildings at all the stations, and they are always surrounded by elaborately laid out flower gardens; we see nasturtiums, roses, lady slippers, cock's comb, mignonette, trumpet vine, a flower like the white one Mama brought from Aunt Julia's, only without the red center, marigolds, bachelor buttons, and many we did not recognize.

The station master at one place had a jeweled ring in the top of his ear. Toe rings, anklets, armlets, bracelets, and nose rings are common, though there are multitudes who wear nothing but one dirty piece of cloth. All sorts of head rigs are seen from tiny round caps to the most stupendous turbans, sometimes put on any way and sometimes the innumerable folds are arranged very evenly, systematically and artistically. Shoes with the toes turned over are the most common except bare feet.

At Itari we saw an immense crowd of natives and their bullock carts; evidently a fair or religious gathering. At 10 P.M. we stopped 40 minutes at Jubbulpore and got out for a little walk up and down, and later saw a Mosque, of which we only saw about three in the whole journey. Excepting these there was nothing to indicate that the people had <u>any</u> religion.

At Miryapur was an elegant depot, and here I saw a man carrying, slung on his back, a skin water jug or bottle; saw the same often afterward. We had breakfast about noon at Mogul Serai. A boy came to the window with fans like that Hattie Perry had, but not quite so nice, and as I have none with me I got one for 2 an. about one foot across when open: it is very thin and light.

At Buxar about 2 P.M. two palanquins were put on the train, we suppose native ladies were in them.

In the afternoon we crossed the River Sone on a grand bridge one mile long, having 25 massive stone piers. Later we reached Patna which stretches for some miles along the Ganges. On one side of us was the beautiful river fringed with grass and palms, on the other an endless succession of yellow clay houses, with tile roofs, the walls being precisely the same as the ground they rose from, only the angle telling where the narrow lanes ended and the wall began. Somehow it was very depressing, though the houses were substantial and neat, none more than one story. But there wasn't one sprig of green or of anything to relieve it. A few were ornamented with white put on in dots.

On the whole the native houses are as good as the country cabins and the city shanties of the negroes down South. But the far deeper degradation of the people is apparent.

We had dinner at Mahapore and at that time, 7 P.M., there were two men and a boy in the car, which made more than there was sleeping room for, even if any of us would wish to go to bed in their presence — of course there were no curtains. Mr. Phillips tried to have the guard change them but he would not; so Mrs. Phillips and Miss Bond sat up all night on one seat and Mr. Phillips slept above them. He had lost his dinner in seeing about it and would have to work more today than the ladies would; besides the ladies wouldn't want to go to bed there even if he did not. We all offered to change places with them for part or all of the night but they would not let us.

Mr. Phillips is a thorough gentleman, always pleasant and obliging; the unfailing patience with which he has looked after our baggage and done the business of the whole party is wonderful. All of the party are nice, Miss Rathbun being perhaps the most unfailingly agreeable one. "Pardon this digression."

We were all up by 4 A.M., packed up our numerous possessions, ate a light lunch out of our baskets and were ready just as the train rolled into the large depot at Howrah where we were to get off. The train does not cross the Hoogley. A man from Mr. Sykes met us, got gharries for us and cooleys to transfer our baggage. We were then sent here where missionaries generally are.

Hattie's reference to "here" was the Walters' Boarding House. The delay in Bombay had resulted in the party for Rangoon missing the connection with the weekly mailboat to Burma and necessitating a wait of several days for the next boat. Hattie and the others used the opportunity to see a little more of Indian native culture and the mission work there.

[Jan. 16, '86, continued]
Mrs. Walter has five immense mansions all near together. Mr. and Mrs. Phillips and Miss Bond are in one and the rest of us in another and we eat in a third. The ceilings are as high as the small rooms at Sibley Hall and the rooms just immense. We have one divided by a curtain to sleep in, with two narrow beds, one exceeding broad one (Miss Rathbun's and mine) and a cot for Mai Myit. Another equally large room for sitting room (I think other boarders use it also), two bathrooms and a large covered veranda with chics to let down are at our disposal, with plenty of tables and easy chairs. We have early tea about 7 A.M., breakfast at 9 A.M., tiffin at 2 P.M., a cup of tea at 5 P.M., and dinner at 7:30 P.M. This is very good, the meals are five hours or more apart and a cup of tea thrown in is not amiss, especially as it is good tea; all the fare is good. We have just returned from a dinner of several courses; all this for R4 a day, and a rupee at the rate of exchange in Bombay is worth 37 cents about. Such accommodations and board couldn't be had at home for that sum.

Jan. 17, '86
Sunday morning we all went to the Bow Boyane Baptist Chapel where we heard a good sermon on Hosea 11:4, by the pastor, Mr. Hook. After the service we were shown the baptistery where Dr. Judson was baptized, and the tablet in memory of [missionaries] Carey, Marshman, and Ward.

Jan. 18, '86

Before breakfast this morning we took a walk to the "New Market," where almost everything is for sale — fish, flesh, fowl, nuts, fruit, vegetables, hardware, dry goods, millinery etc. etc. each in separate parts of the market. We met numbers of Eurasians and English, but of course the great crowd are natives, in every stage of dress and undress. I wanted to get a "puggeroy" (i.e., veil or sash) to put on my hat as it looks like a man's without one.

The proper time to call is between 12 noon and 2 P.M. so today we Burmese folk got a gharry and called on Mr. and Mrs. Thomas at the Baptist Mission Press. They were hoping to see us, and we had a very pleasant call. Then we went to the American Zenana Mission Home. Two American ladies have charge of it; they have thirteen schools in the zenanas of the city and stations in Carnepore and in Allahabad. We found one of the ladies, Miss Hook, and had a nice call. Miss Rathbun and I are to go to visit the Zenanas with some of them tomorrow.

Jan. 20, '86

We took a gharry to the "Doremus Mission Home," generally called "American Mission Home." We found Miss Marston and Miss Hook, who introduced Miss Rathbun and me to an Eurasian lady (their helpers are all Eurasian or native) who took us in her gharry and we started off.

Soon we were in the native part of the city. We passed a small gaily painted, closed, temple; on the next corner was a plain, small affair through the doors of which we could see the idol <u>Siva</u> decked out with jewels and tinsel, a gaudy ugly affair; next to this a little temple to Kali, their favorite goddess, because they fear her, as she is the goddess of murder. She stood on a prostrate figure and her long red tongue hung out. Two or three natives came and bowed before her as we sat there. Close by was a little building and through the open door we could see "The Great God" which was merely a block of black wood which looked as if it might be the ornamental top to a fence-post, except for a curved gash near the top painted red.

We stopped but a moment and then drove on through still narrower streets, only wide enough for the gharry to go and leave room for a man to pass at each side; and presently stopped to take

in a native young woman who is one of the outside helpers. While
we waited a little Mohammed girl, about 11 years old came to the
hydrant to fill her little brass chatty. She had a pretty, bright,
sweet face, her black hair was done in a knot at the back of her
head, as all the women and children wear it, the one long breadth
of cloth, which is a woman's only garment generally (called
"saree" one yard wide and four yards long) was dark red with a
border: her little ankles had heavy silver anklets, her wrists
numerous bracelets and bangles, in her ears immense silver bells,
and through one side of her nose a light gold ring fully three
inches in diameter with several large pearls and other jewels
attached. Her feet of course were muddy, her garment not
overclean but somehow I found her wonderfully attractive, and
would have liked so much to have talked with her.

We saw two other children in a fresh pink garment with
books in their hands on their way to school, also young men
students, for the Bengalese are in the habit of sending the boys
to school and now the girls are beginning to be sent, for the
young men are being educated and they sometimes examine a
girl and won't marry her if she is ignorant.

After riding some distance farther we reached the first
school (average attendance over 100): it has four grades, in
four small rooms open to each other, and in charge of four
native Christian girls. In the lowest grade they were from 3 to
8 years old, and in the highest from 10 to 12 years. At that age
they are married and shut up in zenanas, generally. One of
these 11 year-olds had her hair parted and the red mark in the
part showing that she was married. All had nose jewels, the
younger in the middle, the older at the side.

Their faces were bright and often pretty, and with their
one light garment (white) and tiny knots of hair they looked
like miniature women. They sang a hymn for us, both words
and tune being Bengali, not very melodious.

After this we said "Goodby" and went on to another
school, like the first — only there were but two rooms and two
native helpers. One little tot recited "The Old Old Story" in
her language for us. All these children are from heathen
families, but they are taught Scripture truths and learn passages
in hopes it will come back to them later. They at least have
Christian training in childhood, if it is not continued long.

We next went to the zenana of a family of the Sudra caste (next to the highest). We passed through a winding way into the court in the center of the house, which is paved with stone, lower in the center and damp, as water was running all the time. We passed up a narrow winding stairway into a room opening on the court. There was a European bedstead, bureau and towel-rack, but things were at loose ends. Two cupboards let into the thick walls contained numerous idols. We saw the lady of the house, a very plump woman of 35 or 40 years, and the pupil, her daughter, a girl of 16 years with her 2 year-old daughter on her hip, as all the children are carried. The baby had a short white jacket on and a pearl hanging from her nose. The two women wore the one garment around and over them, of white with a bright border. The older wore on each wrist a massive gold bracelet and a dozen smaller ones, two rings of gold in each ear (one of those school girls wore a <u>fringe</u> of rings on the outer edge of her ears) and a ring 1-1/2 inch in diameter with several pearls and other jewels in one side of her nose; also the rings. The younger wore the same except that she had for a nose jewel (from the middle) an immense pear-shaped pearl fully 3/4 inches long. She squatted on a bit of carpet at the feet of the teacher and recited her lessons in reading, Arithmetic and Scripture lessons. The family are heathen but do not object to learning of our religion. The older woman has said, "It might be easy to <u>believe</u> but very hard to <u>confess</u>." Should one of them confess the whole family would be degraded entirely. The daughter was very pretty though her lips were scarlet with betel nut, which is quite common, as well as the red or white caste marks on nose or forehead, tho these had on the mark in the parting of the hair. There was hanging in the room a Rampore chudda shawl like Mama's, and an India cashmere (of many pieces embroidered) which the son-in-law had worn at his marriage. The <u>men</u> wear these shawls here.

At the second zenana, the family were of the highest caste Brahmins, and consisted of a widow and her daughter and son-in-law. The daughter was 17 years old and had lost two children. These women were lighter in color and more intellectual. The widow wears no jewels and has but one meal a day and must not fix herself up nice; still she looked well. The daughter was robed and jeweled like the other, except that her hair was braided with mock pearls and put in a green silk net. She was also pretty and had very pretty hands as all these women and girls have. She was studying English so as to help her mother take care of her large property, which is in the hands of a man appointed by Govt. These people think the Bible a bad book and won't have it; but they will take and read the tracts the teacher leaves at every lesson.

The third household was of the same caste but very poor; the pupil was a widow of 19 years, widowed when 14 years. We squatted on little stools in a small room 1/2 filled with a bedstead. There was present a married sister (wearing the iron bangle on her wrist which is the marriage ring), an unmarried one, the widowed mother, several men, and two naked children. They afterward put a gray cashmere jacket on one, and a heavy black band close under its eyes giving it the strangest appearance. Two visitors came to the room across the court; they squatted on the floor and food was placed on plantain leaves on the floor before them and they ate with their fingers.

All the women were glad to see us; they admired our hair, and one took note of the chain on my glasses.

On the way home we passed a hovel where an image of Kali was set up. As Brahmins must not kill animals or eat meat, they manage it by offering an animal to Kali, kill it before the image and offer her the blood, and then sell the meat. Since it was offered to her, the gods won't object! There was a pool of blood, a slaughter block and some meat hanging before the image. We reached the Mission Home before 4 P.M. and then returned here, having ridden about 12 miles in all and had nothing to eat since breakfast.

The last evening before boarding the steamship for the voyage to Rangoon was spent in a visit to the Thomases' of the American Baptist Mission Press, which provided an opportunity for Hattie to meet other missionaries working in a variety of fields.

Diamond Harbor, S.S. *Africa,* Jan. 21, '86

We had such a very pleasant evening at Mr. Thomas'; we met Mr. and Mrs. Ellison who were just married and who left for the Garo plains after dinner, and also the other English Baptist Missionary and a Mr. and Mrs. Jones on their way to Dinapore, about 20 in all. I had a nice visit with Mr. Thomas, and one with

a Mrs. Ellis, a Zenana Bible Woman of the English Baptist
Mission who goes freely to the native houses and teaches <u>nothing</u>
but the Bible. She is gladly received, and asked to come again.
One heathen mother tells her with pride how her little eight year-
old daughter says, "Think I'm ever going to bow down to idols —
wood and stone things, made by men — no, I <u>never</u> will." She,
Mrs. Ellis, has 300 houses (12,000 people) that she visits regularly, taking six weeks to go the rounds, and she teaches the Bible
in all. Of course there are houses where she would not be
received, but it is evident that it is no longer absolutely necessary
to teach secular things to gain an entrance. Her people are of all
castes but mostly middle class.

The strength of Brahminism lies in these very Zenanas and in
the prejudice and bigotry of the women in them, and this sort of
work is undermining all that; the men don't thoroughly believe
anyway; they are becoming too well educated. Heathenism is so
vast and powerful that it was cheering to learn of this work.

On January 21, Hattie and her party embarked on the last leg
of their journey to Burma on board the S.S. *Africa,* just two months
to the day since leaving New York.

[Jan. 21, '86, continued]
We were all up in good season this morning, and two gharries
took us all to the river where this steamship was waiting. As soon
as the gharry stopped, and before, we were surrounded by 4,673
cooleys all clamoring at the top of their voices for the privilege of
taking our hand luggage to the boat. A man of Mr. Sykes (Cook's
agent) was among them, and he and Mr. Phillips kept them from
snatching our things and rushing off. We were finally put onto a
native boat, we seven ladies packed under the covering as tight as
possible, and taken out to this steamship which is a three-master,
and seems like a very nice ship. Our cabins are roomier and nicer
than before, tho we shall be visited by immense cockroaches. The
others saw us settled and then we said "Goodby" all around, and
thanked Mr. Phillips who has been exceeding kind and painstak-
ing, and then they got into the boat again and departed.

At about 10:30 A.M. we started down the river, reaching
Diamond Harbor at 4:35 P.M., where we are waiting for the
mail early tomorrow morning.

<u>Friday</u> The mail was brought out in two boats this morning about 11 A.M. and also some more passengers, making 18 in all, 12 being ladies. All are English but us. There is no ceremony, dressing for dinner nor anything of the sort. There are very many second class passengers, Burmans, Karens, Shans, Turks, Chinese, Bengali, Eurasians, etc. etc.

We started about 11:45 this morning and passed out of the river about 4 P.M. The Bay is very calm so far.

I have done little but rest and read and sing Burmese with Mai Myit a little: "He leadeth me," "Nearer my God to Thee," and such familiar ones; if I don't know the tune <u>very</u> well I forget it while trying to read the Burmese fast enough.

The three days on the ship passed quietly but the landing itself was not without incident.

Jan. 27, '86

I was awakened about 4 A.M. Monday by the steamship stopping. I looked out and saw the pilot come aboard and we thought we were going right up to Rangoon. Mrs. Hancock got up and packed, then I got up. After a while we stopped and the engines reversed a long time and then we stopped again. I had the impression that we had gone backward for some distance, but when we were ready and went up on deck, behold there was the green bank right in front of us only a short distance away, and we were stationary. It looked as if we had attempted to go to Rangoon overland! I had noticed that a fog suddenly shut down shortly before we started to back up. It lasted but a very short time but in that short time we were run aground.

After the fog lifted a steam launch was seen in the distance and was signaled and a boat sent to her. After a little the S.S. *Enterprise* was signaled and we were told we could go up in her if we wanted to. We almost decided to do so, when I thought that possibly Frank might come for us and we would miss him, so we stayed on board. Very soon we saw another launch coming toward us. We mistrusted that it was Frank; the English folks were greatly exercised to know how anybody could have learned so soon that we were in distress. Presently a big white hat waved and we were quite sure, and then we could distinguish faces and were certain. He very kindly informed us that "<u>that</u> wasn't the way to Rangoon!" a fact that we had been painfully aware of for some time. He and Mr. Eveleth came up, and there was a very pleasant meeting all around.

We ate our breakfast while our trunks were being got out of the hold and then we started up the river, about 16 miles to Rangoon. The heat of the engine with the sun heat made it very hot, and was probably the cause of my having a headache the rest of that day and the next. We two stopped for tiffin at Mr. Eveleth's and then came on here to Kemindine and found Mrs. Douglass, Misses Williams and Clark, and also Miss Rathbun and Mah Myit who got here ahead of us. The latter two took the steamship early the next morning for Moulmein.

In 1886, Hattie was 24 years old — Frank's age when he left home for Burma. For Hattie, the physical journey from America to Burma had required little but patience and some acceptance of the discomforts of travel; the personal journey — from her first appeal to her arrival in Rangoon — had required considerably more: determination and an unwavering belief in her goal and her ability to reach it. In the end, her persistence had won over the person who was initially the most vehemently opposed to her plan and whose help she needed most, her brother Frank.

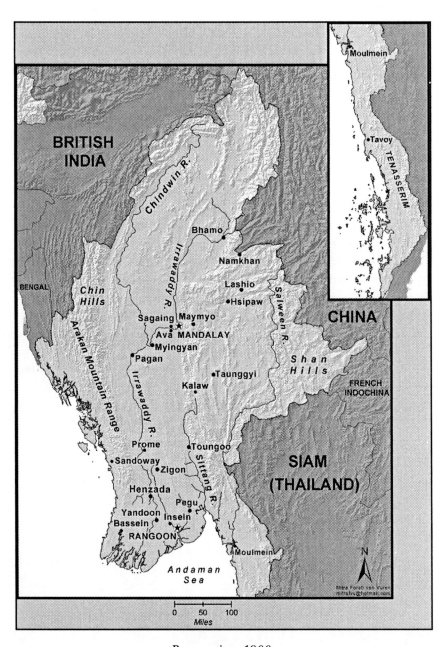

Burma circa 1900.

Part II

Introduction to Burma

The Baptist mission in Burma to which Hattie had been assigned was an historically important and well-established mission. Founded by Adoniram Judson in 1813, it had been the first American mission to be established on foreign soil.

Burma's history as an identifiable nation dates back some 1,000 years, although its boundaries have shifted over the centuries with the migration of various tribes, the fortunes of warring kings, invasions by foreign armies, and the success or failure of Burma's own invasions of neighboring territories. With an area roughly the size of the state of Texas, Burma comprises 261,789 square miles and encompasses three very different types of terrain. Two major mountain ranges run north and south: one along the Arakan, the western borders; and the other along the Shan plateau along the eastern edge of the country and down the Tenasserim coastal area. Between them lie the lowland areas known as Upper and Lower Burma; Upper Burma, the region around Ava and Mandalay, is extremely dry, while Lower Burma, the delta area around Rangoon, is excessively humid and subject to heavy rainfall in the monsoon season.

Although, geographically, half of Burma lies in the temperate zone, its climate is tropical. There are three major seasons, each experienced differently according to region: the "cool" season from November through January; the "hot" season from February through April, and the "wet" season (monsoon season or "the rains") from May through October. The "wet" season is the most variable in its effect: Rangoon has an average rainfall of 100 inches, Mandalay, 33 inches, some other areas of Upper Burma as little as 24 inches a year, while the Tenasserim and Arakan coastal areas receive over 200 inches per year.

In 1886 the geographical and political unity of Burma was a newly achieved result of British occupation, the culmination of Burmese conflict with the British, which left its borders largely as they are today. In three English-Burmese wars over a period of 60 years, the British had appropriated first the western coastal and mountain areas of Arakan and the southern coastal area of Tenasserim (1825); then Lower Burma, the southern delta region, with Rangoon as its capital (1855); and in a final conflict with the last Burmese king, Thibaw, in 1885 (even as Hattie was on her way) the British gained control of Upper Burma, deported the King and his family, and designated the whole of Burma a part of British India. It was not until 1938 that Burma was granted independent status separate from India, and 1948 before its independence from Britain was achieved. During the years that Hattie lived in Burma, the British controlled the country.

Burma then, as today, was a nation of many different ethnic groups, of which the Burmans* were and are the majority group and the predominant landholders. Other major groups include the Karens, the Shan, the Sgaw Karens, the Chins, and Kachins. Prior to British rule, perhaps the only characteristic that many of these groups had in common was Buddhism; for while some of the native tribes had their own religious practices and beliefs, the vast majority were Buddhists.

Burma's economy in the nineteenth century was almost entirely agricultural, with rice its major export and source of wealth. Teak from the northern jungles, and mineral deposits, including rubies and jade, were other exports much sought after by foreign traders. These constituted the basis for the British interest and ultimate takeover and colonization of the country.

The city of Rangoon, the political and commercial center of Burma at that time, served as the headquarters of the British government, protected by a large cantonment of British troops. The most heavily populated city in the country and a cosmopolitan port,

---

*The use of the terms *Burmese* and *Burman* can be confusing. In general the term *Burmese* has been used to refer to anything or anyone that pertains to the country of Burma, while the term *Burman* refers to individuals who are members of the Burman ethnic group, a specific subgroup of the total population.

its citizens reflected not only the ethnic mix of Burmese native groups, including the Burmans, Shans, Karens, and others, but comprised a large number of "natives of India" (Tamils, Telegus, and Hindus brought in by the British to fill a variety of service roles) and Chinese, attracted by the opportunities for trade.

In his work with native populations, Baptist pioneer Adoniram Judson had believed strongly that it was necessary to reach the people through the use of their own language. He himself directed his efforts to the conversion of the Burmans and became proficient in Burmese for that purpose. His accomplishments included not only the conversion of the first Burmans but also the development of a Burmese-English dictionary and the translation of the Old and New Testaments into Burmese. The majority of Burmese were literate, having learned to read in village schools, and thus were able to read the pamphlets and tracts that Judson and later his fellow Baptist missionaries prepared and distributed. A printing press with Burmese type, obtained early in Judson's time, was of major importance in advancing the work of the Burma Mission, as was the American Baptist Mission Press. Cephas Bennett (Frank's immediate predecessor as Superintendent at the press) had been a contemporary of Judson's, having begun his work with the press in 1824. The Bennetts, their granddaughter, Ruth Whitaker Ranney, and many of the missionaries still serving in Burma at the time of Hattie's arrival, were members of missionary families that dated from Judson's day.

In preparation for her work as a foreign missionary, Hattie began the study of Burmese on the voyage to Burma and it remained the language in which her work was carried out. Mission work among the large populations of non-Burmans required missionaries with mastery in a variety of different languages. At the time of Hattie's arrival, missionaries had been recruited to undertake work for each of the major ethnic groups, and worked in a number of different fields.

By 1886, the American Baptist Mission was a well established presence in Rangoon. The mission was looked upon favorably by the British as providing a civilizing influence over the natives and the mission's more influential members were included among the non-governmental leaders in the city. Several of the mission's institutions were located in or near the city's center, an area with which Hattie was soon to become familiar.

Most of the missionary families stationed in Rangoon lived just outside the downtown area on Mission Road or Ahlone, generally attended the "English Church" (Immanuel Baptist Church), and associated little with other Europeans in the larger Rangoon community. Their contact with the native population was limited almost entirely to their roles as pastors to native churches or teachers in the educational institutions set up for the natives. Single missionaries assigned to Rangoon usually boarded with a family or another single member of the mission. Missionaries from other parts of Burma joined in mission activities when they were in Rangoon for business or health reasons, and were accommodated in the homes of one or another local missionary family or in the Mission Guest House, a small building set up for this purpose. There were no suitable public accommodations available in the city and little mixing with other residents.

The map of Rangoon provides a guide to the major places and institutions mentioned in Hattie's letters.

[1] Immanuel Baptist Church, the principal Baptist church in Rangoon, was referred to as the "English Church" because its services were conducted in English. It was located on Fytche Square at Dalhousie and Barr Streets, a major thoroughfare surrounding the Sule Pagoda near the government offices. Frank had played an important part in the acquisition of the land for the church and was instrumental in getting it built. At the time of Hattie's arrival, he served as Superintendent of the Sunday school there, and Mr. L. J. Denchfield was the pastor.

[2] Within a few blocks of the church, the American Baptist Mission Press on Merchant Street was close to the Strand and the wharves lining the Rangoon River. It was the center of much Mission business. While its primary purpose was to supply the Bible and biblical literature (educational materials, tracts, innumerable flyers, bulletins, and pamphlets for use in the mission schools and churches) in a variety of native languages, the press undertook a variety of commercial ventures that made it self-supporting. In addition to his position as the superintendent of the press, Frank also served as the treasurer of the mission, and in that position played an important role in the mission's affairs.

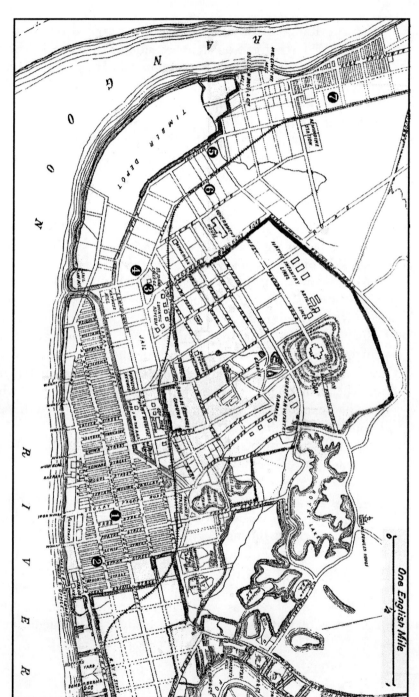

Rangoon circa 1880.

[3] The Rangoon Baptist College was situated on St. John's Street, a little farther out on the west side of the city. It provided education in English for native young men and boys at the secondary level; its goal was to raise the level of educational achievement of its students to meet college standards. Dr. John Packer was the president at the time of Hattie's arrival.

[4] The purpose of the Karen Theological Seminary, located directly across the street from the college, was to train young men to serve as native pastors to the Karens. D. A. W. Smith was the head of the Seminary.

[5] Lanmadaw Baptist Church conducted its services in Burmese and was the principal Burmese church in Rangoon. Hattie was to become active in the Lanmadaw Church after she had attained enough skill in the language to participate.

[6] Mission Road/Ahlone, the area in which most of the members of the mission lived, was a little away from the commercial area of Rangoon and consisted of a number of single houses, many of which belonged to the American Mission Union and were rented by missionaries as they were assigned to duty in Rangoon. Two of these were Russell Place and the Bennett House, immediately next door. The former had been Frank's first home in Burma, and where Hattie had expected to live with Frank when she arrived. Instead, she found Frank still living at Kemindine.

[7] The Kemindine Girls' School, Hattie's first home in Burma, was located in the Kemindine area, a short trip from downtown Rangoon by train or buggy. Kemindine School was a major boarding school for native girls, including elementary grades through high school and normal school training. It provided teachers for schools throughout Burma. At the time Hattie arrived in Burma, Misses Clarke and Williams were responsible for the educational program of the school; (Mrs.) Dr. M. C. Douglass administered the school compound, and the small hospital it contained. The hospital served not only as an infirmary for the girls in the school but on occasion for missionaries who needed special medical care.

6

Rangoon at Last: Getting Acquainted

January 1886 to May 1887

Hattie's long anticipated arrival in Rangoon brought her into a world at once alien and familiar. The exotic setting, with its tropical climate and the customs and peoples of many different cultures, required significant adjustment. At the same time, the normal round of mission activities — the weekly prayer meetings, Sunday school, and church affairs — closely resembled those she had known at home and blunted somewhat the strangeness of her new life.

Even before she had an opportunity to unpack, Hattie embarked upon the series of social calls expected of a new arrival. Many missionaries were already known to Hattie by name, through Frank's letters, mission reports, or personal acquaintance at home in Rochester. Frank's prominent role in mission affairs, not only as superintendent of the press, but treasurer and Sunday school superintendent, assured Hattie's place in the Mission community.

Jan. 27, '86

Early yesterday morning Mrs. Packer called and then Mrs. Stevens, Mrs. George from Zeegone, [and] Mrs. Johnson (Western Society) from Tavoy called. Before breakfast Frank and I went out in his buggy and called on all the missionaries. The rest of the day I rested and unpacked. In the evening we went to the mission prayer meeting. Besides those mentioned above there were Mr. Bunker, Mr. and Mrs. Hale and three children, and Mr. Thomas, in addition to the Rangoon missionaries. Today are the anniversary exercises for some of these visitors. In the prayer meeting Mr. Bunker spoke of the work of Moung Se Dee — of the three strong pioneer churches that he had founded besides smaller ones, and he is still doing pioneer work.

Mr. and Mrs. Brayton gave me the most cordial welcome when we called there, and they wished to be remembered to Father and Mother. I like Miss Ranney very much; she is older than Frank.

Later: I am curled up now in Frank's invalid couch with Robbie side of me and Madge at my feet; they are Scotch terriers and look very much like their pictures. They have big brown eyes and look out through their "bangs" in a very cute way.

I have taken most of the things out of my trunks, sent off my washing and got about as much settled as I can till my box comes. My clothes held out very well and I have plenty to last till my wash comes in, even of handkerchiefs, etc.

Jan. 30, '86

Last Friday I went to the Press with Frank by train, and went over it. I thought things looked very well considering who had charge of it!!! I got a book, *Bible Lands*, for Mah Myit, as she had been very kind in teaching me.

My washing was brought back, 47 pieces, looking very nice indeed, no buttons off, or marks on.

In this close-knit and interdependent community, members of the mission were frequently called upon to help out in one way or another, as need arose.

[Jan. 30, '86, continued]

The night of the prayer meeting I was asked to take a class of little girls in the English Sunday School that was in need of a teacher. So Frank and I got up early and went to 7 A.M. Sunday School this morning in his buggy, and I took the class of girls. There are 15 of them, about 12 years of age. They pay better attention and know more of the Bible and the lesson than the class Ada now has. We also attended the opening of the Sunday School here, and attended the preaching service, and I went into Mrs. Douglass' prayer meeting.

Wednesday I spent, by Mrs. Smith's invitation, at the very pleasant home of Drs. Stevens and Smith. Miss Ranney was

there to tiffin, and Miss Johnson and Frank to dinner. I had a
pleasant day.

Thursday morning [at Kemindine School] I went into a
class of little tots learning the catechism from 7 to 8 A.M. Then
did some writing, had breakfast, etc. and went into the same
class learning the alphabet and going through the spelling book
you have at home. I sit down on a low backless bench side of
the little girls or on a chair side of the teacher.

Hattie had expected to live with Frank in the house on Mission
Road where he had resided previously with Mrs. Binney and later
with Dr. Cushing. Upon arrival, however, she found Frank still
living at the Kemindine School compound, where he had moved
the previous July (his letter explaining the situation having reached
Rochester after her departure). Despite some of its inconveniences,
the Kemindine arrangement proved to be an excellent way for Hattie
to begin her life in Burma. The school setting, similar in many
ways to Spelman, and the care provided by Dr. Douglass and the
companionship of the teachers, Miss Clarke and Miss Williams,
made Hattie's initial adjustment easier.

Feb. 7, '86

We might have <u>more</u> room if we were keeping house, but
scarcely more comfortable room. The days are full and if I had
charge of a house and the trials with servants that I hear Miss
Ranney tell of, I don't know where the Burmese would come
in. Besides I should be alone all the hours that Frank is gone,
and should hear but little Burmese. I could learn to read it but
not to talk it, which is the hardest as well as the most important. And I could not go into a class of little ones. I have begun
translating the Catechism they study and to go through the
phrase book.

By the end of the week, Hattie was to experience her first taste
of the British Raj with the arrival of the Viceroy of British India,
Lord Dufferin, for the first official visit since all Burma had been
proclaimed a part of British India. It was an important state occasion which engaged the entire community, including prominent
members of the mission.

The Kemindine Girls' School, a major boarding school for native girls.

Jan. 30, '86

I spent some time helping Frank in making decorations for
an aisle Dr. Packer is getting up for the Viceroy procession
next Saturday. Frank will send papers telling about it. What we
did was to make an Irish harp in gold on one sheet of card-
board and a shamrock on another, to be out at each end of the
aisle. The lettering will be red and blue on white. The harp etc.
is because the Viceroy is an Irish Earl.

Feb. 7, '86

Frank and I went to Mr. Eveleth's to tiffin by previous
agreement and about 3 P.M. Dr. and Mrs. Packer called for me
and we went to Pandol to see the arrival of "H.E. the Viceroy
and Countess of Dufferin."

Dr. Packer had secured tickets for us before, and our places
were near the front and near the entrance so we saw all there
was to see — which was little: an ordinary gentleman and lady
with Mr. and Mrs. Bernard met in the center of the Pandol by
a group of men (mostly European) — the Reception Committee — one of whom read a short address of welcome to which
the Viceroy responded and then they all moved on and took
carriages to the Government House (residence of Mr. Bernard)
followed by a few mounted soldiers.

The show was the Pandol, arches, etc., and the crowd of
people of many nationalities all in their best bib and tucker.
The silks, satins, brocades, gold, and jewels displayed by the
natives was something to see. You never saw such brilliant and
rich dressing in America. The Pandol was a big tent of coarse
matting lined with red and white; seats at the side and a
passage down the center, carpeted with red flannel; through
this the company passed on coming up from the wharf. After it
was over we went back to Mr. Eveleth's, or I did, and soon
they drove off to see the sights and Frank and I did the same.
We took the route the procession had, so saw all the arches.
The one we had a finger in making looked very well though of
course not so elaborate as the others.

In the evening we went to the Reception given the Viceroy
by the Chief Commissioner, Mr. Bernard. As my box had not
come, I had no choice but to wear my black silk. We got ready
and also the three ladies here. Miss Williams went in Frank's

buggy with us, and Mrs. Douglass and Miss Clarke called for
Mrs. Rose.

We all went in together, stood near the door for a while;
the room was full. Then Dr. Packer found us and took Mrs.
Douglass up and presented her to the Countess. Dr. Packer
was on the Reception Committee. We followed and were
handy so when she finished her chat with Mrs. Douglass he
presented each of us, and she spoke for a few minutes with
us, particularly Mrs. Rose. Then we met Mr. and Mrs.
Bernard, and the latter asked us if we wouldn't like an ice
and took us out on the veranda to get it. The ice seemed
like frozen coffee, strong and unsweetened. We came away
immediately after, and as we waited for our carriages we
heard the band play "God Save the Queen" and that of
course ended the whole affair, at 11 P.M.

The Countess wore a very low-necked and short-sleeved
black dress, diamond necklace and bracelets, and a magnificent diamond coronet or crown, which made her conspicuous but she was by no means handsome. I did not see one
real pretty woman, and none that were dressed really
handsomely, though I suppose they thought they were. The
scarlet coats and gold lace of the men made them as brightly
dressed as the women.

Frank's letters had acquainted Hattie with various aspects of
life in Rangoon with which she now became familiar in practice. Many of the daily routines reflected British India tradition
rather than Burmese: the day started with chota haziri (early
morning tea), followed a while later by breakfast, a more substantial meal, then tiffin, a light meal in the middle of the day.
Dinner was served as the heaviest, evening meal, its degree of
formality depending on the occasion. Afternoon tea, in the British style, does not seem to have been an everyday practice, but
reserved for social occasions.

Responding to letters from home requesting detailed accounts
of living conditions and customs, Hattie felt called upon to explain
and defend the daily routine, which was sometimes perceived as
acceding too greatly to British custom.

Oct. 24, '86

As to conforming to American customs, very few in this
climate could or would care to sit down in the heat of the
day — thermometer 90-110 degrees — in a dripping perspiration and eat the chief meal of the day. No business man could
go from two to four miles to his home in the noon heat and
glare for his dinner and go back again. Besides, as each day's
meat and vegetable must be bought and used the same day (or
spoil) few servants could go to the bazaar, make purchases and
get back and cook as early a breakfast as you can have at home
where everything is on hand overnight and where marketing is
a short operation. If we have breakfast at 9 A.M. we don't want
dinner at 12 noon even if anyone had time to eat then. It is not
that we ape the English but simply live the best we can considering the demands of the climate — which alters everything.

As to what we eat: fowl and beef steak (neither as good as
at home) are the cheapest and most common meats; occasionally roast beef, rarely mutton. Rice is always served as a
vegetable and I eat it in preference to any other. The potatoes,
onions, beans and peas when we have them are not first class.
In Moulmein they have good bread of American flour both
from Chinese and Kulah bakers. But here native flour is used
and the bread is generally very poor, sour, gritty, alum in it. I
seldom eat it except as toast for lunch.

We never have rice and curry here except when company is
invited who are accustomed to it. Miss Clarke don't like it,
Mrs. Douglass don't approve of it, Frank can't eat it and so
Miss Williams and I go without it and are doubtless just as well
off. Dessert is generally a plain pudding of rice "sugy" or
custard — or custard on toast — or a pancake or two apiece,
or a fruit souffle minus the boiled custard, just fruit and soft,
light, uncooked frosting — very good if the canned fruit is
good underneath.

The pervasive influence of the British was felt in other ways. The
majority of the household servants were natives of India who had
accompanied or followed the British to Burma. Terms such as "dhoby"
(washerman), "dirghi" (tailor), "mali" (gardener), "syce" (groom),
"gharry wallah," "box wallah," "pani-wallah," and other "wallahs"
(vendors) originated in British India and had become assimilated into

common usage. (Cooks remained "cooks," however, and "boys" of any age performed any number of assorted tasks.) Almost all the general service roles were carried out by men, though female members of the family had a "girl" assigned to help with personal affairs and "ayahs" were employed to assist with the care of young children.

Goods and supplies were obtained either from the native bazaars, stores selling imported items from England, or from native peddlers, "box wallahs," who brought their wares from house to house. Shopping was not easy, and many goods that Hattie wanted were not available locally or were unsatisfactory. These were often requested from home.

Another inescapable fact of Hattie's new life was the climate. Although she had arrived near the end of the "cold" season, the heat was already intense, giving way to the "hot" season, which would last from February to April. The rains beginning in May would bring welcome relief from the heat, but their own discomforts as well.

Feb. 21, '86

Here we are as usual in our sitting room. Frank on the couch resting, Rob on the floor and Madge in a chair and I in my big rocker between my bookcase and the table. The thermometer on the table says 97 degrees and when it stood by the south wall it was 106 — that was heat off the wall, which being one thickness of board gets very hot when the sun shines on it. My bedroom wall gets quite hot with just the morning sun.

I have decided to take Ne Mah and see how we get along. She will take care of my room, wash out handkerchiefs and such things (which saves on the dhobies) and teach me. Don't know what I'll pay her. Yesterday in making up sentences in Burmese with her I went to say, "The pillowcases are not clean" but made the cheering remark, "They are not <u>black</u>"!

Saturday: Last night I took the 5 P.M. train for Rangoon and Mrs. Eveleth met me with her two wheeled cart and took me to the Park to hear the English band play. The Park is very pretty indeed and the music good. I spent the night with her and so was on hand for Sunday School this morning.

I think our situation here has been explained. We neither of us have anything to do with the housekeeping or the school. Everybody has their own work and attends to it. We have chota haziri about 7 A.M. then I often go into a Catechism class till 8 A.M., study with Ne Mah till 4 P.M. or a little after, have a bath and dinner, rest, read, write, and study till 8 P.M. when we have a cup of weak tea, and continue the same till 9 P.M. when we retire.

Frank generally takes the 10 A.M. train for Rangoon and returns by the 4 P.M. Sometimes we have a ride and make a call after dinner. Sometimes a box wallah comes and displays his wares but I've seen nothing different from what you have.

Beyond the routine affairs of the mission, Hattie was eager to glimpse the customs and lifestyles of the various native groups which made up the population of Rangoon.

[Feb. 21, '86, continued]
Tuesday there was a funeral next door and all day very lively music was kept up, flute, drum, triangle, and tin pan, I should think. Frequently a funeral goes by and always with lively music and bright banners, and a very gay and gaudy arrangement to hold the coffin. A Chinese procession went by with lots of bright banners, quick music, and a fancy arrange-ment in which they were carrying off the evil spirits they had drummed up somewhere. They went toward the river. The folks here thought they didn't get them here, the girls had been so naughty!

In the evening we went to the Commencement of the College, and stayed but half through as we had about 100 girls [from Kemindine school] with us. Coming home they put their silk shawls on as turbans, tucked up their skirts (loon'gy) and no one would know them from boys. They always do so as a matter of protection. Mrs. Douglass, Miss Clarke and I led the procession in Mrs. Douglass's buggy and Frank brought up the rear on pony-back.

On Monday after dinner Mrs. Douglass took me to a family she is visiting to see their little Chinese baby. We saw two Chinese women, the baby's mother and a friend — both had their feet bound. The man could speak a little English; they have charge of the Chinese mission the Presbyterians have just begun.

Immanuel Baptist Church, the principal Baptist church in Rangoon, often referred to as the "English Church."

Mar. 28, '86

Saturday was "worship day" and I saw ever and ever so many of those open silk skirts [Burmese notations] te main. They all come out on those days. They wear nothing under them and they flap and show their limbs half up above the knee, but we see so many worse things that that is nothing at all. The closed skirt is loon'gy, the jacket, in'gy.

Despite the British military victory in the overthrow and deportation of King Thibaw of Upper Burma in November 1885, peace was not accomplished immediately. The resulting civil disorders, in the form of plundering "dacoits" (bandits), threatened many areas in which the Baptist missionaries were working, eventually reaching Rangoon itself. During this time, the missionaries were

uncomfortably aware of the dangers that the Christian natives —
and themselves — faced.

Reports of dacoit activities were regularly reported amid other
mission news. It was not always possible to tell fact from fiction
with regard to the various reports that filtered down to Rangoon.

Mar. 7, '86

Tuesday evening Mrs. Douglass, Miss Williams, and I went
to the prayer meeting at Mr. Cross'. Mr. Eveleth told about
what he heard when away. The native preachers all report the
heathen as saying that since the king is gone, Buddhism is
doomed. The respect for priests is passing away, the Burman
dacoits murder them the same now as they do others. And the
idol in Mandalay which was most revered of all, and was called
the living image, has lately been robbed of its jeweled crown
and the valuable offerings it contained and the gold overlaying
has all been scraped off by Burmans. All of which indicates that
Buddhism is losing its power.

Mar. 21, '86

Both Henzada and Bassein have had big scares. The dacoits
come down on a village, steal what they want, destroy what they
don't want, burn the houses, and not content with simple murder,
they pour oil on women and babies and set fire to them and cut
them horribly; there is a woman in the hospital here was burnt,
but managed to put the fire out when they had left her to die.
Then they force the men of the village to fall in with them, and
carry off the rest of the women and children. When hiding, if a
child cries it is killed, and the mother, if she makes a fuss. When
they meet soldiers they put these innocent men in front to be shot
while they run away from the rear; if hard pressed, they drop the
children and leave them to die in the jungle.

Mr. Bunker says the bottom of it all is hatred to the
Christian religion; they fear the Christian's God and tell the
native Christians that the English have power because they
have prayed so hard, and they are going to kill them off and so
many English as they can, and so get back their power. But one
Englishman has been killed so far and he was reckless. The
worst of it is that the Burmans who have not joined the dacoits
hate the Karens and white people for fighting them and in

Henzada they threaten to kill the Karens. All over the country
they put miniature pagodas out in front of their houses to
protect them from the dacoits, and to bring back Thibaw
(though many don't believe he's out of the country). It shows
the dacoits that they are in sympathy with them and when they
come won't resist and will very likely help them. There are
pagodas out at almost every house across the street from here,
and all through Kemindine. But mounted police watch all
around here at night as well as ordinary unmounted ones.

The dacoits are very near Thongai and they have no
protection except their Christian people. Fifty sepoys are
stationed two miles from them but Miss Evans says she is more
afraid here than there. Think I would rather be here tho. Don't
think any of us sleep very sound o'nights.

Mrs. Thomas, senior, says "the only use for a dacoit is to
kill him and kill him quick."

This letter of Hattie's also related news of personal interest
regarding Marie Van Meter, a good friend of Ada's, who had arrived in Burma only a short time before Hattie.

[Mar. 21, '86, continued]
Saturday morning we were all up early to see Miss Stark off
on the 6:20 A.M. train for Zeegone. After that I studied as usual
and after tiffin word came up from Frank that Mr. Kelley and Dr.
Van Meter were married at 7 A.M. that morning (Mar. 20)!!! We
knew that something was going to happen there, but not what it
was, and were immensely surprised and amused, because she has
only been there twelve weeks and when she was here she told
Miss Williams and Mrs. Douglass that she never would marry (in
a very decided, not to say scornful way) and that she would show
folks that she did not come to Burma for that!!! And now she has
gone and done it and on such very short notice, too. Everybody
speaks very highly of Mr. Kelley and thinks that both have done
very well indeed, and that it is a suitable match, but it is just as
funny for all that. They were to take a trip to Thatone, but I
suppose Ada will hear all about it from "Mrs. Kelley." She did not
write to her friends here, or anywhere that I know of. Perhaps she
remembered her words.

Mar. 28, '86

We had a real April fool scare Thursday evening at the tea table; we heard some men coming, and a little noise from the girls. Of course we thought of dacoits at once and jumped up and went in all directions to see; it turned out to be only the preacher and teacher who live on the compound and a young man studying with them. We have them [dacoits] in mind all the time and so are easily startled. Rangoon was in a turmoil all night, the night watchman calling continually for the people "to sleep with one eye open." There were threats of firing it again. At the lakes five miles away a rich Bengali was robbed and murdered and goods destroyed within earshot of the police. Mr. Eveleth has not been heard from for three days in Henzada and Mrs. Eveleth is about sick with anxiety.

Later — has heard and is better.

When you get this the rains will have begun and we hope that will cool the ardor of the rebels.

Apr. 4, '86

This is a very anxious and uneasy time as there is a plot among the Burmans all through the country to rise next week (their New Year) and kill all Christians and foreigners; 2Rs 8ans is offered for every white head and 1Rs for a Kulah (native of India). The missionaries are very anxious and have been to the Government officials who know of it and in their slow English fashion will prepare for it. It seems to be their plan to wait till harm is done and then send out soldiers to see about it. If anything serious happens you will have seen it long before this in the paper; if it were not so I would not write about it beforehand. Mr. Rose says he has never in 30 years seen the country in such a state.

Thursday Frank has brought up four Kulahs to watch the place nights. The greatest danger will be Sunday and Tuesday, the last of the old and the first of the new year. Troops are to be garrisoned here at Kemindine. We hope the rebels will be intimidated but they trust in the charms which the priests give them to make them invulnerable. The Christians in the villages about are coming in for fear. Miss Clarke, not having a pistol, has bought her a dah, a big knife, blade 1-1/2 feet long in a sheath.

I'm thankful indeed that I have a revolver. The other young ladies haven't. Mrs. Douglass has a little one. Frank has a big government gun besides his revolver.

Between the heat and the anxiety, studying is hard work. Miss Stark sleeps with me, because I sleep better than when alone. I'm glad she is here.

Friday. This morning I studied and this afternoon I made a tie for Frank and put a pocket in my flannel gown which I keep on the foot of my bed with the boots to match, ready to flee if necessary; the others do likewise. Frank would send papers to tell but they won't tell the true state of affairs.

We "trust in the Lord to keep our powder dry."

Apr. 15, '86

Here we are all alive and perspiring (103-109 degrees) with our heads still on our shoulders and enjoying the prospect of keeping them there some time longer. The week has passed quietly here; a number of Burman merchants suspected of having a finger in the pie were arrested Monday and left in jail till next Monday and that doubtless had a soothing effect on some minds. One hundred houses were burnt one night in another section of Rangoon but there have been no fires out here. I think we're getting used to the disturbance. You know anyone could get used to being hung if they were only hung often enough!

Apr. 23, '86

Saturday we learned that Prome, Zeegone, and Thonyi were all troubled and threatened by dacoits. The missionaries at the first two places used to p'shaw the whole thing but we hear no more of that now. It is so easy to be brave when the trouble is at somebody else's home. Mrs. Stevens thought it would amount to nothing but their own straw-stack was set on fire and consumed, and they saw the two Burmans who did it running away, and that done right in Ahlone [section of Rangoon].

A less exciting but more pervasive fact of life were the ups and downs in health commonplace throughout the mission. Most often simply uncomfortable, irritating and discouraging, more serious illness at times proved life-threatening.

[Apr. 23, '86, continued]

This intense heat is bringing out prickly heat on most of us — no fun in that. In fact it is quite distressing and can't be appreciated by one who has not had it. My feet puff up some, which is usual with a newcomer; glad my foot gear is all good size.

Mrs. Packer is quite ill, and Dr. Stevens "very bad," so Dr. Pedley said last night.

Apr. 25, '86

Saturday noon Miss Evans left for Thonze, not entirely cured but as well as she is likely to be. The dacoits are still troublesome there as elsewhere. The English are so aggravatingly weak, dilatory and careless, they have actually run from the dacoits more than once. Near Henzada they met and fired at the dacoits till they turned, then instead of pursuing and capturing and ending that band and their performances — because they <u>hadn't had their break-fast!!!</u> — they returned to the steamer to get it, with one sepoy killed and two wounded, leaving the dacoits to carry on their festive operations unmolested!! And that seems to be the English of it. Everybody is disgusted with the way they run around like a fussy old woman, looking at the remains of burnt villages while the offenders go on to burn another (found nine dead afterward).

Wednesday afternoon Miss Williams, Miss Stark and I went to the bazaar here in Kemindine. It is a big open building divided into squares by narrow passages, the people sitting on raised platforms with their goods around them, and such an exhibition of nakedness and filth can't be described. We bought us some Chinese and Burmese combs, some Burmese rosaries and a betel nut box about the size of your largest. I'll send my Chinese (fine) combs, and the rosary home sometime. The box is for use, it's not pretty, called "it." In the evening we all borrowed ingys, loon'gys, handkerchiefs, breast pins, and necklaces of the girls and prepared to have our pictures taken this morning and Frank took them about 6 A.M. Mrs. Douglass dressed as an old woman and we as young ones, hair dressing and all — that's what we wanted the combs for, they are like the one you have.

Miss Stark, Hattie, Dr. Douglass, and Miss Clarke dressed in Burman women's costumes.

You should have seen Mrs. Douglass perform exactly like an old Burman woman, the girls were immensely tickled at it and at the whole performance. We had a large audience.

Friday. The negatives were taken to get proofs from today and I think by next mail you will get some photos or some of the paper negatives to print from. Our positions, dress and accessories are thoroughly Burmese, except floor and background; they don't count.

It was the understanding under which Hattie was sent to Burma that her first year would be spent in language study and acclimatization without additional mission responsibilities. She reported her progress regularly.

[Apr. 25, '86, continued]
I finished reading Mark and think I'll read John next, along with Mr. Eveleth's book. There are great trials in speaking for there is such a difference in the pronunciation. No one can give exactly the sounds the natives do and the old missionaries have one theory and the young ones another, and each

think that they come nearest to the native sound. If a native is
called to give the disputed sound <u>each</u> one exclaims, "There! I
said they said it <u>so</u>!" If I speak according to the old missionaries, the girls correct me, and if I speak as I think the girls do,
the missionaries correct; for, as I hear, the younger ones come
nearest right. Between all the authorities one don't know what
to do.

Before long, however, circumstances required a change of plans,
and the opportunity — or necessity — for Hattie to become a more
active participant in the work of the mission arose.

May 2, '86

It is probable that I'll not have as much time soon, as
Mrs. Packer is very poorly (as she has been for a long time)
and is just recovering from a severe pull down, so she is not
able to do her work in the College and I expect to take two
or three classes a day in her stead. It is almost if not quite a
matter of life and death with her, and this is the only reason
I do it. It is not a permanent thing or even looking toward
anything permanent as the College needs and must hire a
<u>man</u>. The teaching is in English of course. I'm not supposed
to be "teaching in the College." I'm simply helping Mrs.
Packer to save her health and perhaps her life. More about
it next week.

(6th) Saturday morning, May 1, we had our first shower
and May 4 the rains seemed to really begin, doubtless there'll
be some let ups though. Instead of perspiring in the thinnest
muslins tonight I'm comfortable in my green flannel at 80
degrees.

May 9, '86

Monday morning Mr. and Mrs. Packer called, he to see the
organ and she to bring me an outline of the history which she
had prepared. As I never studied Indian history I've something
to learn!

Sunday night I discovered that black ants had got into my
bathroom very thick. Mrs. Douglass and Mah Moe and I
heated water and scalded them thoroughly, but they were even
worse Monday; one of the servants scalded them three or four

times and put earth oil on the posts underneath and we
thought they were gone, but after a few hours I found they
were thicker than ever, the floor one side, part of the walls and
my water jar were just black with them, the bottom part of the
jar was coated with them solid, jar invisible. I had that carried
out and then scalded the rest and they put kerosene oil around
very thoroughly and they finally vanished. The rains brought
them up from the earth I suppose, or a nest hatched out
somewhere, nothing uncommon.

May 15, '86

We've had no rain for a few days and the weather is
exceedingly oppressive. This morning when we started for
Sunday School at 6:15 the sunshine was decidedly uncomfortable as we faced it. At noon it is almost <u>directly</u> overhead just a
perceptible bit to the north.

Friday Frank brought some camphor gum home and I
sewed some up in bags and put in and around the organ and
scattered pieces through my (and his) drawers, trunks, and
almira to keep bugs out. Those ants or more like them came
back to my bathroom again but a liberal dose of kerosene
discouraged them again. The tiny red ants so high (-) bite like
everything and annoy some very much by getting into bed,
whole trains of them, and spoiling the night's sleep or by
getting into and under one's clothes and biting.

Mr. and Mrs. Kelley will be here in two weeks on their
way to Mandalay. She has written to Mrs. Douglass, but
without mentioning her marriage! Miss Payne says that Mr.
Kelley does not want her to practice as a physician! It is to be
hoped she will have a mind of her own after all the time and
money spent, and with her very elaborate medical outfit. And
<u>this</u> after all she has said about not destroying her usefulness by
getting married!!! The irony of fate!

Her new teaching responsibilities notwithstanding, the mission
board at home continued to plan for Hattie's assignment to missionary work in the field at the end of her year of acclimatization
and language study.

May 30, '86

The Board hope I will be ready to go where I'm most
needed next cool season. So do I — shall be glad to find my
own place and work. The Board have been troubled by ladies
objecting when called to leave here for more needy places and
they seem to fear I will make a fuss too but I don't intend to.

June 13, '86

Wednesday after dinner Frank and I went out and prac-
ticed firing at a mark with my revolver and Frank's rifle. I
came within three inches of the center with each I think, but
Frank can tell better. Thursday after dinner Frank and I took a
ride out through Kemindine along the river; the doctor advised
him to ride out each day as this is the time of year when he is
most likely to break down, and he is looking thinner. In fact,
we are a decidedly thin company. All day I had felt very tired
and languid, but as that is not unusual in this delightful (?)
climate I didn't think much of it. Later in the day my bones
from head to feet began to ache and continued to do so worse
and worse so that I got no sleep until about 4:30 A.M. Mrs.
Douglass having come in and given me a dose of bromide a
half-hour before. She was suffering in just the same way and so
was Miss Williams. Of course I could not teach or study and
we grunted around all day with the pain and soreness. Saturday we had not so much pain, but I at least felt as if I had been
used to scrub floors or wash windows. It was a touch we think
of a kind of fever that goes the round sometimes at this season
of the year. We all feel better.

June 27, '86

The past week has been much like its forefathers! I've been
able to teach and study each day as usual. At present Frank and I
in common with many of the Rangoon folks, are having colds
which affect our throats and lungs only. There is much sickness
around. Mrs. Packer is very poorly, and Dr. Packer is never really
well during the rains. Dr. Smith and Miss Ranney also ailing, but
none seriously. Mr. Roberts who has just come down from Bhamo
thinks the Rangoon folks look rather dragged out.

Saturday morning we discovered for the second or third
time the top of my mosquito curtain to be alive with small red

ants, which have eaten the top of the curtain till it looks as if it had been stuck full of big pins, being perforated with minute holes all over. So I got some shallow glazed earthenware bowls about six inches across and put under the legs and filled them with water. Think my bed is fixed now.

Saturday evening Frank and I rode out and went to a lumber mill where we saw two elephants at work, but only for a few minutes as it was closing time. They looked like animated gray hills meandering around. One dragged a big beam which was hitched to chains, off to its place and the other dragged a big plank to its place by taking one end between his tusks and trunk.

Aug. 6, '86

Saturday I dried things as usual, and put the braid and buttons back on my white jacket. The dhoby washed it very well and also my white and red bedstead. Saturday evening Mr. and Mrs. Brayton came with Miss Ambrose from Toungoo who is down to meet Miss Eastman. But she is so badly off (liver trouble) that Mrs. Douglass has ordered her home at once by the next steamer if possible, and yet Mrs. Douglass says she is afraid to have her go for fear she'll not reach home; there is no one to go with her. Between sickness, death, and dacoits it is a blue and discouraged time in Burma.

Just at sundown tonight there was a great racket from the Burman houses all around, beating of tin pans and of wood. There is cholera around and they were driving the evil spirits out of their houses by beating them (the houses) and making a noise generally.

Monday night about 2:30 I was awakened by a rattling among the flower pots under my window. I seized my revolver and peeked out of the upper slats of the blind and saw two white shadows disappearing toward the gate; my revolver being a little rusty failed to go at first and then I peeped again and thought I saw another form, then I fired over its head. Of course it wakened everyone and Frank came to see about it. Before many minutes two Burman policemen appeared with lanterns but too late to catch anyone. The thieves were doubtless Kulah gharry wallahs from their white clothes and from the fact that they have been acting very ugly and impudent since we have needed them, Mrs.

Douglass' buggy being out of repair and Frank's pony lame. So they refused to come when called, demanded outrageous pay, and were too saucy for anything, and were even reckless in their driving. But this morning one actually offered his services and the one who brought me back from College was as sweet as a basket of chips and asked no baksheesh!!! Good effect of a shot — guess they think it's time to behave!

We are just over our colds, but Frank is not very well, liver not quite straight. It is only care and prudence that keeps him going.

In September of 1886, Frank asked William H. S. Hascall to come to Rangoon to assist temporarily at the press while Frank attended to straightening out the mission's treasury affairs. Now a missionary in Henzada, Mr. Hascall had worked at the press under Cephas Bennett and was familiar with its operations. Accompanying Mr. Hascall to Rangoon were Mrs. Hascall and their children, with whom Hattie soon became acquainted.

Sept. 5, '86

Tuesday: Monday evening Frank and I went to see how the Hascalls were doing and found Mr. and Mrs. Hascall at the Packers. They had just got into their house but were not at all settled. They have four boys, from five years to four months in age. Like most children here, they are sickly looking. Mrs. Douglass says their coming here is well for the children, thinks she might have lost some of them in Henzada.

As her facility increased, Hattie put her knowledge of Burmese to use in a number of activities. Translation, or more accurately, as she explained, adaptation of English hymns into Burmese for use in church services, became a lifelong hobby. Assisting in the work of the press, an activity initially undertaken to help Frank with his heavy workload, also became a major part of Hattie's later life.

Sept. 26, '86

I enclose a Burmese version of Ada's "favorite hymn" (that I used to sing to her after tea) which I have just made. When I come home I'll sing it for you — if I don't forget!!

I've begun to help Frank on the Dictionary by going over the copy first and crossing out the Romanizing and false definitions and seeing that the spelling is right. This will save him a good deal of time, and just so much work. I spent most of Saturday at it.

Oct. 3, '86

Thursday and today I had written examinations of my classes, and today College closed for a three weeks vacation, opening November 1.

Mr. Eveleth was taken very sick again Wednesday, and they have decided to go home soon. He has tried his best to stand it here longer but can't. I presume Mr. Richmond will go with them or soon follow, as his health is very poor and all the Doctors in Rangoon have ordered him home — say he can't live in this climate; lung trouble, I think.

What the Burman mission is coming to nobody can see. Three of the best Burmese missionaries gone since I came and no one to fill their places.

In the eight months since her arrival, Hattie had gained an increasing understanding of the mission activities and nature of the work to be done. The challenges to be overcome in undertaking it were also increasingly apparent to her.

Oct. 10, '86

Haven't you noticed that though some call this [civil unrest] a religious war, others with equal chance for observation say it is not. It is my private opinion that both are right; with some it is mere lawlessness or hatred of the English Government, with others it is hatred of Christianity. In spite of the trouble, there were more baptisms reported in the last *Messenger* than for a long time before and the next number will have a good list, too. Instead of drawing off Burman missionaries more ought to be sent to fill vacancies and get ready to begin when the time comes. Because some think it is a long way off is no proof that it is. And even if the present generation must go as some think, there are the children who ought to be taught now, or where is the hope for the future? If you could see how the streets swarm with the little naked imps you would think there was work for any number of missionaries.

I think Papa's questions are already answered in regard to my teaching. Miss Ranney takes Mrs. Packer's Bible class and I her other two classes, one in History and the other in History and Geography (two days a week for each and one for Composition). Mrs. Packer has no salary apart from the Doctor's. No missionary's wife has, whether she does a great deal of mission work or none at all. The Board appropriated full salary for me from the time I began to teach.

The college vacation provided Hattie her first opportunity for travel outside the Rangoon area. Such excursions were an important aspect of life in Burma, providing a change of pace to offset the effects of climate and hard work on the missionaries and their families. These trips were often to other mission settlements, where the visitors were absorbed into the homes or living quarters of the resident missionaries. Moulmein, reached by steamship from Rangoon, was an historically important Baptist settlement and the site of a large Baptist contingent.

Moulmein, Oct. 14, '86

It's <u>awful hot</u> !!! Monday I spent getting ready to come here. Frank packed in a pah and his photographics in a box, and I had a satchel and another pah. Folks always take a number of small packages that can be carried on gharries and by house servants so as not to have to hire coolies.

We left Rangoon at 6:30 A.M., had a quiet day, just rolling when out in the Bay. After entering the mouth of the river here we passed through a tremendous rainstorm, but had a clear time to land. Mr. Armstrong met us and brought us here. I sleep with, or rather in, Miss Sheldon's room, she having two single beds in her room.

Wednesday we rested all day being quite tired. We have seen all the folks here. Dr. Mitchell took me out with her this morning; we were out from 6:30 A.M. to 9:30 and I got very tired in the gharry on such rough roads. It was pleasant to see Miss Rathbun again and Mai Myit; they are nearby.

Mrs. Armstrong has a Tamil school in the house, so it is not very quiet, and Misses Sheldon and Whitehead are in a large Burman Girls' School, so it seems quite natural.

Moulmein, Oct. 17, '86

Thursday evening we all went out to the Bulkleys' for the evening and had a very pleasant time. Mrs. Webster and her daughter are there for the present. Friday morning I had another long ride with Dr. Mitchell before breakfast and after dinner Mrs. Armstrong took us for a nice ride along the river bank. Saturday morning we walked up the hill back of the house, the top of which is covered with pagodas, and the establishments of the priests. We saw a dead priest, or rather the coffin in which he was. The latter was gilded and had a gilt image on top covered with elaborate jeweled (?) cloth. Around were numerous large white umbrellas etc. etc. A number of Burman women were bowing down and paying reverence before it. Nearby they were building a large and very pretty house from which to have the funeral.

Moulmein seems full of pagodas and poongye [monk] schools or houses; many new and elaborate and nice. Much better than the mission buildings. Talk of Buddhism being just ready to fall!

This morning Frank went to the English Sunday School and between that and the Burmese we had breakfast with Miss Rathbun and then went to the Burman chapel for the last of Sunday School and the preaching service. The English and Burman chapels and Miss Rathbun's school and the house for the Burman missionary (now empty) are all close together. A little ways off is Miss Sheldon's school and the Armstrongs' house, and farther still Miss Bunn's Eurasian school. Then two miles or so away is Miss Garton's school and Mr. Bulkley's house.

This morning Mrs. Armstrong took me on a nice ride down the river and back through the paddy plains where we saw the people reaping by hand, of course. They have been up to their ankles in mud and water while cutting the paddy. The landscape here consists of level plains with steep hills rising abruptly from them.

Oct. 24, '86

Here we are at home again all right. The trip back on Friday was very calm and pleasant. The Armstrongs, Miss Whitehead, and Dr. Mitchell saw us off. We had a very

pleasant time and found the Moulmein missionaries an
exceedingly pleasant and agreeable set of people. Miss
Sheldon seems to be everybody's favorite. She expects to go
home (to Lynn, Mass.) next March and I gave her your
address and told her to go and see you if she ever was near
Rochester. I like her better even than Miss Eastman, and
think you will. She is more quiet — perhaps not so easy to
become acquainted with. She came out in '76; is a little
gray-haired lady with a nice face.

Hereafter I shall pay Frank 35 rupees a month for board
and he will settle with Miss Williams and his boys as before.
This is about what it costs single ladies in all stations who
board in mission families.

Over the coming weeks, Hattie would make the acquaintance of yet more missionaries, as they traveled to Rangoon for
two special events. One was the wedding of Miss Clarke, the
other the annual Convention, an important event for the entire
mission. Held in different locations each year according to the
capacity of the local community, the Convention provided an
opportunity for the mission to come together, native Christians
and missionaries alike, to attend to mission business and renew
old friendships.

Nov. 5, '86
This has been a very busy week. I have taught all the week
as usual again. And as the wedding of Mr. Case and Miss
Clarke is put for next Monday morning, everybody has been
busy getting ready. She is bound to have a "swell" occasion,
two bridesmaids and grooms, white dresses, train, wreath, veil,
gloves and all in style. So three dirgies have been sewing here
most of the week.

Miss Whitehead is expected this morning and will stay
with Miss Williams; and Miss Stark [will come in] the afternoon and will be with me. Mr. Case is with Frank most of the
nights and Mr. Eveleth has the front part of the hall curtained
off. So we will be <u>about full!</u> The wedding and Convention
together draw lots of people.

Baptist missionaries, Rangoon, November 1886.

Nov. 9, '86

Friday Misses Whitehead and Stark arrived and Saturday morning we fussed getting ready for the wedding. In the afternoon as it was cloudy and so not too hot and bright. I took them in the buggy to call on the Braytons, Bennetts, and Stevens.

Sunday we went to Sunday School as usual and stayed to a prayer meeting for missionaries, as it was the day set apart at home for that. In the evening we went again to have the annual Convention sermon by Mr. Case. After the service Mr. Denchfield baptized six children from the Sunday School, two girls from my class.

There are or were 22 missionaries from other stations present for the Convention and wedding. Only Mrs. Kelley of Thatone, Mrs. Crumb and Miss Palmer of Toungoo whom I had not seen before.

Monday we all worked as hard as we could getting ready. Misses Whitehead and Stark and I trimmed the school room somewhat, with green vines and pink blossoms and plants, put all the mats and strips of carpeting we could get together so that the platform and where they entered was covered, and we arranged the chairs for the missionaries and other guests.

Then we got ready (I wore my new olive silk for the first time) and Mrs. Douglass, Miss Whitehead, and I received the folks. Forty-two missionaries were present and eight outsiders, Presbyterians and Methodists and Captain and Mrs. Wells (Mrs. Bennett's daughter). A little after 4 P.M. Dr. Rose and Mr. Hascall walked in followed by ten little native girls with flowers in their hands, then Mr. Richmond and Miss Stark, Frank and Miss Williams, Mr. Case and Miss Clarke. Dr. Rose married them, Mr. Hascall offering the prayer. They were very thoroughly tied together.

After the guests were gone we had dinner, 11 of us, including Mrs. Eveleth and Mr. Richmond. In the evening some of us went to the mission prayer meeting at the Smiths' — a good meeting.

Dec. 19, '86

I'm "all alone in my glory" this Sunday evening, but have had the company of two home letters and many papers. Your 255 and 256 came this afternoon. It seems queer that you should be shoveling snow again.

No, we don't have any snow here, why don't you preserve a little in a bottle and send to us? Miss McAllister brought in a tight tin pail some homemade cookies perfectly good when opened. She has things for a Christmas tree for the girls, too. If cookies, why not snow?

I think my "fate" is settled at last. When Miss Barrows knew that I will go to Henzada if she did not and that Mrs. Gates had suggested me to Mrs. Hascall, she decided at once for Moulmein. So I shall doubtless go to Henzada when freed from the College. I doubt if that will be before March — the end of the school year. Mrs. Hascall wants me when she returns to Henzada, but I can't leave Mrs. Packer without help and she wouldn't wish me to either. Besides, the class would suffer from a change in the middle of the term. Of course the Board have not yet designated me but will doubtless as soon as they hear of Miss Barrows' decision. Better not say anything till you hear the Board's decision.

Although it would be some months before her departure for Henzada, Hattie began looking forward to her new situation. The decision was met with expressions of concern, however, from the family at home. As usual, Hattie's reply was emphatic.

Mar. 13, '87

It is rather late to object to my leaving Rangoon when I came with that expressed understanding. If comfort and convenience were all, I might stay, but I'm needed more elsewhere than here. At present there is not one missionary in Henzada, the Thomases have left for home, Mrs. Thomas (elder) has transferred her work to Sandoway, and next rains the Hascalls and myself will probably be alone there. Number three is not needed as much in this school as Number one in Henzada: besides, I would be very much averse to going into this or any other mission school under the [British] Government. The Henzada school is one of the few that is not. Miss Ranney is taking up the house to house work, the jungle schools round about, and work in the Burman Church. I never should amount to a row of pins if I settled down comfortably with Frank in Rangoon. I don't think he will suffer without me, being quite able to take care of himself.

Change and shifts in mission personnel were ongoing. A major loss for Kemindine was Dr. Douglass' departure for a new position, unconnected to the mission.

[Mar. 13, '87, continued]
Wednesday and Thursday we had a grand upheaval; Mrs. Douglass moved down to the house at Ahlone which Government has fitted up for a woman's hospital and training school for native nurses. Mrs. Douglass has thus not only left Kemindine but left the Mission and is now under Government and paid by Government: Rs300 a month and the profits of her outside practice, instead of Rs100 a month and no perquisites as before. She expects to train a class of native women and girls as nurses. She is the only lady doctor to be had, which accounts for Government taking a Baptist and a Missionary. She has not agreed to the rule of absolutely no religious instruction being given. But it is my private opinion that if she does find time and persist in giving religious instruction Government will shift her as soon as they can find someone who will agree to their rules. She expects to teach four hours a day; as she has not been teaching for years, I fear she may break down. It is a good and important work but with so many more missionaries needed it seems almost too bad that one should be taken. It will make it very hard for Misses Williams and McAllister here, as, though she did not teach, she had charge of the sick and of much of the discipline of the school, had a class in the Sunday School and took charge of the Wednesday evening prayer meeting and Thursday evening singing (after Miss Clarke got married).

Mar. 11, '87
This is my last week of teaching [at the College] and I'm very glad, for it is most tremendously hot and "glaring" going and coming, and the boys are too dreadfully stupid for anything. It has been the hardest week's work I've done for a long time. My eyes burn all the time from the glare on the road, though I wear a veil.
Friday evening. Next Monday evening occurs the closing exercises of the school then begins my vacation.

With her college duties behind her and the prospect of a new and demanding job ahead, Hattie took advantage of her last weeks of freedom from responsibility to make two trips, one a long-promised visit to Mrs. Ingalls in Thonze and the other to K'serdo with Frank. The trip to Thonze was Hattie's first journey by train alone outside the Rangoon area.

> Thonze, Mar. 23, '87
>
> Here I am in Mrs. Ingalls' big barn of a house. Monday I went to bed early and got up early Tuesday and took the 6 A.M. train which was due at 10:30 A.M. at Thonze. We got as far as Wanetchaung and there waited 1-3/4 hours, while a special with troops caught up, stood side of us for 1/2 hour, and got ahead of us. Then we went on at a slow pace stopping from 15 to 20 minutes at every station and finally reached here at 1:30 P.M. and Mrs. Ingalls' about 2 P.M., having taken over 7 hours to go 62 miles. So I had my breakfast in place of tiffin; I had a few oranges and bought a few plantains which were not extra good, but I did not suffer from hunger.
>
> I was met by one of my College boys (whom Miss Evans supports) with an oxcart in which I rode to Mrs. Ingalls'. The jolting was something tremendous, but not as bad as the heat and light which gave me a headache for the rest of the day in spite of a thick hat and umbrella.
>
> Mrs. Ingalls' house has a great open hall through the center with numerous rooms and verandas on each side all open up to the rafters and shingles. It is not built of teak, and the walls are neither as good a color or as smooth as the Rangoon houses, while the posts are just big round hunks of trees. There is no paint about it and all the pictures can't keep it from looking like a big barn minus the hay. The big hall is used for services, Bible classes, etc. I suppose it is just as comfortable as if it were handsomer. In front of the house is the little shed for wayside preaching under an immense banyan tree, which the people used to worship; I suppose because Gautama attained to perfect wisdom [under a banyan tree]. Just the other day a jungle woman came along and bowed down before it. While I was writing just now Mrs. Ingalls was hunting up a skeleton leaf of the tree to send Papa, not

knowing I was writing about it. The tree is bare now but will
be beautiful in the rains.

A little ways off is the Chapel used also as a school house
for Miss Evans' school.

Hattie's trip to K'serdo, one of the mission's vacation settlements in the mountains, introduced her to some of the more primitive aspects of travel in the areas outside the cities. These vacation
settlements were the missionary equivalent of the British hill stations of India, though considerably less well-equipped.

Mar. 23, '87

Wednesday morning Frank and I went shopping for our
trip to K'serdo. I got a jungle bed, i.e., a narrow cotton mattress to sleep on, on the floor: also two pahs, a plate, cup, and
saucer of flowing blue for jungle use. All will be of use hereafter, as well as for getting to the mountains.

Glen Dale, K'serdo, Apr. 10, '87

We left Rangoon at 6:30 with Misses Garton and Payne;
the latter had her boy, the former a Karen girl, and Frank had
his boy, but they went in another car. It was hot part of the
time but we passed through a shower so did not suffer much.
We reached Toungoo about 5 P.M. and were met by Mr. Crumb
and Dr. Johnson. We had dinner with the Crumbs and stayed
at the Cross house which was left open for us, the Crosses
having left that day for K'serdo.

Tuesday we called at the other mission houses, and rested
till 5:30 P.M. when we got ourselves and our baggage into two
open Burman boats (like very long rowboats) and were poled
and paddled down the Sittang River by twilight and moonlight
reaching Yazani, a Burman village, by 8 P.M. There we took
ponies, and coolies took our baggage, and we walked single file
through the woods and jungle grass which towered over our
heads even on pony-back. We arrived at Kopolo, a stockaded
Karen village in the midst of the forest at 9:10 P.M.

We lodged in the mat and bamboo chapel — my first
experience on a bamboo floor — rather shaky and insecure
feeling. I lighted my oil stove, made tea and we had some
bread and butter. Then we unrolled our beds and cots and

rested as well as we could till 4:30; had some more tea and bread, the coolies took up their baskets and we mounted on our ponies (lent by Toungoo folks) and in the early twilight filed out of the stockade and off through the forest at 5:30. For a long way it was level, then rolling land, and after some hours we began to go up the mountains. It was a long hard ride, up steep ridges and down as steep gullies. Miss Garton's saddle slipped and tumbled her off. She is pretty heavy for a pony to carry up hill, so decided to walk the rest of the way. We all walked a small part of the time for a change. We arrived at 10 A.M. considerably lame and tired, but a day or so rested us from that.

Miss Payne and I are at the Cross house, Miss Garton with Miss Eastman in her house. The Hales have a bamboo house, the Cases a board and thatch, likewise Mr. Crumb and Mr. Bunker. Six in all, but "shanty" would be a more appropriate name for all. This one has two rooms and two tiny little bathrooms, the walls and roof of grass-thatch and the floor a spiderweb of bamboos. Miss Payne has a cot and my mattress is on a frame covered with split bamboo which serves as a bedstead.

It is very pleasant here, warm in the middle of the day, 92 degrees on the veranda, but cool nights, and the air is clear and pure compared to the dust and smoke-laden furnace of town.

I read some Burmese every day and have begun to study Sgan Karen with the girls here. It is easier than Burmese and the consonants are similar to those, so I was able to join in the Karen singing this morning. There was a Karen service on Miss Eastman's veranda. I shall not have time to learn much but want to read it so I can sing if I get into a Karen service.

We had a service Sunday evening, one of Spurgeon's sermons was read and we sang a number of pieces after. Monday evening we heard a tiger call every now and then during the evening, but he kept at a respectful distance.

This morning we have had a nice long walk in the woods up and down hill; can walk much better up here than in town.

K'serdo, Apr. 19, '87

Last Thursday evening after dinner Frank suggested "Duck on the Rock" and we all went out and played — found it very good exercise and lots of fun. The weekly prayer meeting was held at Miss Eastman's, Mr. Case led, and we had a good meeting.

Friday morning we got up early and took a long walk to the "Bear's Den," a nice natural cave made of great boulders piled up just as they have stood for ages. The most interesting things in these woods are the mounds of great granite boulders, the immense fantastic creepers, and the banyan trees with two or three trunks. There are few flowers and little of interest to be picked up.

Saturday we heard that the Burmans were going to attack the three Karen villages nearest us, Kopolo and two others. All are stockaded and armed so the Karens were likely to get the best of it. Have heard nothing more.

Monday was my birthday. Mrs. Bunker sent over a leaf canoe full of pretty white flowers, the first real nice flowers we've seen. We had plenty of ferns so the folks trimmed up the veranda very prettily for the Concert in the evening. Mrs. Case and Miss Payne were the prime movers in this. I enclose a program. Mr. Case's was a ridiculous parody on a college song, telling what each came up here for and ending with a verse each in Burmese, Karen, and Shan. He sang with great gusto and it was the hit of the evening. The two Karen girls sang "A Rain Song" in English very nicely. It was all delightful. Mrs. Cross had a birthday cake baked for me, very light and nicely frosted. On the whole, as nice a birthday as I ever had. At the close of the exercises they had Frank make a nice little speech and present me with a tiny alarm clock, the whole about four inches high. Someone happened to have it on hand.

Apr. 29, '87

Here we are at home again, and I will begin where I left off.

Owing to the dacoit troubles last year the roofs of the K'serdo houses were not relaid and so the floors got soaked in the rains and became rotten and tender. The day we arrived Miss Payne went through the floor in our room and got bruises that lasted all the while we were there. Miss Garton is large and heavy and so took great care, but the last Saturday she went through in Miss Eastman's house, bruised one limb badly and twisted the other ankle. It did not look as if she could possibly start with us on Monday. I bound it up with a long bandage wet with witch hazel several times and she used lots of hot water, so on Monday she put on her shoe and was helped onto the biggest and best pony in the mission and Mr. Crumb led him all the way down the hill, so she arrived as well as anyone. I started to ride down back of her, but after going a short distance, while descending a steep place, my saddle slipped down on the horse's neck, spilling me into the arms of Frank and the Karen boy who was leading the pony. If both boy and pony had not stopped I should have had a bad fall on the rocks. I concluded to walk to the foot of the hill after that, but rode from the foot on to Kopolo.

We lodged in the chapel as before. It is like lodging in the midst of a barnyard for the Karens tie two or three cattle under the Chapel and right side of it is a cattle shed with six or eight more under it. Every breath they draw can be heard and the smell is not exactly pleasing; neither is the company of hosts of cockroaches. We started about 6 A.M. for the other half of the journey, about 10 miles. We forded one stream, the Da'lo, a nice rapid clear stream that I wanted to get right into. Clear streams are a rarity. The water came over the horse's knees.

About 9 A.M. we reached the Sittang River again and after some delay were ferried over on bamboo rafts and reached Toungoo about 10 A.M. I was very tired but rested the remainder of the day. The car ride the next day was very hot, and the heat by contrast with the mountain air seems more depressing than ever. It was 102 degrees in my room yesterday, but I did not stay there.

Shortly after Hattie and Frank returned from K'serdo, final confirmation of Hattie's appointment to the Henzada mission was received.

May 6, '87

We received our mail Sunday and I heard from Dr.
Murdock and Mrs. Gates of my appointment to Henzada.
Am just waiting for repairs to be finished before I go.
Besides the bath and storeroom which had to be added, I
will have a board ceiling instead of the old mat one, which
continually drops dirt. The floor matting will come out of
my own pocket. I am determined not to have barn-like
surroundings if I can help it — don't think it is improving to
a missionary who must see nakedness, filth, vileness, etc.
etc. every time he steps off his compound, to have a dingy,
unattractive home to come back to. I can't help the walls
being homely but I can the floor and ceiling.

I am sorry enough to leave Frank but see no other way.
Even if I had the choice I should hardly like to settle down to
teach in the College; it is not just the sort of work I want to be
confined to, and beside a woman twice my age would do ten
times better with those great boys and young men. I could do
little more than mere classroom work.

Hattie's year at Kemindine had seen several major changes in
the school. Miss Clarke, who left following her marriage to Mr.
Case, had been replaced by Miss Stark, and then by Miss McAllister.
Dr. Douglass had left the school in March. These changes and
Hattie's projected departure from Kemindine School had an unex-
pected consequence for Frank's living arrangements.

May 10, '87

Until last Thursday we thought Frank would stay on
here, but it appears Miss McAllister is afraid of the talk that
it may occasion, so of course Frank can't stay. It is not
English custom and might excite remark among them and
the Eurasians and natives even though he would be in a
separate building. I am exceedingly sorry and the more so,
now that he finds he can't even have half of the Packer
house, but must fix up the only thing left, a room in the
College. I don't like it much but hope it won't be longer
than the rains, and that he can have it made comfortable. It
is the room I taught in and has a good outlook, and not far
from the Cushing-Calder house where he'll board. That is a

good thing, that he will not have his meals alone. I would
like to see him settled but he wants to get me off before he
tears up.

On May 13, Hattie left Rangoon for her first real assignment
as a foreign missionary. Her year of acclimatization had introduced
her to many different facets of missionary life in Burma. She had
made excellent progress in mastering Burmese and had some
familiarity with several of the other languages prevalent among
the natives — Karen, Tamil, and Hindustani. She had endured the
hot, rainy, and cool seasons, and survived a series of discomforts
and illnesses that were typical of life in Burma. When needed, she
had taken on the responsibilities asked of her and proved her resourcefulness and ability to carry an uncongenial but needed
workload. She was ready to move on.

7

Work in the Field: Henzada

May to December 1887

Henzada, a small village on the Irrawaddy River about 75 miles north and a little west of Rangoon, had been the site of a Baptist mission station since 1855, shortly after the second English-Burmese War had opened Lower Burma to extensive mission work. When established, the Henzada station had been served by missionaries to both Karens and Burmans; by 1887, however, only the Burman work was being carried on. Despite Henzada's relatively long history as a Baptist mission, the Hascalls found much work to be done in rebuilding the school and congregation following their four-month absence in Rangoon.

Hattie's official assignment was to Mrs. Hascall, to assist in the administration of the mission school and in evangelical work with the natives — work which Mrs. Hascall, with the management of the household, could not carry out effectively herself. Mr. and Mrs. Hascall, their four boys (ranging in age from one to six years), two women teachers for the school, and Mrs. Hascall's Bible woman, Nellie, along with the usual household servants, made up the Henzada mission family.

The Hascalls having returned to Henzada several months earlier, Hattie made the journey alone, except for the small kitten given her by Mrs. Packer. The "boy" whom Hattie mentions as caring for her luggage, was, as usual, essentially anonymous and invisible, though his assistance was extremely useful. He returned to Rangoon when Hattie was safely delivered and settled in.

May 18, '87

Here I am in my own room, by my own lamp, with my puss on the floor, Papa's table and shelves close by, the former covered with the fringed spread Mama sent (the other being on the bureau) and things generally being as indicated in the outline [plan of house enclosed].

As you will have heard from Frank, I left Rangoon on the steamship on Friday the 13th. We stayed in the river opposite the city till 5 P.M. then ran for one hour and stopped for the night. Saturday we went till about 4 P.M. when we reached Maubin. Mr. Bushell met me and I took dinner with them and Miss Putnam, going back to the steamship at dusk.

There is no pier, so we went off on a plank and literally slipped up a very muddy bank. It was just after a very hard storm. When we went back, the planks were too slippery to use and one of the officers brought the ship's boat to the bank and took us on, and then took the Bushells back again.

I was the only saloon passenger and so took breakfast alone, with three young Englishmen — ship's officers — and dinner alone with the Captain at 7 P.M. All were very pleasant and the ship was newly fitted up. I had the ladies' cabin with bathroom annexed, and kitty and I spent our days by ourselves. It was a dull journey and puss was a good deal of company. Sunday was a long quiet day, two stops were made and some cargo taken on; most of it was gnapee (?), their delightfully (?) fragrant fish-food.

We came in sight of Henzada at 7 P.M. Sunday. All the Hascalls were down (except the youngest) and they waited on the bank and I on the steamship in plain sight for nearly two hours before planks were arranged and I and my baggage could be got off. Mr. Hascall came on in less time, and he and the boy I had with me got my trunks, etc. off, and the steamer folks were responsible for my furniture, which arrived at the house early Monday morning. We reached the house about 9 P.M.

Tuesday I began settling and the boy helped all day unfastening boxes, placing furniture after untying it, etc. etc. The big fan I bought is put over a big door in the sitting room. The big doors opening into my room are of cretonne tacked onto frames, and there are curtains also. I have white muslin curtains with a red border in both edges at my windows and the old gold ones Mama made for Frank between my bedroom and sitting room, and at the front door. My room is 34 feet 5 inches by 15 feet 8 inches with a little bath and storeroom off from it. The house is old, has thatch roof and mat ceilings which let down a lot of dust and dirt. Part of my appropriation for repairs went into a board ceiling and a mat for the floor which is old, rough, and cracky. My ceiling looks very well; the matting is rather rough and coarse, and the walls are decidedly barn-like; the light shines through the cracks in them and in the floor through the matting. The small rooms are not ceiled, showing the rafters and grass thatch. I expect after your white walls it would strike you as dark and dingy, but the house is most too old and worn to pay to paint it up, and with my things in, it is about as pleasant as anybody's, at least in out-stations.

Monday evening the Christians, school children, and a few heathen were invited here to meet me and drink tea. The natives made two mottoes, one "Welcome" and the other in Burmese "Praise the Lord with Joyful Mind," and they were put over the steps. About 88 were present — Burmese, Chins, Karens, Eurasians, and Kulahs. The Chin women had their faces tattooed all over with dark blue — as is their custom, to render them unattractive, and they had succeeded perfectly.

The folks sang several pieces and there were two prayers and then refreshments, tho first I shook hands with them all around.

Today I went into the school awhile. Only 25 have come, so far; they are always slow in coming at first.

Friday. I am now entirely settled and beginning to get into the work. The school is run down and in a mixed up condition, due to the Hascalls' long absence — lots to do. Shall introduce some changes on Monday, and gradually get hold of affairs.

Henzada was a far cry from Rangoon in every way. It was a small village with paths and unpaved roads instead of streets, a native bazaar instead of stores, and no other missionaries. The only other foreigners, to whom Hattie was soon introduced, were connected with the British District Headquarters stationed there.

[May 18, '87, continued]

This noon Mrs. Hascall took me to call on the one English lady in the place — the Deputy Commissioner's wife, and on the only other lady, a French woman, mother of a Gov't surveyor. So one English, one French, and two Americans make up the society available. The English lady, Mrs. Butler, has just left four children, from four to ten years in age, at home and is here with a two-year-old and her husband.

It rained very hard while we were there and she had two servants take us in her hand-carriage, like a big baby carriage, that held us both with a little crowding. One man pulled it and another pushed. It saved us muddy feet and wet clothes.

I begin with my teacher tomorrow, Mah Chin, one of the two who have carried on the school. The other is a Eurasian, but dresses Burman fashion.

Hattie soon became familiar with the routine of the mission: Sunday services, Wednesday night prayer meeting, visits to the families of the students, and "walking out" to preach. School duties and Burmese language study took the major part of the days; walking out was an early morning or evening activity.

The school itself was a time-consuming assignment. It had suffered from the lack of supervision during the Hascalls' absence and needed considerable re-organization and additional staff. Student enrollment had fallen off and recruitment of students was a necessary part of the missionaries' activity.

May 26, '87

To begin at the beginning — Saturday morning I went into school which is held from 7 to 9 for the study of the Sunday School lesson. The pupils are mostly from heathen families yet they come. The school is badly mixed up, and we have done a lot of talking and planning. The school needs a native teacher, a man, to carry on the big boys who come. Neither of the girls here are at all well educated. The Hascalls don't want me to take classes in English, etc., for if I do it will put an end to all other work, and we regard school work as secondary to preaching and teaching the Bible. We mean to have as good a school as we can without sacrificing other things.

I have had Mah Chin one hour a day 8 to 9 A.M. for my teacher, and I have taught my Bible class from 10-11 A.M. They are very ignorant, only one professes to be a Christian. We are studying Acts, as they had been over the Gospels a good deal, and I thought they would be more interested in what they had not had.

I am also in school from 3 to 4 P.M. teaching sewing and writing and one afternoon a week we give a dictation exercise in Aesop's Fables (Burmese) and another is spent in singing.

We have devotions here in the morning in English, and at 7 P.M. the Christians round about come in to Burmese service.

Wednesday evening the church prayer meeting is held at different houses, this week in the school house. All these things with my studying and preparing for them fill the days full. Mrs. Hascall wants me to walk out twice a day, don't think I can manage that, tho we must do some visiting. We called on one of the Christians Tuesday morning and Oh! dear, how they do live! Filthy is no name for it. Of course, there are some exceptions.

I have a girl from the jungle to take care of my room, etc., for which I pay her board in a native family (41) and her schooling (-18) here and give her clothes. Amounts to nearly Rs5 a month, which is a good deal for the little she does. I'll have to train her a good deal. It is an experiment and is more for her good than mine. She was baptized last year.

The practice of holding the weekly prayer meeting at a different home each week enabled more native Christians to participate, as many lived at some distance from the mission. For Hattie, it provided an opportunity to become better acquainted with native life.

June 3, '87

Wednesday evening (5 P.M.) we went to the weekly prayer meeting, held this time at the Bible woman's — Mah Koo. She lives a long way off so we had to go by cart. There are no gharries here, and it was too muddy and the roads too bad for ponies. A buffalo cart was brought to the door and we all climbed in over the wheel, and the children were lifted in after us. I sat on a rattan stool but Mr. and Mrs. Hascall preferred to sit on the bottom of the cart, so did the three boys, but the baby was held. Three grown people, four children, and the cartman all packed in a cart 3 feet by 4 feet with a projection in front for the driver. After we left the town limits, the roads were dreadful — mud and water a foot deep. The cart went bumping over, into, and swishing through water, and the hoofs and tails of the buffalos spattered us with mud and water. I thought it was raining, but looking up saw clear sky, and put down my umbrella, concluding that the water came from below.

When we arrived we found between 30 and 40 of the Christians and school children there, and when we began to sing, a good number of the heathen neighbors gathered round. Children with little or nothing on, women with a single scant skirt reaching from the armpits to the knees, a naked baby on their hip, and a cigar in their mouth. The men much the same. We met on the lower floor, which has no side walls; there was a chair for Mr. Hascall; I sat on my stool, and Mrs. Hascall on a rude bench, the children on the floor. The pigpen was under the same roof a few feet away and the chickens everywhere. Nice mats were spread for the folks to sit on.

Mr. Hascall and the native pastor preached and several of the heathen men listened attentively. After the preaching and several prayers we returned as we came, getting a few finishing touches in the mud line. The baby being hungry began to wail. Mrs. Hascall's feet got so numb she could hardly move, so I tilted up my stool to give her a chance, and having tilted it there was no place to put it down again; to stand was impossible, to sit on a slanting stool and hold it in that position was a laughable predicament, but after some engineering room was made and I sat comfortably again. We arrived home safely, not having been caught in a shower, and feeling very glad that we went.

Monday I taught and studied as usual, and we made two calls in the morning and three or four in the evening and Mr. Hascall had a chance to preach to one hardened old heathen in one of the Christian houses. Mr. Hascall is preaching all the time. I have heard the Gospel preached more in three weeks here than in all the time at Rangoon.

June 10, '87

This has been a busy week as usual. Sunday I had thirteen in my Sunday School class and at noon I led the woman's meeting, which is the first time I have led a meeting in Burmese. I have taught as usual during the week: Monday evening we called at two native houses and Tuesday evening Dr. Dawson called and then we all walked out with him. I am getting to be quite a walker for me — go out every night. It tires me a good deal but there is no other way, and I must have some sort of exercise. We want to get a hand carriage but they are not easy to find.

Our new teacher Maung Chan Min arrived from Moulmein on Wednesday. He is a quiet pleasant man of about 30 years. The school has never been graded or classified, so Thursday Mr. Hascall and I spent the whole day in school, examining and classifying according to the Gov't standard. We have five classes — and about 55 pupils and more coming.

Maung Chan Min takes the place of Nellie, who is to help Mr. Hascall on some translating he is doing for Frank (getting up a geography) which he can't find time for himself, and also be ready to go out with me nights when I want her.

June 17, '87

Monday I began with Maung Chan Min as my teacher. He is a great improvement on Mah Chin. I have begun to write in a copy book myself. Maung Chan Min sets the copy in Burmese, of course.

Wednesday evening we went to prayer meeting at the house of one of the well-to-do members, a frame house better fixed up than most. About 30 were present. The old man of the house is one who, when a boy, threw stones at Dr. Judson. He was pastor of the church a long time; is very feeble now.

June 24, '87

Last Saturday morning I went out with Mah Nellie and called at the homes of several of the scholars, if such places can be called "homes." I don't wonder they have no such word in their language, they have nothing worthy the name, at least very few have. In the evening Mrs. Hascall and I called on one Chin and two Karen families nearby. I rather like the Chin women in spite of their tattooed faces; all that I have seen are Christians.

Sunday passed as usual. I ventured to lead in prayer in the woman's meeting. Their solemn form is as different from the common as with us or even more so.

Monday, as we had got to Paul's first missionary journey, I made on a sheet of brown paper (had nothing else big enough) a map to illustrate the journeys extending from Jerusalem to Rome, the names in Burmese of course. As we study along I mark the journey by blue pencil. It helps to interest them.

Thursday after dinner I went out again with Mah Nellie,
and called on a number of pupils who live on the Karen
compound. Karens and Chins and on one Burman family
elsewhere. I think there are about as many Karens and Chins in
school as Burmans. Shall go again tonight if it doesn't rain.
Have had none for three days now and it is very hot and
oppressive.

June 30, '87

Sunday afternoon I started the Bible readings at 2 P.M.
Thirty-four of the young folks came, which was more than I
expected. The reading I gave was "Ten thoughts about God"
and they found the references and read them very well. I think
they liked it. I have prepared another for next Sunday on the
Christian character which Maung Chan Min will lead. The
Hascalls don't want me to every time, it makes five services for
me, not counting our morning and evening worship.

The prayer meeting this week was at Ko Tke's — the
pastor. They had put a patch-work quilt on the table for a
spread, not a perfectly clean one either. Yet their home looks
quite as well as any and better than most.

Once the school was in better order, Hattie had more time
to engage in the evangelistic work that had brought her to Burma.
It required much walking, and, as Hattie became more experienced, much talking — not always with as much success as she
could wish.

[June 30, '87, continued]

Thursday evening I made two calls with Nellie; as we were
coming back we stopped to see a man making mats for walls.
Someone asked Nellie what I had in my little handbag. She
said tracts, or little books rather, so I asked him if he wanted
one. He said yes and when I gave him one, others gathered at
once and held out their hands till I gave all I had. I told them
to read and consider, so did Nellie, but they may not. They
seemed to want the biggest piece of paper; perhaps that is all
they wanted, and perhaps they will read and come to hear
more.

July 8, '87

After dinner I took a walk with Mr. Hascall and for the first time heard him do some street preaching. He certainly has a talent for it, making any sort of an incident open the way to a "preach." There is nothing particularly encouraging in the work here; a good many say they are "considering" or are almost Christians, but they stand right there for years at a time.

July 15, '87

In the evening or just after dinner I went out with Mah Chin and Nellie on a preaching trip. It was a big worship day and many had their rosaries in their hands. I stopped to speak to an old man with one. He said by repeating on the beads over and over "Impermanence, Tribulation, Insubstantiality, God" he would reach the Nat country. I tried to talk a little to him but Nellie would not help so I soon walked on, but a woman listened and when we stopped at a house, where they were making those wooden dancing figures, and got to talking, she followed us and paid better attention than anyone. At this house Nellie woke up and spoke well for some time. Some said they had never heard but it was doubtless a lie to hear me talk; they didn't gain much by it, however. One man said, "O yes, you come to teach us about being good, and then kill chickens which is a great sin." Nellie reminded him that they ate chickens after someone else killed them and also fish in their gnapee, to which he had nothing to say.

On the way home we stopped at an idol house near an old pagoda where a good many people were bowing down to a lot of idols sitting and standing behind iron bars; all the people had rosaries which they counted off just like Catholics.

In addition to her language study, her work in the school, and learning the ropes of "walking out," Hattie continued some of the work she had carried for Frank in Rangoon, spending time each week reading proof that Frank sent up to her from Rangoon. She also undertook the translation of articles for publication by the press.

July 15, '87

This week I have translated a short article for Miss Ranney or for Mr. Hascall, as, if I had not, he would have had to do it. Miss Ranney is getting out some tracts; the illustrated papers are given by an English Society if the receivers use the English article to translate into Burmese. Mr. Bunker has them and puts the articles into Karen. Mr. Hascall had a half-dozen articles to translate so I helped out by doing one; my teacher corrected it for me, though but slightly.

July 21, '87

Lately I have made my lessons almost entirely conversation lessons, and Wednesday morning I had a very interesting talk with Maung Chan Min. I told him to take the Buddhist side and I would take the Christian and we would have a discussion. So he did, but took the side of the highest sect of them, which believe in one God who created all things and of whose beginning and end no one knows. His first appearance was Gautama, who did not sin, but bore the various penalties for the various sins committed by man. His next appearance will be Ajinbadaya. But though he bore the penalty of sins every man must keep the law or be lost, and no one ever yet kept it. So they have no better hope than common Buddhists. I did not know of these sects before; there are three, one is called Bara-mot, the others Su la-gande and Ma hah-gande. The latter two think Gautama has reached M'gban but by good deeds man may better his condition next time he is born. The last one call the idols and pagoda — "God" and worship them as such and also worship a multitude of Nats. But the second one say they are not "god" but are to be reverenced by way of doing honor to Gautama. Those who belong to the first sect are the hardest to answer as there is much of truth mixed with their errors. We talked over an hour and I finally got the best of it.

July 27, '87

Last Saturday morning I went out with Mr. Hascall when he went out to preach. We sat in one house and he talked a long time. It is quite easy to make these folks acknowledge the folly and worthlessness of their own religion, and the superiority of Christianity, but to get them to give up their own and accept ours is quite another thing. Their minds are convinced in many cases, but they <u>will not accept</u> Christ; they would rather go on believing that they can save themselves.

Tuesday evening I took my girl and went out to read some Scripture to a Christian woman who cannot come to Chapel. She has a heathen sister who came and listened, but she is a hard case, has been preached to any amount, like lots of others here. The road was <u>dreadfully</u> muddy, did not seem as if we could get there even when in sight of the house. Of course, there is not a sidewalk in the place.

Thursday I read some proof, had my lesson, taught my Bible and English classes, copied off my next Bible reading and after dinner I went out alone for the first time to preach. I meant to find some women to talk to in some house but they seemed to be eating rice, so I went on till I came to a corner where there is a pagoda and idol houses. Here I saw a girl reading a notice so I stopped and spoke to her and then another and some children. So I asked what those idols were and went on to talk. In a few minutes I was in the middle of a crowd mostly of men and children, the latter would have been "clothed in sunshine" if there had been any sunshine. One man had a mind to be flippant but he soon quieted down and listened well and asked sensible questions. They were all respectful and hushed up the children in a hurry if they did not keep still, saying "Hey! listen! she's preaching!" I read a leaflet that was to the point and gave a few away with some cards.

Friday after dinner I went out by myself again, saw a girl at a well and stopped to speak to her. She said she had believed for two years but I saw it was only with her head. She asked me to go home with her so I did, and preached to the household. Her mother did most of the talking back. When I spoilt her arguments she tried to make out that Christianity was just like Buddhism!

Aug. 6, '87

Monday after dinner I went to the house of one of the scholars, but found them too satisfied and indifferent to listen. A man next door called across for a tract, so I went over and gave him one, and talked awhile; he listened better and the woman of the first house followed me. The idea that some at home have that the heathen wait with outstretched hands for the Gospel is as far as possible from being true of the Burmans, at least. They as a rule are perfectly satisfied with their own religion of gaining merit by works; if they do not do well in this life, why, there are an endless number of lives still before them.

Tuesday had classes as usual and after dinner I walked out again, stopped to speak to a woman at a street stand. An old hag came along who stoutly maintained that her religion was absolutely perfect and satisfactory in all respects, and she was entirely happy in worshiping Gautama! She would not listen, and the men began to gather round so I walked on.

Thursday morning I went again with Mah Koo, this time to a section of the town called Ca-they'don where the silk weavers live. They are not pure Burmans, and they seem to mix Buddhism and Braminism — worship Krishna mostly, I guess. Those we saw were very pleasant and listened well. One man when asked by Mah Koo to come to the Chapel on Sunday, said he already kept the Burman worship days as well as his own. They have been preached to a good deal.

The Hascalls want me to give up my Bible Reading (it makes Sunday such a very hard day) and let the girls have a prayer meeting at that time. Think I shall have to do so; may occasionally prepare Bible readings for Mr. Hascall to use Sunday evening.

Aug. 12, '87

Tuesday I went out with Mr. Hascall when he went to preach as he does most mornings. We stopped at a carver's house. An empty coffin occupied the middle of the room. A woman was cooking in one corner, and the man was carving a handsome bracelet in another corner. A horse had his stall just outside of a door in the third corner. The whole front was open and we sat on the edge of the floor and let our feet hang down.

Wednesday I read proof, and began to get ready for my Bible class which have finished and reviewed Acts; and now I shall take up the prophesies of Christ in the Old Testament and their fulfillment in the New.

I sent one of my Bible Readings to Dr. Jameson for the *[Burman] Messenger.* I see it appears this week. Miss Ranney says the articles we translated (Mr. Hascall several and I one) shall be published first!

Wednesday evening the prayer meeting was at Ko Tilar's. His wife is down with fever; Mrs. Hascall's ayah has been sick with the same for several weeks; she is not yet able to work, and has gone over to the Karen compound for a change. Now my girl is down with dysentery, a most obstinate case; Mr. Hascall thinks there may be worms to blame!

This morning before breakfast I went out a while with Mr. Hascall. He preached at a house where the son is in the Gov't school; knows English and Geography enough to know that the Buddhist Scriptures lie and yet he worships Gautama "because his forefathers did." He had just had his photo taken and Mr. Hascall asked why he had that and why he studied English, his forefathers did neither! He laughed and saw the point, but said that "every man thinks his religion the best." So he was told to find out about the Christian religion and judge for himself. Education does not mean evangelization by a long shot. They will cling to their books and bow down to their idols long after they know by their education the falsity and uselessness of both; or they dispense with religion altogether.

Aug. 19, '87

Monday morning I went out with Mah Koo to the silk-weavers again. She preached some in two houses where she had many times before; the people were utterly indifferent — "gospel hardened" I should say. After dinner I went alone and called on three scholars' houses, and preached a little; found them even more indifferent than those of the morning.

This morning Mrs. Case, being on the steamship which arrived at 9:30 A.M., sent her girl up to the house and we three went down to see her. She has been ill for some time, fever, etc. She was looking wretchedly, but she always does when at all sick. She is the first missionary we have seen since May (when we came) so it was quite an event for us. The steamship left at 12 M. so we had quite a visit and rest between the two very hot walks to and from the steamship.

We expect to have some baptisms Sunday and another Sunday School Concert. The outside Christians have been invited in and are beginning to arrive today.

Saturday morning we rehearsed the Sunday School Concert in the school. At noon came the church meeting, then eight candidates were examined for baptism tomorrow. There were three girls from Christian families, four women (two from out of town) and a Karen man. The meeting lasted two hours; the folks answered pretty well, some have believed for a long time but have just got up spunk to ask baptism. This evening we have a prayer meeting in the new schoolhouse in the center of the town.

Aug. 27, '87

Sunday we met at 7 A.M. and two more girls were examined and accepted. Then we all went down to the river, which is not far off. There were in all, including the schoolchildren, about 130 of us, and the heathen formed a crowd around us at once. There was singing, prayer, Scripture reading and a forcible talk by Mr. Hascall. The Ko Tike, the pastor, baptized the ten candidates and we sang a verse between the baptisms of "Ring the Bells of Heaven." Everything passed off nicely, the women and girls being baptized being calm and dignified. At 11 A.M. came the preaching but I was so tired from the 2-1/2 hours service of the morning I stayed at home and went over at 12 M. to the Lord's Supper. The hand of fellowship was given to the 10 new members. At 2 P.M. we had the women's and the girls' meeting for an hour or so. At 5 P.M. came the monthly Sunday School Concert: over 100 texts, answering the questions, "Who, what, why, and when shall I believe?" were recited by pupils and Christians; they had been learned before. There was frequent singing and all had a good time. About 20 Christians from out-stations were present and it was all a great treat to them. One woman thought it must be like Heaven, and when Nellie told her Heaven was far better she said, "Then let me die at once." We were tired out with so much service — seven hours in all — but it is seldom these out-station Christians have any such privilege at all and as baptisms are by no means frequent, we can afford to make an extra time of it.

Tuesday evening we took dinner with the Dep[uty] Com[missioner] (Mr. Butler), one young man in the police service was the only other guest. It was pleasant enough but they are worldly people who not only have no sympathy with us, but positively disapprove of missionary labors.

Sept. 3, '87

I have taught as usual this week, and been out two mornings. Once, to the house of Mah Nellie's grandmother who had just died. She was a heathen and was very much afraid to die: had been preached to but had not accepted. She called on Gautama, the "Law" and the "Assembly," and on "Mah Nellie's God" to save her. The same day the old Chin Christian across the way died. He said he was not afraid, and afterward, "they have come to call me, don't you see them?" He asked someone to pray and during the prayer died.

Friday morning I went with Mah Koo to see the heathen wife of one of the members of the church. Did not receive any encouragement; she says there is no occasion to preach to her, she understands perfectly, and is "considering." As I told her there is danger of her "considering" till she dies and never getting any farther. The truth is she is afraid of the ridicule of her friends.

We have two boarders now and expect two more, one is my girl and a Burman in town pays for the other three. Rs4 a piece a month, but it will be tight squeezing at that. They do the buying and I keep the money and take the account.

There is no news as I see. The week has gone in teaching, study, and a little proofreading, etc. etc.

Sept. 7, '87

I sent off an outline of the Old Testament books which I condensed from Barron's *Companion to the Bible* and then translated. It is long enough for two papers and I mean to do the same for the New Testament. Dr. Jameson wants something every month. I am able to sympathize with Editors in need of "copy" so will do the best I can for him, especially as it is good practice in Burmese.

I have also made a version of the hymn "He Knows" for Mrs. Hascall; I say <u>version</u> advisedly as it is almost impossible with Burmese to get into the same number of syllables the same amount of ideas as in the English. All the songs lose by translating. Some of those we sing are nowhere near the original.

Hattie had been stationed in Henzada barely four months when
Mr. Hascall received notice of a new assignment.

                                        Sept. 12, '87
    The event of the week is the arrival of a letter from the
Rooms sending Mr. Hascall to found a new station between
Mandalay and Bhamo, a work he is well fitted for. A new man,
Mr. Cumming and his new, young wife will take this station,
sailing in October (as a letter from Mr. Cumming says). The
work is so well organized here and there are so many helpers
that a new man can do very well. But a new man in a new
station, to build, etc. would be useless.
    Nothing was said about me; but last year both Mrs.
Hascall and I asked that I be appointed to her, rather than
to the place; and as, if she needed me here, she will ten-fold
more in a new place, with few if any native helpers, it looks
to me as if I better go along too. I should not think the
Board would care to give a helper to a new fresh couple
with no family cares. Mrs. Hascall with her four boys to
teach and with her housekeeping does not pretend to do any
missionary work to speak of. She wanted me especially for
house to house work, and I feel as Mr. Hascall does about
it: if I am to spend the best of my life preaching to the
heathen I would like to preach to those who have never
heard, rather than to these in Henzada who have heard and
turned away over and over again; to whom the Gospel has
been preached for 37 years. Of course it would be easier
and more comfortable to stay on here (providing the new
couple cared to have a third party in their new family) and
it is nearer Frank, and nearer civilization generally. But if I
am going to look out for No. 1, I better come home and do
it comfortably. When the new road, now being built from
Toungoo to Mandalay, is done, it will not take so much
longer to reach Rangoon after all. About 24 hours from
Mandalay to Rangoon.
    Mr. Hascall has telegraphed today to Mr. Kelley and to
Mr. Roberts to ask about the stations. Of course, he will
choose a large one, where there will be English troops, a
Deputy Commissioner, doctor, etc. — a civil station if
possible.

I do not know what the Boards think I am going to do, if indeed they have thought about it at all, but I shall write to find out.

Mr. Hascall is, I think, pleased with the plan, and Mrs. Hascall is not afraid to go anywhere with him, as he is prudent and will take the best possible care of all.

We are considerably "shuck up and down in our minds" so to speak. But "nuff sed" for this time.

While Hattie waited to hear what this new assignment for the Hascalls would mean in terms of her own future, plans were made to attend the upcoming Convention, held this year in Moulmein.

Sept. 20, '87

The Hascalls think of going to the Convention at Moulmein in November. It is their old home and they want to revisit it before going farther away, besides improving the opportunity to attend the Convention. There are to be special meetings of missionaries after the Convention for prayer and conference. If they go, I shall go also, in preference to being left alone in the station for the better part of the month that the trip will take. Besides if we "go up" this cold season I shall like to go to Rangoon again, tho I rather dread the trip, it is such an undertaking with all these children — not that I am responsible for them, of course.

By the time plans for the trip to Moulmein were in place, Hattie had become reconciled to the undertaking and began looking forward to a visit with Frank and Rangoon friends on the way. Preparing for Convention added to an already busy week.

Oct. 18, '87

Friday morning I went to two scholar's houses with Mr. Hascall who preached a little. In the afternoon I made seven soldier hats of pink blotting paper with tassels of various bright tissue papers furnished by Mrs. Hascall for Willie's birthday. The Eurasian children of the place which are in Mrs. Hascall's little Sunday School were invited. They all had caps and Mr. Hascall trained them. Cake and sweets were served and they had a fine time.

Saturday I fixed the sleeves of the two sateen basques which were a trifle too long and large, also put under-sleeves in the thin white basque. And tried on my two batiste dresses to see if they were ready to wear in Rangoon and Moulmein.

The white ants have been working in the house and part of the partition, though solid in appearance, is as rotten as paper; can poke your finger right through. So with everything else on hand the carpenters must be around repairing.

And to cap the climax, the Prices are coming Thursday to go on to Rangoon Tuesday just when we expect to go, which makes it decidedly hard on Mrs. Hascall to have company to the last minute. As they expect to take up the [Karen] work here, they want to come and see things while Mr. Hascall is here.

On the S.S. *Brama,* Oct. 25, '87

Here I am steaming down the river toward Rangoon.

Monday at 9 A.M. we heard a steamship whistle and while Mr. Price went to see which it was, we hurried around to get ready. It proved to be this. It has no cabins, is not designed for passengers except deck-passengers. Mrs. Hascall said at once she would wait till the next in a day or two (she was not ready anyway). But the Prices and I being all ready and being able to rough it a little decided to take it, and so have a day or so more in Rangoon. So we came aboard.

The Captain is very pleasant and obliging, has made us two rooms on deck with canvas wherein we can sleep in tolerable comfort though we are right over the wheels and engine and near the smoke stack so it was very warm the first part of the night, and is very jiggly all the time as this writing shows. There are lots of natives aboard on the same deck. They have no cabins, just unroll mats and hang up a thick mosquito curtain and crawl under. I hastily put in a mat, two blankets and a curtain, and the Captain furnished canvas cots which are quite spring-like.

This morning we had a nice visit with the Bushells and Miss Putnam at Maubin. They came aboard, were on for an hour.

On the steamship Tuesday when it had stopped to wait for a tide and was quiet enough to talk I had a chance to preach to the 20 or so at hand. Most were from the jungle, going to

Rangoon to worship at the Shway Dagon Pagoda. So I held forth to the best of my ability and gave some tracts and scripture cards.

I had a note from Miss Whitehead [in Moulmein] saying in answer to a question that I need not bring a bed, as she has several hooks in her room not in use and she could hang up the spinster sisters on them if beds give out!!

<u>Packer House, Ahlone</u> We arrived at the city at about 8 A.M. Wednesday and I took a gharry at once to come up so as to catch Frank before he went down to the office. I arrived just before his breakfast so we ate and talked and <u>talked</u> and <u>talked</u> till he had to leave for the office. I spent the day in draping his lace curtains at doors inner and outer and fixing around generally. With his furniture and new curtains the house looks nice and homelike. At noon I went over and visited Mrs. Bennett and Miss Ranney and took tiffin with them.

This morning Frank and I went out and called at Kemindine and on the Roses and Mr. Vinton. After breakfast I went down with him and did a little shopping, then came back and darned a purdah which Madgie had torn, and when it was shady I went and called on Mrs. Douglass and Mrs. Kelley; found both looking very well.

It does seem nice to be in a quiet house once more with not the noise of many feet and many tongues, and still nicer to sit at table with only Frank and have a chance to do some talking myself. I do get tired of the continual clatter and chatter of the children.

Despite Hattie's initial reluctance to undertake this trip, her attendance at Convention proved to be a very positive experience and a needed change.

Moulmein, Nov. 3, '87

Tuesday morning Mrs. Roach and I took the new steamship for Moulmein; there were seventeen grown folks and nine children who went. We had a calm, pleasant passage arriving before 3 P.M. Miss Stark and I are staying with Miss Whitehead and taking meals with her at Mr. Armstrong's.

Wednesday we attended the meetings all day; from 7:30 to 10 A.M., 1 to 3:30 and a sermon in the evening by Mr. Calder.

The meetings were very good, such a treat as we have not had in this land before, at least I have not. After the afternoon meeting Miss Garton took me home with her to dinner.

Today we have attended the meetings according to the Programme. This evening we dine with Miss Barrows; there will be five "old maids" and Mr. Calder!!! Don't you pity him?

In the evening there will be a meeting of the missionaries at Miss Bunn's; of course we will all go.

I have enjoyed myself very much since reaching Rangoon. It is very refreshing to see other folks, hear other talk, have some rides, be in a quiet house, and attend services in English. (I have not yet heard a half dozen English sermons since I came to Burma.) I have gained enough already to pay for the trip, which will not be expensive; Rs8/3 took me to Rangoon and Rs.18 pays for the trip to and from Moulmein.

Packer House, Rangoon, Nov. 10, '87

After mailing my last letter I took dinner at Miss Barrows' and we all gathered in the evening at Miss Bunn's and had a very pleasant conference meeting. The question of school connection with Gov't was discussed, also Mrs. Ann Judson's grave, which it was decided must be moved back 70 yards on the same compound to save it from the sea which is within 21 feet of it now. Then the case of Mr. Rand who is in poor circumstances and who does not receive anything this year from the Executive Committee was discussed. It was thought that he had given it up as he told Mr. Price that it was his greatest trial to have to take it. He is all drawn out of shape, can hardly feed himself, but is bright and cheerful as ever. Has four girls to educate, so we took up a collection (or rather made a subscription) amounting to over Rs500 (31 missionaries) and the Karens next day added Rs.60, which will be sent to him at once. His memory is very fragrant in this country.

Friday the meetings were continued, the subjects being the missionaries at home, schoolwork, medical work, Presses, etc. They were interesting and profitable to the end.

In the evening there was a mass meeting of all — Burmans, Karens, Tamils, Telugus, Shans, and English. Each had singing prayer, and a speech, closing by the doxology in each language. About 1000 were present, I think.

Monday and Saturday the Convention meetings were held, and each day the Adies, a Eurasian family living near who have known the missionaries back to the time of the Judsons, gave to us all a substantial tiffin.

Saturday evening we met again at Miss Bunn's to continue the discussion of the school question, and it was decided to send a protest to Gov't in regard to some objectionable rules. Sunday I attended the Burman and English preaching services.

Monday evening dinner was served to all in Miss Whitehead's school, a very pleasant affair; besides the 31 grown-up ones, were a dozen children or so.

Tuesday most of us came back to Rangoon.

Almost immediately the Henzada contingent began the journey home.

Prome, Nov. 17, '87
Wednesday the Hascalls and I came by train to Prome, leaving at 6 A.M. and arriving at 5 P.M. This morning Mr. Hascall took the mail steamer for Mandalay to seek for a new station, and we will take the next convenient steamship for Henzada.

In fact, the return journey was accomplished neither as conveniently or easily as one might wish.

Nov. 24, '87
Here I am again in my own room and very glad to be here at last, after an absence of a month. We had to stay [with the Carsons] in Prome a week waiting for a steamship which we finally got and went aboard Tuesday evening having to cross a bar of sand and a ledge of rock in the river bed, and then four "flots" (a sort of freight scow attached to the sides of the steamship) and a Steamer before we reached ours. We left in the morning and arrived in the evening — yesterday.

I enjoyed meeting the Carsons, but we were so crowded it was not comfortable enough to enjoy having to stay so long. I had to use the same bath and sleeping rooms as Mrs. Hascall, the four children, and two ayahs; an arrangement not nice in this climate, if in any. While there a young English lady gave me two rides around Prome and along the river; both were

very pleasant indeed. Prome is a more desirable place of
residence than Henzada — prettier, pleasanter, etc. etc. Sunday
I attended their Sunday School and preaching service in the
morning and Communion service at 5 P.M. While there I read
The Life of Aunt Lizzie Akin and several short stories, and
sewed some for Mrs. Carson.

The decision regarding the new mission was finally made, and
preparations for the move began. Hattie's position was still un-
clear but her expectation was that she would be allowed to accompany the Hascalls to the new station.

Dec. 13, '87

Last Wednesday we heard from Mr. Hascall that he had
decided to settle in Sagaing, which is just below Mandalay on
the other side of the river. It is the head-quarters of a district
and so has a Deputy Commissioner, doctor, etc. like Henzada.
It is spoken of by all, both English and natives, as the most
desirable place in Upper Burma. Mr. Hascall found that the
Burman population above Mandalay would not warrant
starting a station there now — very sparse. Around Mandalay
it is very dense. There is a daily steamer between Sagaing and
Mandalay and next year the railroad between Mandalay and
Rangoon will be done, then we could get to Rangoon in less
time than from here. Mr. Hascall hopes to get the land purchased and carpenters to work and get back here before
Christmas, but he may not; things move slowly in this land. He
expects to move at once to Mandalay and live there while he
goes back and forth seeing to the building; thus having the
cool season to brace us up for the hot.

The new folks, the Cummings, to take the Hascalls' place,
have arrived here. The steamship came in Sunday; we went to
meet them and all got back to the house at 3:30 P.M. in time to go
to the 4 P.M. preaching service. Nearly the whole church went to
meet them and followed us home, and were in to worship and a
sing in the evening. Mrs. Hascall gave tiffin of bread and tea to
scholars and Christians. They are pleased with the Cummings I
think and they are pleased with everything. They are a small
couple, good looking and pleasant, he with blue eyes and light
hair, and she with brown hair and black eyes.

We hear that the Prices are to come to the Karen mission and Miss Wepf perhaps will come. So it will be very pleasant for the Cummings, not so dull as it has been during my stay here.

My former girl NeMah writes that she can go with me; her father is willing. I expect to call her soon.

Dec. 20, '87

Today at 4 P.M. Mr. Hascall arrived, amid great rejoicing. He has bought land in Sagaing, and given the contract for the building. The house is to be done in three months from December 15. We expect to move to Mandalay as soon as we can get ready. Each of the folks [missionaries in Mandalay] invite us to stay with them, but Mr. Hascall expects to rent a house for the time we shall be there.

The Cummings are taking hold nicely and the people take to them. Mr. Cummings is going to get the "talk" quickly, I think. They are going to take my room for theirs. Though they say they would like to have me stay, I know they don't expect me to, nor feel any need of it. I have made a list of common sentences in anglicized Burmese for Mrs. Cummings so she can manage before she learns to read.

Mrs. Butler met Mr. Cummings on the street and told Mrs. Hascall afterwards that he did not look at all like a clerical gentleman; when asked why so? she said "Why he wears a <u>blue</u> tie!!!"

Hattie's second Christmas in Burma was celebrated in style.

Dec. 27, '87

We all took Christmas dinner at the Butlers; there were 14 at the table which was profusely decorated with flowers. Mrs. Butler borrowed Mrs. Hascall's organ and so after dinner we had music and singing; on the whole, a very pleasant time.

Monday we gave and received presents. I gave Mr. and Mrs. Hascall two large fans for wall decoration, and Mr. and Mrs. Cummings two scrolls, and to the helpers, handkerchiefs, jacket, ink stands etc. etc. Mr. and Mrs. Hascall gave me a beautiful silver and glass double photo holder; the base is of silver ivy leaves. It is for Papa's and Mama's cabinets when they come. Mr. and Mrs. Cummings gave a nice card and a pair of nice salmon pink gloves. From the children a folding Burman slate, a tiny decorated plate and a box (I gave them some round boxes). Nellie and Mah Chin gave a string of mock pearls and a silver star. Maung Chan Min gave a "Book of Worthies" and from others I received two handkerchiefs, a glass dish, a floor mat, a box; just now the mail brings three more cards from Burma friends and a lovely little book *Pilgrim Songs* from May and Tony. So you see I fared very well indeed.

At 4 P.M. we all went to the Christmas got up for the Eurasians at Mrs. Butler's; refreshments and presents were given to all the Eurasian children in town, about 30.

Both Saturday and Monday evening we prepared the gifts and filled the candy bags for our tree. We had native peanuts and sweets and English candy for the bags. This morning we put them on the tree which was at one end of the veranda. Many gifts were glass dishes which looked very pretty. The tree was something like a little oak tree with green leaves all over. No pines here nor snow! Over one hundred came and we all had a good time. There were 163 presents and 149 bags made up. Those who could not come sent friends. The folks came at 11 A.M. and went after 1 P.M. Now the rest have all gone to see the sports got up by the English on a common back of the jail. I did not care to go.

The Christmas celebrations marked the end of the Hascalls' and Hattie's Henzada responsibilities. To her relief, Hattie's assignment to Sagaing with the Hascalls was finally confirmed.

Jan. 3, '88

The mail is in bringing a letter from Mrs. Gates to the effect they were pleased to transfer me to wherever the Hascalls went. Very good. I am more and more decided that it is the thing to do, and it would not be at all well to stay on with this young couple, both younger by a year than I.

Henzada duties completed and the new missionaries in place, the mammoth job of packing up for the move to Sagaing began in earnest.

Jan. 8, '88

Things have been in a great state of upheaval this week. The Hascalls and myself packing, the Cummings unpacking. Pictures and curtains are down, furniture tied up and the house forlorn generally.

Mr. Hascall is half-sick with dysentery; so is Charles. I have done my packing with what Ne Mah could help, which was little, as I could not trust her to put in things. There are plenty of servants here but all are so busy it is hard to get help.

The Prices and Miss Wepf arrived about 9 P.M. yesterday and are staying here till their things arrive. Everything is in great confusion. The municipal overseer sent about 50 or 60 coolies today to take our goods to the river bank, ready for the steamship tomorrow. My things have all gone; will have to camp most anywhere tonight. I take one almirah with my mattress in it and two rugs. I also take my bedstead and book case and chest of drawers. Of course, everything I have from home goes. Twenty-one pieces in all counting pahs and trunks.

I have done most of my packing. Mr. Cummings helped tie up the furniture and NeMah took down my bedstead and helped what she could. We are all very tired. When settled in Sagaing we hope to <u>stay</u> till we go home.

S.S. Rangoon. Nowhere in particular, Jan. 11, '88

I slept the last night with Miss Wepf in the Karen house, their bedding having come, and at 7:30 A.M. a whistle was heard and the rush to get off began. The Hascalls as usual were not near ready and the amount to be done the last minute was appalling. Mr. and Mrs. Cummings, the servants and I all pitched in, so to speak, and worked as hard as we could. In spite of all that had been sent off the night before, there were trunks, pahs, bath tub, two boxes and several bed rolls to be done up. I never saw a family with so much in the line of goods.

When everything but the numerous boxes of plants had gone, we learned that the first whistle was not the *Rangoon*, which had just then come in. Mr. Hascall was at the shore and Mrs. Hascall at the house. The things were put on as fast as possible and at last Mr. Hascall had to send for her to come. She just got on before starting, and one box of plants had to be left.

If we had not had the false warning of the first steamship we would have missed this <u>sure</u>. The Captain had heard nothing of our coming — if everything had not been right there, they would not have waited. Did not like what delay we did cause them.

If Mr. Cummings had not helped me, putting in my organ, taking down and tying up my bedstead, protecting the glass and tying up my bookcase, I should not have been ready either. I could scarcely get hold of a servant for a minute even, and Mr. Hascall was too weak and had too much to do to help at all.

I did nothing yesterday after we started but lie in my berth and try to rest. I doubt if I was ever more tired. I mean to unpack just as little as possible in Mandalay; don't ever want another such siege of packing.

As an established mission, Henzada had provided a relatively comfortable, if somewhat uninspiring, opportunity for Hattie to learn about missionary work in the field — observing and assisting in school for local children, attending prayer meetings in native houses, "walking out," and trying her hand at convincing the heathen to accept Christian doctrines. She looked forward to Sagaing as an opportunity to work with less worked-over natives.

8

Upper Burma: Sagaing

January to August 1888

The capital city of Upper Burma and the site of the palace of the deposed King Thibaw, Mandalay was an historically and politically important center of Burmese culture. It was also home to a number of Baptist missionaries, and therefore provided a convenient place for the Hascall party to stay while the Sagaing facilities were under construction.

Hattie and the Hascall family began the 300-mile river trip from Henzada to Mandalay aboard the *Rangoon* on January 10, but soon encountered a series of delays and inconveniences.

Jan. 11, '88

Here we are, not stuck in the mud ourselves, but stopping to help the *Danoon* which <u>is</u>. This ship's officers were trying hard to get to Prome tonight when this steamship, the *Danoon*, appeared in sight. Our flots have been anchored, the *Danoon's* taken off and now they are working at the steamship.

Thursday 12th. We got off from the *Danoon* at 10:15 A.M. today and at 5 P.M. we went aground ourselves hard and fast, between Myanaung and Prome.

Friday 13th. I may as well begin again for here we lie where we stuck, and no very bright hopes of being off tonight either. We have had exciting times: they took one big anchor and coils of heavy chain and dropped the anchor up the river as far as possible hoping by winding up the chain to pull off the steamship. Fearing one chain would break, they started to take another. A big boat with the anchor and lots of chain, a dozen men, and the mate, capsized. The latter and six men jumped in time into another boat, but six got into the water and as the current is exceedingly swift here, they were swept downstream till almost out of sight in a moment. They kept up till boats got to them, however; some caught oars. Both rudders and most of the oars (oars recovered later) were lost: the capsized boat was entirely out of sight under water, but the anchor kept it from being lost and it was finally pulled up and the leaks stopped. It was an anxious time all around.

Saturday 14th, 3:30 P.M. The *Burma* and the *Mindoon* steamships have come up to us from below and the *Mandalay* from above, so now we hope the latter will help us off.

I have written my annual report, and three letters besides this. After my report was sent off I began and have finished translating the Outline for the New Testament, since they have published the first half of the Old Testament Outline.

Monday 16th. The *Mandalay* hindered instead of helping, so we only got off Sunday afternoon and could not go on till this morning. Three days on the sand!! Are steaming along now to Prome, expect to arrive about 1 P.M. but make no stop to speak of.

Jan. 21, '88

Tuesday noon we reached the last Lower Burma station — Thayetmyo and saw the fort there. Wednesday we reached Minhla where is another fort. At night we reached Minboo, noted for dacoits, and had a walk on shore in six inches of sand.

Thursday evening we reached "White-Elephant-Island Town"; the bank here is almost straight up from the water some 30 feet. We climbed up and had another walk. The view is seldom pretty or attractive at all. Just now (Friday) we are passing some hills bare and reddish brown, prettier than usual. Water, sand banks, and jungle grass make up most of the view with now and then hills, seldom towns, once in a while pagodas on the hill-tops.

The mate is a Christian man, about the only one on this steamship. He comes up and has long talks with us evenings. The Captain is an American, has been up and sang with us, and last night he got up a candy-pull. We all pulled some of it, and we took the almonds out of a jar of raisins and made nut candy. Had a very pleasant evening. The journey has been very pleasant though four days longer than anticipated. Reading, writing and sleeping make up the days.

Friday we passed Pagan noted for its pagodas, and I do not wonder. The river front for miles was studded thick with old pagodas and ruins of them. A few were white and in repair but most were very old. They were different from most in Lower Burma.

Jan. 27, '88

I believe I mailed my last from Mingyan where Mr. Case met us and took us to his house, which is in good condition to live in but not yet finished. Mr. and Mrs. Case came down to the steamship and we had a sing before we again started at 4 P.M.

We had steamed off about 10 minutes and were on course in sight of Mingyan when we stuck again. The steamship drawing 4 feet 9 inches and there was but 4 feet 6 inches to be had. At 9 P.M. the Captain received a telegram to the effect that he must drop his flots and go at once to Mandalay to take back the mails Tuesday morning. So the flots and part of the cargo were left for another steamship to bring later and we got off (being lighter), and steamed away at mail-boat rate. It was inspiring, after the way we had poked before. We had to stop for a little to fix the engines but went then till dark.

Tuesday we ran aground twice but quietly got off and arrived in Mandalay at 9:30 A.M. We passed Sagaing an hour before. It looked very pretty, hills all along covered with pagodas and idol houses and priests houses almost as thick as Pagan but with a newer aspect. Mandalay is just fearfully dusty, words fail to do it justice. You have a description of the city in the mission magazine, so I'll not enlarge.

Fourteen days out from Henzada, on January 24, Hattie and the Hascalls arrived in Mandalay, where they would stay with the local missionaries. Of their hosts, four were already known to Hattie: Mrs. Hancock and Miss Rathbun had traveled with Hattie to Burma; Mrs. Kelley, the former Marie Van Meter, who came to Burma in 1885 after completing her medical degree, had been a friend of Hattie's sister-in-law Ada, and had visited at 4 Brighton Avenue several times. Hattie had met Mr. Kelley in Rangoon.

This week-long interlude permitted time both for sightseeing as well as participation in mission activities.

[Jan. 27, '88, continued]

Mr. Kelley and Mrs. Hancock met us, the former took the Hascalls and the latter me. Mrs. Hancock gets her own breakfast and takes dinner at the Wesleyan Mission, Mr. Winsten's, an arrangement I do not fancy but shall not be here long. After dinner that day Mrs. Hancock took me a long drive partly on business. We returned through the city, entering by the north gate and going through the palace grounds and out by the south gate. The cantonments are to be within the walls and all residents are moving outside of the walls.

Wednesday morning we went and called at the Kelleys', and Miss Rathbun. Mrs. Kelley is well but not strong, does nothing but take care of the baby. Mr. Kelley keeps house. Mrs. Kelley is having trouble to find food for the baby.

Mrs. Hancock has a woman's meeting Wednesday morning and I led it for her. Of course only the few in the house were present, six of us in all.

After dinner we went to see the ex-queen's poongyee kyoung. It is very elaborate covered within and without with gilded carvings inlaid with bits of looking glass and imitation precious stones. At a distance pretty and rich looking but tawdry on closer inspection. Mrs. Hancock stopped later to preach at a house but the dust soon choked her and we moved on. She stopped again and sold about 16 tracts. Then we went to the Burman prayer meeting at Miss Rathbun's. A good attendance of boarding pupils and neighbors. Mr. Hascall preached and two native helpers.

Thursday we all, i.e., the Hascalls, Mrs. Hancock and I with three girls, a servant, and two men, went to Sagaing, taking the little steamship which plies up and down around here, at 9 A.M. and returning at 1 P.M. by another. We had breakfast under a tree on our new lot, saw the post-holes for the new house and the posts being made. There is an old Burman house on the land which we will use for school. Nearby is a good mat house owned by a Deputy Commissioner which Mr. Hascall is trying to buy for us to live in at once. The land joins ours and goes to the river bank. The situation is pleasant, lots of trees, and not dusty as Mandalay. Though of course everything is very dry and brown under the trees, no grass. It does not rain here but a few weeks in the year and hardly a day that could be called rainy. No trouble with mildew, mold, rust, etc. etc., but the dust that lies white and thick on everything in the house, in spite of two or three wipings a day, is to my mind almost as bad. It is awful on shoes if one walks a step as one must sometime.

Mandalay, Jan. 31, '88

Last Saturday at 6:30 A.M. Miss Rathbun called for me and we went to the "Unrivalled" poongye-kyoung, built of brick outside, lined with wood covered with gilt and glass work. There was an immense idol in it, and lots of big plate-glass mirrors. Evidently built by a European architect. Across the road is another kyoung in true Burman style, with hundreds of gold-covered posts; the whole inside and out overlaid with gold and bits of glass. All these places are surrounded by a substantial brick wall, four-square with a gate on each side. Sometimes these walls are 3 or 4 feet high by 2 feet thick and sometimes 10 or 15 feet high. The amount of labour required to build all these pagodas, kyoungs, walls, idols etc. etc. is appalling. Nearby is a pagoda with a chamber in it, in which are many marble tombstone-like tablets on which is written the Buddhist bible.

I spent the day with Miss Rathbun and after tiffin, her school being dismissed, she took me to the "Big God," a large gilt idol on the outskirts of the city, under the usual gold and glass house of many roofs. It is called the Arrakan idol. The entrance and the ceiling were being re-gilded, re-glossed etc. where needed. There were some old broken brass figures, life size, in the compound and many sick people come and rub these figures and then themselves expecting to be cured. Not far off was a long row of sheds where men were making idols and images of alabaster. I bought a reclining figure of Gautama and a turtle for Rs.1/4. The figure is five inches long and the turtle two inches or three inches.

Less than three years after the third English-Burmese War, the British were firmly in control of the city. The King's palace compound was still in the process of being cleared for occupation by the English troops stationed there to maintain order and to convince the Burmese that Thibaw would not return, a fact by no means entirely accepted by the Burmese people.

[Jan. 31, '88, continued]

This morning Mrs. Hancock took me to see the palace. We first went into a little gold and glass-covered kyoung which is now used as a chapel for Church of England services! The Wesleyan chaplain has held services in the throne room of the palace itself. Before going there we went into the King's court house [Burmese characters] and the man who watches the place let us take from a big chest full of palm-leaf Pali books, two apiece. One of mine is in the old square Pali character, quite a prize I think. The chest was side of the throne. We then went into the palace and saw the throne but I was disappointed in it. The gilding was tarnished and dusty and the whole not as fine as the interior of the better kyoungs. Back of the palace are numerous houses formerly for the queens. One was entirely of lattice work gilded and inlaid with bits of glass. There is also a building of brick in French style, and a high round tower with spiral stairs on the outside; this we ascended and had a good view of the city, which looked very well, as the houses were hidden by trees to a great extent. The man on the tower said visitors were not allowed there, but we had had a good look before he spoke! All the buildings in the palace compound, which is raised eight or nine feet above the rest of the city, are now used as offices by the English. In the Court we saw a lot of idols, some had been gilded till the form was lost and one would be puzzled to know what the figure had been in the first place.

Sunday I attended the English Sunday School here at 8 A.M. (very small) and the Burman preaching here at 10:30 A.M. Went to Burmese service again at 4 P.M. at Miss Rathbun's school, and after dinner there, came to 6 P.M. evening English preaching service here.

Monday Mrs. Hancock and I started early and went to one of her regular places of preaching and teaching. Some children here are learning the catechism and songs. She got me to preach for her; there were several men and women and lots of children present.

The Queen's Golden Monastery, Mandalay.

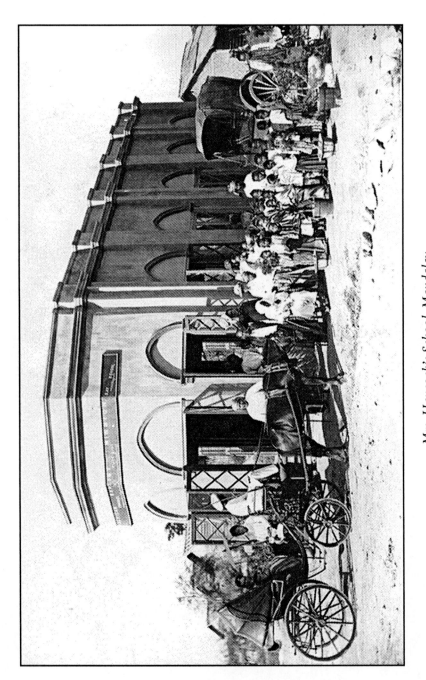

Mrs. Hancock's School, Mandalay.

The mornings at this season are decidedly chilly. We have had three days that were cloudy, cold, and rainy part of the time, most dismal. But since those showers it has been delightful. There is no rainy season here as in Lower Burma only semi-occasional showers from now to October.

On February 1, 1888, the Hascalls moved to Sagaing to set up the new mission station. While construction on the mission house was far from complete, Mr. Hascall had bought a house nearby to serve as temporary quarters.

Feb. 3, '88

Wednesday we took the little steamer at 8 A.M. to Sagaing, took a native boat at the Sagaing landing and came down till about opposite the house, thus saving a long walk, and arriving at 10 A.M.

The house is like this [drawing]. Underneath, a cement floor and one storeroom. The walls, partitions, ceiling, doors and windows are all of matting with wooden frames; no glass in the house. It is very small compared to the Henzada house but is near the new one and is comfortable enough for a few months till the other is done.

We can begin school as soon as the Burman house on the place is emptied and fixed up a little, thus getting several months more of work here and saving rent and board in Mandalay. The house is shaded by four or five immense tamarind trees, the home of some grey squirrels. Rats are abundant.

This morning (Friday) I took my girl and went to bazaar, a 25 minute walk through the woods and jungle by a cart-track. I got sweet limes, a gourd, and plantains. Layams [servant?] finds trouble in getting food at these native bazaars — [who] want to sell by the 100. He had not been to the one I went to, so I went to see what there was to be had. Vegetables, meat, and fish which we can eat seem somewhat scarce, though this is called the "garden of Burma!"

The women up here all wear the open skirt — te-main instead of the closed loon'gy of Lower Burma. The people so far seem very respectful, using to us the form they would to king, priest, or god.

We were cold the first few days but now it is considerably warmer. There are two pretty flowers growing by the way-side here, a shrub bearing a long morning glory shaped blossom, pure white and fragrant, and a handsome thistle, the leaves tipped and edged with white and the blossom like a yellow portulaca. I tried to pick one but desisted!

There are a very few English officers here but no ladies at all. One road has been built from the fort to the steamship landing, but it does not pass near us. The rest are winding cart tracks or foot paths. Many of the houses have high bamboo fences around them.

Feb. 5, '88

This is our first Sunday in our new station and a very pleasant and quiet one it has been. We had Sunday School at 8 A.M. Mrs. Hascall took the children in English Sunday School, I had the three girls we brought, and Mr. Hascall the preacher and teacher. We made the latter treasurer and took up a collection. At 10:30 we had preaching service; besides those here, the chief clerk in the Deputy Commissioner's office, who is a Christian from Moulmein, came bringing his cousin, another from Moulmein, a servant, a sister-in-law, two children, an old man also from Moulmein and a neighbor's child, so we had quite a nice congregation. Some of these are only on a visit but the clerk is here for good, we hope. Some of the neighbors came and listened a while. After an interval we had a prayer meeting before the folks went home.

We have had some visitors from the natives but not many. At sunset we took a walk along the river bank and back by a lot of pagodas, and we each got the toenail of a big griffin, one of a pair at the entrance of a pagoda compound. There are four entrances, two griffins to each, about 15 feet high; they are built of brick covered with plaster, but the toenails are of white marble about seven inches long.

Feb. 10, '88

I have been out every morning this week telling about the school we hope to open next week and preaching when I had a chance, every morning but this. Several times I had some women to talk to. I like the appearance of the people generally very much. Of course they never are particularly impressed at once — decent attention is as much as we expect.

Feb. 26, '88

We opened school Monday with two little boys and two girls. No more came for two days, but by Saturday night (we kept Saturday, as we heard some were coming that day) we had thirteen, though two are only five years and come and go as they please. One or two are orphans whom we let come without fees. Most are children of Burman officials. I go over four times a day to keep my eye on things but not to embarrass either teacher or pupils. The children enjoy the singing and seem to like the school.

While Hattie had particularly looked forward to the opportunity to preach to those less familiar with the Gospel, her efforts were nevertheless often frustrating, with some good listeners but many "ignorant and indifferent" ones.

[Feb. 26, '88 continued]

Thursday morning I went east to get a chance to preach to a group, mostly of women, on the river bank. I handed a tract to a man and he read off two pages. I asked if he wanted to take and read it and he said, "No" and would not have it. Evidently he saw his peace of mind would be disturbed if he did. One woman said she had forgotten the name of her God, so a man prompted her!!

Friday I went farther in the same direction and had a talk to another group of women and children. Such ignorance, such utter stupidity, such blank minds! They are like children — cannot keep their minds on any one thing but a few moments. In the midst of most earnest preaching they will enquire what wages I get, or how old I am, or lift my dress skirt a little to admire my petticoat! My girl gets disgusted with their lack of manners, and indifference to school.

This morning we held Sunday School in the school house; a good many outsiders hung around during the singing but did not stay to the teaching. A big nat feast was going on nearby. These people are given to nat worship which is contrary to Buddhism. We often see offerings of rice on tiny shelves on tree trunks. The crows get the rice; the nats are supposed to be benefited by the smell of it.

Sagaing mission house (circa ?).

Monday morning I went out the north gate (or rather hole in the wail) and found a group of more intelligent folks than ever before, had a good preach to about 25. One man in particular was interested and took to read the tract that the other man refused. I think he is the first I ever met who showed any real interest. He went and called an old man to hear, and some younger men also came, besides a lot of women. The most encouraging time yet.

Mar. 3, '88

All of Tuesday morning before breakfast was spent in the school with Mr. Hascall putting up some black-boarding, maps, etc. It looks quite like a school house now. We have about seventeen in regular attendance. I spend some time daily in teaching the oldest boys English. Saturday morning I gave them all a conversation lesson and one in Geography. We have school Saturday from 8 A.M. to 9:30.

Wednesday morning I went to the quarter of town where the Musselmen live who are largely Burmanized. I preached in two places and had good attention. We have two or three pupils from there. Thursday I went to the east and found the people there, as I have before, very ignorant and hard to reach. I walked far and got tired but did no preaching. Coming back I tried to talk to an old man chopping wood but he did not care to listen. Afterward I saw an old woman kneeling down to an immense ruin of an unfinished pagoda (begun by a former king) and counting over her beads. She would not listen either.

The next morning I tried to talk to a household on the same road but met with the greatest indifference. One kept on her work, going here and there, one turned her back, and others after a moment walked away.

Once the school at Sagaing was underway, an attempt was made to start another at Ava, a village on the other side of the Irrawaddy that once served as the capital of Burma but was now a sparsely settled area.

Mar. 10, '88

This morning Mr. Hascall and I (and three Hascall children) took a native boat and went across to Ava, and opened school there in a little Burman house which the owner lends for that purpose till the water comes up to it. I put up maps, Scripture cards, etc. and we took a table and chair and four mats. We began with the three children of the one Christian of the place. Others are promised. I hope to go frequently as we've no one to teach sewing.

Despite a promising start, however, recruiting and holding students at either school proved difficult.

[Mar. 10, '88 continued]

Three pupils left school and Ko Tha Nyo (that Christian clerk) wrote me the enclosed note. You see the school has made an impression.

[Enclosed letter]:
Dear Mama [Hattie],

I am very sorry indeed to hear that you are losing pupils instead of gaining them. I hear children are complaining to their parents about their school mistress (Ne Mah) who they say is little too hard on them. They are so young that I think they want little training as to attending to their lessons. I mean to say that they like to play more than to learn their lessons so the Saya (teacher) is to allow them to go their own ways until they can confess their own faults.

The chief objection of the parents to keeping their children in the School is — teaching their children not to worship other gods but Jehovah. They say that they keep their children in School to be educated but not to be taught of English Scripture. When children come home they fight with their parents by telling them not to worship idols. Children believe what their Saya says but not what their parents say. Parents did not like this.

Excuse penmanship.
Yours sincerely, Tha Nyo.

Mar. 17, '88

Friday morning I took Ne Mah and the preacher, who hired a native boat for me, and went over [to Ava] to see how things were going. Found that one new pupil had come. I got them together and gave the two boys a lesson in English while Nyee Mah taught the two girls sewing. I had to be back by 9 A.M. to give Ne Mah time for her use before school opened here, so could not stay long.

Thursday I called at the houses of two pupils, at the first I tried to talk with them but found them so very self-righteous it was no use. Needless to say, they were from Lower Burma and understood Christianity very well.

The rest of the time out of school has gone in writing, etc. I answered the letter of the Worcester lady, who promised $25 for a pupil. I asked her to let it be used for our Ava school.

One day I heard a funny little sound and on looking around saw two young rats having a grand frolic on the mat in front of my chest of drawers. They were jumping at each other on their hind-feet and rolling over and over each other just like two

kittens. I went close to them and called the others to come and
see, and stamped on the floor before they ran away. I never sit
down here without seeing from one to a half-dozen; they are
more at home than we are and wake me nights gnawing.

Sunday evening we had a sing on the veranda and a dozen
or so heathens came in. We sang a song and Mr. Hascall taking
it as a text, preached a few minutes, and then we sang another
and so on. Afterward a Christian clerk in the Commissioner's
office who is in town spoke to them very well. Today is their
worship day. I went out the King's road quite a ways and
preached to a group of comers and goers, part Burman part
Kulah, one or two listened well. Two little girls have entered
school. Their father is a Chinaman and mother a Burman; such
children are often very bright.

Mar. 26, '88

We are having hot weather. The thermometer has not gone
over 99 yet, but a very strong south wind prevails; it feels like
a blast from a furnace. The rest enjoy it, but it is inclined to
give me a headache, and I find it weakening instead of refreshing as the others do. Today it is quiet, but for three days before
it was windy. The temperature is 80 all night in my room, and
rises in the morning.

One morning I preached at a house where the people are
given to nat worship, are nat-guardians, and have a row of
images in the house which are worshiped by the whole neighborhood. They said it made no difference whether we worshiped or not, but if they did not the nats would at once injure
them. They said Thibaw lost his kingdom because he neglected
nat-worship!!

Friday morning I took my two teachers and went to the
school in Ava. I found that the one new pupil had left to
become a priest, and two of the remaining three were sick. But
I had Nyee Mah give the one who did come a lesson in sewing
and then we returned. The boat was a little one and the river
rough but we arrived all right. Shall insist on a big boat next
time; these winds may hinder my going as often as I'd like.

This morning I went where I found the man so interested
before, took him a tract and talked some more to him. Then
went across the road and had a long preach (about 40 minutes)

to about 25 people who listened well. These are not pure Burmans but Katheys, who have adopted the language and religion of Burma. Came down from Munapore long ago and settled; they are often silk-sewers, and, to my mind, superior to the Burmans.

A boy has come from Minmoo to enter school; we find he is in love with one of our girls and came to be near her. Her folks do not like it and so the girl leaves the school. Mr. Hascall is trying to get the boy to go to Miss Rathbun's school. We do not want to lose the girl and her sister.

Apr. 1, '88

Wednesday at my request Mr. Hascall and the preacher and teachers went with me to Ava. We did not stop at the school but went around the place, which is only a lot of tiny hamlets scattered here and there, within and around the old walls, the intervals being wild jungle, with nothing to suggest a former great city, except that in some places the ground is covered with broken bricks, and there are numerous holes, as if for posts. A square tower of grey stone still stands in the center. It was the King's watchtower, and we tried to find a path through the jungle to it but failed.

We stopped where there was a group of houses, and sang a song or two, and Mr. Hascall and the preacher and two teachers (young men) preached to 25 or 30 people who gave good attention. Afterward before coming back we went within the walls and found in the midst of the jungle a big brick tank with sloping sides and four flights of stairs leading into it. They called it the "King's Bath" and it was in good preservation tho all the buildings once surrounding it were leveled to the ground and completely overgrown with bushes and brambles and inhabited by snakes and, it is said, wild animals.

The school has not grown any there; the people up here do not appreciate an education and are not in the least ashamed of not knowing even their letters.

Apr. 8, '88

This week has passed as usual. It has been very hot, 100 degrees every day, and my head feels as if it were baked. Constant wetting down is all that keeps it comfortable.

Thursday I took a walk with Mr. and Mrs. Hascall, came across an idol shed with 50 or 60 images in it. Mr. Hascall preached to a couple of poongyees. I had a caller to preach to later in the day, and Saturday morning five came in; two were from another place and had never heard of Christianity; they came again today.

Friday morning I went to Ava, with Ne Mah; that school is not growing at all and may have to move elsewhere. Neither is this one. I fear Ne Mah is too cross for one thing; besides it is a bad time of year — the hottest — and some think Thibaw will yet return and then they better not have been friends of the foreigners. And then there is the fear of our religion, and the general indifference to education.

The coming week is the great water feast of the Burmans and my pupils had said they would be absent, so I concluded to close the school for a week. It is too hot to keep it anyway. No other schools in Burma are open at this season.

As I have been often invited I mean to go to Mandalay for a few days, not that it will be cooler (Mr. Kelley said 104) but it will be quieter and I am so tired of the noise of the children; the house is so small there is no escape. I could do nothing here during the feast anyway.

I shall take a boat front of the house to go the 1-1/2 mile to the steamship landing, to take the daily steamship to Mandalay.

Services today as usual but it was so hot I could not take any comfort in the midday one. There has been a <u>very</u> strong and <u>very</u> hot wind that takes the <u>sprall</u> all out of me!

Hattie's visit to Mandalay included a short trip to Oung-pen-la, the site of Adoniram Judson's imprisonment during the first English-Burman War. It remains today an important historical site for Baptists in Burma.

Apr. 16, '88

I went to Mandalay as I planned and had a pleasant time at Mrs. Kelley's. My head did not feel the heat as much as here, as their rooms are so much higher and have board ceilings. We had rides night and morning most of the days. Thursday morning we went to Oung-pen-la in their dogcart. The drive is along the top of an old dike which separates the marsh called "Oung-pen-la lake" from the paddy fields which it irrigates. Beyond the marsh are the high Shan hills dimly seen through the smoky air. In the fields Burman buffaloes were ploughing in water up to their bodies. The road was English make (tho the dike was not) and was fringed with trees. It was about the pleasantest ride I ever had.

There is nothing at all to see when one arrives at Oung-pen-la — just an ordinary little native village. The site of the prison is just a bare plot of ground near a tiny priest school and ruined idol house. I picked the enclosed leaves from the ground, absolutely all there was to be had as a memento.

Apr. 23, '88

This week, I have been so miserable with a heavy cold, nausea, lack of appetite, and swimming head that I have done nothing at all, except to go over a few minutes a day to school. I feel pretty well now except weak. This roof is so low and thin that my head feels bad every day from the heat.

At the evening service Po Myit, our water carrier, asked for baptism. He seems to have experienced a real conversion, very marked for a Burman. Think he will be baptized next Sunday.

A number of Government clerks have attended our meetings and Ko Tha To asked to have meetings every evening this week — expect to do so.

Dacoits were a continuing problem in Upper Burma at this time, and became a matter of local concern.

Apr. 30, '88

Last week five dacoits who were under guard here waiting trial, made their escape by cutting through the bars with a spoon!! Two only were retaken. The guard was sentenced seven years in prison, but that don't retake dacoits. It is English style to shut the door <u>after</u> the horse is stolen!

One morning I went to my zinc-lined book box for a book, and found a scorpion on my big cloak I had put in the top of the box. He went out the window with more haste than dignity.

Thursday evening we planned to have a change (we get so dull and lonesome at times) so took a native boat and were all poled two miles up the river by twilight and moonlight. All the helpers and children went, even to the cook's little girl. It was very pleasant till we got half-way home when one of those sudden wind and rain squalls struck up. We had no umbrellas and feared to stay in the boat, so landed and ran under a rice shed till it held up, then went on a ways by land. When it rained again we went under a house: and at last running and walking we arrived at home, hot, tired, dusty, and wet with both rain and perspiration — we had our <u>change</u>!!

May 7, '88

Sunday we had the usual services (in the new house) and at 6 P.M. we met on the riverbank and after singing and a short talk, Mr. Hascall baptized three young men (a crowd of natives on the bank). One is our water-carrier, a Sagainite, and two clerks from the Court, natives of Lower Burma. The conversion of all three is due largely to the faithfulness of Ko Tha Nyo and our teacher we brought from Henzada. In the evening we had a prayer meeting. The young men looked very happy.

Have done very little this week; my day's work has to be done before 12 M. it is so hot: 92 degrees at 6 A.M., 106 in the middle of the day, and 95 at bedtime. I doubt if it went below 92 all night. We can't rest such nights. I felt just as tired this morning as last night. The worst is I can't get a nap in the daytime, my room is too hot to stay in after 12 M. and there is no other place in this tiny house. The new one is promised by May 20 and this is rented from that date so we move in whether it is done or not. Hope it will be nearly so.

May 12, '88

We have had two evening meetings this week — Tuesday evening a short Bible reading, and Thursday a prayer meeting. The two clerks could not come Tuesday but one did Thursday. Somebody stoned their homes the night after their baptism! No harm done and they are not at all ashamed. The wife of one is angry and a relative-priest tells her she must give double to the priests now!

Four others have entered this week beside an orphan boy whom Mr. Hascall has taken to feed and educate. They are two Hindoos, a Mohammedan, and a Burman man from near

Henzada. Have 13 boys besides the cooley, and 3 girls. No native Burmans of Sagaing have entered. They do not appreciate an education.

The Ffords (Deputy Commissioner) who have rented this house have arrived. They must be staying over the courthouse or in the fort; there is no house for them in town but this. Unfortunately, they are not such people as we care to have much to do with.

I send a plan of the lower story of the new house. Upstairs the center hall is but 8 feet so making the Hascalls' two bedrooms 24 x 17, I could have had one of the other bedrooms but did not like to run up and down as much as this climate and frequent changes of clothes would necessitate. Shall be so glad to get into it and unpack once more after five months of being unsettled.

May 19, '88

Monday night about 2 A.M. we were suddenly awakened by firing at the military police barracks, across the road and a stone's throw from the new house. As there had been rumors of coming dacoits we thought at first that they had come sure this time. We were up, dressed and gathered in the middle room in no time. A lot of scattering shots and two volleys were fired, but we heard no yelling and orthodox dacoits always make a perfect pandemonium so we concluded it was a false alarm and we feared stray bullets through our mat walls more than dacoits. None came, and after an hour or so we retired, but did not sleep till dawn. One of the sentries heard or saw something and fired, the rest following suit. They are just up from Mimoo which has been twice attacked lately, so were easily startled.

The natives around were panic-stricken; all forsook their houses and fled to the river bank. They are not over it yet and so my school is very small. It collapsed entirely the next afternoon, not one pupil daring to come. They (the natives) are desperately afraid; those who could, left the place for Mandalay, or elsewhere. They say the dacoits have put notices on trees that "they are coming" — and they believe every rumor they hear. Tuesday night the Commandant of Military Police sent us a guard of four sepoys and we slept beautifully. The Commandant lives just next to us on the road and the Deputy Commissioner will be in our mat house on the other side. Both will have sentries all night who challenge every passerby. So I think we will be pretty safe from sudden danger. Besides, we number fifteen grown people and nine children on the compound, Burman helpers, cook and family and dhobie and family.

I have not been out preaching; little use when the people can talk and think of nothing but dacoits.

June 16, '88

Ko Tha Nyo says the people are continually looking for Thibaw's return and say that when he comes all who have learned English or been friends with them will be killed. That is why no native of Sagaing will come to school.

In the midst of illness and dacoit scares, time was running out for the Hascall family's occupation of the mat house. The new house was slowly nearing completion.

May 19, '88

As lumber gave out and the carpenters had to stop work yesterday (Friday) we thought we would begin to move. So we did, and with the aid of our helpers and six Burman cooleys we got moved, with the exception of a very few boxes, which were brought over this morning. Of course we are not at all settled. As the bathroom doors are not yet in, and my room is not particularly secure, I slept upstairs for a few nights. Not all of the downstairs partitions are up yet but my room is enclosed.

May 26, '88

The past week has been spent in settling; but now I am settled I think. As all my possessions are within a space of 25 feet x 16 feet I do not have far to go for anything. Am very glad I decided to sleep downstairs. Ne Mah sleeps in the little room next to mine, side of the stairway. On the whole I am very well pleased with my quarters and the house as a whole.

The move to the new house, coinciding as it did with cooler and more comfortable weather, should have been the beginning of more auspicious times for the Sagaing missionaries. It was marked, instead, by illness that affected the whole station.

June 9, '88

There is nothing at all to write this week as I have not been able to go out or do much of anything in. The first three days I was used up with diarrhea but China and Phosphate cured it. Then for a few days I felt well but too weak to work much. Last night the trouble came on again but I hope to conquer it again; living on corn flour porridge and crackers.

Mrs. Hascall is no better off, only it is stomach that makes trouble. Mr. Hascall is up and down too. We all got badly run down during the long hot stretch and have not begun to pick up yet, though the weather is cooler.

June 30, '88

This has been a week of it sure enough. Mrs. Hascall is still confined to her room and to the bed most of the time. The doctor left for good Friday (yesterday) but said she must stay in her room and have nothing but milk for a week longer. Three of the boys have had sore eyes, got from a Burman boy whom they would play with though warned not to. The other oldest boy has had a very high fever indeed and one of the Burman ayahs, not quite so bad.

As for me, from having to see the children so much at table, etc., I took sore eyes too. By taking Belladonna and Merc[ury] and using witch hazel I think I am cured but I have not used my eyes at all since Tuesday morning. Then on Tuesday my trouble (diarrhea) returned about as bad as ever. So with it all I did not go out even to the school two days of the week, and since Monday morning when I had a little preach not far away I have not been off the compound. Wednesday Miss Rathbun and Mrs. Kelley came and spent a few hours (between steamships) with us. Mrs. Kelley said I must not walk much, and not to eat meat or fruit; as we have no vegetables, not even potatoes now, there is little left to eat, except soups and spoon-victuals generally (mushes). On these and one raw egg a day I have lived since Wednesday. My trouble is gone but don't know when it will return, so shall continue that diet for some time. The Hascalls have some American meal so we have mush same as you. Pineapples are the only fruit to be had, and beef (tough) and chicken the only meat.

Mr. Kelley and Mrs. Hancock called today and the latter stayed and will go back Monday. As Mr. Hascall is nurse for all the folks upstairs, it will be a great help to have her here tomorrow when he must attend services. I am no good at running up and down stairs.

July 7, '88

This has been a hard week; everybody sick. Mrs. Hascall is not able to be down and ought not to be moving around much but the children and one of the two Burman girls have been ailing all the week and this morning the oldest and youngest have very high fever (as they have for several days), the other two sore eyes, and Mr. Hascall has <u>very bad</u> contagious sore eyes. The doctor was called yesterday, and this morning when he came he said there was danger of Mr. Hascall's losing his eyes. Mr. Hascall does not think so, eyes always weak and often look bad at nothing.

I have telegraphed to Mrs. Hancock to come again to help us. She will have to come in a native boat if at all today and that is not nice when these high winds are raging. She will be seasick. The cause of so much sickness is the lack of rain (none in two weeks) and these long continued high winds.

I have kept along "so so"; hope to pull through by taking diolized iron, beef extract, a raw egg a day, etc.

I have made a big shade for Mr. Hascall's eyes, lining it with a piece like my silk dress — all the green silk there was in the house. Have also entertained numerous Burman callers who always seem to come at the most inconvenient times, sent notices about tomorrow's English services which will be omitted, and the Burmese which Ko Tha Nyo and Mg. Tool will take.

Mandalay, July 14, '88

Another hard week has passed. Mrs. Hancock started to come to us Saturday afternoon but the waves were so high the boatmen had to go back. Their fire for cooking their rice set her dress on fire and about ruined it. She started again Sunday at 6 A.M. and arrived about 8 A.M. We were glad to see her, you may be sure. Mr. Hascall's eyes are improving, quite out of danger, but the baby has grown steadily worse, has typhoid fever, and it hardly seems possible that he can pull through the three or more weeks the fever will run. The others are some better. Willie seems over his fever though the other two still have sore eyes. Mrs. Hascall is worn out with watching, she cannot rest even when someone else is caring for the baby. She did not begin to take solid food till Thursday. We fear she will have the fever next.

Friday morning the doctor said the three older boys must be got away, so we flew around and got them ready, and I brought them with their Burman ayah here to the Kelleys' in Mandalay. Our former Ava teacher came with us. The Kelleys were planning to telegraph for me to bring them and were very glad when we appeared. They (the children) were all run down, and it was the only way to be sure they would not have typhoid also. They have been shut up in the house for so long on account of their sore eyes.

I mean to go back Monday morning, leaving them here; they are content and happy.

Sagaing mission is under a cloud, and it will be long before it is out, even if the baby lives and Mrs. Hascall does not take it.

Mandalay, July 20, '88

I did not go to Sagaing as I intended on Monday. Mrs. Kelley and baby had colds, and the boys needed so much attention I could not leave it all for her to do. Mr. Kelley went over Tuesday and returned reporting the baby the same, but Mrs. Hascall prostrated again, with dysentery followed by diarrhea, and Mr. Hascall just worn out.

I felt that I <u>must</u> go to see them and see about the school, and Wednesday Mr. Kelley and I went, arriving at 9:20 A.M. (July 18).

The baby had died at 6 A.M. and the doctor had ordered Mrs. Hascall to be taken on a litter to Mandalay <u>that day</u> and no one was to live in the house for some weeks. So it was Providential that we went.

Mr. Kelley got the coffin made and Mrs. Hancock and I padded, lined, and covered it with white dotted muslin (a gift to the baby for a dress long before). We had reading, prayer, and one song in the upper hall, Mrs. Hascall on a bed in the room on one side and the baby in his coffin in the other room across the hall. (He was carried in and laid side of Mrs. Hascall just before he died — passing away as if falling asleep.)

Mrs. Hancock had laid him out; his mother was too ill to do it, though it broke her heart not to. He looked very pretty in his white dress and white coffin. After the service they carried him in to Mrs. Hascall. She said, "It is all right." Then they took him downstairs and the crowd of natives saw him and four Christian young Burman men bore him to the grave in the Cantonments cemetery, followed by Mr. Hascall and Mr. Kelley who could not stay to see it filled.

Mrs. Hancock and I stayed and got Mrs. Hascall ready. Word was sent to the steamship to wait, which it did, and our goods were put on a cart (they had had to be packed also that morning). Mrs. Hascall was put on the litter (Mr. Kelley carried her down in his arms) and we walked as fast as we could to the steamship, 1-1/2 miles. We could not take a boat, the wind and the waves were so high. We all got off safely, leaving Mg. Tool to keep up the boys' school and Mg. Tone A to air daily and watch the house.

We arrived here all right, though Mrs. Hascall was exceedingly tired and nervous. Mrs. Kelley, though not expecting us, had got a room all ready and Mrs. Hascall was laid right on the bed where she still stays. Dr. Pedly was called (Mrs. Kelley would not take the case, not feeling able to). He speaks more hopefully; the Sagaing doctor said they must go to America. Mrs. Hancock is taking care of her and I sleep at Mrs. Hancock's, the Kelleys' house being full.

Not only we in the new house, but the cook's and dhobi's families are ill with fever, some of the children seriously. The Hascalls' three are much run down.

The Burmans in Sagaing say that we were all sick because we removed Burman houses and the children had a nat image to play with — someone gave it to them — so the nats were offended and injured us.

It was clear that the illness in the Hascall family would require an extended stay in Mandalay. Hattie, however, was determined to return to Sagaing and carry on the school work there as best she could.

[July 20, '88, continued]

I mean to go to Sagaing for a day (not night) once or twice a week till it is safe to stay there, and then stay if I can find a companion. The work must not stop for the sake of the effect on the heathen. No telling when the Hascalls will be able to return, though they hope to after having a change. I shall be so much more comfortable there in my own room and bed and with a bathroom to use etc. etc. It is very noisy at each of the houses here.

Rangoon, July 31, '88

Much to my surprise I find myself in Rangoon. The Monday after my last letter I went again to Sagaing with Mr. Hascall and after helping him get several trunks of clothing ready to go to Mandalay, I found myself too tired to go back and decided to stay all night, and have the cook sleep in the house, there being two Burman teachers (boys) in the school-house. I got along all right and was not too lonesome.

I found that my absence had nearly put an end to the school, no one coming that afternoon. So Tuesday morning I made some calls and got half-a-dozen back. I saw there would be no school if I did not go and stay, so I decided to return to Sagaing on Thursday bringing Ne Mah and one boy for my cook and live there and keep up the work as best I could till the Hascalls could return or someone else come.

When I told my plan in Mandalay that afternoon they all objected, though acknowledging the need. When discussing what cook I should have, Mr. Hascall, who was much troubled, said, "Well, we'll sleep on it. Perhaps you'll be sick tomorrow and can't go!" Sure enough, at midnight I was taken with a chill and then fever. I knew at once I could not go to Sagaing, the friends would veto it, and my own sense agreed. So, as I had no really comfortable place in Mandalay (all houses were so full and all were so busy) and as I could not work in Sagaing or even go back and forth — it tired me so — and if I was in for a course of fever it would be the last straw to break down the folks, who were doing all they could stand under, I at once decided to take the mail steamship the next afternoon (Wednesday) and come to Frank.

In the morning the folks all agreed that it was altogether the wisest plan, and Mr. Kelley got my ticket and took me and Ne Mah on board the *Tomah*. It was the steamship and the cabin I had in moving to Henzada from Rangoon.

I think my coming staved off a course of fever, and the change of climate will cure my bowel trouble; so I hope to go back well and able to carry the Sagaing work alone or with a Eurasian helper for a time if necessary. I left Mrs. Hascall improving but very weak indeed. The doctors who ordered them home give a little hope of their staying awhile at least. It is still an open question.

I was bitterly disappointed at having to close my school for a month, and at not going back to Sagaing, to which I had fully made up my mind. But evidently the Lord means us to let Sagaing alone for a spell, so I try to be content.

Hattie remained in poor health for several weeks. Frank attempted to treat her with his homeopathic remedies, and Dr. Douglass tried a variety of medicines. It became clear that Hattie, like the Hascalls, could not return to Sagaing in the near future.

Aug. 28, '88

I shall not have a chance to try living alone yet awhile, for Mrs. Douglass advises me to stay here during September. It is a particularly feverish month in Sagaing and I am far from strong yet. I don't feel able to go back and live alone even if folks would let me, so shall follow her advice unless the Hascalls should go back before October when I should probably follow. Am sorry to keep the school closed but can't help it.

I have had a queer upset sort of life in Burma. I don't know as if I'll ever be settled.

At the time Hattie returned to Rangoon, Mr. Eveleth, a missionary expert in the Burmese language, was at work with Frank on proofreading and correcting materials for publication by the press. Several important works, including a new edition of the Bible in Burmese, were in the final stages of preparation when Mr. Eveleth's health, which had been failing for some time, finally required his immediate departure from Burma. Mr. Eveleth, whom Hattie had been helping at the press, suggested that she be considered to take on the work he had been carrying. Frank, as superintendent, took part in the decision making.

Sept. 13, '88 [FDP]

As soon after Mr. Eveleth had decided to go, I had a talk with him about his work, and he then advised me the plan now being carried out. I told him I would not propose it, or advise it. I really have not had occasion to find out how much Hattie knows or how accurately she knows it, and I did not want anyone to say that I was putting her forward, or picking out a soft place for her, which others were more in need of or better able to fill. At the meeting which I called to consider his work, Mr. Eveleth proposed the plan, and I proposed that we call for a man to take Dr. Jameson's place and ask him to take up the work. Both plans were fully discussed, and the conclusion was unanimous, and Dr. Jameson will be here before or by the time Hattie gets to Sagaing. The *News* and Hattie's letter give you nearly all there is to be said further.

[Enclosure]
Burma News September 1888:

At a meeting of all the Rangoon missionaries September 3 called to consider this matter, after considerable discussion it was resolved that we approve of Mr. Eveleth's plan for his Bible work, that Dr. Jameson be asked to come to Rangoon for three months to take charge of the work and that Miss Phinney be asked to assist him and to take charge of the work at the end of that time.

As might be expected, Hattie had mixed feelings about the assignment.

Sept. 8, '88

Except for the pleasure of being with Frank while he stays here, I would much prefer going back to Sagaing. It is not at all easy to give up my home and work there, and settle down to the monotonous and uninspiring work of proofreading. But if I refuse, Dr. Jameson must leave his field, and a new man be sent there, which will rob some other stations waiting for help. There is Toungoo, Tavoy, and Sagaing to be supplied this year, not to mention new stations for which appropriations are made but men not forthcoming. So there is nothing to do but agree to the plan.

The next thing is to go back, sell off, pack up, and come down again. I dread it very much. I am so tired of moving. I expect to leave here Wednesday next —12th — by the morning train and Prome Thursday morning and reach Mandalay Saturday. I plan to take Ne Mah to help me and also a boy to cook, as I shall probably be alone in Sagaing.

Mrs. Hascall writes that except for Theo they could return at once, but he is so poorly that they may have to leave the country before February and may possibly not be able to go to Sagaing at all. So even if I were not coming here, I might not find the way open to live in Sagaing.

I shall sell everything that I can replace here, to save the expense of moving. I don't mean ever to try to feel settled in Burma again.

Hattie's decision was a hard one. Clearly the interests of the mission must be put before her personal inclinations, but giving up her plan to return to Sagaing was difficult to accept — not only for Hattie but the Hascalls as well.

[Letter from Mrs. Hascall to Hattie]

Mandalay, Sept. 9, '88

My dear "Eldest,"

Your startling letter was handed me as I was driving with Mrs. Kelley, and startled me at once from its unusual size, but as I was holding baby Kelley I could not read it till I got back to the house, when I found "pair" [Mr. Hascall] and together we sat down by the verandah railing and read and wondered! One thing is certain, Hattie, the Lord has taken us into His keeping and means to place us where we shall carry out <u>His</u> plan, not <u>ours</u>. I cannot tell you how grieved and disappointed we are at the prospect of losing you, just when we need you <u>so much</u>. You have ever proved yourself such a valuable worker, and true friend in every way, that the Sagaing home will never seem the same home without you. I had such bright hopes of working with you for the next five months, and you seem to belong to us so much that somehow all day long I have felt as if something dreadful had happened, my knees shake, my hands tremble, and I somehow shrink from going back to that home again without you. And yet who can say that the Bible work is not more important than the work in Sagaing, and where is the man or woman so well adapted to that work as you! Yes, 'tis true we must have separated when March comes; but I wish we might have just three months together since you must come back — I cannot undertake to run the girls' school. I am not strong enough, nor could I look after it, and be faithful to Theo who needs almost as much care as a baby. Mr. Hascall says he will try to keep on the boys' school with Moung Toob, as school hours do not interfere with morning and evening work, and he is very desirous of doing all he can in the few months that remain, and while he had not planned school work, if this is of the Lord we must not rebel.

We wish the Rangoon Missionaries could have waited till our already overburdened hearts had finished the work we planned for the remainder of our stay, with you as our helper as heretofore —but as I said at first The Lord is doubtless in it all, and, as in all our trials and disappointments of the past three months, we must submit our will and plans to Him.

We went yesterday to the marble workers and ordered a stone for baby's grave. The grave will be cemented and the stone laid on it, and besides "Our Baby," we shall have engraved in English and Burmese "Jesus loves me, this I know."

This evening four were baptized at Miss Rathbun's and Will preached to over six hundred people, who remained very quiet and some listened most earnestly. One of the candidates was the boy from Ava who entered our school in Sagaing, so one of your pupils has entered the church and is very promising, Miss Rathbun says.

May the Lord help you in all your decisions, and lead you where you may win many stars for your crown of rejoicing is the earnest prayer of your loving friend,

Emma A. Hascall.

For the fourth time in a little over a year, Hattie was faced with a major move. In this she was assisted by Abraham, Frank's most trusted assistant at the press, who arranged to take his vacation "up country" at that time.

Sept. 26, '88

Since I wrote last I have traveled about 1200 miles and have once more packed and moved. I arrived in Mandalay Sunday at 6 A.M. and the following morning I went with Abraham and Ne Mah to Sagaing. Mr. Hascall went for the day and their boy also went. Abraham and I worked hard all day and got four boxes and my trunk packed: two of the boxes came from home, i.e., the folding-table box and the picture box. Both I used in moving from Rangoon to Henzada and Henzada to Sagaing. Shall keep them for further use.

I sold, either in Sagaing or Mandalay, my bookcase, almirah, bed-stead, chest of drawers, bathroom furniture, one canvas chair and even my <u>organ</u>! I went back to Mandalay Tuesday and Abraham brought my things in two boats the following day, shipped my boxes and delivered the articles bought. A few chairs and one little stand is all I brought down besides the table and my big rocker from home.

I stayed at the Kelleys' though somewhat against my wishes as they were already full; but Mrs. Hascall insisted on my being with her while I could. They are all <u>very</u> miserable, thin, weak, and discouraged. Theo's temperature is never normal and when I left Willie was having very high fever. They would start for home at once if it were some other season, but the doctor forbids taking Theo to America or England in the winter. So they don't know what to do: they hate to stay longer at the Kelleys' and yet have not been able to leave the doctor a single day since they went there.

I left Mandalay Saturday morning, reached Prome Monday noon, and came by the night train to Rangoon.

Despite its disappointing outcome, Hattie's first excursion into missionary work in the field proved to be an excellent introduction. Under the Hascalls' direction and guidance, she was able to observe and participate both in the work of an established mission, with its native congregation, native pastors, and ongoing routines, and then in the founding of a new out-station mission and the recruitment of students and church members from a native population that had not been served before.

Hattie had thrown herself fully into the work of both missions which, despite its negative aspects, clearly appealed to her and suited her interests and skills. Given her choice and the strength to carry it through, Hattie would undoubtedly have returned to Sagaing or taken on an assignment to another mission field. In the end, however, her health and the need for her services by the press returned her to Rangoon.

9

Rangoon Redux

September 1888 to March 1891

Hattie's return to Rangoon provided the opportunity to slow down and settle into what was by now a familiar setting, one considerably more comfortable than Henzada or Sagaing. The previous four years had been a time of dramatic change and challenge, as Hattie had tackled one new experience after another: Spelman, appointment by the mission board, the trip to Burma, learning the language and ways of life in Rangoon, and the sixteen months of out-station work with the Hascalls. Each experience had required and provided new learning and new skills. Each had followed so closely one upon the other that there had been little time for Hattie to fully master one situation before being called upon to embrace and master a new one. Her new life in Rangoon would now give Hattie the chance to assimilate and integrate these experiences, and consolidate the wide range of skills she had acquired.

The first order of business was to find a home for herself and Frank. During her illness, Hattie had shared Frank's rooms in the Roach house; now that she was to be in Rangoon on a permanent basis, it was necessary for other quarters to be found.

Living arrangements among the missionaries in Rangoon often resembled a mammoth game of musical chairs. The limited number of mission properties combined with a community of missionaries whose comings and goings were at the mercy of climate, health, and family exigencies, as well as the dictates of the mission board at home, created a constant shifting and reassignment of accommodations.

Frank, as Treasurer of the mission, was in a good position to know what properties were available, and he was soon able to secure the Russell House. In keeping with the spirit of musical chairs, this was

the house from which Frank had moved to Kemindine in 1885, and
the one that Hattie had expected to share with Frank when she first
came to Burma. Hattie and Frank moved in almost immediately.

Oct. 12, '88

We are moved and very nearly settled. I have a long room
divided by my curtains into study and bedroom: also a very tiny
dressing room and an equally small bathroom. The rooms are all
small and our necessary furniture fills them full. I have not got my
bookcase yet, but I have a study table, a great convenience, in fact
a necessity. My curtain is not hung as the pole for it had to be
made. Things have been upset by men to set the broken glass,
others to finish and fix the mat, and also to paint, carpenters to
fix the shutters, etc. I suppose all will get through in time.

Friday we heard that Miss Rathbun is very ill, and Saturday
a telegram telling of her death. Friday October 5 at 9:30 P.M.
She had typhus fever. She began to break down last year and
has been urged and urged to take a vacation and go away for a
change, but she would not — has not since she went to
Mandalay — so she had nothing to rally on when the crisis of
the fever came. I feel sure if she had taken a vacation in time,
she might have pulled through. Mr. Kelley does just the same. I
would not be surprised to hear of his being down at any time.

Oct. 26, '88

Three mornings Frank has gone to town at 7 A.M. for some
meeting and I've sent his breakfast to him. This makes long days
for him and for me. I spend much more time alone than I did in
Sagaing tho I like living in the city! The Hascalls are back in
Sagaing and hope to stay till February 1, but there is much fever
there, and Theo's temperature is seldom normal. They have been
asked to open school, and will, I think. Mrs. Hascall has telegraphed for a Henzada helper Mah Nellie to come to her.

For some time after Hattie's return to Rangoon, her health continued to fluctuate between periods of relative comfort and bouts
of illness, fever, nausea, and diarrhea, despite Frank's medicines
and Dr. Douglass' advice and ministrations.

[Oct. 26, '88, continued]

I don't seem to conquer my trouble, so Sunday I sent to Dr. Douglass for more medicine and she gave me some more <u>horrid</u> stuff which I am making a faithful trial of. I feel better this last week.

In bed, Nov. 8, '88

I got to the end of my rope last Friday and on Saturday I stayed home all day, not even going to prayer meeting in the evening. Sunday ditto except that I did go to the preaching and communion service in the evening. Monday evening Frank and I went to the Annual Meeting of the YPSCE at Mr. Gahan's house. It was very successful and pleasant but I felt dead beat, and Tuesday morning my trouble was so bad that I went again to Dr. Douglass and she said that the only thing to do was to go to bed and stay several days and give the medicine a chance to help me. So I did and this is the third day. I only took Homo. Phos. Acid, and am much better, in fact, no diarrhea at all now. Am living on "slops" so to speak but shall have more tomorrow.

The neighbors have been very kind about dropping in, i.e., Mrs. Roach, Miss Ranney. Mrs. Bulkley invited me to go home with her [to Moulmein] to get well, as they have cows and lots of good milk. Our milk is largely water and has a sediment of mud. The Roaches have a cow and will soon let us have milk. I don't care to go away, I have gadded so much lately. Mrs. Douglass sent one of her girls — daughter of a Karen pastor — to stay with me, as I couldn't be alone and lie abed. With her to read copy I have gone over No. 49 again, shall look it over tomorrow and send to Dr. Jameson on Saturday. I expect to be around again soon.

Nov. 15, '88

Not much to write this week. I have got some letter writing done, and helped some of the *News* proof, revised the translation of a song I made in Sagaing, i.e., "None but Christ Can Satisfy" and translated another, "Have You Been to Jesus?" They will be put in the new addition which I hear is to be gotten out.

I have not been out yet. My trouble is better but I don't get any strength. Mrs. Douglass advises a trip to Moulmein. I think I shall have to go, as I must get strong soon to take up the Bible and *Burman Messenger* work.

The trip to Moulmein was helpful and gradually Hattie's health improved, enabling her to take on more of the responsibilities she had been asked to assume. The major work for which she was to be responsible, following Dr. Jameson's departure from Rangoon in December 1888, was a revised edition of the Bible. In addition she would take on the editing of the *Burman Messenger*, a monthly publication (in Burmese), covering news of the Burmese-speaking missions and native Christian churches. Another monthly publication of the press, the *News* was published in English and contained news about the work of the mission. It was distributed not only to members of the mission itself but also to mission circles at home. Hattie became increasingly responsible for the *News* as well as for the *Messenger*.

> Dec. 7, '88
>
> I have had proofreading to do, the 12 new galleys, and today and tomorrow the form. I am not sure that one of my books was sent home as I did not direct it myself; so I send one this mail. Miss Evans says she likes it and shall make use of it.
>
> Mama thinks I've "stepped down." I'm not sure whether it's down or up. This [work for the press] is quite as important as anything I could do in Sagaing. I am serving not only all future as well as present Burmans who shall ever care to know the truth, but also all Burman missionaries. Besides there is no one else to do it if I did not, as Dr. Jameson must go to his own field.

> Dec. 14, '88
>
> Dr. Jameson has given the *Burman Messenger* into my care, and I have done some for that, and have read Bible; written some letters, fixed my velvet bonnet and done alot of little jobs.

As her health improved, Hattie entered more fully into the life of the Rangoon mission, something which had been less convenient during her first year in Burma. Unlike Kemindine, the Russell House was closer to the city center. It was also immediately next door to the home of Mrs. Bennett and her granddaughter, Ruth Whitaker Ranney. Mrs. Bennett at 81 was still an active and important member of the mission community. Hattie's growing friendship with Ruth, whom she had known and liked during her earlier stay in Rangoon, involved Hattie in a number of the activities in which Ruth was engaged.

[Dec. 14, '88, continued]

Wednesday morning I went to the Burman woman's prayer meeting with Miss Ranney for the first time, and it was the first Burman service I had attended in five months. But I was able to lead in prayer, so I have not forgotten everything. Went to evening meeting at the church also. It was a lovely moonlight night and I enjoyed the ride as well as the meeting. You see I am getting a great deal stronger for we are having really chilly nights and mornings, so a cooler dress is needed till about 10 A.M.

At last I am really getting acquainted with Miss Ranney as we are next door neighbors. She is a sister, and a good one; also one of the most efficient workers in the mission.

Jan. 18, '89

Last Thursday form 53 was printed and today form 54 will be; so I have got out a form a week, but the whole was ready to read when the other was done. Have also begun the February *Messenger* and today began reading the little Burman church hymn book which must be reprinted.

Miss Ranney starts this morning for a town on the river where there are over 20 asking for baptism — a most wonderful thing for a Burman town. Dr. Rose has gone, no "Mama" [woman missionary] has ever been, so she is going, and I will do some of her duties here — in the Band of Hope tonight, the WCTU [Woman's Christian Temperance Union] tomorrow and Burman Sunday School. Can't go myself, though I'd like to much, but am glad to help her go. She could not unless someone did take these things.

Feb. 15, '89

Thursday afternoon Miss Ranney and I went down to the Baptist Mission Tamil and Telugu school and organized a Band of Hope. As the pupils are Burman as well as Tamil and Telugu, and some know English, a teacher put it into Tamil and two other teachers and I between us put it into Burmese, so it took a long time. I got 18 to sign and as many more of the other races were ready to.

Mar. 8, '89

Last Friday the *Burman Messenger* was printed and today
the Bible form is to be printed. During the week I have worked
some too on the "Minutes of the Pegu Association" proof
which the Association voted to have me see to. The spelling of
the copy is simply awful. The same names of persons and
places scarcely spelt twice alike. The galley proofs have the
margins written full.

Saturday afternoon I went to WCTU and afterward we all
attended the wedding of Abraham's nephew and brother. The
service was all in Tamil and very long, followed by Tamil
singing which was queer but very pretty, at least part of it. We
went to a friend's house where there was more singing and lots
of sprinkling with scented water. The brides and grooms were
given milk to drink and anointed with a paste of sandal wood,
which was equivalent to wishing them to have abundance of
milk and honey! Then we went to the Tamil school which was
prettily decorated and the wedding cake was cut and all had
some.

Sunday I went to Burman service and Sunday School. It came
to pass that it was time to get out the next Burman Sunday School
lesson leaflet and the copy from America was not on hand and
none to be got, so Miss Ranney and I picked out lessons for April
and, with commentaries and reference Bibles, we made the copy
for translation and sent to the young man in Moulmein who has
charge of the translation. So we tided over the break, and hope
for the copy in time for another month.

In April of 1889, Frank took a short vacation trip to K'serdo,
which provided an opportunity for Hattie to become even better
acquainted with Mrs. Bennett and Ruth Ranney. Hattie continued
to pursue many activities within the mission.

Apr. 12, '89

My Old Man has decamped "leaving me lone and blighted
like a dried up mullein stalk in a sheep pasture" in the words
of the poet. I sleep and have my meals at Mrs. Bennett's and
spend the hottest part of the day there, too, as that house is
larger and much cooler than this.

Missionaries on holiday in K'serdo, one of the mission's vacation settlements in the mountains. Back row: Mr. Bunker, Nellie Bunker. Standing, Second Row: Miss Palmer, Mr. Eveleth, Miss Stark, Mr. Case, Mrs. Mix, Mrs. Douglass. Seated: Mrs. Bunker, Ruth Bunker, Frank Phinney, Mrs. Eveleth.

The last page of the Old Testament was printed on Monday April 8, since then I have been reading hymn book, tract and *News* proof. Shall get the *News* out next Monday I think and then begin the *Messenger.* Am trying to get my letters answered too. I am keeping very well considering the heat, better than I expected to. Have attended the regular meetings this week.

It is a great blessing that Mrs. Bennett and Miss Ranney will take me in. I could not stay all alone of course, and don't know where I should go. They are very kind indeed to me always.

Apr. 19, '89

During the week I have read proof of the hymn book and tracts, written a number of letters etc. etc. It has been extremely hot, yesterday 106 in my room at 4 P.M. but I stay most of the time after the early morning here at Mrs. Bennett's, which is much cooler. Could not stand it to stay in that house all the time.

Yesterday was my birthday and Miss Ranney gave me a large volume *Life Mosaics* by F. R. Havergal, illustrated with

numerous colored plates, a beauty. Mrs. Bennett gave me a
dainty little one in the shape of a shell. Mrs. Rose and her
mother sent me a pretty little flower holder, and Miss Evans
and Mrs. Smith sent me cards. Mrs. Bennett made a dinner
party for me. Mr. and Mrs. Roach and Miss Coté were invited
and we had a pleasant time. On the whole it was a very pleasant day indeed, thanks to Mrs. Bennett and Miss Ranney.

May 14, '89

I have been made chair woman of the "Temperance Committee" in the YPSCE to get up Gospel Meetings in the Coffee
Room once a month. The Methodists won't do their share so
the WCTU can't very well continue them and as they draw
some who would not come to church, it was too bad to give
them up.

May 28, '89

Last Wednesday morning I led the Burman prayer meeting
at Miss Ranney's, giving a review of all of Paul's journeys and
the last chapter of Acts. Now we think of taking up some of
the Psalms. Miss Ranney and I called on Mrs. McAllister
(nearby) to see some new books and tracts she has had a
present of, for the Hospital work, etc. Went to prayer meeting
in the evening. Thursday I had hymn book proof, new titles to
put into the index, etc., *Burman Messenger* proof and New
Testament copy on hand. Went down with Frank for the ride
and came right back. I also translated "Daniel's Band," that
temperance song. I imagine it is the first temperance song ever
translated.

Saturday I translated the temperance Doxology and
wrote on the index of English titles, a new feature I am
putting in the hymn book for the convenience of missionaries. In the afternoon went to the WCTU meeting, and had
company to dinner. Sunday I rested, only going to Burman
Sunday School, though at 2 P.M. we had one of the College
teachers and a few of the boys come and have a sing — to
help keep the boys out of mischief.

Monday morning we had a WCTU committee meeting to
arrange for our 5/28 annual public meetings at Miss Barrows.
After breakfast I got off *Burman Messenger* form proof, two

galleys of hymns, and then wrote a series of questions and answers on Daniel in Burmese for a Band of Hope Exercise. Shall have this (or the WCTU will) and the Daniel Hymn printed as a leaflet and sent around, in hopes of getting Burman Bands started. The flower of the Burman young men are being ruined through drink by the influence of the English. Before the English came, drunkenness was all but unknown.

Monday evening the Mission's meeting was <u>very good</u> and pleasant. There were 32 missionaries and 6 children and they had all sit down and then stood up all children of missionaries; there were 15 in the room and 6 of these were also grandchildren of missionaries.

June 11, '89

The first form of the New Testament is to be printed today, and Shwey Dway is coming with the next galley proofs. The hymn book was done last week. I have translated another Temperance song and added a 4th verse out of my <u>inner consciousness</u> and begun a tract, "Little Henry and his Bearer," which will go into the *Burman Messenger*.

Aug. 12, '89

As for my week's work: Wednesday morning I led the Burman meeting here, 17 present. Wednesday afternoon read No. 5 form, which is No. 6 really, to Shwey Gyon and was <u>tired</u>! Two hours steady reading aloud is no joke. Also prepared for my talk at the Parlor meeting and my No. III tract. Thursday I finished No. 66; translated a little on "Little Henry," prepared New Testament copy. Wrote two notes, went to Burman YPSCE, 75 present.

Friday afternoon I went to the Parlor Meeting at Mrs. Roach's. Twenty-four present, all ladies of course. I gave a short talk on the Sandwich Islands and temperance work there, Mrs. Roach followed on Australia, Mrs. Freiday on Japan which she had just visited, I on China, Miss Fells (Methodist) on Siam, Miss Barrows on India, Miss Coté on Madagascar. The whole with singing took one hour. Mrs. Bennett went and said she enjoyed it so much she could have cried. She has not been out to a meeting since February. We got hold of some who never come to the regular WCTU meetings.

Sept. 13, '89
Thursday morning (yesterday) Miss Ranney left for a trip
to Toungoo, Mandalay, Sagaing and Myngyan, to be gone
about a month. She has been very poorly all the rains and
needs a change. I miss her dreadfully, but am glad she could
go. Shall be alone more than ever.

The relatively peaceful life Hattie had enjoyed with Frank in
Rangoon since her return from Sagaing a year before was about
to come to an end. Frank, who had been in Burma without a
break since April 1882, was due for a furlough. His health had
been somewhat precarious ever since the period of illness in
1885 that precipitated his move to Kemindine under Dr.
Douglass' care, and for some time there had been talk of his
taking a furlough in America. For two years and more, Frank's
letters had described the difficulties he had finding a replace-
ment for himself at the Press. In March of 1890 Frank and the
Mission Executive Committee agreed upon a Mr. Miller to take
over the superintendent responsibilities. Frank prepared for the
voyage home.

The family at home, looking forward to Frank's coming with
great anticipation, was also anxious that Hattie accompany him.
This was not Hattie's plan.

Sept. 20, '89
Last Sunday I read *Sarah Judson* and enjoyed it too. She
had my trouble (Mrs. Bennett says, who knew her well) and
yet she lived here 21 years without once going home, did a lot
of work, and [had] two husbands and ten children!! So I've no
idea of trotting home with Frank because it would be pleasant
and convenient and I've not been very well for a year or so. It
rather annoys me that so many take it for granted that I will, as
if I only came to be with him, and would go at the first opportunity. I believe I shall be given grace and strength to stay on,
and that a work and home will be provided. I am best fitted for
the work I am now doing.

Sept. 26, '89

I fully expect now to get right along and be well again and
stay and work on indefinitely. I should think you would rather
we would come home one at a time and sort of spread out the
performance over a longer time. At any rate I should not feel
justified in coming home now because it would be pleasant and
convenient, and I expect to be so well by the time Frank goes
that my health will not demand it. With so many (3 couples
and 1 lady) going home after such short terms, I don't want to
make another. So please don't expect me. You don't want
people saying — "There, I told you so! She only went to be
with her brother!!!!!"

Frank, often pessimistic where Hattie was concerned, added at
the end of the last sentence: "Might as well say that as to say a little
later 'She couldn't stay without him.' But time will tell." Meanwhile, Hattie's letters continued to report the variety of activities
that occupied her.

Dec. 13, '89

This has been a busy week too. Saturday afternoon I had a
meeting of the WCTU here. Twenty-two ladies came and we
made up 300 card packets for Christmas gifts to soldiers,
sailors, train conductors, etc. etc. The four holes in each card
had to be punched with Mrs. Smith's eyelet punch and that
was slow, hard work. A Methodist lady insisted on doing the
most of it, the rest tied the cards together with narrow gold-
colored braid. They had cake (Miss Ranney furnished it) and
got through and left at 5:30 P.M.

Sunday I rested and read some to Mrs. Bennett and Miss
Ranney. The latter had granulated lids and last Friday (a
week ago today) went to Miss (Dr.) Coté who put in and
<u>rubbed in</u> some very strong ointment which brought the
inflammation to a head so furiously that she was totally
blind, did not once open her eyes (unless Miss Coté forced
them open) till Monday and could not open both wide till
yesterday. Cannot see well yet, and of course does not use
them at all. When I want a doctor I'm not going to Miss
Coté! Everyone has been very indignant at the treatment.

Staff of the American Baptist Mission Press.

American Baptist Mission Press on Merchant Street, Rangoon.

Detail of Press Staff.

Dec. 26, '89

Christmas morning I received from Frank a gold fountain pen, and a bottle of Colgate's perfume with a pretty card, from Mrs. Bennett a pretty locket and from Miss Ranney a silver napkin ring of Burman work and cards from several people.

At 4:30, Miss Ranney and I took my organ and went to the General Hospital; the Church Choir had been asked to go and they were there and also Mr. Brayton. We sang a lot for the patients, Mr. Brayton made an address and Miss McAllister provided cake and tea for the convalescents. They seemed to enjoy it very much.

Jan. 24, '90

Rev. Roach came in and to my surprise invited me to come to live there when Frank goes. They will give me the two rooms on this side which Frank had before. This leaves them no guest chamber but as the rooms are large I can have an extra bed in my room and so take in some when necessary. I shall have larger rooms and cooler than these and altogether it is the best place for me. I am very thankful for it.

As the time for Frank's departure neared, work at the press was being put in order, jobs completed and plans for the work to be done under Mr. Miller outlined. In Frank's absence, Hattie's responsibilities would increase.

Jan. 31, '90

Last Friday I went to the Press with Frank and went over it somewhat and got samples of book paper etc., also list copy, and the copy for the reprint of Miss Evan's Grammar, and in the evening learned how to compute the cost of printing a book — so when he's gone I'll know something.

Feb. 14, '90

Last night we went to a reception for Frank given at the Millers' where all the Press employees came and presented him with a splendid big silver bowl, a silver cup, and various curios, and a big box of chutney etc. All of which you will see later. They decorated Frank and I and the Millers with garlands of

flowers. Frank's was a <u>stunner</u>! He'll bring it home as it was
not all flowers.

Feb. 28, '90

This week sees the completion of the Bible. The last one
was printed Thursday so <u>that's done</u>! It was begun by Mr.
Eveleth in Feb. '87. Dr. Jameson also worked on it. I have
several jobs of proof on hand and some bigger ones waiting till
I have had a vacation.

This morning the household goods bought by Mrs. Bailey and
Miss Coté were sent to them, including Frank's desk, paper
shelves, a rocker, tete-à-tête, the big screens between our parlor
and dining rooms etc. The house begins to look like moving.

Mar. 12, '90

Frank goes aboard tonight, I expect, and Mr. Roach will
see me off early tomorrow. I suppose you will see Frank
shortly after you get this. You'll know him by one <u>very</u> small
tin trunk, and one <u>very</u> big hand-bag <u>and the rug</u>! It is needless
to say that I shall miss him dreadfully and be very lonely, but
he needs the rest, and everybody here is very kind. I hope
you'll have a jolly good time with him.

I shall not try to catch Frank with a letter as I doubt if it
would overtake him in England. Hereafter he'll be part of the
"Dear Folks." If he don't behave well you mustn't blame <u>me</u>!
I've "done the best I could with the material I had to work
on," in bringing him up.

The wrench of Frank's departure was mitigated somewhat for
Hattie by a vacation trip to Amherst with Ruth Ranney and Mrs.
Bennett. Hattie had earlier received "a very cordial invitation" from
Miss Haswell of Amherst to spend the hot season at Amherst and
accepted it with pleasure.

Amherst, Mar. 26, '90

Here I am "by the sand of the seashore." I came last
Wednesday night in a boat with the Kirkpatricks, the Seagraves
and the Vintons in another boat. I have part of Thé Po's (Miss
Haswell's adopted daughter) room curtained off. She, Miss
Haswell, and three little children have their part. The house,

which is not large, contains now eight grown people and six children and various natives, so of course it is noisy, but as Mrs. Bennett and Miss Ranney have a separate building to themselves, I can escape there.

I have been in bathing once and liked it. Had not forgotten about swimming and floating. I enjoy too the walks on the beach. The rest of the time I read, study, sew, etc. etc. I want to prepare for a Bible class in College next rains.

Wish you could see how we live here; it's pretty much <u>a la native</u>! Miss Haswell's heart is too big for her accommodations; she talks of several more coming!!!

Apr. 30, '90

We have had a very unusual 10 days past. The monsoon seems to have broken!! Beginning the 20th we had very hard thunder storms and rain every 24 hours and it seemed in all respects like the beginning of the rains. Today the spring tides begin and there is a change; no rain last night and this morning clear and bright, so we all feel better. As we are in a very open building and could not escape the wind and dampness it rather upset us. But we shall be all right now; we leave day after tomorrow, i.e., Friday May 2, and go on to Rangoon Monday.

We bathed for the last time last evening, got onto the rocks and into the mud somewhat then, but the waves were good and we enjoyed it. The water here is not clear but muddy always. One night it was fairly <u>hot</u>, as hot as one would use if taking a warm bath at home. There are no shells to gather, but I have found several pretty stones. The rocks are very porous, volcanic mostly, with white stone formed in the openings of the red volcanic stone. The mixed red and white ones are very pretty and also the white just tinted by the iron of the red — as if blushing.

Rangoon, May 8, '90

Here I am at home again and very glad to be here too. We left Amherst in boats at 8 A.M. Friday and reached Moulmein at 2 P.M. Mr. Stevens met us and I went to Miss Barrows' and stayed till Monday. I enjoyed my stay so much; it was nice to be civilized once more, and have things comfortable and dainty. We took breakfast at the Bulkleys' and called on the others.

On her return to Rangoon, Hattie was soon settled into her quarters at the Roaches'. The weeks were busy, filled with press, college and mission duties. With WCTU, Band of Hope, YPSCE, and mission meetings and events, many of which she shared with Ruth Ranney, she had little time to miss Frank. In addition to her duties at the press, Hattie had undertaken to teach a Bible class at the college.

May 16, '90

This has been a very busy week. I've been out somewhere every evening and sometimes in the day. Don't know what I should do without the buggy. Saturday I went to WCTU, 19 present and Mrs. Kirkpatrick gave a Bible reading. Sunday to Burman Church and Sunday School and to English Church and Coffee Room meeting, 30 present, good meeting, one new soldier-convert spoke. Monday night to YPSCE, room full, good meeting. Tuesday went to Press on business, *News* etc. and had ride in evening. Wednesday to Burman prayer meeting at a sick woman's house, 21 present. In evening to prayer meeting where Deacon Twidale and a long-winded soldier took <u>all</u> the meeting and Dr. Cushing was <u>wrathy!</u>

Thursday I rushed down and got the *News* off in the morning. The Burman YPSCE will meet here (in the College) during the rains so last night had but a few steps to go. 40 out.

Have got off the *News* (short number) and sent in *Burman Messenger* copy and Geography copy. Got Band of Hope No. 9 translated, also a story for *Burman Messenger*; have rewritten the Subscription List of latter in the new book, and scribbled first draft of my report on Burman work for the WCTU. Preparing for my Bible class takes considerable time.

Work at the press in Frank's absence did not always go smoothly.

June 27, '90

Tuesday I could get nothing at all at the Press. Dictionary stopped: "Man sick." Geography ditto: "Engine under repair." WCTU Annual Report, ditto; Mr. Denchfield kept a form up

one month and so no type for it. Thursday things had begun to
move on but the *Burman Messenger* stopped: "Shwey Dwe
away!" and it's time it was getting out. I'm <u>trying</u> to rush the
YPSCE topics but it don't rush much. I've only got off two
forms each of Geography and Dictionary.

July 4, '90

    The week has gone much as usual. Proof goes so slowly
that I have time between for preparing the hymn book copy,
revising "Little Henry," reading *Mahanthada*, translating
songs — I've done two more in No. 5, i.e., Nos. 4 and 66.
And Wednesday I began taking lessons in Karen, a boy from
College (one in my class, Po Sein Oo) gives me a half hour
in the early morning and I study the rest by myself. I can
read it and we are reading the Catechism and he translates it
as we go along so I'm picking up the vocabulary — have no
dictionary but I have borrowed Mr. Bennett's copy (inter-
leaved) of Mason's Grammar, and have Bennett handbook.
The three gutturals are <u>awful</u>!

Busy as she was with all of these activities — proofreading, translating, Bible class, YPSCE and WCTU responsibilities in addition
to regular mission activities — Hattie nevertheless accepted additional obligations when her help was requested.

Sept. 4, '90

    Now for the news of the week. The Tamil and Telugu
School is in connection with the Tamil and Telugu Church.
It has been nominally under Mr. Denchfield who wanted to
close it before, and it was rescued by Miss Ranney's taking
the Burmans and starting her Pazundaung School, leaving
this purely Tamil and Telugu. Now the head teacher Mr.
Noble is going to be a preacher. Mr. Denchfield says "Close
it" but the church people object so after considerable ma-
neuvering it is arranged that I am to be Superintendent of
the School. Mr. Denchfield is willing to make the transfer (it
is under Gov't) and Dr. Rose, to whom the appropriations
were sent this year (!), will give me the money, 400/- and I'll
"boss it" as Miss Ranney does her Pazundaung School. That
is, visit it frequently, pay the teachers, take the fees and see

that it's kept up to time. There are two men in view as teacher in place of Mr. Noble and his assistant, who has also gone. I'm writing today, Thursday, because I shall go to visit it tomorrow.

When the new helpers come, of course, I shall drop my Bible class in the College and shall have so much more time.

The possibility of even greater responsibility soon arose. Kemindine School, still under the direction of Miss McAllister and Miss Williams as it had been when Hattie left for Henzada, was in serious need of help. Miss Williams was in poor health and threatened with the possibility of having to leave the country.

[Sept. 4, '90, continued]

If Miss Williams <u>does</u> go home, I've offered to help out there some, but I've no idea of moving out, or offering to take her place, for various reasons. I can accomplish more and live longer where I am; to go out there would cut me off entirely from <u>everything</u> I am doing now, and very likely send me home in a year. Miss McAllister writes for someone to be sent this Fall anyway.

Sept. 12, '90

This has been a busy week. I had a long talk with Mr. Denchfield about the Tamil and Telugu school and yesterday he made everything over to me and wrote to the Inspector of Schools about the change. There is a balance of 113/2/2 and some due from Gov't. The money sent from America, Mr. Miller says, he can't make over till he hears from home! I'm going to see him this morning. I've been twice this week to the school and am going today. Mr. Noble, the former teacher, leaves today and I have three new ones — an old man and two young ones. Of course I can't afford this long unless the school grows a good deal. It is a most forlorn place and I'm trying to fix it up with pictures etc. I want sewing material for the girls and if somebody wants to send I shall be glad. I have all the various and sundry Gov't Registers in hand — there are <u>five</u> to be kept up all the time.

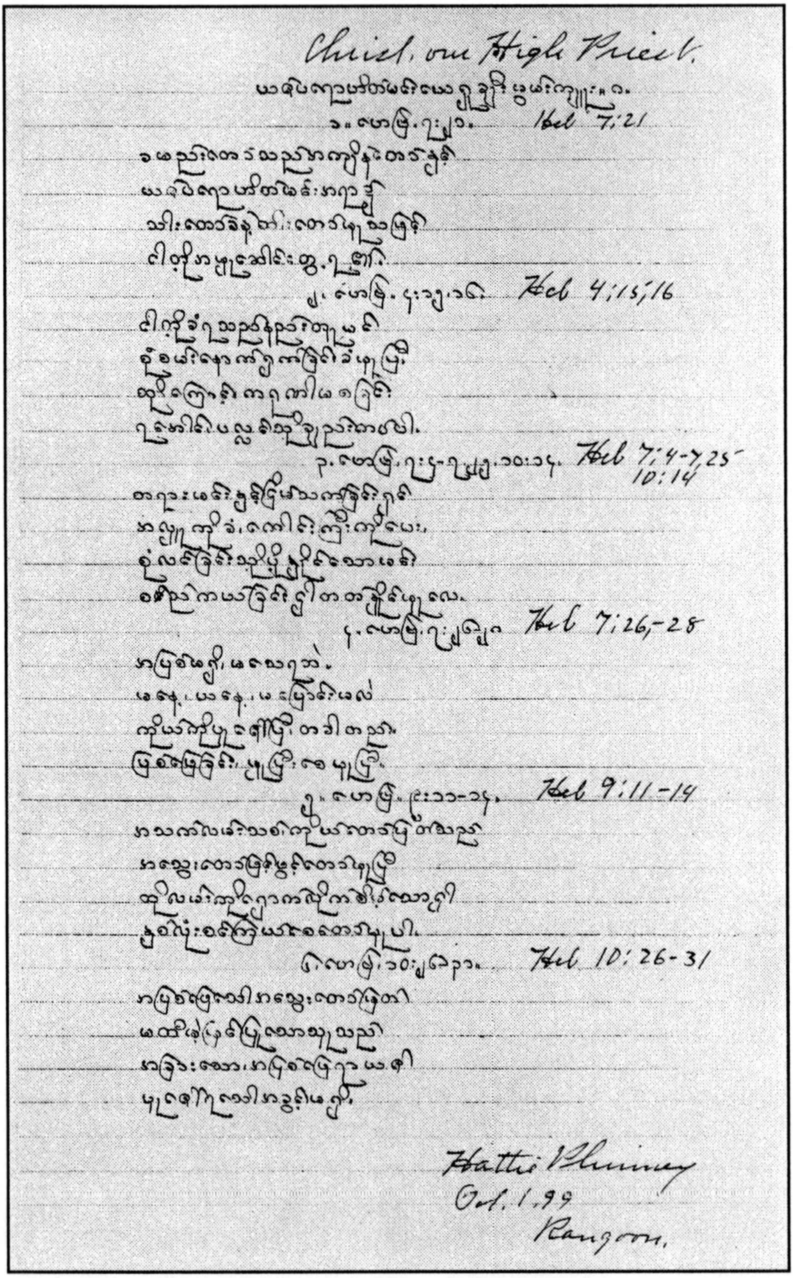

Christ, our High Priest.

Heb 7:21

Heb 4:15,16

Heb 7:4-7,25
10:14

Heb 7:26-28

Heb 9:11-14

Heb 10:26-31

Hattie Phinney
Oct. 1, 99
Rangoon.

Hymn written by Hattie in her handwriting.

Sept. 18, '90

Tuesday I spent from 10 A.M. to 2 P.M. downtown reading two last proofs of *News* and visiting my school. Thursday I was down from 10 to 12, doing various errands at the Press, 1/2 hour at school where I found 36 pupils against 17 the first time I went. I've had the blackboards painted, had the sign brought up. Ponapa painted the background and I'm ordering the letters.

Thursday I examined my class on Creation, Flood, Call of Abraham, and Friday on the Prophecies; have not read the papers yet. During the week I've cut and fitted two basques for Miss Ranney. She's not easy to fit and the dirgies are just awful.

Today Miss Ranney dismissed her Bible women [at the end of the school term] and I went over for the closing. It is time for she is worn out with the four-month siege. She has done splendid work with them.

This afternoon Dr. Cushing brought in a Doctrinal Sunday School lesson to see if I'd try to get it printed in time. I seem to be the only one who can get things done on time, go straight to the foremen, and they'll any of them do any thing I want.

As the situation at Kemindine became more critical, Hattie offered to help out on a temporary basis. Inevitably, however, bit by bit, "help out" became "take on."

Sept. 27, '90

Monday and Friday morning I went to Kemindine before breakfast. <u>Both</u> Miss Williams and Miss McAllister are to go home soon, and both need to if ever any one did. Miss Williams has had beri-beri severely and is in danger of heart failure any time, and now it appears that Miss McAllister's health is in even more critical condition. It is a matter of life and death with her. They have cabled home for two to be sent. I may be called on to step in there, at least to fill the breach, and I may not. I don't offer to take the place of either because I feel pretty sure it would simply kill me off, or send me home in no time, and they and everybody here thinks so too. Still if it comes to the school being left or their staying at the risk of life, I'll do what I can.

Nov. 14, '90

The Kemindine ladies sail next Saturday and I shall hold
the fort till the new ones come. We hear indirectly that Miss
Stark is appointed to Kemindine (doubt if it is true). I hope I'm
not expected to play second to her. I don't feel able to go into
the school in any capacity and don't see who would do some
things I am now doing. I've not had a day's real vacation since
May last; have tried to twice and failed: and I feel about at the
end of my rope.

Kemindine, Nov. 22, '90

Here I am installed as sole mistress of this school. I came out
with my clothing and table linens etc. Thursday morning. The
ladies were too busy to tell or show much and were downtown
several hours, and they left here at 8:15 Friday morning so I had
little chance to get hold of the ropes. But both ladies passed over
the multitudinous accounts in good shape and plenty of cash on
hand. I have settled myself in Miss McAllister's room and yesterday evening Miss Manning came in from Insein to stay with me,
so I am not alone. She can't help me much for I don't know the
work well enough to have help.

Have had *Burman Messenger* and Dictionary proof to read
with everything else out here.

The next party of missionaries to arrive in Rangoon included
Prof. David Gilmore and Miss Gertrude Clinton, the two new teachers for the college whose arrival had been anticipated to ease Hattie's
responsibilities there. It had been expected that Miss Clinton would
come to live in the Roach house with Hattie, but those plans were
upset by Hattie's move to Kemindine and the Roaches' imminent
departure for America.

Nov. 29, '90

Mr. Gilmore and Miss Clinton are engaged! And more
than that the Roaches are going right home with the baby. This
takes Miss Clinton's home as well as my former one, and so it
looks now as if I might have her here.

You see I am forced to take the school with such help as a
new one can give. There really seems no other way. They must
send new ones as soon as possible. I can't do it long, I fear. The

worst of all is having to move again. I did hope not to have to before Frank returned. The very worst is being so far from everybody and everything. As Mr. Whitman is to take the Tamil and Telugu work I mean to pass the school over to him. But the proof etc. I must keep.

I might as well not try to write this. I can't tell how many times I've stopped and got up to tend to somebody. A family of 96 or 97 has many wants; the last item was to buy rice for them, a bill of 30/- and over for 10 days or so.

Misses Stark and Manning are with me now. I'm keeping house with Mrs. Douglass' remnants of crockery and Frank's silver and table linen (I mean <u>cotton</u>!).

Two Normal classes are to be examined all next week at the Convent. I'll have to go some and I '<u>spose</u> move out too.

<u>Oh my</u>!! I don't know which way to turn or what to do first. "Jordan am a hard road to trabel, I believe."

Dec. 6, '90

Well! Here I am all moved and settled at Kemindine in Miss Williams' room. It's been a hard full week.

Monday I got a gharry and took out my trunks and some small things from the Roaches', who were preparing to sail on the next Singapore steamship on Friday or Saturday.

Tuesday I went again to the Examination, stayed a little while and then came back to the Roaches'. They had so much to do, and both Mrs. Roach and baby needed so many new warm things that I sat down and sewed till 2 P.M. Then, just as I'd called a gharry to take some more things, word came that the steamship went on Wednesday (the next morning) at 4 o'clock! So I just sat down again and sewed till 5 P.M. when things were about ready so far as clothes went. Then I came home and sent her my heavy underwear as she had none. They left that night, got aboard about 1 A.M. Of course the house was left as it was and Miss Clinton is there yet straightening up, but will come out here today. Mr. Gilmore will live there and David [Frank's boy] will stay and look after their things and Frank's which I have left there. I have only brought what things I must have, i.e., bed, 2 almirahs, desk, chairs, trunks etc.

Dec. 13, '90

Tuesday I had to go to town on school and other business; got
the Bibles off; otherwise I've been busy at the school. Have
inducted a member of the Normal Class as teacher, making six
girl teachers and one man. Have introduced the new Burmese
spelling and set all to learning it. Have bought rice for the school,
33/-, two carloads of wood, 48/-. Seen to no end of Gov't work,
getting money for teachers on Gov't half-pay stipends for Normal
pupils, scholarships, etc. etc. Led the Wednesday Prayer Meeting,
worked on my translation for *Burman Messenger* and Dictionary
and Grammar proof and wrote to Miss McAllister all about things
and to Mr. Pope asking various questions. Wrote up arrivals and
departures for *News*. Dr. Cushing promised to read it, but this
morning brought the galleys to me to arrange as he is going to
Toungoo and to somewhere Tuesday, so I'll finish it.

The Kemindine work, combined with the ongoing work for
the press and participation in mission activities, was becoming a
heavy load. The frequent trips to the press and to attend to other
mission activities from Kemindine were time-consuming and tiring. The separation from Ruth Ranney and Mrs. Bennett, who had
served as a refuge and support for Hattie, was an additional hardship, made harder by Ruth's health problems. The latter had been
evident for some time, even before Hattie's move to Kemindine.

Dec. 13, '90

Miss Ranney's eyes have got so bad that she is going to
Madras [India] to see Dr. Brockman and for the sake of the sea
trip as well. She expects to leave Tuesday next and be gone a
month or more. I scarcely see her now that I am at Kemindine but
I shall miss her dreadfully all the same. Still, I know she needs to
go very much. Wish I could go with her, but I couldn't afford it
even if I were free. She has money in the Bank, so can.

Jan. 10, '91

Abraham brought the man to see about re-tiling the roofs. I
bargained with him and the Chinamen came and set to work
on the ventilator, which is now well underway, and so is the
tiling, five Chinamen and seven Kulahs on the place!! Then
there was a woman to sell rice and I bargained for <u>that</u>. Then

there arose a fuss between the girls and I had to settle <u>that</u>. Altogether it was a tremendous day.

Tuesday I got up early and oversaw the moving out of all the girls from the big dormitory which is to have the ventilator. Later the deputy inspector of schools came and I talked over the new Normal Classes with him and the next day organized them. Also prepared and led the Wednesday evening prayer meeting and reckoned up the averages in attendance registers. It's lots of fun when you have Burmans, Chinese and Tamil boys and girls, day and boarding pupils all on one register (there are seven registers) and the average for each to be kept separate and total also to be given!

Have read Dictionary, Grammar, and Band of Hope proof.

Feb. 6, '91

Last mail I wrote to Mrs. Safford that I did not wish to be responsible for the opening of school in May, it was all I could do to hold on till after April 1st, and suggested Miss Stewart of Prome as a good one whom I thought could be got for the rains at least. But this morning very sharp letters come from Prome dashing all hope of relief from there. I don't see how I can hold on, they simply <u>must</u> send someone. This school furnishes teachers for all Burma, and, except the Moulmein one, is the only Normal School, so it <u>must</u> be kept up.

If Frank hasn't started [back to Burma] I hope he'll say a few things where they will do good.

On her return to Rangoon, Ruth Ranney's health continued to deteriorate. The emotional support which her friendship provided, and on which Hattie relied, could no longer be counted upon.

Feb. 21, '91

This has been the hardest week I ever lived, I think, not on account of work, for I've done almost nothing. As you know Miss Ranney came from Madras two weeks ago, and we all hoped was improved in health. I knew she did not seem better but hoped she was. Tuesday last she sent for me and told me that the doctor said she was on the verge of complete nervous prostration and in danger of paralysis of the right side and ought to go home at once. I knew she had had numbness and prickling on that side but I never dreamed it meant anything so serious. It was a crushing blow, more than I could bear up under, the thought of her danger and that we must be separated, for I didn't see how I could leave this school and go just as I suppose Frank is coming and I did not feel any more ready or willing to leave than last year.

I was prostrated for two days, in fact have not got back yet. Finally one morning (Thursday) I realized that I was broken down; as long as I had Miss Ranney to go to for sympathy, advice, and comforting companionship I could stagger on under this triple load, but when she broke, the last support was gone and I collapsed.

Still I wasn't ready to give up and let go of Burma and my work, that I'd held onto so tightly the last two years, but that morning as I lay abed, I let go, or rather it seemed as if the Master unclasped my hands, and as one objection to going after another came to my mind, I found I had let go of <u>everything</u>, even to missing Frank. Still I hoped to stay (with Miss Ranney) for a month or two, but last night I found that it was about decided that she ought to go at once, say March 11 on the S.S. *Irrawaddy* and it was such a satisfaction to her and, if possible, more to Grandma, to think of my going too that I said I would. She ought not to go alone anyway. But she has decided, at least plans now, not to go to America but stop in England with her Aunt, and if well or much improved return here in November. This plan makes it much easier for her to leave.

I have no plans beyond going with her to England. What the Lord will show next I don't know. If that much will set <u>her</u> up I <u>certainly</u> don't need more, and I don't want to spend more of the Board's money than necessary in this time of stringency — but I have no plans yet, and this whole plan may be utterly upset before night, as several others have been in the last few days. Last Monday, yes, Tuesday morning I had no more thought of going home than I had of flying, though everyone keeps saying I ought, and have all along.

At present the idea is for Prof. Gilmore and Miss Clinton to be married at once and come here and run things till May 1st. Then Dr. Rose <u>must</u> make some provisions, <u>everybody</u> says. Dr. Rose and Mrs. Rose might come themselves. I shall close the school earlier than I meant. I've got a lot of things done while here and leave it all in good condition.

When you get this I <u>may</u> or <u>may not</u> be on the way to
England. More next week. Shall leave all furniture for Frank,
taking only clothes.

Feb. 28, '91

Our passages are engaged for the S.S. *Irrawaddy* which will
sail about March 20, if it does. Don't expect me till I get there.
Don't know anything beyond the fact of sailing.

A few more odds and ends needed to be cleared up before the
trip homeward: the Clinton-Gilmore wedding and the assignment
of someone to take over the *Burman Messenger* and the press work.

Mar. 7, '91

The event of the week was the wedding on Tuesday. The few
missionaries in town came, and the few girls here and a few other
natives; in all enough to make a fair audience. I spent the forenoon in having the platform trimmed with plants, palm branches,
flowers, etc. so that the whole back of the platform which they
faced was a mass of ferns and foliage plants and white fragrant
blossoms. The post near the platform I draped with Frank's flag
and white blossoms. Everybody spoke of its being so pretty. It was
a pretty wedding. Dr. Rose gave her away and Dr. Cushing
married them. It was all very pleasant and no hitch.

Mar. 14, '91

I've nobody to take the *Burman Messenger* yet, the English-
Burman proof or Band of Hope. Almost <u>no one</u> cares for or is
prepared for this work.

Mar. 21, '91

I've had to get Ah Sou to do the *Messenger* one month and
leave to Mr. Cummings the rest, if he'll take it. Can scarcely
get my work off my hands. I suppose a Kulah will be seen
coming down the Irrawaddy in a sampan after we start, franti-
cally clutching a parcel of proof!!

Hattie and Ruth sailed from Rangoon on the S.S. *Irrawaddy* on
March 22nd, 1891. It had been just a year since Frank had left on
furlough and a little over five years since Hattie had arrived in Burma.

Hattie Phinney & Ruth Whitaker Ranney, 1890.

Part III

Charting A New Course

March 1891 to October 1892

Hattie and Ruth's trip home on the S.S. *Irrawaddy* was without major incident, although both women were in poor health and found the five weeks' journey to London long and uncomfortable. The time was spent in reading, Bible study, and sharing ideas, plans, and hopes for the future. Once in England, the two joined Ruth's aunt and uncle in London. Hattie, after a brief visit, traveled on to America, arriving home in May of 1891. Frank, still on furlough, met her in Boston and accompanied her to Rochester.

Hattie's return to 4 Brighton Avenue brought the family living there to seven members; Herman and Ada's son, Sedley, had joined the family, and Frank was living at home between trips on business for the Mission Union. It was a large family for a small house, but no consideration seems to have been given to other living arrangements. In August of 1891, Frank returned to Rangoon to begin his second tour of duty as Superintendent of the Mission Press.

Hattie spent the first few months at home quietly, resting up from the strain of the last months in Burma and the long journey home. By October she was feeling well enough to accept speaking engagements at local church groups in Rochester and began to receive requests to visit and speak at mission circles in other towns. Such speaking trips became a major feature of her remaining months in America.

Hattie and Ruth Ranney stayed in close touch during their furlough home. Ruth returned to America from England in September, stopping off in Rochester for a brief visit before going home to Homer, New York.

In October of 1891, Ruth's grandmother, Mrs. Bennett, died in Rangoon. Following her death, Ruth undertook the task of writing a memoir of her grandparents, the Cephas Bennetts, covering their lives in Burma since the early Judson days. Ruth enlisted Hattie's assistance in gathering resource materials and preparing the manuscript, their collaboration conducted by correspondence over several months. By March of 1892 the memoir was finished and plans for its publication were underway.

By that time, too, Hattie and Ruth had formulated their plans for the future. The friendship between the two women, strengthened during their long voyage home and their collaboration on the memoir, had deepened to a commitment to live and work together after their return to Burma. The center of their plan was the establishment of a school for native women to train and prepare them to serve as Bible women, able to aid missionaries in their work. A second aspect of the plan involved traveling to outlying areas in the jungles of Lower Burma. Aside from their evangelistic purpose, the jungle trips were important in the recruitment of prospective students — Christian women who were interested in participating more actively in Baptist work. Another aspect of their plan involved the furtherance of other work in support of the mission. For Hattie, this meant using her excellent language skills in a variety of ways, including the development of materials in Burmese.

In March the two women set out on a trip they hoped would elicit the financial support they would need to realize their plans. For two months, they traveled to a series of meetings, visits to missionary friends, and speaking engagements throughout the East Coast and New England, from Philadelphia to Boston. Both women had improved in health by then, Hattie reporting Ruth to be "so much better than in September, hardly the same person." They used the time to tell about the work they hoped to undertake in Burma and to solicit interest and financial support for the school. They were successful in finding sponsors — Miss Chapman of Brooklyn for Hattie, Mrs. Brooks of Boston for Ruth — and other funds to cover the first year after their return to Burma, as Hattie later reported:

Oct. 21, '93

Our trip about that March and April has brought in alot of money. The one visit to Morristown has resulted in our two salaries for two years, that's $2,000 and two Bible women and now a preacher = $110, besides the cash they gave us at the time, some $22. I think it paid!

Frank's stay in Burma this time turned out to be a short one. On his return to his duties in Rangoon, he met Lenna Smith, who had joined the mission during his absence in America. After a brief courtship, he and Lenna were married. Lenna, who had been ill before the marriage with what was diagnosed as consumption, became seriously ill almost immediately. She was ordered to leave Burma as soon as possible. The couple left Rangoon in May of that year and returned to Rochester, arriving in July.

While Frank made it clear in his letters that he expected Hattie to continue to make her home with him when she returned to Burma, she had other plans.

Feb. 14, '92

As to my living with you, I think it very doubtful. If Miss Ranney returns as she now hopes, in the Fall, and we work together, as is quite likely, it will be more convenient and suitable for me to live with her, and I should be perfectly happy in such an arrangement.

Lenna's illness made the whole discussion moot. After their return to Rochester, Frank again found work with the Mission Union, and he and Lenna moved into a home of their own. Lenna never recovered completely from the consumption that had sent them home from Burma so precipitously. She died shortly after giving birth to a stillborn baby boy in May 1894. Frank himself did not return to Burma until July 1895.

A second death occurred in Ruth Ranney's family during Ruth and Hattie's time in America. Her uncle, Captain Wells, died after a lengthy illness. His death and that of Mrs. Bennett had an important effect upon Ruth and Hattie's plans for their return to Burma. Mrs. Bennett's death released Ruth from her responsibility for the care of her grandmother, but also deprived her of her Rangoon home. Captain Wells' death left his wife in need of a change and willing to return to Burma to live with Ruth and Hattie, sharing expenses and handling the housekeeping affairs of the household.

In October 1892 Hattie and Ruth sailed again for Burma, having spent 17 months in America — time well spent in regard to their future plans.

10

A New Life in Burma

December 1892 to December 1893

Hattie returned to Burma a different person in many ways from the young woman who had left nearly two years before. The questions and uncertainties that had characterized her first term in Burma were gone. While the plans she and Ruth had formulated during their furlough remained as yet untried, Hattie was now sure of the direction of her career, independent of her brother Frank, and to a greater extent than before, independent of the mission board. She had found the person with whom to share her life and work, and was ready to take on, with vigor and dedication, the task she and Ruth had set themselves. Hattie was 31 years old, Ruth 35.

The two women had learned important lessons from their first years in Burma, during which both had assumed a variety of positions and responsibilities within the mission, as the need arose. In Hattie's case, this had meant substantial changes in living arrangements and occupations, often with little warning or preparation. From Rangoon to Henzada and Sagaing with the Hascalls, to press work in Rangoon, and finally as administrator of Kemindine School (among other duties), Hattie's willingness to take on more and more responsibility had finally overwhelmed her.

Now Hattie and Ruth returned with a well-articulated plan that would allow them to better pace their energies and avoid the risk of overwork and breakdown. By setting their own priorities, they hoped they could more effectively direct their energies toward the goals they set out to achieve. As Hattie explained a few years later:

Nov. 30, '94

When we returned [to Burma] this time, we came with the purpose of putting native work <u>first</u> always and letting nothing hinder that. . . . This plan we have followed out.

The threefold activities of their plan were divided according to the calendar year and the exigencies of seasonal climate. The Burman Woman's Bible School would be in session during the rains, roughly from the middle of May to early October. Trips to the jungle were to be undertaken during the cool season, November to February. The hot season, March to May, would be given over to more concentrated Burmese language work, and other mission work as time and energy allowed.

Arriving in Rangoon on December 10 after the two months' voyage from America, Hattie and Ruth quickly settled back into the life of the Mission. In her role as housekeeper, Mrs. Wells had preceded them and prepared the house for their return.

Home!! <u>Wahklu Lodge</u>!!! Dec. 10, '92

We had a very calm passage from Calcutta, took on the pilot at 4 A.M. and just <u>scooted</u> up the river as if we were a mere little steam tug, reaching the wharf at 7:30. The Roaches, Roses, Prof. Gilmore, Mrs. Carson and Mrs. Wells were there to meet us and of course <u>Abraham</u>. Mrs. Wells took us to Mrs. McCall's (where she had been staying) for breakfast and now we are fairly in our own house. Most of my things had been brought over, though several <u>haven't</u> come yet. Mrs. Wells' things are very nice and pretty and we shall have a very delightful home, I'm sure. The *Tenasserim* with our goods from N.Y. is in three days ago, so we'll soon have our boxes. We are very glad to get home and shall enjoy settling.

Dec. 16, '92

It seems as if it might be a month since I wrote last but it is only six days. They have been very busy ones. Sunday we studied our Burmese Sunday School lesson early and went to Lanmadaw at 10:30 A.M. We had a quiet restful day and went to English chapel in the evening. At both churches the congregations were larger than we had feared they would be from the reports heard.

We called at the Gilmores' Monday evening and went to the mission prayer meeting Tuesday at Dr. Rose's. Friday we dined at Kemindine and had a very pleasant time. Miss McAllister has made great improvement in the buildings. Gov't requires Kindergartens in the Normal Schools (!) so there is that to be seen to.

We have spent the bulk of the time in <u>settling</u>, and in receiving natives and other callers. Our home is getting to look settled and homelike and is very pleasant. It is large but as there are three to furnish it, the center and east half are well supplied. The great room is a trifle bare and the study not exactly full!

We learn from Dr. Smith that we are to have this house without rent, or as he expressed it, it is now in our hands and he does not feel any responsibility about it. I shall have a small bathroom added for myself and return the rest of the appropriation made for rent.

Everyone asks after Frank and Lenna. Mrs. Carson tells that her Carl, four years old, was preaching to a Kulah and telling him about Christ; the man asked him how he knew about him and he said by the Bible. So the man asked where the Bible came from and he said "Oh! God wrote it on two flat stones and gave them to Moses, and Moses gave them to Mr. Phinney and he made the books"!!!

Dec. 23, '92

Saturday morning we went to the WCTU meeting which has run down in Miss Ranney's absence. Sunday morning at 7:30 we began a Sunday School at Ko Shwe Aung's house in Kemindine — the pupils being her day pupils; 41 were there and we had a pleasant time with them. Then we went to Lanmadaw for Sunday School. We each had a class. In the evening we went to English Church and heard Mr. Whitman.

I agreed to take the English/Burmese Dictionary proof as far as I could, and also took over charge of the *Messenger* but it was given to me without a single bit of material on hand, so I've had to gather straw and make bricks this week for sure.

Wednesday at 11 A.M. we had our first Burman woman's prayer meeting. Twelve came which was a good number considering how many have died and moved away. We had a very good meeting.

Once settled in their new home, the two women lost no time in undertaking the jungle work essential to their plan. Their first trip out of Rangoon, a two-day trial run, was taken less than two weeks after their arrival. A week later they undertook a four-day trip to Syriam, across and a little ways up river from Rangoon. By the middle of January, they were ready to undertake a more extensive trip.

Jan. 14, '93

We expect to get off for a long trip next Wednesday, to Dedaye, Maubin, etc. A preacher, Saya [teacher] Timothy (formerly a Mandalay priest), and his wife go with us and Ko Tha Din's wife and a girl with her.

Maubin, Jan. 25, '93

There is so much to tell I don't know as I shall get it all told but will begin. We went aboard the steamship for Dedaye about 11 A.M. a week ago today and found it <u>full</u>; however we didn't take a cabin but found place to stow our goods and on the upper deck just space to put our chairs. All around us were Burman men and Chinese and Kulahs [Indian natives] with their beds spread out and they sprawled on them. It was by no means pleasant and the cigar smoke was distressing. However, we stood it very well and Saya Timothy and his wife preached about all the time. It began by their asking about some text so we got out our Bibles and began talking with them, which drew some heathen about and they preached to them all afternoon.

We did not reach Dedaye till after dark and learned that the Gov't rest house was removed, and we were warned by a woman not to try to go out the mile or so to the Christians' village as the road was bad and thieves abounded. So we sent Saya for the head Burman official and he came to the landing and said we could spend the night at his house. Just then the only Christian in the town appeared and took us to the heathen house where he lives as a sort of helper (he has no family). They took us in and gave us a corner of the upstairs to sleep in. We had had nothing to eat since 10:30 A.M. so the bread and cold roast beef we had with us tasted good and after worship we went to bed. We went to sleep to the sound of Saya's preaching downstairs and Mah Oo's upstairs!

After tea in the morning we started out and walked to the village where about four Christian families live, and were <u>most cordially</u> received, and given a place in one house which had evidently been put in order for us. There is no privacy to speak of in a native house, our own curtains were all there was to screen us day or night from anyone in the house or on the road.

After breakfast we had a service (Bible reading) with the Christians (a dozen or so) and a lot of children. One or two heathen were always present when we met. At 3 P.M. we had a children's meeting, three Christian girls from 14 to 22 years old being there. The oldest we expect will come in for the rains to us. In the evening all gathered and I gave a lesson on Prayer. Friday morning we had another meeting (on the Sabbath) and much visiting and general teaching and a singing lesson.

After a very early dinner we walked to Dedaye again, the Christians carrying our goods. We had been urged to preach to the heathen in Dedaye and the entire evening till 10 P.M. was spent in that way. The head Burman officials came and listened and talked back and were very nice, but one man was there simply to gainsay and was so unreasonable the rest turned against him. When they got too heated we'd sing a song and get them cooled off a bit and then go on. They talked some time after we went to bed. Early Saturday we called on the two leading men, preached a bit. The headman asked for a Bible and said to be sure not to forget to send it.

We left about 2 P.M. in a sampan (open row boat) and had a very pleasant trip to Keiklot, arriving after dark again (had to go by the tides). We found the house of Mah Kin, who had invited us, without trouble. She is an SPG Christian [Society for the Propagation of the Gospel] now converted by our Saya when he was an SPG preacher. She is now most exercised about baptism and will, I doubt not, come to it before long. She is by far the most earnest Bible student I ever saw among the Burmans, if not among <u>any</u> people, and the sweetest disposition. Has made wonderful progress for one but three years out of heathenism, is one of the few <u>prepared</u> ones.

When we went up in her house (a very large and good one) we wanted first to have our food as we'd not eaten much since breakfast. As we were eating off the floor, the SPG priest (Mr. Ellis) came in to have a singing lesson with his Christians! and a poongye in yellow silk robe was there also to hear and discuss Christianity!!! It was very funny and a trifle awkward. As we were eating, a crowd of Burman women, heathen, who heard we were there rushed in to see us and hear us preach and their remarks on us, our food, etc. etc. were comical.

We kept still till the SPG priest (in his black robe) got through having them sing — regular Church of England droning — and then Miss Ranney began to talk to the women who had often asked in a whisper — "When are you going to preach?" One of them was exceedingly interested and when asked to come again said, "I can't, I must go on with our boat tomorrow — we live on a boat — and I must go without this matter being settled." We gave her a tract and hope she'll find someone to read it to her. The SPG man was quite polite to us and seemed anxious as to how we were to get food and a place to sleep — he stays at the Gov't guest house. We were finally, about 10 P.M., given a corner of the room and we got up our curtains and beds and retired.

Early Sunday morning the priests returned — both yellow and black — and a regular Church of England service was held — Scripture, songs, and prayers were intoned in a high whining tone; I never heard anything like it in Burmese and it did seem most heathenish. There was not a thing really helpful to anyone. I gave a lesson on Ps 121 for one morning prayer and afterward at Mah Kin's request we went over with her all the texts on Baptism. One of our own Christian women, Mah Nyet, came with her daughter; the former, we expect, will come for the rains and possibly Mah Kin also. Both will be great additions and very useful afterwards.

Another of our folks, Ko Moung, who has been much among the Karens, came to see us and on leaving gave Miss Ranney 10/- for our expenses! We were much encouraged. He thinks of starting a school. After dinner we had a long walk to his house and I led a meeting there, mostly heathen.

About 3 P.M. we set out again, this time in a very large nice Burmese row boat having a roof in the middle. We had hired it for 6/- to take us all to Maubin, but when we were in and started we discovered two great fat black Kulahs snugly settled on their beds under the roof. This we couldn't allow as we were to be all night in the boat and there were we four women beside the men to sleep in it. So we said so and made them go back and find another boat for the men. We had to pay 8/- but were glad to for the sake of decency and comfort.

It delayed us a half hour or so but finally we were off again, had our dinner, a private Bible study and then sat out at the bow and saw a grand sunset and remained in the moonlight singing, asking Bible questions with our helpers etc. till bedtime. We could not put up our cots and the floor was <u>very</u> hard so the night was not so restful as might be. It was very cold too.

We had a breakfast in the boat — the boy cooking it — and morning worship. I gave a lesson on "Obedience" and at 11:30 A.M. (Wed. 25th) we landed in front of the Bushell house. Mr. Bushell is out in the jungle but the two ladies, Misses Putnam and Knight are here and received us most cordially.

We have had meetings in each of the houses of the two Burman Christians in town, and twice had street preaching toward night. We have each taken the Burmese Bible class in the school, and last evening I led the regular prayer meeting. Saya preached all day yesterday in different places. Tonight we'll visit some Burman houses nearby and then have a Temperance meeting in the school, and tomorrow at 9 A.M. or so take the steamship for Neyoung-done. The ladies have been so glad to have us come and do something for the Burmans, in the town and in the school. There is no preacher here and no Burmese service. We are eating and sleeping well and keeping well every way. We have an excellent boy — a Christian, who knows Burmese and is first-rate for jungle work, can get up a meal out of almost nothing and with no conveniences.

I stand an amount of walking and talking that would have quite laid me out formerly. The Lord is blessing us every way wonderfully. The opportunity to teach Saya and his wife is worth the trip almost, as they are anxious to learn and to have <u>us</u> teach them. The Saya wants us to preach whenever we are along and he keeps still unless called on. This is very remarkable for a Burman! He can fight Buddhism, Catholicism and SPGism beautifully but doesn't know how so well to simply preach Christ. He is learning, however.

Somewhere between Pantanaw
and Neyoung-done, Feb. 1, '93

Here we are packed in a big row boat but not nearly so big
and comfortable as the one we went to Maubin in, and we
have the preacher's wife and daughter and nephew of
Neyoung-done added to the party of six.

To begin where I left off: we had, Thursday evening, a
temperance meeting in the school (Maubin) and both spoke
and I showed the red, white, and blue pledge cards that are
to adorn a woman's building at the World's Fair [in Chi-
cago]. To our surprise our Saya got up and gave a splendid
talk and actually signed the first card pledging himself not
to use coon or tobacco. This is a wonderful step for a
Burman and one who is around among folks all the time and
constantly urged to take it. He had before given it up when
he was a priest but had used it again afterward. He is
constantly urging his wife to follow suit. About 30 of the
pupils also signed and as this is the first public effort in that
school they were much encouraged.

We left the next morning about 11 o'clock on the big mail
steamship. There were few passengers and so we had plenty of
room and a chance to preach to a man who is very "<u>near</u>" we
think, and to a crowd that gathered. The man is from Obbon
and we promised to go there as soon as we could.

We reached Neyoung-done about 3:30 and had a very long
walk to the preacher's house and had to enquire along the way.
We asked, among others, an Eurasian young man, who assured
us there was no mission in the place except Catholic. As this
preacher had been there eight years, we knew better. We finally
found the place — a very tumble-down and dirty house, even
for a native.

As we were having dinner the same young man appeared
with a young Englishman, the head school master of the
Gov't school. He invited us to call on his Mother and so we
did and she asked us to sleep at her house. We were glad to
do so as the floors at the native house were so rotten we
were in constant danger of going through (Miss Ranney did
once) and the place was too dirty for anything. We considered it a special mercy to be called elsewhere and the lady,

Mrs. Colloden, considered it so too, for she had not seen any women whatever to speak to since she arrived a month ago. We found she was of a family well known by the old missionaries and she was very kind to us. Of course our boy did our cooking, etc.

We went out early Saturday morning and had a long preach to 60 to 80 people in the front of a Chinese shop. Then we had worship with our folks and the preacher's family (there are no other Christians). We always give them a regular Bible lesson and it takes a good deal of study but as they <u>want</u> to learn, it is too good a chance to lose. About 3 P.M. we went to see a woman who they said was "considering." We found her one of those who say, "Yes, yes" to <u>every</u>thing but who are the hardest cases of all.

Monday we were up at 6:30 and off in this boat at 7:30. It is a <u>very</u> unsteady one and we have to keep still all the time or the man hollers at us. We stopped about 10 A.M. for the boatmen to eat, and going up on the bank and through some grass 15 feet high we came out onto a bit of a road and ran across a Karen who turned out to be one of Mr. Bushell's Christians. Going on a bit, we came to a Karen Christian's house and climbed a bamboo ladder to greet the inmates. It was a very pleasant break in the journey.

We arrived at 3:45 P.M. and found the preacher's house, quite a great deal better than the other's was. But the man had separated from his wife and things were anything but pleasant or hopeful. Our Saya and wife took hold and tried to reconcile them and when we left they promised to live together and do better. The Saya actually cried over it. We visited the school but there was little chance to preach. The preacher was well known and his crooked life didn't recommend Christianity. Dr. Rose has stopped his pay. The river is closing up and the place fast running down.

In going, the rowers, our boy, and the preacher's wife and girl all got out and dragged the boat over the sand bars! We only stayed one day and two nights and left at 7 this morning and are getting back to Neyoung-done and from there to Mayales.

Thursday evening, Mayales. We stopped at Neyoung-done from 5 to 7:30 P.M. and called on Mrs. Colloden and had dinner in the larger boat we hired on arrival. It was bright moonlight and very pleasant; at first we were hindered once by running into a nest of big rafts of logs from Upper Burma. We didn't reach here till 11 A.M., stopped to wait for the tide at a place called "Not-Enough-Rice." We are staying in a native house that is <u>dirty dirtier dirtiest</u>. These are Burmanized Karens; 25 or so of them Christians. I led the meeting this evening.

Saturday P.M. We had another meeting Friday morning but early, before breakfast, we took a <u>long</u> walk to see a Christian household and had prayers there and then another where a very worldly Christian had to be reproved.

We left in the boat — a large comfortable one this time in which we could put up our beds and sleep comfortably. This morning we had to wait from 2 A.M. to 8 for the tide and found we were at a tiny village so went ashore and all had a good chance to preach; had some very good listeners. We reached Kemindine at 11 A.M. and took gharries home.

If you want to appreciate civilization and a good clean comfortable home, just try living in native houses for two or three weeks! We've learned to climb perpendicular ladders, eat with our food on the floor and plates in our laps, watched by a crowd of naked children and their parents, wash in dirty water, go without bathing, live "in the eye of the public" as Miss Ranney says, walk miles to shake hands with a Christian, and talk and sing by the hour.

Our trip has resulted in about five Bible women promised, two or three girls for Kemindine School, some subscriptions for the *Burman Messenger,* and some Bibles bought. I think the folks that went with us got as much good as anyone. A good many heathen heard the truth very plainly and a good number of Christians were taught.

This first extensive trip of the jungling years was typical of the many that Hattie and Ruth would undertake, with its uncertain traveling conditions and living accommodations, encounters with "hard cases" and hopeful ones, polite listeners and hecklers, solitary English families anxious for English-speaking companionship, not to mention the discomforts of heat, cold, dirt, mud, insects, and irregular meals. Typical, too, was their visit to a mission station, as at Maubin, where Ruth and Hattie could provide support to the local missionaries by leading meetings and utilizing their language proficiency to work with Burmans not served, in some cases, by the non-Burmese speaking missionaries assigned to the area.

Three more trips in February, March, and April of that year completed the "jungling," as Hattie called it, for the first year. Having identified a number of prospective students, who would be "coming for the rains," the next step was to prepare for the classes and ready the house and grounds for the Bible school.

While these preparations and later the daily classwork engaged the greater part of their energies from this time on, Hattie continued her work for the press, the *Burman Messenger*, and preparation of the monthly Sunday school lessons. Ruth undertook the supervision of the Lanmadaw and Pazandaung schools. Both women remained active members of the Lanmadaw and English churches and Sunday schools, entertained their share of visitors, and attended the mission prayer meetings.

The Burman Woman's Bible School opened May 16, 1893, with six women in attendance, but grew quickly in the following weeks. By July, the school would be filled to capacity.

May 6, '93

This has been a week of housecleaning and we have had coolies every day till today, and had the small house in the compound (San Tay's) cleaned for our women and this house has been thoroughly cleaned. All the walls and ceilings swept and all the floors scrubbed with sand and cocoa-nut husk, everything moved and everything on the walls down and dusted. The servants helped of course but it's been a busy week.

I've made a map of Palestine for the class and we finished going over Mark in Burmese for ditto.

Miss Ranney received Rs49/11 from a friend in Philadelphia and this with the $5 Eva Campbell sent me will carry us through the first month — house rent and all; we pay 10/- for the little house.

Wahklu Lodge, first home of the Burman Woman's Bible School, 1892-3.

May 13, '93

This has been a week of odds and ends getting done up and all ready to begin the Bible class on Monday. Po Min and his wife (our preacher from Mingaladone) have moved and we shall have some of the women tomorrow.

Saturday. <u>Four</u> women from Mandalay have come today, and three are coming from one place instead of <u>one,</u> two in another place <u>asked</u> to come so I think we'll not lack material to work on! It looks as if we'll have a dozen at least.

May 19, '93

This has been a full week; we began with six women and now have eight and there are several more who expect to come. Four are from Mandalay, one each from Henzada, Insein, Mingaladone and Syriam. All can read and seem bright and anxious to learn. We've had good times with them every day. I teach Mark the first hour; Miss Ranney follows with Genesis and the afternoon is to be spent on Luke, tho to begin on, Genesis has been taught after tiffin also. I take the last half-hour or so giving the outline on the board and seeing that they copy it. The rest of the time I have for the *Messenger* and Sunday School paper and Miss Ranney also has to oversee the Bible work in the town schools but think she'll manage not to be away much of the time she would otherwise teach here.

May 26, '93

We have nine women now and have settled down to regular work. They all seem to be contented and are on the whole bright and in earnest. Four have been Bible women. We expect a few more.

June 1, '93

This has been a full week. Two more have come so we have eleven bright women, and have to enclose part of the veranda of the little house for them to sleep in. We expect more next week. I teach them in Mark and the Old Testament prophecies of Christ and give the outlines to commit. Miss Ranney teaches Luke and Genesis. Generally I take the first hour and quarter in the morning and the last hour in the afternoon but when she goes to the schools I take all the morning and she all the afternoon.

June 9, '93

Monday morning another woman came, Mah Kyu Oue, who lives in town and comes every day. Yesterday a girl we expected from Syriam came, Mah Hnin E. Her father is an evangelist and an unusually nice man; she, though only 20 years old, is, they say, a good "preacher." We are very glad to have her: she makes <u>13</u>.

The students' training included opportunities to participate in Christian work throughout the community and to apply their learning through teaching Sunday School, attending women in their homes, and participating in other activities and events.

[June 9, '93, continued]

Thursday after school we took six women and went to the house of a Christian in Lanmadaw district and held a meeting. I opened and spoke a few minutes and then four of the women followed and did <u>quite</u> as well as Mr. Thomas's men [students] do. There were twenty or so women and some men who gathered in the house and listened quietly all through — rather unusual. We mean to hold such meetings with Christian women, who because of little children can't come to chapel.

June 23, '93

Monday afternoon we all went to the house of a Christian nearby who can't get out to chapel, and held a little meeting with her. Her near-neighbors are mostly Kulahs so we had only four Christian women beside our own.

Another girl came Monday, so we have 15. Two of these are from the only Christian family in their village and we are especially pleased to have such come in. We have now as many as we can well take care of. There has been no sickness to speak of so far, which is a great mercy.

Wednesday evening at the Lanmadaw zayat at Mr. Thomas' invitation four of the women took hold and exhorted the heathen listening to them just as well as to the men. Mr. Thomas has meetings Tuesday and Thursday evening also but we shut down on the women's going to so many — they are too sleepy the next day.

I have begun the Old Testament miracles with them as we'd finished the prophecies.

July 7, '93

Monday Ko Shwe Aung's eldest daughter, Mah Chone, who has kept the little day school at Kemindine for many years, entered our class. Her niece keeps the school and so she has a chance to study the Bible — she needs it! This makes 16 in the class and we hear that Mg. Tha Din's mother is coming. That will be quite as many as we can take.

Monday morning we held our neighborhood prayer meeting at Ah Sou's house, and had a few unconverted in beside the household and Christian neighbors. I led on the subject of "Obedience" and we had a good meeting. The women take part freely.

July 21, '93

The teaching has gone on as usual and I've added a map showing the land in the time of the judges. Now we have four large maps on our walls, and the women are very much interested in them. Two more have entered, an old woman, mother of Tho Din of Maubin, and Theim Kin, Miss Ranney's old girl. She asked to come and does on the same ground as all the rest. So we number 18 now, 3 of them day pupils.

Wednesday morning one of the younger women led us and we had an unusually good meeting. The women are learning at last to pray for definite things and for people by name and it's a great improvement. As I had them all day today, after an hour on the Old Testament this afternoon, I set them all to drawing maps — copying one on the wall of Palestine. Most of them never drew a line before and there was considerable excitement and laughing over it. Even the old women took hold and did very well too — much to my surprise.

Aug. 4, '93

It's a pleasure to see how the women grow. They can now write very good outlines of chapters that we've studied and lately we give them a character to write a composition on, and they do very well indeed. Miss Ranney gave them "John the Baptist" and for Monday I've given "Elijah."

They grow spiritually too; at first if we reproved them or
made a rule as to their going and coming etc. some were apt to
be sulky or sour for a time, but this week we had to lay down a
strict rule about having visitors and they all took it with the
utmost sweetness and good nature, for which we say, as we so
often have occasion to, "praise the Lord."

Aug. 11, '93

Our <u>19th</u> woman arrived this morning from Mandalay,
Mah Gyi, a helper to Miss Fay, and formerly in the King's
household. She is bright and anxious to learn, has not been a
Christian long. The women are so thick in the house that we
asked them first if they could take her in, before we gave
permission for her to come.

The teaching goes on as usual; they all did very well with
their story of Elijah, the only trouble being that they made
them too long; like some other folks, they can't "boil it
down"!

Aug. 18, '93

One thing that has taken time and strength has been a
small disturbance among the women. There are two from
Mandalay that have very trying dispositions and they clashed
and there was an unpleasantness that made all unhappy. Both
have publicly begged pardon and peace is restored. Considering how <u>thick</u> they are in the little house they have been
wonderfully kept from quarreling.

Aug. 25, '93

Tuesday the women were all in a tangle; had been for a
week but as the leaders had begged pardon publicly we hoped
it was over, only to find that they were all by the ears and no
one could say a word without a fuss arising. We felt it was
worse than useless to go on so and were much burdened about
it. When they were called, Miss Ranney read and talked on the
Fifth Psalm and there was a general breaking down all around,
particularly the leaders — those at fault. They all one after
another prayed, making confession, and we felt that the Lord
had cast out the evil spirits. The atmosphere has been clear
since. We <u>could</u> rule them by <u>rules</u> and keep them straight by

outside pressure but we don't want to — have seen too much
of that sort of work. Just as soon as the pressure is removed
they fly back to their old way of living. We want the Lord to
work from the <u>inside</u> and then it will be permanent. We see
signs that He is doing so.

Sept. 1, '93

In the afternoon Mah Sein, the leader in the fuss last week,
came up to say how differently she felt towards the others and
they toward her. She has evidently experienced a change.

This morning we found that one of the girls had stolen a
bit of spicing from Po Min and lied about it. She finally confessed to us and before the class.

Sept. 8, '93

The girl who stole the curry stuff and lied about it, confessed it under pressure but we couldn't see any signs of true
repentance and were troubled over her. Yesterday Miss Ranney
had a little talk with her. This time she didn't accuse others but
still showed very little sense of guilt. However at dinner time
she and her sister came quite broken down, begging to be
forgiven and taken back into our good graces again. We think
there has been a change in heart in these cases too. There is a
spirit of love and good will among all the women that is really
refreshing and is manifestly of the Lord.

Sept. 22, '93

When we got home at 9:15 P.M. we found the women all in
a ferment over the last arrival, the "Princess" who misunder-
stood a money affair with Miss Ranney and Miss Fay (who
sends her) and who had been slandering Miss Ranney all day.
The girls were crying and in a dreadful state over it. It was all
explained to them and the woman called. She professed to
understand it but went off with great stiffness and wasn't
happy or good all Sunday. But Monday morning Miss Ranney
sent for her and she came in a very different spirit, said she
awoke at 2 that morning and began to pray about it and had
repented. All day she seemed very different, taking an interest
in the study which she had not done before. But Tuesday her
friend came up early to say that she was all broken down, was

over at the house crying and confessing her sins; the woman
added: "She has never listened to any human being's voice
before and this is nothing but <u>the power of God</u>." She came to
class with tears in her eyes and when I, in the course of the
lesson, spoke of the power of the "Word" she burst out afresh,
saying, "Yes, the Lord spoke to me through the <u>Word</u>!" and
then she made the woman next read the passage she had
exhorted from the Wednesday before: 2 Tim 3:1-5 and as she
read it she kept sobbing out, "<u>That I</u> dared to take that text
and exhort the rest from it as if I was perfect and it meant <u>me</u>
all the time." The others were much touched and one said,
"Yes, when she picked that out just carelessly, I said, 'That fits
<u>you,</u>' and she answered, 'Yes, yes' without seeing it at all."
They all realize that only the Holy Spirit could have broken
her down.

Sept. 29, '93

The two Mandalay women have been recalled on account
of sickness in the family and another left Monday for Insein
for the same reason. Two day pupils have dropped out as well,
so we are reduced to 14. We close Oct. 10th.

Five or six of our women have given up coon and tobacco,
and one at least testifies that whereas before when she has tried
to give it up in her own strength she has had such a craving for
it she couldn't stand it and had to take it up again; now it is by
the power of God and tho she stopped short, He has taken the
very taste for it away so it is no temptation to her. Our
preacher too has given it up. It is not because we've preached
it for we have never asked them even to stop it, but simply
because we've taught them 1 Cor 3:16,17 and the Spirit has
shown it to them. Our old woman from Mandalay has given
up tobacco and finds it hard work so far; a good proportion of
the class do not use it.

The school's first year ended on a high note, with a sense of
achievement and pride on the part of teachers and pupils. It was an
occasion that called for celebration and sharing of the women's
accomplishments.

Oct. 13, '93

Sunday in the evening we went to Lanmadaw and walked home with the women for the last time. Monday we finished up all the lessons and in the evening Mrs. Wells invited all the women to the house. We showed them pictures and had the Thomases and Gilmores in. Mr. Thomas asked them some questions on what they had been over. They recited the contents of each chapter of Genesis, Exodus and Acts — a sentence to each chapter. They can do the same for Luke. We had a good deal of singing and surprised Mr. Thomas by my Burmese version of "There is Sunshine in My Soul" of which he is very fond. He took my tambourine and put it through in great style. We heard that one of the women "cried all night because she wouldn't hear the tambourine again." Mr. Gilmore had translated the song into Karen and one of Mr. Seagrave's pastors on hearing it, in his prayer asked that someone would translate it into Burmese so they, the Burmans, could hear it too! He was very much pleased when he heard that it was done. After singing etc. we had tea and cake all around and the women went home. Though last of all, we all sang (in a ring) "God Be with You till We Meet Again."

Tuesday morning we had a prayer meeting, everyone praying. We couldn't help noticing how wonderfully they have improved: the best prayer offered was by Mah Kay Kin who could hardly put two sentences together in prayer when she came and had only been a Christian two months. In the afternoon we had a praise meeting, each one telling what she had to be thankful for and what she wanted us to ask for her. The experiences of some were most interesting; the oldest going back to Mr. Kincaid's [contemporary of Judson] time! They didn't want to go and we didn't close till after 4 P.M. They asked for some parting songs and before we got through, Miss Ranney and I were left singing alone, they all being in tears.

With the winding down and completion of the school year, Hattie and Ruth could once again involve themselves more fully in the concerns and activities of the mission community.

[Oct. 13, '93, continued]

This has been a red-letter week. In the first place at Kemindine Sunday morning I had 49 youngsters who all seemed interested. I wish you could see some of the <u>very tiny</u> ones — "knee-high to a grasshopper" — repeat a text or catechism question. It is very funny, they can hardly talk plain yet. Then at Lanmadaw there were three young men and a woman baptized, followed by the Lord's supper.

Monday, Wednesday and Friday mornings Miss Ranney and I have gone to help Mr. Seagrave with his preachers. He wanted personal testimony and the Bible to back it up. Miss Ranney spoke Monday and I Wednesday in Burmese as they all understand it. Miss Fredrickson, Miss Williams and Miss McAllister have done the same — the first and last through Than Bya as an interpreter. Miss McAllister <u>could</u> use the Burmese but thought they'd understand the other better. The men (20 of them) take very kindly to it and seem in fact to enjoy it. They take down all the texts quoted and are very cordial afterward. It is quite an innovation but the men are getting a blessing. Mr. Thomas and Prof. Gilmore help also. Mr. Seagrave has them all day. We have enjoyed it very much.

Monday evening we had the regular mission meeting, 58 missionaries were present, though that included George and Herbert Vinton who had never come before. They too seem to be waking up. It was a good meeting and a pleasant social afterward.

Tuesday evening we went to the prayer meeting at Dr. Cote's and it was another grand meeting, as good as the last.

I was left alone Wednesday evening and improved the time by translating another song — "Happy in Jesus."

Thursday evening we had the usual circle here and also the Sharps, Miss Hopkins, and Mrs. Carson. Prof. Gilmore gave a Bible reading and then we had experiences and lots of singing and a good time generally.

Sunday Lanmadaw was crowded and at 2 P.M. there was a mass meeting and College hall was packed solid and some outside. It was a praise meeting with singing in all sorts of languages. There were baptisms at both Lanmadaw and the English Church. Several young men from the Gov't High School have joined at Lanmadaw and things are looking up there.

The rest of the housecleaning has been done and things are nearly in shape for Convention. We expect Misses Hawkes and Watson and Dr. and Mrs. Cross.

The Conference and Convention was, as always, an important mission event. This year's provided Hattie and Ruth the opportunity to catch up with old friends and to meet some of the new missionaries who had come out during their furlough in America. With the Bible school closed for the season, Wahklu Lodge had room to accommodate its share of out of town missionaries.

Oct. 21, '93

Wednesday our four guests, Dr. and Mrs. Cross, and Misses Hawkes and Watson came and we had 13 callers beside, so that day was full.

Thursday and Friday we attended the Conference. There has been very little that could be called spiritual food, but some very important business on burning questions has been done and all in a peaceful way. They answered the questions sent by the Woman's Board. The points were (1) no more high schools or 7th Standards at present and new ones to be only to the 4th Standard, (2) Mission money to be used sparingly and with discretion on schools for heathen children, (3) examinations in future for missionaries (in the [native] language). A committee was appointed to consider having an Advisory Committee for Burma as per the enclosed slip. Also noted that attendants at these meetings pay their board so smaller stations can afford to have it.

Today the College Chapel was packed with natives and missionaries and the Convention business was carried on. Another important item of the Conference was a unanimous vote of approval of the College and a desire that it be supplied with suitable instructors and given an endowment! We feel these things are in answer to the many prayers that have been going up for the last few months.

Oct. 27, '93

Well, the big meetings are over and guests gone. We went to some of the Convention meetings but not to all. About 60 missionaries were in attendance and a larger number of natives

than usual — 300 Burmans, they said. All the meetings went
off nicely and there was great unity all around. Saturday
evening there was a good prayer meeting at Mr. Seagrave's and
some Karens standing outside were heard to say, "See how
those missionaries love one another."

A number of us wanted a more spiritual meeting as the
Conference has become so largely business and we knew that
several had come hoping for a blessing; so a meeting was called
here of such for Wednesday from 1:30 to 4:30 and from 7 to 9
P.M. Twenty-eight came in the afternoon and 72 in the evening.
Many had gone home. We had a very solemn and yet very
pleasant time and many were greatly helped. There were
different leaders for an hour each.

The Crosses left Wednesday morning and the Bassein ladies
Thursday morning, so we rearranged the rooms again and now
my desk is back in the study and my bedroom is more roomy
than it was during the rains.

The school year and Convention behind them, Hattie and Ruth
began to anticipate their next round of jungle trips.

Nov. 11, '93

I did more fixing for the jungle and we are expecting to
begin short trips on the RR [railroad] this coming week. The
rats got at our cots so the canvas of one must be replaced. We
hunted the town through for braid for our new jungle dresses
and it is not to be found. Next time you send please put in, say,
<u>four</u> rolls, to match sample. We expect the dresses to last a
long time so the braid will be in time to refresh the bottoms.

Nov. 25, '93

Thursday morning we went to town to get things needed
for the jungle — a new canvas for one of the cots — an oilcloth sheet to do up our bedding, a wash basin (!), stores, a
lunch box tin [sketch] etc. etc.

This is a red-letter day, for the box came from home with
the cookies and shoes (woolen) and best of all the photo of the
children [Hattie's nephew and niece] but it's hard to tell which
is sweeter that or the candies! Both are greatly admired and
<u>appreciated</u>! Sedley looks as natural as possible and Ada looks

very sweet but I shouldn't know her. The pillowcases from Mother are just what I needed as I had but two for that pillow which I use, liking it better nights than the big ones. Very many thanks for them. The sweets we sampled and found them the "right kind" so I've put them away for Christmas and will give the various packages to the others at that time. But, Oh the peanuts! Words fail!!

The shoes fit Miss Ranney and are "just elegant." She got her Christmas box today too. Her Mother and sister each sent me a little book, very handsome. There were candies for her too (though not as nice as mine!) and lots of cards and booklets we can use for gifts and in the work. She had material for two very pretty thin dresses.

December 1893 marked the end of Hattie's first year back in Burma, a year that had brought "great blessings." The Bible school had been more successful in attracting pupils than anticipated, no major accidents or disruptions had interfered with the work, and both women had maintained their health. Hattie and Ruth had demonstrated that they could carry not only the work of the school but their share of the work in the mission community as well. Having proved the soundness of their plan, Hattie and Ruth followed it, with little modification, for the next 38 years.

This first year also confirmed the women's compatibility as coworkers and companions. From the time of their return to Burma in 1892 until Ruth's death in 1937, Hattie and Ruth lived and worked as a team — "yoke-mates," as Hattie termed their relationship — with common goals and values that enabled them to work in harmony throughout a lifetime of shared affection and endeavor. Indeed, the relationship between the two women was so close that any attempt to ascribe specific features of the school or decisions regarding practice to one or the other would almost certainly distort the situation.

The following chapters offer a more in-depth look at each of the central aspects of their lives: the jungling trips, work with native women within the context of the Bible school, and Ruth and Hattie's work within the larger community, both native Christian and missionary alike.

11

Jungling

1894 to 1906

Over a span of twelve years following their return to Burma, Hattie and Ruth spent the cooler months of the year, November through February, in a series of trips into the jungle, preaching the gospel to the heathen and providing encouragement to native Christians. Many of the latter lived in primarily heathen communities, without the support of other Christians, and were often subjected to open hostility from their neighbors. Varying in length from one-day excursions to nearby villages, to tours of four weeks or more, the jungle trips were an important part of the "native work" to which Hattie and Ruth had dedicated themselves.

In the early years, recruiting women for the Bible school was an essential function of these trips; in later years, they afforded Hattie and Ruth the opportunity to visit the homes of their students and graduates, and observe the work they were doing. Their travels were also a chance to spread word about the school throughout the native Christian community and generate needed financial support for the school. On occasion, the two women joined forces with other missionaries for special events or evangelistic efforts, and often they were called upon to assist in mission stations where there was a special need.

Travel in the jungle was never easy or comfortable. It involved many forms of transport: oxcarts, ponycarts, native dug-outs, sampans, rowboats, sailboats, steam boats, railroads, and, almost always, a good deal of walking. Accommodation was often uncertain, and ran from non-existent to moderately comfortable: a corner of a local chapel, a native house, the deck of a boat, or (a luxury) a room in a government rest-house or bungalow.

Most of the trips were taken in the company of one or some-times two native preachers and a "boy" or cook to help carry the goods and provide the meals. Sometimes the preacher's wife would accompany her husband, perhaps with a "girl" to help her, and one or more Bible women. The party carried as much of its own food as possible and relied on native markets for additional supplies on longer trips. Canvas cots, folding chairs for long boat journeys, canvas curtains (to provide privacy in open native houses and the open decks of boats), mosquito netting, and utensils for cooking and eating were part of the usual traveling gear.

Their first year back, Ruth and Hattie made six trips, the one reported in the previous chapter being the longest of the 1892-93 season. In 1893-94, they repeated the Maubin-Dadaye-Keiklot-Mayale circuit and made seven other shorter trips as well.

In November of 1894, Hattie and Ruth began their third year of jungle work, this time with a more lengthy stay in a single town, Yandoon, a station they were to visit several times in their jungling years. As always, preparations were necessary before heading out.

Oct. 20, '94

We went to town and got our jungle topees, of the mushroom variety, which protects the back of the neck beautifully. That is what we need, for you can't hold an umbrella and climb up a narrow plank over rods of mud, or creep along on a native bamboo bridge or walk a slippery log! We also got a bottle filter for the jungle.

Oct. 31, '94

We are all packed up ready for a start tomorrow to Yandoon. Mr. Kelley spent last Sunday there and baptized five converts. He says the house we are to have has roof, upper and lower floors but no sides as yet. He told them to hurry up and said he would telegraph that we were coming, so we hope there will be part walls up at least. If not, curtains must do.

The rest of Monday, Tuesday and today have been full with gathering up our jungle outfits and getting them packed up and doing a thousand and one things preparatory to being away a month. As we go into an empty house we must take all we need for eating, sleeping and living generally besides lots of tracts, etc. etc. This time we'll take the organ too. I think we do well to get off with ten or eleven compact bundles — three clothing pahs; two baskets (cooking pots and tinned goods neat and ready); one folding table in a mat (Father's make); two folding chairs tied up (Frank's), and our two canvas chairs loose; one long bundle in canvas (the two cots and walls, i.e., curtains around them); one big bundle in oilcloth (bedding and pillows); and the organ in a mat. In our hands a little satchel and a tin lunch basket — our little filter, shawls, and umbrellas and that's all!! It is not half what the Roses take for a few days' trip but I've reduced packing to a science. I have bags for everything, one each for kitchen towels, knives and forks, dishes, bread (8 loaves to start on). The dishes are ironware and the bags go in the baskets.

We go this time by native steamer, no cabins or anything much but deck and awning — takes all day.

Yandoon, Nov. 7, '94

We left by the native steamship at 2 P.M. (it follows the tide); had few passengers, did some preaching, curtained off part of the deck at the bow and had our dinner and went to bed. Arrived at midnight but did not go ashore till light when the preacher here, Ko Myat Tha Done, came to meet us. We found the house we had engaged had a good tile roof, a good upper floor, but no walls at all! So we went into the Gov't rest house and stayed two days.

Saturday afternoon we moved to the new house, the walls being partly up. The man had enclosed a good-sized room with mats, no windows, and no door to the doorway, and in this we settled and still remain. Since then he has enclosed a small room in which Po Min and wife live, our boy sleeping in the still unenclosed space. The house, if ever finished, will be a substantial two story building. It just suits us for it is on the main street where there is constant passing to and fro, is high and rather conspicuous, so whenever we go out on the veranda we attract attention.

Every morning till 9 or 10 and every afternoon after 3:30 we go out. At first we went to the houses of the three men who were baptized two weeks ago and then to those interested and now we seldom appear in the street without being called in to preach in some house, and can have an audience any time by appearing on the veranda and sometimes without even that. Every day we have from three to five audiences with various number in attendance. The first two nights we had evening prayers at the preacher's house nearby but in a side street. I led and we made it a <u>real</u> prayer meeting, all praying even to the preachers' wives! a new departure! Since coming here we have followed the same plan, different ones leading off and all of us taking part.

Thursday 8th. Saturday morning and again yesterday we went to a big heathen school kept by a smart but very self-satisfied heathen woman of middle age. We visited her two years ago when here; she is one who says "yes, yes" to everything but really accepts nothing and ever since we have called her the "yes, yes" woman. She is just the same now but we got permission to come now and again to teach her children the Catechism and hymns. Yesterday there were nearly 60 present and we got them started on the Catechism, first two questions, and on "Jesus Loves Me." They and the idlers about get a good bit of preaching by the way.

After leaving there we were called into a nice big house by a Karen woman and had a good number of heathen Burman listeners. She was a Christian though ignorant. Coming on farther we were again called in and asked to preach to a household and their neighbors. Before we got home were twice again invited in but put these off till afternoon. We started at 2 P.M. this time and went to these two places and also to the home of a girl who had come here to call us.

We had callers in the middle of the day, and in the evening the veranda was fuller than ever, mostly men this time. Po Min had been over the river in the middle of the day and in the morning to a big funeral and was tired as were we. We shall try to be fresh for night hereafter if folks are coming at this rate.

This morning we went again to the home of one of the new disciples and had a long talk with his wife and mother, not particularly hopeful cases.

I've not told about Sunday yet. Before breakfast we all got together — three preachers, wife of Po Min, daughter of Myat Tho Done, three new disciples and we two, ten in all and went to the bazaar and stood by a tiny pagoda; got a big crowd by singing and then I began and Miss Ranney and the preachers followed, with plenty singing between, then we each spoke twice and before going home gave out tracts or rather leaflets. The people are eager for them. Altogether our reception is very different from anything we've found before. After breakfast we held a regular service in the house, quite a good number of heathen and all the Christians coming. Two men of the place have asked baptism but one is called away to his work so may not be here while we are here. After the morning service, in which we all took part after Po Min, we had Sunday School using the regular lessons. In the early evening we had another meeting — a good day.

I think we are getting to be quite Salvation Lassies ourselves! We have hats quite as astonishing as their pokes, and except for the drum and tambourines, I think we do about as they would. Perhaps they would not have so big a house, but the big house in a well known locality (next to the Hospital and near the Gov't School) is a distinct gain, for we can always invite anyone in any place in town and they know at once just where we are and often come from some distance to hear.

Yandoon, Nov. 15, '94

Two weeks today since we left home and the past week has been as full as the first of opportunities and blessing.

Every evening we've had a crowd in the house — Sunday night 40 grown men stayed quite two hours and could hardly be dismissed. Monday evening about 20; Tuesday quite 75 at one time and many others who came for a little while and went again. Each evening the meeting and talking has lasted from two to three hours. It has been moonlight and there have been no end of pwes and performances but most of those who have come have come here in express preference to heathen performances, and because they really wished to hear. There has been absolutely no reviling, fault-finding or anything disagreeable, and little effort to make out Buddhism the same or as good as Christianity. The fear of the Lord seems to have fallen upon the people and they are held in check; even the Mohammedans, so violent and bitter, have let us alone, though this house is owned by one (possibly <u>because</u> owned by one!).

Every morning and evening (except one morning) we have gone out and preached in from two to three different places each time. Twice we have visited the Burman wife of an English official now on leave in England. They were married Burman style with all the big men present etc. So far as she is concerned she is a <u>pukka</u> wife. I don't know that <u>he</u> is so straight. The Burmans respect her as properly married. At the first visit she was curious about our religion (he has taught her nothing; very likely don't know religious Burmese!) but rather bold and brazen. The second time we saw her alone, or with her parents, and she appeared very much better. Just as I wrote that, she herself called on us. I think she is sincere and would like to be a Christian but does not move in the matter till her husband returns.

Friday a man who was baptized last year came in bringing his heathen wife to whom we gave a talk. They live some distance off but he promised to come in for Sunday. That evening a young married man avowed his faith and asked baptism. Sunday evening the sister of one baptized just before we came did the same. The wife of another, whom we have several times visited, appears very differently, and instead of saying that her mind is all confused (literally "had many minds") she says emphatically that she believes Christ has forgiven her and she wants to be baptized, but she holds back a little for fear of heathen parents and friends. We hope she will decide this week. There is a man and wife who are <u>near</u> but not quite <u>in</u>. Neither can read and that makes it harder.

This is a very noisy place for three or so families with endless goats and children live in shanties under the eaves and keep things lively in Burmese and Hindustani all day and into the night; among them a pretty <u>girl</u> of <u>19</u> with <u>3</u> children, wife of a Mohammedan. But that is nothing to the theatrical performance held in a poongye-kyoung, very near us, for two nights the dreadful din of the band (!) and shouting of the actors being steadily kept up right through till dawn. It wasn't restful to say the least.

Then the people have been having the "rope-pulling" performance to bring rain. It did rain a little and they take all the credit for it. The rope-pulling <u>is</u> like a College rope pull exactly and quite as noisy or more so. Then someone gave a big offering which was paraded all over town to the sound of gongs and Burman bells (K'gees) and bands of music (?). First there were 6 fancy boxes (2 ft. high lacquered inlaid, etc.) 11 big trays of food, 32 immense fancy paper and bamboo figures of men, animals etc. etc., 12 boxes of plants and flowers, 2 bands(?) and numerous followers. Each of these articles was carried on a pole between two nicely dressed young men, though part of the heavier ones were on coolies' heads. Later a funeral of some big man went by, the coffin carried on a large funeral cart drawn by ten yoke of oxen! It was covered by very gay rugs.

Yandoon, Nov. 22, '94

Just then there was a great racket going along and we supposed it was a funeral or an offering to the priests; it proved the latter — an oxcart with white palings all around and a bright scarlet cover and yellow flags etc. and reposing under this cover an <u>immense black pig</u>, alive and wagging! A lot of young men followed, singing(?) and making a noise generally. One of them had almost nothing but <u>mud</u> on; as Miss Ranney remarked, "evidently belonged to the same family as the pig." The pig will be presented to the priests and set free and I suppose the offerers think they will lay up some merit.

Just now the wife of one of the new converts comes along with sweet meats to sell. It is the glutinous rice <u>popped</u> and mixed with native molasses. It is <u>very</u> good and we bought two pice worth! A big handful.

The work this week has been much the same as last week. I had thought that the dark night and lack of performances to call people out would keep them away from us evenings, but we have had from 20 to 30 men up every evening and often a number of women. The woman who keeps the school let us come three times in all, but was so ungracious and spoilt all we said and hindered the children from learning so that we have given that up.

Late Saturday night Mr. Kelley arrived with Saya Timothy, three Christians who used to live here and come on their own accord for a visit, and Arthur, his son, for a little change. Mr. Kelley and Arthur stayed at the preacher's and the rest here.

Sunday morning early we had a prayer meeting and then examination of four men for baptism. At 11 A.M. a preaching service and immediately after it we all went a long walk to the river and Mr. Kelley baptized the four, in the presence of a great crowd.

In the evening another meeting, to which two men from Meyale came. They have long wanted baptism but always just missed Mr. Kelley. So they were examined and answered so well that Mr. Kelley baptized them early Monday morning before taking the steamship for home. We shall stop to see them on the way home.

Monday afternoon we went to see the sister of one of the Christians, a girl of 15 who has a most fearful cancer, the result of an injury to her knee over a year ago. It is quite twice the size of her head, extends from the knee nearly to her body and is hard as a stone, an awful looking thing. She spent a month in the Hospital here (which we have visited) but has been home two months or more and in all that time since returning home has not been bathed or even her face washed. I never saw anyone so filthy in my life. We urged them to bathe her and I gave her some soap and soft cloths but the native doctor thought it wouldn't do and so they have left her as she is. Such are the tender mercies of heathendom! The doctor in the Hospital said the only hope was in amputation but they'll never agree to that. If they would allow it, Mr. Kelley would bear the expense of removing her to Rangoon Hospital where she would be kept clean and fed. They are so poor sometimes she has enough and sometimes not.

Wednesday morning we went for a long, long walk to visit the house of the three brothers baptized on Sunday. They were very cordial and we had a pleasant time. A number of relatives and friends gathered and Po Min preached to them. They are fishermen.

This morning we went a long ways in the opposite direction to visit the other one of the four. He and his wife live in a tiny house that would go into Mother's bedroom and leave space to spare. We sat on the edge of the tiny veranda and were nearly eaten up by mosquitoes while we talked with them. They were preparing the popped rice I spoke of at first and offered us some. It is about as nice as popcorn and never has any hard kernels. He brought out his Gospel of Luke and wanted the miracles pointed out.

I forgot Tuesday. In the morning we went by invitation of some women to the bazaar and had a little chance to talk; then to the wharf and had a crowd. On the way home got into houses on two streets we had not had a chance on before, and in the afternoon took a long walk in a different direction to the home of a back-slider. A poor, weak, inoffensive man who, in a Christian land or community would make a good Christian, but is kept in abject fear by his wife and relatives who simply won't let him be a Christian, and he has not force or faith enough to leave them or withstand them. Po Min and I each gave them and him some plain truths in plain language. His wife actually beat him when he was baptized a year ago.

There are five or six women connected with the Christians who, we believe, will before long come out on the Lord's side. One we feel sure has been truly converted since we came.

Last evening Ko You Gin, the pastor at Lanmadaw, arrived and will help for two or three days. He was anxious to come and is a real help. Has been a Christian for 40 years, and his life has been straight all through and that is a good deal to say. Is about 60 years old. He said when he was converted there were only about 75 Burman Christians!

We leave here Tuesday or Wednesday next and get home by Friday, the 30th. We left Rangoon on the 1st.

Nov. 30, '94

We intended to take a boat and stop in at the villages by the way, but could not get a boat and so had to take the steamship and stop off at Mayale to see the two new Christians and the old ones. It is the third year we have visited them. We spent two nights and days with them and went to the Upper Village to see the two new ones and preach to the heathen. Miss Ranney went in a dugout just broad enough for her to sit in nicely and paddled at the stern by one man. I preferred to walk and did so crossing various small ravines on a single <u>narrow</u> plank and going through a big plantain grove. The mosquitoes were so thick I had to beat them off all the way. I dislike little tipsy boats and Miss Ranney dislikes narrow bridges. I enjoyed the walk and she her ride and we returned as we came.

Both nights we had meetings before dark and were simply forced to go to bed at 7 P.M. because by that time we were tired of keeping ourselves in motion, and then not succeeding in keeping off the mosquitoes — great big ones the size of Rangoonites.

We left by the steamship at 11 A.M. yesterday; gave out some tracts and after a while a group of middle-aged men asked us to talk to them so I gave them a summary of Bible truth and they listened respectfully and well, till we neared Kemindine where they left. Had we tried to force it on them they might not have done so well — not that we wait for an invitation generally, but it seemed best this time.

We reached home about 4:30 and got ourselves cleaned up. As we had no proper bathroom the whole month you will see that we needed it!

As a summary of the work done — we presented the Gospel 96 times (to groups varying from 2 to 80) on 22 streets and many more than that houses. On most of the occasions we both spoke. We distributed 1,050 leaflets, 175 Burman and 13 Tamil and Telegu tracts to those who really wanted them, and might have used a few more. The preachers reached an entirely different set, though I doubt if they preached more than half as many times. This does not include any of the evening meetings at which we, for any reason, did not take part. We held Burman services every evening for 27 nights in succession, from one to three hours long.

The first trip of the 1895-96 season was another month-long visit to Yandoon, followed by six additional trips farther afield. The 1896-97 year began with a short visit to Yandoon, followed by a longer boat trip to Kyeiklat, Bogalay, Kyun'-la-moo. The latter ended in an all-night ride.

Nov. 18, '96

After starting at midnight we came to a sentinel post, and were told to stop and tie up for the rest of the night, which meant waiting till noon again for the tide and not enough food for breakfast on board! The preachers and men replied there were English passengers on board and went on, but they sent a sampan after us in a hurry and the preachers told us to put on our hats and go out; so we did and I called out in English to come alongside and say what they had to say. The sight of our big hats and the English voice was quite sufficient. They didn't come alongside but after profuse apologies went back and we went on, though a dozen similar boats were tied up. It is a Gov't arrangement to stop paddy stealing and the men were all right in what they did, and so were we!

We reached home about 11 A.M. tired, dirty (only one bath in two weeks) and hungry. It seemed good to be civilized again, eat from a table and stand up straight!

On December 4, 1896, less than a week later, they were on their way to Upper Burma for a trip of more than a month. The trip up the Irrawaddy to Mandalay was a familiar one to Hattie; the rest of the way to Bhamo was a new experience for her. A brief stop at Sagaing gave her an opportunity to revisit the mission there.

Dec. 9, '96

The place is not much like the Sagaing I knew in '88, the old wall leveled down a few feet and made into a beautiful road, a strand road and lots of other roads all over the place (where before there were mere cart tracks and byways), gharries and street lamps, a steamship landing, a railroad depot etc. etc. The mission compound is all leveled, sodded and is, with its grand big tamarind trees, the finest place in Sagaing, and in the best location. The little mat house we lived in is now a school and meeting place. There is a little girls' school. We occupied my old room in the mission house.

Before leaving Sagaing we went and saw the Hascall baby's grave in a tiny plot walled in, with the graves of soldiers killed by dacoits. No more will be buried there. The cemetery is elsewhere.

After stops at Mandalay and Shwebo, the trip continued on to Katha, and then to Bhamo.

Katha, Upper Burma, Dec. 26, '96

I mailed my last from Shwebo. We got our goods packed and on a cart before dark and arrived at the depot just at dark, though the train wasn't due till 8 P.M., for we have no lantern and the hand lamp has to be packed. The train was 3/4 hours late and after we got aboard we learned that the boiler had cracked and we must wait for another engine to come. We had a Tamil lady with us and we all went to bed, I up aloft, and slept some. The train finally started about 1:30 A.M. and five hours late! This is the only through train to Katha. The next morning we enjoyed the scenery very much, a range of mountains each side and finally before changing cars we went through a beautiful pass, high hills, deep valley, clear stream cutting through rock, etc. etc. When we changed cars we had to go into the first class apartment as the second was full of native men, and so were with two couples of English officials, one from Burma and one from India. They were very nice to us. The scenery on the branch line was most wild and beautiful, high hills covered with lovely jungle impenetrable to anything but wild beasts, and they say there are plenty — leopards, wild elephants, bull-bison, deer, etc. We didn't see any!

We reached Katha on the Irrawaddy River about 3 P.M. instead of 10:25 A.M. We knew these English people would fill the Gov't. rest house and we didn't care to go there if we could find any other place. There is a house here owned by the American Baptist Mission Union and rented, so we went there and asked the man, who is the doctor here, if he knew of any empty house we could get. He said he thought there were no empty houses but if we liked he could let us occupy an empty ward in the (Punjabi) Police Hospital. The preachers went back for our goods and we went to the Ward and waited for them. They couldn't get a cart for a long time and so didn't arrive till dark and then we had to send for oil to get a light, and after much trouble the boy managed to get us hot water and we had bread and coffee. Had very little all day but were thankful for something hot, and got to bed.

The Ward is a great building, 18 by 80 feet with 17 wooden cots on a side and a big veranda on three sides; very high but well-built and as warm as it could be, being so immense. We curtained off one end and camped out there, the preachers taking two cots and the boy one farther on in the building; our tiny lamp didn't begin to light up even one end of it, altogether a striking contrast to the tiny bamboo structure we've just left in Shwebo, which had bamboo floor, mat sides, and thatch roof, while this is teak all through, the posts being immense tree trunks. The native doctor in charge of the other like ward is very kind and has helped us to water etc. Our boy is a most helpless creature and doesn't know how to do under any new circumstances. The food is scarce, chickens being all there is and those not plentiful just at Christmas time. The cook went Christmas morning to buy some, but after a long time returned with nothing at all!! Saying they asked too much and the chickens were so small one wouldn't make a meal! Whether he thought we would therefore go without eating in this place or not I don't know but we fortunately had a tin of salmon, which we had him open and cook some rice and we had our Christmas breakfast and dinner of salmon and rice and coffee. It wasn't bad.

We went out morning and evening and worked among the people, who are Burmans and Shans all mixed up. And are not very ready to listen or take leaflets, yet we had a fairly good time. We got the preachers to buy us two chickens which <u>are</u> small to be sure but will make us three meals and then we expect to be on the steamship for Bhamo, which we take tomorrow morning if all is well.

<u>Dec. 28</u> We were told the steamship would leave yesterday, so we were up early and got on board only to find it would <u>not</u> leave till today as the English mail is late. We couldn't go back, but took second class, i.e., a canvas cabin on the deck with a table, two chairs and two canvas cots. We settled and had a quiet day, going ashore and holding a street meeting in the afternoon. We slept fairly well and will start this morning, we suppose.

S.S. *Mandalay*, Irrawaddy River, Jan. 4, '97
My last was mailed at Katha as we were leaving. We had a quiet pleasant passage to Bhamo, passing through a very beautiful defile where the river was narrow and on one side the rock rose straight up from the water, I don't dare say how many hundred feet. We had to look right <u>up</u> to see the top at all. Next to Gibraltar it was the finest rock scenery I ever saw. There was one English woman on board, and when we had evening prayers with the preacher on deck she came and sat with us and seemed to like the singing. There were <u>very</u> few Burmans on board, a dozen and a half at most.

We reached Bhamo about noon Tuesday. No one met us, but we got to the Mission houses all right and found that it had been telegraphed that our steamship wouldn't arrive till 3 or 4 P.M., which was why we weren't met. Mr. Roberts and his daughter Dora entertained us, and we enjoyed sleeping in a proper bed (after two weeks on our cots) and being quite warm enough.

Dr. and Mrs. Griggs (Shan) and Mr. Hanson (Kachin) are the only other missionaries here now. Neither we nor our men were able to do much work, for the people are mixed to the last degree: Kachin, Shan, Chinese, Natives of India, and a few Burmans, not of the better class, and more or less mixed even then. Dr. Griggs took us a cart ride of two miles out to a Shan village but only his man could do any preaching. He also took us over to a very old and fine Chinese temple, which the Chinese held as a fort against the Burmans at one time. A very curious interesting place with no end of images of all sorts, grotesque and ugly enough to frighten anybody. A theater is also provided in the temple. Mr. Roberts took us there in his old dogcart and showed us where his home was when he was driven out by the Chinese, where the land was that Thibaw gave him, etc.

Miss Ranney and I drove out in the dogcart and Mr. Roberts and Dora rode ponies (or rather one pony and one <u>mule</u>) to a Kachin Christian village 5-1/2 miles out. The Kachins are tiny folk, very picturesque and very dirty, except a few who have been Christians for some time and have put off their barbarous jewelry and cleaned themselves up. They are the folks that wear some dozens of light black rings around their loins and more just below the knee, and astonishing earrings — rods 6 inches long with red streamers from the front end. Ears pierced not in the lobe or outer edge, but through the main part of the ear rather high up. We saw one woman weaving, sitting on the ground with no loom whatever. Two sticks in the ground held one end of the web and a band around her body drew it tight, she bracing her feet against two other sticks and the shifting of the threads and putting the bobbin through was all by hand in the most laborious manner possible; another was pounding out rice, and others freeing it from the chaff. The women do all the hard work.

We got home again at 10:30. The ride was mostly through a very beautiful woods, wild jungle, grand old trees and big creepers over them. There are beautiful high hills all around Bhamo. I couldn't find any curios at all, Shan or Kachin. Walnuts, chestnuts and persimmons seemed to be all there was different from Lower Burma to be had. The caravans of Chinese or Shans or Kachins with their pack bullocks or pack mules (tiny ones) were very interesting and quaint.

Shan village.

One day Miss Ranney led a girl's meeting in the afternoon and I a general one in the evening at Mr. Roberts' request. Some could understand Burmese, but it was all put into Kachin besides.

Mr. Roberts saw us aboard the steamship and it will take three days to reach Mandalay. There are five French and seven German tourists on board and we hear French talked all day. Two of them can't speak English. <u>Very</u> few Burman passengers. This is the <u>bazaar</u> boat, fitted up like one, and on the way up it makes stops of several hours and all the villagers come aboard and do their shopping. But going down it makes very short stops and we've not gone ashore at all.

Mandalay, Jan. 6th We couldn't reach here last evening, but did reach the great Mingone pagoda and bell (you have pictures of it, I think) and the Captain took us all ashore in the ship's boat. It was dark, but with plenty of lanterns we managed to see the big bell and over a dozen of us went in under it and there was room for as many more. The Irrawaddy Flotilla Co. has raised it and hung it between two great iron pillars, the Burmans paying the base cost. A log of wood thrown at it brought out the sound, as loud as we cared to hear. We went up to the front of the pagoda and viewed that also, and then back to the steamship. We had wanted to see it but had given it up and so were glad of a chance without a pice extra expense.

Think that is all this time. Next from home, I trust. Upper Burma is all very well, but we've no desire to move up here yet!

Jan. 15, '97

My last was from Mandalay, I believe. We left there Thursday A.M. and reached Meiktila about 4:30 P.M. The Packers were very glad to see us, and so were our two girls who are working with Mrs. Packer — Mah Yone and Mah Tha Tha.

The next day we and all the workers took two oxcarts and went out five or six miles to visit two villages. Mrs. Packer had thought of going but wasn't able to, so we went and had a fairly good time. Dr. Packer has a bad leg and it takes Mrs. Packer an hour a day to dress it. She is poorly too, and they are going up on the mountains near Mandalay soon. Saturday Dr. Packer took us on two nice long rides in his dogcart and another on Monday morning, which we enjoyed all the more from not having any trap of our own. We also helped in the woman's meeting Saturday noon. It was the week of prayer, and our men took their turns in leading, and Po Min preached Sunday morning. Altogether we felt the last was the best; we enjoyed our visit there very much. The situation is very pleasant though now for lack of rain everything is perfectly dry and brown, and the lake very low indeed.

We left Monday about 2 P.M. and got home next morning at 7 A.M. and were not sorry!

The 1897-98 trips began with the annual visit to Yandoon, then on to Shwegyin to assist in that field.

Shwegyin, Dec. 13, '97

Miss Knight has no companion or Bible woman so we have brought our preacher and intend to travel with her for a few weeks. We left Rangoon Thursday at 8 A.M., reached Nyounglebin at 3 P.M., took carts four miles to the river, then a big boat towed us for an hour to a big sand bar across the river, over which we walked or waded in sand, children coolies carrying our goods, and then about three hours in a small steam launch to Shwegyin. We had six parcels and Miss Knight had a <u>lot</u> of things for other folks as well as herself — 22 in all, of all sizes, shapes, and kinds which had to be handled for all of the changes!

Friday and Saturday I just worked hard on the next Sunday School lesson paper which must be handed in Jan. 1, and hence done <u>now or never</u> as we shall not be in again before then. I got it done and was very thankful.

Sunday I taught the Sunday School and in the afternoon we had a service in the jail, much work has been done there and a good number converted in the past. Three preachers went with us and we had an hour service. Then one of the two English families in the place came to the house for a little English service.

Today we have been packing as there are three of us and we are going for three weeks or so, out in the district where there is little or nothing to be had; we have to take <u>every</u>thing. We expect to leave the house about 8 A.M. — one hour by cart, eight hours by launch, spend the night in a native house at a village, by cart or boat to another and then 20 miles by cart to destination "Belin," way off southeast of here, a big town. Three preachers are going with us and two Burman men Miss Knight wants to have learn how to preach, so altogether we'll have a party of nine, including our cook.

Shwegyin, Dec. 31, '97

After my last, we finished working in Belin, not meeting with any encouragement except that, at the last, one old man seemed to be quite a hopeful inquirer. We think he will come out. One night drunken men came and broke up the meeting.

Wednesday morning (Dec. 22) we got up at 4:30 and got off by cart to go to a village eight or ten miles off to return the next day. In crossing a little plain we came to a stream which must be forded. The oxen didn't want to go at all and when we got into the middle of it, with the water close up to the bottom of the cart, one ox kicked about and finally turned short about and took us back onto the bank we had left. So the driver went farther along and drove them into the water again. We reached the middle of the stream and <u>stuck</u>, the oxen wouldn't or couldn't go another step and there we sat, unable to get out backward or forward. If the three preachers and boy had not come up then I don't know how long we might have sat there. The preachers waded in and tried to help but it wouldn't go, so they went back and laid aside their good clothes and came in again and by dint of much yelling, pushing and pulling got us started again and through the stream. It was not an experience we cared to repeat nor did the driver, for he brought us home next day by another road and avoided the stream.

At the village we found an empty native house and took it. The people and children just swarmed in almost on top of us. We talked all day long to them, and gave leaflets all through the village. Found one man quite a hopeful case. To eat our meals we had to shut up the doors, fasten them, and then the children peeked in at every crack and even enlarged the cracks!

On our way back next day we stopped at another village a few hours and had the best listeners of all, and gave leaflets through still another hamlet.

We were quiet the next day and Christmas we got up at 4 A.M. and started off for some more villages. Had to cross a stream again but got over all right, though in returning one ox stuck and fell in a mud hole just as we came out of the water and we all jumped out over the muddy wheel so he could get up and go on. We had to walk behind the cart for a ways through high grass which had wiped the mud from the wheels, and our dresses forthwith wiped the mud from the grass. We were a sight to be seen when we clambered into the cart again!

We visited three villages and got home just at sunset for our Christmas dinner. Miss Knight and I went up the stairs with our hands full and Miss Ranney stopped to see to dinner, sending one of the boys up with our chairs and several other things. He is a tall strong man and had his hands full, and as he reached the third step from the top, it fell through to the floor with him, all the things flying in all directions with a great clatter. He was hurt on his head and somewhat dazed and bruised but no bones broken, and we were so thankful that it was not Miss Ranney who would naturally have come up next. We found that the stairs were just put together and put up in place and not a nail about them, and the side pieces had gradually spread apart till the steps finally fell out. We sent for the owner (Miss Ranney was downstairs and we upstairs and no dinner for any of us till those steps were again in place!) and he came and was much disgusted, but he, a coolie, and our men all went to work and put the sides and steps together — all had been taken down and laid on the floor — and then with new ropes <u>tied</u> the two side pieces together at top and bottom and with a great effort lifted them into place and <u>tied</u> them to the upper floor! And then after dark we had our Christmas dinner — meat, potatoes, parsnips (tinned), and a tinned plum pudding.

We left Belin at 5 A.M. in carts coming back over the 20 miles as we went. At Kyeukin we stayed in the Gov't rest house.

We left the next evening at 7 P.M. in a row boat to go the 12 miles by canal to Winpedaw. It was moonlight and two men towed that boat with 11 people and no end of baggage in it that 12 miles in 4-1/2 hours, without stopping! When we arrived we took our chairs up into an open native rest house, hung up curtains, and we spent the rest of the night also in our chairs, though Miss Knight lay on the bamboo flooring with her bedding. We left by launch at 7 A.M., left the launch for a rowboat at 3:40 P.M., and reached Shwegyin sawmill at 6 P.M.,

being poled and towed these two hours and getting stuck
several times. Then Mr. Harris met us and we rode two miles
in oxcarts up to the house. The canal rowboat and the launch
were both very tipsy and rolled dreadfully, so it was a very
tiresome journey and we were very thankful to get here, wash
up, and have dinner. We shall go back to Rangoon Monday
(Jan. 3) and we shall then have had 88 miles of cart ride, and I
don't know how much by boats.

Jan. 8, '98

Monday we were up at 4:30 A.M. and got off in a cart
for the steamship landing, where we took a sampan out to
the launch which was a tiny one and simply packed solid
with natives and the holds packed with their goods. There
was an Eurasian man on board and our three chairs occupied the entire width of the deck!! It was not a pleasant four
hours and we were thankful to get off. As there was such a
crowd we preferred going all the way to the railroad by cart
rather than be re-packed in a rowboat, so had a mile or
more of very rough riding and four miles on a good road
and at last reached the railroad and took the train in a half
hour and then at 2:30 P.M. we broke our fast, having neither
eaten or drunken since 5 A.M.

We reached the house about 8:40 P.M.

A year later Hattie and Ruth were off on their third long trip of
the 1898-99 year.

Thongua, Jan. 19, '99

We left by steamship on Saturday and went to Kyouk-tan, a
three hours' ride. We put up in the Gov't bungalow, worked
the town, and on Sunday went to a tiny Methodist Sunday
School whose teacher is a Baptist. On Tuesday we had an
oxcart and went out three miles to Kyaik-a Maw and visited
that old girl of ours who is dying of consumption. Found her
quite bright and comfortable but very thin and her voice very
husky.

We left Kyouk-tan at 4 P.M. and came up the stream to
Thongua. We were forced to take first class (a very tiny cabin
and deck place) because the rest of the steamship was packed

with a theatrical troupe and belongings, a rough hard crowd,
dirty and noisy; and to have sat in their midst would have been
misery, even if there had been space for us. We made our
dinner on a little cold hash, bread and butter, and a cup of
coffee. The boy managed to boil some water so we could have
at least that. We expected to stay in the Gov't bungalow here
but it was full and so the clerk of the steamship (a Kulah) let us
have a small corner of his front room in a house nearby and we
got to bed there about 11 P.M.

The next day a family of Methodist Christians here engaged for us an empty Burman house next to them and we
moved here. It is ordinary sized and as it has been empty for a
month is not too <u>lively</u>! As we weren't expecting to take an
empty house, we had nothing to use as a table so had to use a
cot till the bed was made up, and then the floor; but now the
woman next door has lent us a <u>table</u>, one foot high and 11 x
18 inches in size! — a great convenience! What the table won't
hold, the floor will. As we never have more than rice and
curry, or else stew and potatoes and something to drink, the
floor is not used so much as it might be. We've been out in
town and have had a good time.

Friday, Jan. 20, evening. This morning we went to another
village near here, where we have been before — the <u>longest</u>
village I ever saw. We were walking and talking for 3-1/2 hours
and we didn't reach the farther end then.

We want to go from here to Tada'ua where there is a church,
but the steamships are leaving in the night now and if the one
tomorrow reaches the town we must get off at, before light, we
can hardly manage it, I fear, as we have to land ourselves and our
goods in a sampan and we know no one in the town. We take a
cart from there to Tada'ua across the rice fields.

Jan. 29, '99

After my last we found that the steamship would leave in
the night, so we gave up stopping off at Tada'ua and sent Saya,
but his steamship stuck on the mud and delayed him so he
couldn't go either for Sunday, so came on home.

We stayed over Sunday, did not have more meetings as the
child of the Methodist man came down with smallpox; another
in the house back of us had it already. We frequently see people

with it just in the drying up stage, in the groups we are talking
to. I suppose we are exposed every time we go out.

Saturday morning we went to a small village just on the
outskirts of Thongua and coming back had to cross some fields
to reach the main road. Half way over we saw a white ox come
towards us full tilt. We <u>ran</u> as fast as we could and were quite
frightened, but the animal went by us and we reached the road
in safety. Some people there said that ox was not chasing <u>us</u>, it
always ran away when it was let out of the cart. If we had
known it sooner we would have felt better! Mrs. Crumb was
very seriously gored by one of her own animals once and the
natives are occasionally hurt by them. But we're not so afraid
of them as of Burmese buffaloes, the ugliest creatures in looks
and hateful to Europeans.

Later that year, Ruth and Hattie were called upon to serve as
hostesses for the annual Burman Association meetings, a task that
their jungle experience prepared them to handle better, perhaps,
than some of the other missionaries.

Feb. 25, '99

It took all Monday and Tuesday to get ready, and Wednesday morning we left for the Association, prepared to entertain
the missionaries attending. We were waked that morning
before 4 o'clock by a big fire nearby. It gave us a great start
and made me feel quite weak, but we got ready and left the
house at 6 A.M. with three small boxes, two baskets, two pahs,
two bed bundles, one bread bag and two chairs, had one hour
on a steam launch and then a five-mile cart ride of 2-1/2 hours
and arrived at the village.

They had just rebuilt the chapel and made it smaller and so
low we couldn't have a dining place underneath as we could
formerly. However, we settled and got our things in order for
our guests who arrived the next evening, Mr. McGuire, Mr.
Cummings, Misses Chapman and Hanna.

Friday, Saturday, and Sunday we had four meetings a day and
an extra woman's meeting on Sunday. Mr. Valentine, Mrs. Roach,
and the WCTU missionary Miss Parrish came Saturday for over
Sunday. Sunday morning we went two miles in carts to a lake at
the foot of the Syriam Pagoda and 10 were baptized.

It was a <u>very</u> pleasant occasion indeed — that and the meetings as a whole. Miss Ranney kept house, and they all enjoyed their food very much. The Christians insisted on paying for all our food, i.e., the stores we brought, beside furnishing chickens, beef, and eggs on the ground.

We were up at 4 A.M. and got everybody off and then we packed up and got off ourselves at 6:30, very dirty, tired and hungry.

A month-long visit to Zigon opened the 1899-1900 season. It was followed by an unexpected request for help from a missionary family in Hsipaw, in the Shan States, Upper Burma, which required a long and arduous trip by a variety of transport.

Feb. 2, '00

We expected to be in Yandoon by this time but we heard that the Leeds in Hsipaw were in great need of helpers, had telegraphed for an ayah, and also sent for our two girls who before agreed to go there, to come up with a young fellow who has been in the Theological Seminary. The Leeds are new to the country or they would not have asked <u>that</u>! Neither the girls nor the ayah could go on with a young man like that, without some responsible party along like a reliable man and his wife or some missionary. The need of the Leeds was so great, however, that we postponed our proposed trip and sent the preachers out to find the two girls. One is ready to go and we expect Saya Po Min back today when we will know about the other. If we get <u>both</u> girls (both graduates of our school) we think of taking them ourselves to Hsipaw. It is quite a big undertaking but it <u>might</u> mean saving Mrs. Leeds' life to have help and company at this time. We suppose she has an infant. She is a frail, young, quite inexperienced lady.

<u>Saturday 3rd.</u> We have just decided to go to Hsipaw at once. We leave by mail train Monday evening; hope to get a pass on the construction train beyond Mandalay for 80 miles and then finish by 52 miles carting. If all goes well we will be on the way back by the time you get this.

Nhamcho, Feb. 9, '00

We started as we expected to on Monday evening by the mail train, with our good cook (in a cast-off suit of Frank's), our preacher Po Min and the two young women we are taking up to Hsipaw. No ayah whatever could be found so we have come on without; had hoped to get someone of some use in Mandalay but failed.

We reached there Tuesday at noon and went first of all to get a pass on the construction train to Maymyo. Got it all right and then went to Miss Spear's. After tiffin hunted an ayah and called at the Boys' School where Mr. Valentine got me to give a short talk to the boys, over 200 of them. Mrs. Hancock and a number of the Christians we know called in the evening, two women who were in our school the first year. One gave us two tins of milk and 16 eggs.

We were up at 4:30 A.M. as we were to take a train at 6 and the Station is a long ways off and our goods had to go by oxcart. We all reached the station in good time for a 6 o'clock train but found it went at 6:30. We took it to Myohoung, 30 minutes ride and waited there for the construction train, in which we finally started at 9 A.M.! We and a lot of natives (mostly of India) were stowed with our goods any-which-way. Most of them on top of rails in open trucks, but we and several others were piled on and among barrels of Portland cement in a covered freight car, so escaped having our clothes burned full of holes from the engine cinders.

It is only 39 miles to Maymyo but we arrived at 6 P.M.!! Needless to say we were not moving all the time. It is most interesting and sometimes "skirful"; the track went up a mountain this way, the three tracks being like this [sketch] (engines at both ends of train). The view was extended and fine but one didn't care to glance <u>down.</u> After that there were various similar turnings and short tunnels. All the party enjoyed it exceedingly.

At Maymyo we started out to find the Gov't bungalow, walked a mile or more and found it <u>full</u>! Walked back, our cartload of goods following and found an empty room at the railroad station which we were allowed to use. We then had a dinner of hot rice and warmed over chicken, the first proper meal all day for any of us. We and the two girls slept on the floor and Peter and Po Min in another room.

Next morning we started again in the same car and with the same barrels at 7:30 A.M. and came on up the line at a better pace, with only two long waits. Had some nice views of mountains but mostly were on a high plateau in the midst of jungle. At one place there was a long deep cutting through the top of a peak and an upgrade. They tried six times to make it but could not, each time running back to the level. At last a coal car was dropped and we finally got through and went on, reaching here at 2 P.M. Walked a <u>long</u> ways to the Gov't bungalow and back again about the goods as there were neither coolies nor carts to be had. Finally a cart was found and the goods got up here about 4:30 P.M. Dinner was the next thing, as we'd nothing hot since a cup of coffee at 6 A.M.

After that we went to the village headman for carts to go on as we are two stages from the place the mission carts are to meet us. He had the one we had just used but no other and couldn't get one for today but would try for tomorrow, so we have been obliged to wait over a day. Everything is in use by the railroad builders and the Gov't and it is hard to get.

Saya came across a man and wife baptized by Mr. Carson in Thayetmyo some time ago. He is a Christian in secret here as he is the only one and not bold enough to let his light shine. He owns carts which have just come in from Hsipaw and the oxen are too tired to start back at once. We feel we must get on to Kok-teik tomorrow (Saturday) and walk ourselves, then spend Sunday there and go on Monday with mission carts if they arrive.

Just this minute a man from Hsipaw has just appeared saying he has been waiting here three days for us with the mission carts, so as soon as two more can be got we start on, so can't send this now.

<u>Later</u>. No carts were to be had before tomorrow morning so we still wait here, and I can mail this. The young man is a Karen preacher who came up three years ago and has never been back. Our girls (who are Karens) are delighted to meet one of their kind; he's already been reading Shan to them, which seems to come easy to Karens. He has one mission cart and as he has goods to take up it will need two more, which are promised. So if they are forthcoming we shall start by daylight tomorrow.

The climate is very different up here, so dry and much cooler. The water this morning was the coldest thing I've felt since we arrived in Burma!

There is a range of mountains to be seen from this bungalow, a very pleasant sight after the endless paddy fields of Lower Burma.

We met a Canadian man, a hard drinker, I fear, who wanted to be helpful but didn't get a chance. He has been in Rochester and Buffalo etc., is or was working on the famous Gok-teik bridge, which we are very sorry to miss seeing. Everybody we met was kind to us but the drinking and swearing is not nice, to say the least.

Hsipaw (Thibaw), Feb. 15, '00

You see we have reached the end of our long journey. We left the place where I wrote last, at 7:30 A.M. being hindered by the difficulty of getting carts. We went down, <u>down, down</u> by winding roads like the railroad I spoke of in my last letter, which were frightsome sometimes, it being so steep and deep down from the roadside, which was often none too wide, nor good. At the bottom we got out and walked across the bridge over a rushing clear stream at the base of high hills on both sides rather too high to call <u>hills</u>.

We walked up the other side to ease the oxen till we came to the first PWD bungalow. Here we had breakfast and rested a while, going on at 2:30 P.M. We walked till about 4:30, climbing up the other hillside by roads not so steep as before. All day we had beautiful mountain views which, after the exceeding flatness of Lower Burma, were very refreshing. We saw a good deal of the earth work for the new railroad which is done beyond here to Lashio.

Having reached high land again we got into the carts and rode till 8:30 when we arrived at the next bungalow, eight miles from the first, and found a room, though there was one Eurasian man in another room. We got dinner at 9:15 and went to bed as fast as possible, thoroughly tired, and thankful the next day was Sunday.

We had two services and the man attended and was very "decent," which all English men met in this way are <u>not</u>.

Monday we were up early and off for nine miles more through rolling country with mountains in the distance. One of our cartmen was a queer fellow, fool or knave, hard to tell which. Our cook was in his cart and in a few minutes he got out and ran on ahead and Peter had to drive the cart most of that trip! He didn't want Peter to ride in his cart. The next day Peter drove the mission cart and the Shan driver walked, and the last day the other driver behaved and let Peter ride with him.

The third day we went 12 miles and had breakfast about 1 P.M. and decided to go no farther, but after dinner a man and no end of followers arrived and our people wished to go on three miles to a native zayat where they said we could stay. So we started out, we two and the two girls, to walk. It was 6 P.M. but daylight. Soon it was dark but for the moon, and, the carts not catching up, we walked all the way by a winding road through thick woods. It was a trifle "scary" but we saw nothing and met no one the whole way. Found the zayat but only three walls and plenty of natives about. However, we curtained off a corner and curled down for the night.

We got little sleep and were up at 3:30 and off as soon as possible by moonlight. After two hours the roads became very bad and we walked for nearly two hours more and finally crossed the big bridge over the Cheng-the River and reached a bungalow about 8 A.M. but as it was but seven miles more to Hsipaw, all wanted to come right on and we did so, reaching here at just 11 A.M., the ninth day from Rangoon. A dirtier set you never saw, for the dust lies three to six inches deep in the roads and the oxen go so slowly we can't leave our own dust!

We found the Leeds and nine-day-old baby all well and bright, and have been getting cleaned up and a little rested. This house is the first one you come to in reaching Hsipaw, the town all being farther on. We came the last 53 miles by cart. When Mrs. Leeds came she had to take the whole 132 miles by cart.

It is very cold mornings here so that a fire is very comfortable, but hot in the middle of the day — a dry heat, not like Rangoon.

Our girls did beautifully on the journey; were bright and cheerful all the way. The food was hard to get till the third day when Saya shot four jungle fowl and all had "a big feed." We had a chicken which a Kulah Christian at one station gave us. At that station there is a little mission house where we put up for the night.

Dr. Leeds took me to the Post Office yesterday in a dogcart; the roads are horrible and it was quite as tiresome as the worst of our cart trip. Not much like any place under the English!

We expect to start back Wednesday next at the latest.

Mar. 3, '00

I believe my last was from Hsipaw. We stayed there 5-1/2 days and during that time we went to a bazaar meeting (there is bazaar once in five days only, and there is a mission zayat to preach in); also we held three meetings for the workers there who are part Karen and part Shan but all know Burmese. We saw the girls nicely settled and provided with a Shan teacher and all they needed.

Mrs. Leeds began to get up and we were afraid it would be too much for her and we needed to get home anyway, so left Tuesday, Feb. 20.

We made 16 miles the first day; 12 the second; 17 the third; and the last 8 miles the fourth. We walked all the way down into and up out of the gorge and enjoyed the views very much. Got a number of specimens which I want HK to see and classify. I think they are black and white marble, slate, and soap stone, the last from a cutting 10 miles from Hsipaw, the others from the gorge.

We also got some Shan baskets which they wear in the place of a bustle! I gave one to Jennie and a small Shan knife in its sheaf to Frank.

We came the first 50 miles by railroad in an empty freight car pretty full of natives, and very shaky. Then we had to spend Sunday at Maymyo and stayed in the room at the Station, where we did before, sleeping the two nights on the floor. There can't anybody tell us about that floor!

We left at 8 A.M. Monday in an empty coal car packed solid with natives of every conceivable kind and condition, and at least ten races. It was most uncomfortable, but before we got to the descent of the mountains we were invited into the private car which was taking some officials and the wife of another down; for two hours we were duly thankful and made the rest of the journey to Myohoung in comfort and with a chance to see all there was to see, and that is considerable. It took four hours to cover the 39 miles and then we waited one hour and took the mail train for home, reaching here Tuesday morning at 9 o'clock, just a week from starting from Hsipaw and three weeks from leaving here to go.

The trip to Hsipaw was the last trip of the 1899-00 cool season. Three trips of varying lengths were made in the following season, the last before Hattie and Ruth's furlough in 1902-03. One of their last major jungle trips was taken in 1905.

Jan. 12, '05

Saturday we took a small launch to go to Kyawyan where we had never been. All said there was a bungalow there, but after five hours journey we landed on the bank to find no bungalow nor any other place to stay. So we put our goods into a sampan and we walked to the next village, Tainkala, of which we had heard. It is a Karen Christian one, and the headman very willingly took us in. The Karens here are noted for their big chapel and big houses. This one had a center room 70 x 18 feet with a wing 24 x 9, and another the same size partitioned off for a bedroom. The upper story was the same and there was a cooking and dining room, at the end of a covered walk, about 20 x 20. We had the back section of the room curtained off and were quite comfortable though there was no bathroom. The house was very clean for a <u>Karen</u> one.

Sunday we spoke in the afternoon meeting and heard both morning and afternoon the choir which is the best in the district (Mr. Seagrave's) and certainly sings <u>very</u> well in Karen, Burmese, and English.

Monday we walked clear to Kyawyan's farther end, selling 60 gospels and having a number of good talks. We went back from the Kyawyan bazaar by sampan, being thoroughly tired; were out 4-1/2 hours.

I forgot to say that two monstrous water buffaloes slept under the house, pigs were under the cook house, and cats and dogs everywhere. The former (cats) took a fancy to sleep under our cots and to <u>nose</u> into our things generally. I fear we brought away some livestock!

<u>16th</u> We had difficulty in getting off to the launch by a small sampan as it could not come up to the bank. We intended stopping at another village to see some Burman Christians but we were not sure of the exact place; there were yards of mud and no bridge over it; no one to help the boy with all our goods, and as the long walks in the sun had rather upset us, we

decided to keep on to Kyeiklat. We spent one night in a bungalow and got a good bath and dinner, and then went on to
Pyapone next day.

Here we found the bungalow full, and had we not known
of some Karen Gov't clerks (Christians), we would have had to
go home by the same steamship. But we went to one of the
Karens' (Municipal Secretary) and though we had never seen
them before, they took us in very cordially. As they had just
moved into a new house, we had a small room to ourselves and
were quite decent and comfortable. The main drawback was
the iron roof without ceiling — intolerably hot through the
middle of the day, but as it was a two-story house we could go
downstairs. The rats ate the straps off our cots, and the Kulah
neighbors were very noisy at night.

There are four Christian Karen Gov't clerks here with their
families and we had a nice evening meeting with them, and
visited them in their homes. It seemed to do them good as they
have no church privileges. We found the Burmans the hardest
of all visited this year; still, we sold 88 gospels.

We went aboard the steamship Friday evening, as it left at
3 A.M. The natives aboard were many and very noisy, so we
slept little, but fortunately had a cabin, such as it was! We
reached home about 2:30 P.M. — very hot and tired and glad to
be back.

Although jungling proved rewarding in many respects, Hattie
and Ruth found the arduous and uncomfortable conditions more
and more difficult as time went on. The 1905-06 cool season was
the last to be devoted to jungle trips. Those they did undertake
were less extensive than formerly and taken primarily for the purpose of relieving missionaries in field stations who were in need of
help, rather than scouring the jungle villages for converts.

Nov. 11, '05
We expect to go to Thonze Tuesday next and go on to
Henzada the next Monday to help Mrs. Case and Miss
Stickney, who are in great need of it. We do not feel equal to
rough jungle work but could help in a station. Do not know
how long we will be there.

Henzada, Nov. 17, '05

Tuesday morning we took the Henzada steamship, the other passengers in the first class being two Burman men. We had a good straight talk with them, particularly with the younger. He is an English educated lawyer, said he "was very broad-minded" and respected Christianity as well as Buddhism!! He freely acknowledged at the same time that "he had no God." We also had a good talk with some on the deck. We reached Henzada at midnight Wednesday and landed in the morning.

The ladies were glad to see us and we got into some work at once, each taking a Bible class in school. Today I taught two and also the teachers' Sunday School lesson class after school.

Monday Mrs. Case will go to one of her out-stations and take our two girls who are here for Bible woman work.

Henzada, Nov. 25, '05

We are quite settled down into regular work. Mrs. Case left Monday morning for a very necessary trip. Ruth and I each have two Bible classes and one English class a day and a Sunday School class. She keeps house and sees to all the school sweeping. I give a five-minute Bible talk at the opening exercises every day, have the woman's meeting Sunday and the teachers' Sunday School class Friday, and Wednesday, the pastor being away, I took the regular prayer meeting — very small.

There is a big school here now, about 200 pupils, but no church to speak of. After school we have called on the families of a number of the pupils and on the Karen pastor. Thursday evening we had a nice little meeting with Mrs. Morgan and Miss Gouch who are running the Karen side as Mrs. Case and Miss Stickney do this — the whole Henzada mission left to ladies. We also took dinner with them and were glad to get a little more acquainted.

Henzada, Dec. 16, '05

Last week was so like the one before that I did not write. This week has been much the same. Mrs. Case returned Saturday evening (9th). She was gone three weeks, and has been very busy since with all manner of cases and work Miss Stickney could not see to. The work is too heavy for her. She and Miss Stickney are doing, and have for nearly two years, done what formerly both Mr. and Mrs. Cummings and Miss Stickney did. Mrs. Case is beginning to break and I hope the Cummings will soon return. We have helped with the classes and meetings as before.

S.S. *Alguada,* Dec. 22, '05

The past week we helped as usual, and also some about the Christmas picnic, which for lack of any who could sing was substituted for a concert and tree. I also took the Wednesday prayer meeting for the pastor as he had a cold. We helped label the gifts Miss Stickney is to take to the jungle schools next week, and count the cards. One evening some of the boy boarders helped us fill the candy bags for all the schools.

We had our Christmas dinner last evening with them as Mrs. Case had had a gift of a nice duck. Afterward the ladies from the Karen side came over for a nice little meeting, and then all four saw us clear down to the steamship, which was to leave at 7 A.M. this morning.

The picnic is to be today and so we thought it best all around to go on board in the evening. They wanted us to stay indefinitely but we felt we ought to go back to see to things. Mrs. Case is far from well and ought to be relieved of the burden by Mr. Cummings returning. If she should break down we might have to go back. Mrs. Harris is calling us to come there for awhile as she is very poorly and Mr. Harris wants to be in the jungle.

<u>Insein</u> — We did not arrive till after dark last evening (Saturday) but found everything all right, of course very <u>dirty</u>.

Dec. 30, '05

Mrs. Harris wants us to come and help her at Shwegyin, but the need of Miss Stark at Zigon is still greater. She is quite broken down nervously and is ordered home. She cannot go at once and we shall go and help her for a time, longer or shorter as the case may be. She had a serious operation a year ago and has never recovered nor ever will in this climate; has not been fit for work for two years and might better have gone home in the first place.

Zigon, Jan. 6, '06

We came up here Thursday. Miss Stark is about now but was very ill Tuesday, has given out nervously, the result partly or largely of an operation had out here, which never pays. She is ordered home and passage engaged, but no one is in sight to take her place and care for the school and the other work here. Some European has to be Superintendent of these Gov't schools. Mrs. Case must also be relieved or break down.

Miss Ranney is keeping house here, much to Miss Stark's relief, for her boy knows <u>nothing</u>, and I've begun helping her on her reports. Fortunately she has a full set of teachers and they seem good ones.

Zigon, Feb. 2, '06

On Wednesday, as the school had no Christmas treat or even vacation, they were all invited to the house (160 of them). They were seated in rows on the veranda and in the rooms, and were given tea, popcorn and biscuits. Then each class was called in and given a very small present. This was after school closed at 4 P.M. but it took all day to get ready for it.

We finally got Miss Stark off, bag and baggage for Rangoon and home on Saturday morning. We and the whole school, teachers, pupils, and the preacher and his family all went to the station, which is not very far, to see her off, the school giving her a cheer as the train moved off.

The house was in a state but we have everything packed away now and a lot of the accumulations of the past six years disposed of. We expect to stay over another Sunday and Mr. Randall (who is to take charge of the school till May) will be up for a day or two. Then we shall probably finish February in Henzada as Miss Stickney is left alone, Mrs. Case having gone away ill.

Henzada, Feb. 18, '06

We came here Tuesday last and Miss Stickney went to the jungle the next day and is still away, so we are running things. As the pastor is out with Miss Stickney I took his morning service.

Feb. 24, '06

We left Henzada early Thursday morning by train and were all day coming, arriving at sundown. We had been away seven weeks and I was most glad to get at my own room and things again.

The following cool season, Hattie and Ruth involved themselves in evangelistic work among the Burmans in the Insein community and surrounding areas, working from their home. In 1907 the Bible school's program was extended to include a second term each year, November to February, the period previously used for jungling. Hattie was 45 and Ruth 49 when they gave up their jungle trips.

Bethshalom with Bible School students, Hattie and Ruth (in window) and benefactors U Pan Di and Daw Oo (by doorway), circa 1904.

12

Finding a Home

1894 to 1928

Opening in May of 1893, the Burman Woman's Bible School continued under the direction of Ruth Ranney and Hattie Phinney until their retirement in 1928. Only during the periods when the two women were on furlough (1901-02, 1911-12, 1920-21) was the school closed.

Any attempt to summarize the 35-year history of the Bible school runs the danger of understating the problems and uncertainties that the school faced for many of these years. The very fact of its longevity, and its survival in modified form a century later, cannot help but give the impression that, once established, the school's course was set and its continuation assured.

With the founding of the school, Hattie and Ruth successfully defined for themselves a place within the mission community that would allow them to carry out the work they felt most called to do. While complementary to other mission activities, the school operated largely independently of the mission board in America, with the exception of two crucial areas: appropriations and housing.

The first year of the Bible school, as reported in Hattie's letters of 1893, was typical in many ways of the years that were to follow. Many of its features, routines, and practices put in place at that time, remained fixtures of the school thereafter. Many of the anxieties and uncertainties, however, were also typical of the years ahead. Financial support was an ongoing concern, as was the uncertainty each year with regard to the number of new and returning students. Illness among the women, problems of discipline and suitability, were only some of the challenges to be met. The problem that was to loom largest, however, was the necessity of finding and maintaining adequate facilities for the school: classrooms and dormitory space for the women, servants' quarters, and a place for the pastor and his family, in addition to a home for Hattie and Ruth.

The ease with which they had found such facilities when they first returned to Rangoon in 1892 proved to be misleading. Equally misleading had been Dr. Smith's statement that he was turning Wahklu Lodge over to Hattie and Ruth, seemingly with no strings attached. In fact, Dr. Smith's jurisdiction over the land was given over to Dr. Cushing, head of the Rangoon Baptist College. Problems began to arise as soon as Hattie and Ruth returned from their second year in the jungle and began to prepare for the opening of school.

Apr. 28, '94

I believe I have said that we had rented the other small house on the compound for our women, who were badly crowded last rains. After renting it to us, the owner, a Karen, went to Dr. Cushing and said if he didn't buy it at once he should take it down and remove it! So as Dr. Cushing wanted it for a teacher who has just married, he bought it. We happened to hear of it or it might have gone on thus till the women came.

We need the room so shall take the rent appropriation and some remnants of specifics and build, side of Po Min's house, one of mat and thatch work with pinkado posts and board floor. Po Min will oversee the buying and building. He was a carpenter one year. It will cost 175/- to 200/- , and if we have to leave this place in the Fall (as Dr. Cushing wants and expects), the College will buy it of us. Dr. Cushing expects another man then and wants this place for him to live in and the grounds for the boys to play.

I find it a little hard to see why Bennett Place (left empty by the Roaches' going) wouldn't do just as well; the boys could still use the most of this place, whereas the Bennett house will not do for us, as there is no room at all for the women to live and we can't have them way out of reach. However, this whole place has been given to the College and of course Dr. Cushing wants it, and we'll be sent out if a new man comes. He hasn't come yet, and we don't worry; the Lord provided this place and he can do the same again.

While the second year of the school was held at Wahklu Lodge, the question of its use for the following year arose just as the term ended.

Oct. 20, '94

Dr. Cushing informed us that a man was coming this Fall and he wanted the house. He professed not to know whether he was single or double but we know through Prof. Roach that the appropriation is only for a single man. So Miss Ranney suggested that it would save the ABMU [American Baptist Mission Union] 500/- or 600/- rent if we stayed here the cold season and someone took the young man in. Dr. Cushing has a house the size of this all to himself and could take him in perfectly well if he thought so. He said he wouldn't take him in, but if someone would we could stay till May, but he must have our house then — (for Eurasian school boys and teachers).

So there it is; we must doubtless move in April or March; where to we don't know at all.

Feb. 21, '95

We had a letter from Mrs. Safford asking us not to move till April 1, or hoping we wouldn't, and saying they didn't want to make new appropriations till then, and that as Mr. Valentine (who arrived Saturday) is single, they don't see why we should move. All of which makes Dr. Cushing mad and he says we must go, and wants us out so Mr. Valentine can get in before he (Dr. Cushing) goes off on vacation, as he "won't leave any man in his house during his absence." So there is nothing to do but go.

Until yesterday we could find nothing at all, houses all taken before being vacated, but we found one on the corner of Simpson Rd. and China St. in Cantonment [section of Rangoon], which will do if we can get permission to build a dormitory for our girls, and that is now pending. I drew the plans to submit this morning. If we take it, we must do so on March 1. The rent is 130/- a month.

The house on Simpson Road was far from ideal; its location at some distance from other mission activities, the size of the house, the noise and dust of the neighborhood, the streams of natives passing on their way to the local pagoda were all detracting factors. Mrs. Wells, Ruth's aunt, who had managed the household since their return from America, decided to return to England in the face of the proposed move, thus adding housekeeping chores to the work already carried by the two women. Despite these handicaps, the rooms were readied and the 1895 school year began.

May 11, '95

This has been a week full of odds and ends of all sorts of work, sewing, study, cleaning and arranging the school rooms, etc. etc. We have covered the walls with the big pictures of the Sunday School lessons, as we had received several rolls, and partly covered the floors with cheap mats for the girls to sit on. We decided too that they <u>must</u> have <u>something</u> to put their books on, so have ordered four long low desks, 18 inches high, one foot wide and 7-1/2 feet long with a shelf 4 inches below the top for books. We shall have to foot this bill 32/- and for two tables 3/8 and the mats etc. etc. ourselves; we've no appropriation for such sundries. If we don't have girls enough to use up the appropriation we may be able to reimburse ourselves.

May 18, '95

Our school rooms are nice and so are our new benches. The only drawback is a lack of glass windows; shutters closed make the room dark as a pocket, and open when it is <u>pouring</u> is too cold for me; I shall have to invest in a glass window next. We can scarcely ask the owner as it would not be a necessity to any other tenant and she has put hundreds in the house now to get it in order for us.

In June, Frank returned from America. Following a short visit to the Simpson Road household, he moved into the Bennett House, which he had left with Lenna in 1892. His return proved very timely for the school. Almost immediately after Ruth and Hattie

were settled in and school started, their use of the house was
threatened by their landlady's death and the proposed sale of the
house. Frank provided them with an ally in dealing with the mission
and the local bureaucracy.

June 20, '95

This house is to be sold next month and Frank discovered
that the agreement we had made was not sufficiently stamped
to hold and unless we got permission to stamp it properly we
could be turned out by the purchaser. So he has kindly seen to
it and we have paid Rs 9/8 in addition to the -/8 stamped paper
it was on and now feel safe for this year anyway. Of course,
someone may buy it to rent and we can stay on. Had Frank not
come just now we might have been ordered out before we
knew what was the matter. Both Mr. Roach and Mr. Kelley
thought our agreement was quite sufficient.

July 26, '95

Thursday this place was sold at auction. Frank came and
hung around and so we knew at once about it. The man buying
it is renting and his lease expires as ours does in February so
unless he changes his mind we will have to move next March
1. We did hope we were settled for several years anyway but it
looks as if not.

With Frank's help, a solution to their predicament was found.

Aug. 30, '95

The matter of our future home is settled. The new owners
want this and find they can sublet the one they occupy, and we
can have Russell Place which is just now vacant. We couldn't
take it before as it is too small for three but large enough for
two. There are no classrooms nor place for any, but Frank will
let us use the lower rooms of his house next door [Bennett
Place] so, though not nearly so convenient as this place or
Wahklu Lodge, it will do fairly well; and the rent is 30/- a
month less, and as it is a trust estate in Dr. Smith's hands we
can never be turned out, a great consideration.

Sept. 13, '95

Saturday we began to pack up for moving and this will go on between times till we get out. We get no time school days to speak of. The other house is cleaned, and a new mat is to be woven on the center room floor as it is too rough to live on. It looks like a tiny box after this and Wahklu Lodge! We shall be very cozy and snug.

Berachah, <u>Mission Rd.</u> Oct. 5, '95

Well, here we are in our new home! We moved Monday.

The business of this week has been to get ready for school. Three rooms under Frank's house have been cleaned and I'm positive <u>you</u> never saw a dirtier place. In a house in constant use dust and cobwebs gather with great rapidity, but these rooms had not been touched for a year nor used for a year and a half, and you can't imagine their state! But now they are very attractive with bright pictures (Sunday School lesson rolls) maps, and Burmese texts on the walls, and the windows nicely cleaned, and the floors covered with mats. As they are cement there must be two thicknesses where the girls are to sit or they will be getting sick. Natives don't like cement floors a bit.

The fourth, fifth, and sixth years of the school (1896-98) were held in Russell Place, back in the mission colony and close to its original location at Wahklu Lodge. Frank's marriage to Jennie Wayte in April of 1897 did not interfere initially with this arrangement. In January 1899, however, the couple moved from Bennett Place to a house on York Road, closer to the press and more convenient for Frank, but leaving the school in a familiar quandary — at the mercy of Dr. Cushing.

Aug. 20, '98

As Dr. Cushing has the promise of Frank's house, we didn't know but we should lose our school rooms, and that would mean another move of ourselves and also of the dormitory! But Dr. Cushing says we can use the rooms at least one year more, and perhaps longer.

The following year, Bennett Place was assigned to Professor Randall of the college, and finding new classroom space became a necessity if the school was not to move again. The construction of a new classroom building was proposed to supply this need. The task of drawing up the plans for the building fell to Hattie, who was by now becoming an expert at the task.

Oct. 28, '99

I prepared plans for our new school house for which we have received an appropriation from home. So we expect another year to be in a more healthful situation — don't think we could stand another year in those damp rooms.

Once the school year was over, Hattie's plans for the new school building were put into play. Chinese carpenters, under the supervision of Mr. McGuire of the mission, were hired to carry out the work.

Mar. 24, '00

Our new school house is finished except oiling the outside and putting in the glass, which we hope to see done early next week. Since the carpenters left, we have been trying to get the compound cleaned up a little. Our preacher is being carpenter and making quite extensive repairs on the dormitory where white ants and weather have made havoc.

May 12, '00

The rest of last week and Monday and Tuesday were spent in cleaning this house, the dormitory, the compound and the school house, with three coolies to oversee. It also took some time to put up the pictures and maps. Now the School is very bright, pretty and comfortable. That we endured the damp, dark rooms [of Bennett Place] so long without breaking down is little short of a miracle. Mrs. Randall considers them much too damp for Mr. Randall to teach in!

Hand in hand with securing adequate facilities for the Bible school was the need to obtain the funds necessary for its operation. Fund raising was an ongoing task that absorbed much time and energy. While their American benefactors, Mrs. Brooks and Miss

Chapman, supported Ruth and Hattie, respectively, funds for the operating expenses of the school itself had to be obtained from other sources. During the school year, room and board were provided to the students from school funds; the women lived in the school dormitory, cooking and keeping house for themselves, but drew on the assistance of the household servants on occasion. Upkeep of the buildings and the compound grounds were additional ongoing major expenses, even without consideration of the funds for needed expansion or improvement.

Initially the major portion of these running expenses was borne by the Woman's Baptist Foreign Mission Board, with the remainder being raised from the Burman Christian community. In 1898 the situation changed, and Hattie and Ruth were left with the full responsibility of obtaining whatever assistance they could from mission circles, locally or abroad. When all other sources proved insufficient, Hattie and Ruth drew on their own salaries.

May 25, '94

One event of the week was the completion of the little house. It cost 200/- and is quite satisfactory. We have 186/- appropriated but the rest we'll have to contribute. We had to have this and Po Min's house — roofs (beside the servants' house) repaired, 20/- more. All the missionaries are putting their salaries into the work just as far as they will go, I think — at least I know a number who are.

Aug. 8, '98

Thursday evening Mr. McGuire called to talk over mission affairs. By a misunderstanding the Board has given no appropriation for our school next year. We hoped the natives would support it <u>some</u> time (they gave half last year) and <u>they</u> [the Board] hoped they would this year, so cut it off. We will see if they will and we won't ask anything from home. Mr. McGuire will help all he can about raising it.

Aug. 20, '98

I'm not sure whether or not I mentioned the fact that my estimates being late, and we having raised part of the funds for the School here and expressed a hope that sometime we might get it all here, the Board have given us a chance to do so at once by giving <u>nothing</u> for it this year! As we have enough this year without touching the native collection or at least not using much of them, we can save that over and the native gifts for two years will doubtless carry it on one year at least. So we have not asked any reconsideration. It will be a good thing to throw it more onto the Christians here.

From this time on, funds to maintain the school were provided from a variety of sources, including native churches. In some cases these were in the form of gifts to the school; in others, they were provided for the support of a specific student attending the school. The latter funds were often from the student's family or from a missionary interested in the individual.

Each year, Ruth drafted a circular letter that was sent to mission groups, churches, and individuals who might have an interest in the work of the school. In her letters home, Hattie often recounted specific gifts made to the school. As the years went by, graduates of the school became important contributors to its work.

> June 7, '95
> Our circular letter was sent to Berachah Southport
> [England] where we spent a week and was read at a meeting,
> and a stranger, a lady from Liverpool, sent us £1 for our work.
> It got here just in time to pay for the two additional benches
> we had ordered but were short of funds to pay for; they cost
> 16/-and the £1 brought 18/-! So the Lord provides!

> Feb. 2, '00
> Sunday we were pleased to have one of the Christian
> women — a "hired girl" in an English family — give 25/- for our
> School; as at home, it is the <u>poor</u> who give the most. Rich women
> and teachers on from 20/- to 60/- a month begrudge -/8 a year!!

While many of the funds received were from individuals and groups familiar with the school and committed to its support, their receipt was often erratic in timing and dependent upon competing demands of other institutions and conditions. It was necessary to make the needs of the school known to the Christian community through newsletters and attendance at meetings of missionaries and natives ("Associations").

> Feb. 2, '00
>
> We feel we must be here for Association on account of our School as we've not travelled in this district at all this year and our money may fall short if we're not on hand to present the needs of the School, lest "out of sight" should be "out of mind."

> Mar. 17, '00
>
> [At the Association in Bassein] we had a woman's meeting and the women of Bassein promised to support a girl in our School this year. Two of our girls who graduate next term are working there and it is one of them whom they take up. Besides this, a wealthy Burman Christian there who practically entertained all the natives (50-75) gave us 50/- toward our new building which is costing more than we expected. As our receipts so far are less than last year we were very thankful that we went, tho it was an expensive trip.

The new school house, completed in March 1900, was put into use for the 1900 and 1901 school terms. In 1902, however, when the school did not attract enough new students to warrant a full first year class, it was decided to close for a time "until a new set should grow up." Hattie and Ruth made use of this time for a furlough to America.

On December 10, 1903, Hattie and Ruth returned to Rangoon to learn that the house they had left was now occupied by a new tenant. They were once again in the familiar predicament of having to find a home for themselves and the school. This time, the answer was found with the aid of the native Christian community.

> Dec. 12, '03
>
> We find our house rented for an indefinite period with the promise that they should not be turned out. So where we shall go we know not.

Dec. 20, '03

We seem but little nearer a home than before, except that we
have given up trying to get our old home, as there is no certainty
but that sooner or later it will be given over to the College and we
be as badly off as now. Meantime property and rents are going up.
Besides, our dormitory will have to be almost rebuilt as it is so
eaten by ants and we do not care to put some hundreds of rupees
into it only to sell or remove it later at a loss.

The native Christians want to give a small plot of land and
have us come out to Insein, but we are waiting to see Mr.
McGuire about it first.

During this time of uncertainty Hattie and Ruth received invi-
tations from several mission posts to locate in other fields in Burma.
Some would accommodate the school; others would have required
giving up the school to carry the mission work of a field station.
None of these options was acceptable.

Jan. 9, '04

We have had now three stations offered us with a chance to
take the man's place and do his work; the Rangoon friends
bemoan our leaving there as it is the "Hub" of Burma, and the
Insein Christians are urgent that we come there. With it all we
feel a great deal pulled to pieces. But it looks as if we should have
the necessary land in Insein and settle there. We do not believe in
women taking the men's places and doing their work, anyway,
and we do think that our School is the first consideration for us.
All the friends who write us elsewhere want us to have the
School, but seem to think we could have it in any out-of-the-way
place as well as at the center. We know better.

Dec. 27, '03

We have rented a tiny house at Insein, near the plot of
ground they want us to build on, and expect to move out there
bag and baggage January 1st. Whether we settle finally in
Insein or not depends on their getting more land for us.

Ruth's circular letter of March 1904 summarized the situation
for their missionary and home friends:

On returning to Rangoon we began inquiries as to a permanent home. We found that there was no hope of our obtaining our old house, or any other in Rangoon. We were invited to take up station work in more than one place where there are vacant mission houses, but we felt we could not abandon the Woman's Bible School work to which we were called eleven years ago and for that we must be in or near Rangoon. While we were away a Burman preacher and his wife, U Pan Di and Daw Oo, bought a plot of land in Insein which they wanted to give for the use of our School; until we found that the old place was not available we would not consider their proposal.

We found the land well situated near the Burman Chapel and within walking distance from the bazaar and railroad station. But it was too small for our house, the dormitory and all necessary outbuildings, and on one side the land was not for sale. On the other side it was owned by a man who was very loath to sell, asking Rs.1200 for what he gave Rs.500 a year ago. But the couple were willing to buy at any price and give to us, so we decided to move to Insein.

A trust fund was found available for building our house, and it is now being put up and will be ready by May 1st. Our hope is that the Woman's Baptist Foreign Mission Society can in time replace the fund and so own the entire establishment.

The building of the house and school, based on plans drawn up by Hattie, was a major undertaking. Progress was slow and frustrating, but in May, just before the school year was to begin, Hattie and Ruth were finally able to move in and start preparing for the new term.

May 21, '04

Here we are at last in our own home. We did not move till last Saturday and the carpenters, painters and glass men were still here then, but all have gone now. The Chinese carpenters were staying in the schoolrooms downstairs and we finally had to call the help of the police to get them out!

School benefactors Daw Oo and U Pan Di.

June 4, '04

During the week a lot of plantain trees have been planted on the compound, and seeds of papaya and mangoes prepared for planting. So we shall have fruit trees, but whether we have any fruit or not remains to be seen!

The contractor's bill for the house is settled and we have a small balance to use for gutters we now see we need. The fund was Rs.8177, and all will be used in the building. All think we have a very good house for the money. It is as convenient and homelike as I thought it would be when I drew the plan. The walls are a very light green and the ceilings white. The floors are bare, but the pictures and curtains and other things make it look very well.

Sitting and dining room of Hattie and Ruth's home, Bethshalom.

Aug. 20, '04

We asked Mrs. Brooks to name our house, and she thought "House of Peace" would be suitable, so I put it into Biblical form to get it into one word and hence "Bethshalom."

Aug. 27, '04

Without our knowledge U Pan Di and Daw Oo collected money among the Christians, Burmese and Karen, bought lumber, and are having made school desks and seats for our girls! Friday half were finished and put in one room, very much to the delight of the girls. They have sat on the floor heretofore and have not complained to us, but say now they do get weary and stiff. The Burmans are adopting English style as far as using chairs is concerned, very fast.

Living in Insein had many of the disadvantages Hattie had anticipated. Though trains ran at regular intervals between Insein and Rangoon, the nine-mile trip took 40 minutes, "besides a walk here and a gharry there" as Hattie put it. This distance often made it inconvenient or impossible to attend the ongoing and special events of the Rangoon mission that had been an important part of their lives before the move.

Mar. 4, '04

We dressed up and went in to a wedding at the Baptist Church and to the reception at Mr. Griggs' house, but the bride was so late that we had to leave before the refreshments were served. Mrs. Griggs had asked us to help cut the cake, but we could not stay so late, as we had not had our dinner, and the next train would bring us out after 8 P.M. That is the disadvantage of living out here, we lose the best half of anything we go to, or lose it altogether, as we shall a wedding at Kemindine at 3 this afternoon which is too early for us to start out for.

Sept. 10, '04

Yesterday afternoon I tried to attend the funeral of Mrs. St. John. The train was late and I waited three-quarters of an hour here, then being too late for the service at the house, I waited an hour at the Press; then Frank and I waited half an hour at the cemetery as they were late in arriving. By that time I was obliged to go for my train home, as the next was an hour later and would bring me home after dark, with no certainty of a gharry, and no dinner till very late. So I simply saw the procession! This is one of the beauties of living in the "Mofussel!"

Opportunities for visits with Frank and Jennie also became more infrequent. While the distance made casual socializing less convenient, the two families nevertheless remained close and affectionate, ready to help in times of need.

Aug. 11, '07

Tuesday a note came from Frank asking me to come in and stay with Jennie as she was in bed. So I went after an early breakfast and stayed all day. Ruth kept the girls busy during the morning and gave them a half-holiday and came in, too. Miss Larsh had been sent for, but we did not feel easy, so Ruth went in early the next day, but fortunately Miss Larsh had come, so came back in time for school, much to my relief. As we both teach all day, if one is away the other has no spare time to give to her classes, and the work is disorganized.

With the purchase of the land for the Bible school, the worries and uncertainties about the location of the school that had plagued them during the early years were gone. In their place were ongoing concerns regarding maintenance of the compound grounds and buildings, expanding the site and facilities to meet the needs of a growing student body, and dealing with a variety of other problems, both natural and manmade.

Sept. 23, '05

The first event of the week was the biggest flood of ten years, the older residents say. It was the fourth this year and the worst we have seen. Last year the water only rose twice. This time the water came up under the dormitory, covering about half the compound and the bridge out to the main road, and the main road itself was quite two feet under water. All the other houses in this neighborhood had from one to five feet of water underneath them. Several lengths of our fence were hidden. It was raining very heavily at 6 A.M. but the water had not begun to rise. At 9 A.M. it was as I have described, and at 10 A.M. we could see by the fence that it had begun to go down. At 4 P.M. some of the girls were sitting out on the grass where the water had been! They did not sit there long after we saw them!

Nov. 24, '07

At 1 A.M. last night I was awakened by hearing a commotion at the girls' house and looking out the window I saw to my horror that their cook-house was ablaze! I called Ruth, she called the boys, and I threw on a skirt and rushed out. The girls drew water and the boys got it out, and when I saw the danger was over I collapsed and went back to bed. Ruth had dressed and went out and stayed till she saw that all sparks were out and the girls had their things back which they had tumbled out of doors. Half of the back wall and half of their cooking platform is gone, and the place will have to be very thoroughly made over. We have never had school in the dry season before and shall have to be very careful about fire.

Neighbors and potential neighbors were an ongoing source of concern, as their actions often impinged, or threatened to impinge, on the school and its occupants.

June 20, '08

The land next to us is now being put on the market and if it should be sold to a native who should build a lot of native small houses or barracks, this place would be much injured, and might easily be made unusable for us or the school, as the house had to be as near the line as possible to give room for the dormitory and all to be above high water. The owner offers a strip of 25 feet side of us and a small plot at the back for Rs.1500. This is a fair price as she is asking Rs.7000 per acre for the high land and Rs.5000 for the lower land. We simply must have at least the strip and plot, not only to keep this from being spoiled but to give place to grow as we now have all the compound will accommodate. We do not know where the money can come from but have told the owner to consider this part spoken for. The ladies at home have said they cannot help us as they have a big debt on the building fund. The Burmans can do something and we can put in all our savings but that will not be enough.

Don't you folks know of someone who would like to invest in this part of the Lord's work? As the Burmans gave the land, the well, the school furniture and most of the dormitory, and support the school all the time, giving Rs.700 or 800 a year, we cannot expect much from them.

July 4, '08

On Monday after school we looked over the land with Miss Beale (the owner), Daw Oo, and U Pan Di, and at that time Daw Oo asked if we would object to her renting the house opposite us to a lot of young men, natives of India. We said we did as it would be most unsuitable for our girls, not to say unsafe, as they could not get out of the compound or be out in the compound without being under the eyes and within sound of the Hindu young men. So she said she would take it back as no written contract had been made. But at 6 P.M. on Wednesday we saw <u>ten</u> young men moving into the house. We called Daw Oo, who said she had sent them word they could not have it, and we, the Morans (in the house next to this), and Daw Oo and the young man she had sent to them, spent an hour on the road insisting that they take their goods out at once, which they finally did, we paying the cart hire. We knew if they slept there we could never get them out and it would mean closing our school, for the girls were thoroughly frightened. The law is altogether on the side of the tenant, who can neither be put out nor forced to pay, as our friends have found to their sorrow. When it was over we were exceedingly tired, you may be sure.

Mar. 16, '13

Our heathen neighbor has built out a high wall, rounding it out into the stream bed, so that another rains would see the loss of some feet more of our land. Dr. McGuire saw him and we both expressed our views on the subject of his stealing land, and he promised to move the wall back. He has been doing this ever since we came here and already has a number of feet of land taken from us by his forcing the stream out at our side, but this last wall was too much to be borne in silence. The only way is to go on and protect our entire side with laterite, which means fifteen tons more; five have gone in now. Fortunately the appropriation will cover it, and when once done it will be sound for all time, so far as the eating of the stream is concerned. Frank is going to write the man a letter to help him do his duty.

Despite its distance from Rangoon, the new site offered many advantages aside from providing a permanent home. The choice of Insein as a location for the school had not been as random as it may have seemed at first. The Burman and Karen Theological Seminaries were already located in Insein, as was the Karen Woman's Bible School. Hattie and Ruth and their women became active members of the Burman Church in Insein, with their school rooms often used for community events. Their weekly Woman's Mission Society meetings were open to the women of the community, and the students from the school participated in many community activities and special events.

Sept. 16, '05

Monday was the great day of the week. We with the girls and Christians from hereabouts all went to the Karen Theological Seminary chapel at 8:30 A.M. About a dozen of the Rangoon missionaries, including Jennie, were there too, and of course all the Karen and Burman students. The affair was to celebrate Mr. Thomas' 50th birthday, and Mrs. Smith had collected from Missionaries and the Christians around here a good sum of money. First Dr. Smith read a very witty and appropriate address, and a Burman teacher read one in Burmese by Dr. Stevens, which was even more witty and was greatly appreciated by the Burmans present. Then 50 young people came up the aisle bearing the presents. First tiny girls with bunches of 50 roses; little boys with assorted fruits; a girl each from Mrs. Rose's school and ours with each a roll of 50 two-anna bits done up in a box and a basket; then the big boys with all sorts of parcels labeled with various articles, and with rolls of all sorts of coins in 50s. U Pan Di presented the gift from the Burmans of over a 100 rupees. A Karen gave an address, and when all was done, Dr. Smith said to Mr. Thomas, "That is all; now don't you want to get up and say 'Thank you'?" He did in a very good talk in English, Burmese, and Karen. As he works for all races it was very suitable.

Sept. 21, '07

Sunday as Dr. Cummings is to preach at the Seminary, we expect to take the girls up there for the afternoon service if it is not too rainy, or they are not too coughy and sneezy.

Sept. 22, '12

Tuesday evening we went up to the Burman Theological Seminary and I gave a talk on our trip in Palestine, showing our framed pictures and a few cards. The young men seemed interested. They have a large relief map on which the route could be very well shown.

July 13, '13

This is the great day, the anniversary of Judson's landing in Rangoon 100 years ago. I suppose all Burman and at least some of the Karen churches have observed it. We began on Friday by having a special meeting, not in connection with Judson, but as a sort of 20th anniversary of this school which has been in existence one-fifth of the time! We had the older girls write to old graduates and ask for letters about their work, and had nine answers that were suitable to read in the meeting. One had been in work 15 years, two 13 years, others for shorter periods, and two were the wives of ordained pastors, a Burman and a Chin. Another Chin, an especially good worker, just now with the Hascalls, and two Shans were also heard from. It made a very good meeting, and there were 17 outside women in.

This morning we and the girls all went up to the Burman Theological Seminary where Dr. McGuire preached to both schools and the Insein Burman Church. Our girls recited Rom. 10:10-17; they had been well-drilled and recited it as one voice, without a syllable wrong. Tonight the 10 older girls give the life of Judson as set forth in the little booklet in Burmese.

During the rebuilding of the Insein Burman Church, which required the destruction of the old chapel, the Bible school facilities were used for weekly services.

May 23, '14

The chapel of the Burman church was taken down while we were away and a new, larger one of brick instead of teak is going up, built mostly by Daw Oo and U Pan Di, though the church is also putting its savings of years past into it. All the meetings both English and Burmese have been held in our school rooms till now, but with the Bible schools in session our rooms will not do for the latter, and Sunday mornings they must go up to the Burman Seminary. The English meeting can still be held here. Even without the schools, part of the Burman congregation had to sit out of doors, and got very little of the service.

June 20, '14

The new chapel has its roof on and we shall be so glad to see it far enough along to be used, for the frequent extra meetings here make us quite a bit of work; and too, we have the pulpit in our front lobby, the communion table in the center passage of our house, and a lot of chairs and two bookcases in the school rooms, besides the organ, which makes things rather "cluttered up."

There was a concert given at the Chapel, the same as last year,
by a number of Burman and Karen choirs from different parts of
Insein. This time it was held downstairs and there were more than
ever present, I think, for the place holds more and was packed
solid with Burman and Karen Christians and their children. Our
girls contributed two recitations of Scripture. Paper bags with two
oranges and some other small gifts were distributed after the
program. There were four short addresses as well as much
singing. The Burmans and Karens like a good <u>long</u> program. The
heathen think nothing of staying all night at their theatrical
performances!

In 1915 the school and the Insein Baptist community suffered
a loss in the death of U Pan Di, the native Christian who, with his
wife, had provided the original land for the school in Insein, and
had contributed most generously to the school over the years.

July 3, '15

U Pan Di died about 2 P.M. Monday, and that and the next
evenings we and some of the girls were over there for meetings
and singing. Wednesday afternoon we had no school and
attended the funeral at the church and to the grave. There was
a big crowd and Dr. McGuire took the services in the church,
and our former preacher Saya Po Min, pastor of the Rangoon
Burman Church, preached excellently to the crowd at the
grave, a few of whom were Buddhists. Ruth took the girls
again to sing at the house on that evening.

Tuesday evening beside the meeting from 7 to 8 at Daw
Oo's there was an English one at the chapel from 6 to 7 P.M.
You remember that Daw Oo and U Pan Di are the ones who
gave the first plot of land for this school, and also Rs.100
toward the addition bought later. They very largely built the
new brick chapel; when it was finished and the Association had
met there, U Pan Di said he was ready to go.

A major fundraising effort to build a new dormitory for the
students was begun in 1913, ending after several years of effort
among the Burman fields and with major assistance from Miss
Chapman, Hattie's source of support in America.

Oct. 31, '15

We have just sent to arrange with Ah Pan to build the new dormitory. He is a younger brother of Ah Sou. We are glad to have a Christian contractor, his estimates and specifications were by far the best offered and came within the amount we have to spend.

Nov. 13, '15

The Municipality sent back the plan of the dormitory and demanded that the bathrooms be built out from the house and on another side. I have replied that the printed regulations make no such demand; that no house anywhere here is so built and that it would cause the drainage to run under the whole width of the house and all across the compound to reach the stream. Yesterday we went and called on the Municipal engineer and he said he would see that it did pass, particularly if we agreed to add a flight of stairs just for the bathrooms, which we did.

Jan. 15, '16

Bricks and sand and lime have been coming all the week, and on Friday Ah Pan came and in the afternoon the building was marked out on the ground. A half dozen workmen are on the place, living in a mat and thatch house at the back, put up for them, and beginning work on the brick feet to the posts. These are Chittagonians, and when they are through Chinese carpenters will occupy the place, so things are beginning to move.

It was a long slow process, with many delays, but eventually the end was in sight.

Apr. 2, '16

Friday we went over to see how the dormitory was getting on and found that things were really moving, all the floors, a low inner partition, most of the veranda railing, and some of the lattice work was done. This morning I found that the rest of the tiles had been put on.

Apr. 23, '16
The dormitory is all done except for some chics for the front
veranda, and they are being made. Our Burman carpenter is oiling
the building, inside and out, and then it will be absolutely done.

After much turmoil during its earlier years, the school had found
a welcoming and permanent home within the Insein community.
The site at Insein remained the home of the Burman Woman's Bible
School for the duration of Ruth and Hattie's leadership.

Hattie, Ruth, and students, Burman Woman's Bible School.

13

The Burman Woman's Bible School

1894 to 1928

The long-term success of the Burman Woman's Bible School was due in large part to the clarity of its mission and the vision and dedication of its founders. The school's purpose was to prepare native women for evangelistic work in their native communities, or, if not to work in the field, to be informed and better practicing Christians, able to explain the Bible to others and to bring up their children in the Christian faith.

From the beginning, Hattie and Ruth retained personal control over all aspects of the school's operations — from classroom instruction, financial and administrative responsibilities, to providing for the care and welfare of their students. The letters reveal a sense of mutual regard and affection between teachers and students, and the pride with which Hattie and Ruth regarded the work of their graduates.

Over the years, enrollment fluctuated widely, and the beginning of each term was marked with a degree of uncertainty with respect to the number of students who would make up the enrollment. While it was a three-term course, students did not always return for the second or third term, and the number of new students was always a gamble — the outcome often not determined until several weeks into the term. Travel problems, family illnesses, sudden marriages or unexpected job opportunities were among the many reasons for changes in a student's plans.

May 11, '95

We begin Monday and at present six <u>nice</u> girls are on hand
and another will be here on the 5 P.M. train. Two of these are
certificated teachers from Kemindine School as well educated

as any girls in Burma. Their coming is quite voluntary and both give up good salaries to do it . . . but they want to do evangelistic work.

We have learned that one who should have returned and graduated this year has gone and got married! We wish she would have waited six months and finished her course. She has married Mr. Cochrane's teacher at Pyinmana which is all right and nice.

May 13, '99

We had fifteen to begin with but Mrs. Hancock got one of the new ones to go to Mandalay with her so we had but fourteen till yesterday when two more returned. We expect another the coming week but evidently this is to be an off year again. Every other year a good number enters and the year in between a very few.

June 4, '05

We now have twenty-four girls in school, the largest number we have ever had. There are twelve in each class. As only one is a day pupil, the dormitory is badly crowded, but none of them want to go to sleep at Daw Oo's, and as it would be inconvenient, we do not insist. We have turned away four new girls, hoping they will come again next year. It is very evident that the dormitory must be enlarged before another year. Not enough money has come in to feed the girls yet, but we expect it will come as the need is known.

Students for the Bible school were recruited from all the mission fields in Burma and represented many of the diverse ethnic groups making up the population of the country. The teaching was done entirely in the Burmese language, since Hattie and Ruth's primary concern as missionaries to the Burmans was to attract and prepare Burman women for Bible work. This was a goal not easily attained, however. The Burmans, as a group, were less responsive to the evangelistic work of the Christians than some others; the Karens in particular made up the largest proportion of Burmese Christians. As the national language, Burmese was spoken by many of the native groups, as a first or second language, and this fact made it possible for a diverse student body to participate in the school. While all women interested in attending the school were welcome if they could speak and write sufficient Burmese, a high proportion of Burmans among the students was always noted by Hattie as a source of satisfaction.

May 26, '06

We now have twenty-three girls and expect two, three, or even four more within a week. One of the new ones is a widow and one of the third year class is a married woman, but the rest are young women. All of the new ones are Burmans except one Shan-Taline and one Karen.

June 9, '06

The event of the week was the arrival of four Chin girls — three were old girls and one was new. They could not find anyone to escort them from their home, which is three days from Thayetmyo, so had to wait till a relative was going to Pyinmana, and so go there with him and so down by railroad. This meant four or five days on the road, and as they could not find carts to hire they had to walk three days, sleeping very little nights for fear of thieves. Of course each had to carry her own baggage. They were a tired set of girls, I assure you, but were heartily welcomed. They wanted to come pretty bad! Since then we have refused four for various reasons, largely because we are full enough, and now it is too late to enter.

May 23, '08

On Wednesday morning we opened school with 23, the largest number we have ever had on the opening day. One more came the next day and there are three more of the old girls who should return. If they come, some of the married women will have to sleep at the neighbors'. We have fourteen new ones and of the whole school all are Burmans except four Talains, one Chin and one Karen. The youngest is 17 and the oldest is 45.

May 31, '08

Our numbers have been added to this week by the arrival of a Shan girl from Namkhan, six days' journey away! Our Toungthu girl comes back tomorrow, when we shall have twenty-six. Have already sent two to sleep at Daw Oo's, two of the married women, whose husbands are in the Seminary, and being new Christians, are a little "difficult" in the dormitory with the younger women and girls.

June 5, '09

A new girl has arrived from Myingyan district. Her name is Miss Silver Nest, but we call her Miss Nest for short. We have a Miss Silver, Miss Circle, Miss First of Many, Miss Victorious Peace, Miss Pleasant, Miss Hanging Fire, Miss Sand, etc. (22 in all).

May 27, '15

Our Chin girls who have been working under Mr. Condict have at last returned, having been delayed by his absence. If they had only written us I would have sent their fares, but they did not have gumption enough for that! We now have 24, and expect one or two more. We can manage it as four are day pupils. Two of the latter are from the family of the retired Gov't official mentioned above, and dress beautifully, and others are as poor as poverty! "The rich and the poor meet together."

May 27, '16

The girls began to arrive on Monday and are still coming, the last being a Chin from Sandoway, who had to come the long cart trip by a terrible road over the mountains, with wild beasts and fearful precipices to look out for. The steamship being taken off, it is the only way to get here.

In addition to the academic proficiency required for coursework, students were expected to meet standards of conduct and behavior. Not all the students who sought admission to the school were found to be "suitable."

June 12, '09

On Wednesday two Shan girls arrived from Hsipaw. One of them we were expecting and she is a very suitable one; but the other we had not been told of and she is not suitable. Was baptized only a few days before (we expect them to have been Christians at least a year), reads Burmese very poorly and does not understand it, and cannot write at all! Mr. Cochrane should not have sent her without our permission, and I have written to see what is to be done. She ought not to be supported here.

June 4, '16

Tuesday we had a very good new girl come and also another of the unsuitable kind. This one too had a pastor's certificate, and we took her in, but three days was enough to show that she was not up to the mark in health, in mental ability, and worst of all in moral character. She said she had a brother-in-law in Rangoon and we sent her there with two older girls, but it turned out she had never seen him, and was no relation at all anyway! The man is a Chinese preacher with a nice Karen wife, and they came out Saturday morning to see us about it, with the cutest baby you ever saw with them. They agreed to care for the girl while her father was being sent for. So letters and telegrams must be sent, etc. etc. These good-for-nothing ones take more time, strength and money than the good ones.

June 11, '16

On Monday Miss Fredrickson called to see about that girl we had to send back, as she was still staying at her supposed relatives near Miss Fredrickson's home. I had written and telegraphed her father and by Wednesday word came to send her by a man at the seminary, so I got a gharry and before school rushed up there only to find the man had gone. So after school we went to Mission Road and saw the girl and Miss Fredrickson. It was finally arranged that her Bible woman was to take the girl as far as Prome and put her on the steamer, and I was to telegraph her father to meet her at the steamer landing and see her the 40 miles of cart journey to her home! A night on the train, a day on the steamer, and a day and night by cart makes the journey, to be paid for, besides the trip to Prome and back for the Bible woman and no end of time for us, not to mention gharry hire, telegraphs etc. etc. All because a native pastor looked upon the Bible school as a reformatory or Refuge for Undesirables!

The core curriculum of the school was the study of the Bible. The 1913 annual report sent to friends and supporters provides a detailed program description.

> During the three years' course all of the Old Testament Historical Books, Daniel and some of the Minor Prophets, the Gospels, Acts, and the leading Epistles are thoroughly studied, an outline of every chapter being copied into notebooks and committed to memory by the pupils, with a "sentence a chapter" outline of some of the books in addition, that they may know where to find any portion wanted for use. A course in Christian Doctrines, an Outline and Introduction to each Book of the Bible, Torrey's "Practical Work," and the best Burman tracts are also studied. Besides this the entire school commits to memory every week a portion of the Scripture, from three to ten verses in length, and a standard hymn. A number of these texts are recited every morning in the opening exercises, and by the end of the year each girl knows them all well. We choose important passages often referred to in teaching. At the close of the rains the six who did the best in reciting these texts receive a prize. [In 1913 this was a copy of *The Life of Paul* presented by the translator, U Pay.]
>
> The girls take turns in leading the opening exercises, choosing the hymn, leading in prayer, and giving a short talk on the passage read, which is always from some book they have studied. In this way they gain confidence and learn to bring out the main point. As they know they will be corrected if they make a mistake, they prepare carefully beforehand.

All instruction was carried out between Hattie and Ruth, each taking turns with the different classes. Teaching proved to be a full-time job. During times when one was called away or fell ill, there was no one at hand to step in. Nevertheless, classroom work was kept up as much as possible.

May 18, '95

> We each have between 4-1/2 and 5 hours in school daily, five classes each and it takes all the morning before breakfast <u>at least</u> to prepare for it.

July 26, '13

A week ago Ruth suddenly developed a very bad throat, and we sent for the doctor who came four times in all and gave various things to spray, inhale, and take. The first week the classes were kept busy by my passing on her directions, and for four days this week she has had them upstairs.

Hattie and Ruth used a variety of assignments in their attempt to increase the effectiveness of their teaching.

Aug. 21, '09

Miss Fredrickson told us a funny thing when here last time. Her Bible woman, who graduated here last year, received a roll through the mail; as she undid it before Miss Fredrickson, she [Miss F.] asked what it was and she replied it was her "Doctrine" book (they write out the doctrines and learn them in Miss Ranney's class). So Miss Fredrickson asked where it came back from, and she said, "Oh, I lent it to one of the students at the Theological Seminary to copy; they study 'The-ol-o-ze' and they don't understand it, but by having this they are able to understand that better"!!! Ours is more within their reach because it is not a translation of an English book, but was prepared with an eye to the untrained Burmese mind.

Sept. 18, '09

We have been having the girls take notes and see how much they can tell about the sermon they hear on Sunday morning. Some do fairly well, but they are apt to leave out the point of the illustrations and in fact the main points of the sermon. They lack in both reason and discrimination.

While the major work of the school was dedicated to classwork and study of the Bible, Hattie and Ruth sought to provide further enrichment through additional lectures, demonstrations, and activities. Some of these were designed to serve educational or practical purposes; others were included for enjoyment and recreation. Ad hoc topics were incorporated into the school work as issues were raised by the students or by events. Presentations by visiting lecturers were often opportunities for others in the community to enjoy as well.

Aug. 13, '09

One day one of the girls brought up the doctrine of soul-sleeping which is taught by the Seventh Day Adventists, one which she had heard. So I took the Friday meeting and went over the more important texts which disprove it, for the benefit of all the women, as they are bound to meet it. Some from our churches have gone over to them. Shall take up Saturday-keeping later on.

Jan. 1, '10

Friday afternoon instead of the usual work we had one of the College teachers who lives out here come and give the girls the proofs that the earth is round; a point that the heathen are very slow to believe, even those who have some education.

Dec. 15, '12

Monday morning Katie Armstrong brought out Mr. Burges, the Secretary of the All India Sunday School Union, to speak to our girls before he went to speak to Dr. McGuire's men at 9 o'clock. We had the girls all ready, and he spoke for 20 minutes or so, on the work in India and the very great importance of work for the children, I interpreting.

Then on Friday, by previous arrangement, we had Miss Strout, Secretary of the WCTU, who is in Burma for three years, come and speak to the woman's prayer meeting. There were 16 in from outside, besides our girls, so she had a nice little audience, and gave a good temperance talk, on all harmful drinks and drugs, I again interpreting. We hear that the use of cocaine is spreading among the natives, and there is always more or less of opium using.

Nov. 20, '15

This evening we have the Woodins from our farthest station off in the Chin Hills to dinner, and to speak to the girls a few minutes. One of our Chin graduates is the wife of one of the Woodins' preachers, so we have an extra interest in them.

Aug. 11, '16

Tonight we are to have something new for the girls. We have borrowed the radioscope of the WCTU and Dr. Thomas is going to show the post card pictures they bought on their trip home via the Pacific. Mr. Wiatt will run the light and all will have dinner with us first.

Aug. 26, '16

We had another picture show for the girls, as we still had the mirrorscope in the house. This time Miss Mack came to dinner and afterward ran the lantern while I explained the pictures. We had a few temperance ones and then I showed a lot of Rochester views of the parks with the flowers in blossom, and some others of striking mountains, waterfalls, etc. Quite a lot of outside people came in without any invitation from us and rather spoilt things!

Dec. 10, '16

Friday we had Dr. Coté come out and give the girls a talk on the care of their health from a Christian viewpoint. I translated the talk which was very good, and was well listened to by our girls and 21 women of the church who came in.

Nov. 24, '07

On Tuesday Ah Sou came out and gave the first of a series of lectures on how to do personal work. It was both profitable and enjoyable; he expects to come out every Tuesday evening.

June 22, '13

We are having drill twice a week to wake them up and give a little more exercise.

Attendance at community social events and occasions was also instructive.

July 17, '15

I took a lot of the girls to a funeral meeting, as a sister of one of our old girls had died of heart trouble at Daw Oo's. All the other relatives are heathen, and the wailing as she was put into the coffin could be heard all over the neighborhood. We started singing and that stopped it. But the next day when the coffin was closed they went at it worse than ever, pounding their heads on floor and walls, jumping onto the coffin and howling terrifically. When you consider that Buddhism offers absolutely no hope whatever of any possible reunion, much less of any resurrection of the body, you can see why they should do so. These people have, of course, heard the Gospel many times, and heard it again now. You would think they would be only too glad to accept. The behavior of the husband and the Christian sister was quite another matter. Ruth took the girls to the funeral Sunday afternoon.

A "social evening" with the women was a monthly event during the school year and held as a special treat on other occasions. Characteristically, Hattie and Ruth made use of the evenings for additional education and exposure to the wider world. From time to time, visiting friends from the mission attended and participated in the activities.

July 12, '94

Last Friday evening we had the girls up and the Kelleys came and after singing some new songs (my translations) we showed them ten rolls of Sunday School pictures, one on Acts and one on Joshua. They had to guess what the pictures were, who the characters, and tell the circumstances. The new class couldn't do much but those who had Acts last year and had read a little in Joshua did beautifully. To bring out the new ones Miss Ranney had them give the subjects in order of the first 30 chapters of Genesis which they did very well indeed. Mr. Kelley was much pleased and all seemed to have a very good time.

Aug. 24, '94

Our Magic Lantern Show was a great success: girls — 80 natives big and little came and seemed to enjoy it thoroughly, the closing pictures of wild animals being especially to their taste. Mr. Hicks brought Alice and the Kelleys their boy and girl, Mr. Thomas had Albert and the Roaches came alone. The Kelleys had to leave at 8 P.M. but the rest stayed to tea after the crowd was gone. All of our women and a number of Mr. Thomas's men were out, even our girl who had been sick all the week bundled up and came and has been well ever since!

June 7, '95

Last Friday we had our first social for our 22 girls and Po Min and baby. Katie Armstrong came and brought her Karen girl and Tamil girl and they sang in Tamil and Telugu and our girls in Pwo, Sgan Karen, and Burmese, and we all sang a verse of "Come to Jesus" in six languages, one after another. Then we showed pictures and photos and all had a <u>real</u> good time.

July 9, '97

We had Mr. Kelley and the Kemindine ladies to dinner Friday and had the girls up in the evening. Frank and Jennie also came over and we had singing, a good talk to the girls by Mr. Kelley, and then we for the first time had games. We had put 35 articles on the dining room table, the girls and the guests, too, went out and looked at them one minute and came back and wrote down all they could remember. Miss Chapman did the best at 27, a girl Mah Delay next, Mr. Kelley and the Chin girl and a Burman next. We gave the girl winners a bright card. Then one person chose some article in the room and all guessed till we hit it. Then a Bible character, etc. The girls entered into it and did very well.

Aug. 3, '07

Thursday evening we had the girls up again for a social hour and a half, which they greatly enjoyed. We played games as before, adding hunt the thimble, and when it was put on Miss Ranney's shoulder and the hunters could not see it when right before them, the rest were convulsed with laughter; it gave them all a good shaking up. As they went out we gave each a few sweet biscuits in a fancy paper napkin.

Sept. 18, '09

Friday night we had the girls up for a social evening, and had a tail-less donkey of Mr. McGuire's, the girls being divided into two sets and seeing which could get the highest numbers in putting the tail on, blindfolded. The donkey has white circles with numbers all over him, and when I asked them what was the matter with him, they said he had small-pox!! It took them some time to discover that he had no tail! After that we played a Scripture game and sang and they had a good time.

July 6, '13

Friday evening we had the girls up for a social, had them write in eight minutes as many names of articles in use in a Burman house as they could, the highest was 54 and the lowest 18. Then they wrote occupations of Burmans and got up to over 30. Then we played "I packed my trunk and put in —," each putting in all that the previous ones had mentioned and adding her own, keeping the same order every time. We went twice around the circle and the last one had 41 things to name in right order and did it. They are good at any memory game. Then we had singing in Shan, Chin, Karen and Burmese. As they went out each had two markers for their Bibles, a card and a Scripture picture.

One practical addition to the scheduled school activities was inaugurated in 1913, and became a regular feature of each year's program from that time on.

June 22, '13

We have started a new thing in the school. We found that most of the girls did not know how to cut and make their own jackets, so we have engaged the nurse who lives across the way and is up on the matter, to come Saturdays and teach them. She began yesterday. We furnish the cloth and each girl is to have the jacket when she has cut it and made it under Ma O Zah's direction. Then the two who do the best work are to have cloth for another one as a prize.

Sept. 7, '13

The other event of the week was the selection of the best made jackets, which the girls have been working over for some time past. We invited Mrs. Smith, Anna, Mrs. Thomas, and Mary Ranney to come at 4:30, and we had afternoon tea at once, and a good visit at the same time. Then they settled down to the jackets, selected the six best, and from them the two best for prizes and two more for honorable mention. Then we all went downstairs and gathered the girls, and Mrs. Smith and Mrs. Thomas each gave a little talk, and a Shan girl from Namkhan and a Burman girl from Mandalay took the prizes, another Shan and a Burman having honorable mention. The girls recited a passage of Scripture, Ps 139:1-12, and sang a song for the guests. Everybody seemed to enjoy the occasion very much, including Ma O Zah who taught them.

In preparation for future work as Bible women and educators, the Bible school students were encouraged to make practical application of their Bible studies through participation in community work, native Sunday schools, and during vacation periods, either at home or under the supervision of missionaries.

May 26, '06

Today many of the women went out in different directions to do evangelistic work. They are to start a Sunday School in a Christian house by the river tomorrow, the people promising to call in the numerous heathen children around. With five classes a day to prepare for and teach, we do not do much else.

Nov. 19, '16

On Wednesday we called school early and then let the girls go for a noon meeting at the house of a Christian family where a child has been sick for a long time and they wanted a prayer meeting for him.

The school did not always run as smoothly as Hattie and Ruth might have wished. Dedicated to their girls, Hattie and Ruth were firm disciplinarians in their efforts to protect them from taking the wrong path — back to heathenism, bad habits, unchristian behavior, or making an unsuitable marriage. Known as "Mama Phinney" and "Mama Ranney" ("Mama" was the term used for the missionaries, a term equivalent to "big sister"), they ruled their family with a firm hand. Disputes among the girls or other forms of unsuitable behavior often required their intervention.

Aug. 14, '96

We had a little fuss in the school between two girls — the only ruffle this year. The Devil tried hard to get one of them and spoil her prospects altogether but he <u>didn't</u> get her! But on the other hand the affair was made a blessing to the school —

we took the first hour for a meeting and had a chance to make practical application of various truths taught in the classes.

Aug. 14, '97

What has really tired us is a little fuss between some of the girls, not of itself of any importance, but stirring up such a feeling that we felt we could not go on till a better spirit prevailed. We had a session of silent prayer and then called for confessions from any who had broken the rules of school. A number confessed to smoking in the house, going by <u>twos</u> instead of <u>threes</u> to bazaar, etc. but after we let them go, the real trouble was aired by two coming up and talking it over with us here. We had prayers with them and they went away feeling some better. It broke out again the next morning and we had Saya who knew the whole matter lead the regular Wednesday meeting which he did most acceptably and now I think the bad feelings are put away. We very seldom have such trouble, but there are two <u>new</u> Christians among them, who don't enjoy being under authority a bit, and have not yet got rid of a good deal of heathenism generally and they are mainly the cause of friction. We felt as if we had been pulled through a <u>small</u> knothole when it was over.

On occasion Hattie and Ruth had to take on the parent or parents of a student in what they felt to be the best interest of the student.

June 17, '97

The mother of a third year Burman girl wants to call her out because she had a sick turn and, as she is very wilful and not a nice woman to get on with, she may succeed. There have been more trials and tribulations this year. Just there the aforesaid girl and her mother came and I talked an hour or so with them and finally the mother gave in and the girl is to stay. We had prayers over it with the girl and her brother who came to call her this morning, and she told the mother that "The Lord knew about <u>this</u> matter, anyway, for the Mama told Him," and I think they were all impressed by it, and didn't quite dare to call her. We've never had a girl drop out of the third year and don't want to. After being fed and taught two terms they ought to finish and be in a position to be useful.

Aug. 26, '05

We have found out that the dullest girl in school, who ought really not to have come, was carrying on a correspondence with a student in the Theological Seminary and clandestine meetings were being planned. Considering the girl's character, or rather lack of character, all agreed that she must be sent home at once. A suitable escort was found and this morning I saw them off for Thonze, where if the girl really wants to study the Bible she will still have a chance. What possessed any young man to write to her is beyond me! The most stupid and least attractive in the whole school!!! We have no objections to the young folks marrying, if they will go about it in a suitable manner.

I gave the girls a lecture Monday morning, and things have moved on at a better rate since. With a drag removed the others have been more in earnest and have done better work.

We called on the Eveleths [of the Theological Seminary] on Thursday. Their young men had been given a stiff talk on the subject of interfering with our girls in an underhanded way, so I think we will have peace now for the rest of the term.

Sept. 23, '05

The only unmarried native teacher in the Burman Theological Seminary is looking toward one of our nicest girls, and as he is going about it in a proper way we are pleased. It would be an ideal match and we hope it will come off.

Oct. 6, '05

We had another disagreeable event this week, being obliged to send Ma Myit back to the Hascalls. She had not been doing well for some time in various ways, and was so under the influence of the heathen woman in bazaar whom her mother had hired to win her back to Buddhism, that we felt she must be got away. Besides, her mother was planning to come for her at the close of school and then we could not hinder her going right back to the heathen, whereas if we sent her back to the Hascalls she would have one more chance to live with Christians. She objected to going but we insisted and Daw Oo took her. She is now with the two Bible women who were our post-graduates of last year and has every chance to be a Christian if she will.

Aug. 1, '09

We have had no less than eight <u>long</u> talks with as many different people, out of school hours, during the week. Part were in regard to the girl we did not allow to come back. She refuses to go home to her father, or to stay with good people, and has settled now with a heathen family here in Insein near the bazaar, where she can have a chance to get our girls into mischief if possible. They have strict orders to have nothing to do with her. The rest were about some not altogether above-board doings of two of the girls when we closed for a week. Everybody seems to be pretty well straightened out now and we hope for clear sailing for awhile.

Nov. 6, '09

The girl turned out came back three times begging to be taken back and her mother came once, but we saw no signs of real repentance or reform, in fact she lied while pleading to return, so we refused.

Dec. 6, '14

The newly appeared mother and brother of one of our girls, whom we supposed had not a relative in the world, wished to take her for over Sunday, but as we knew nothing about them or their surroundings, we did not allow it. It looks as if they wanted to marry her off to a heathen Burman.

We had a call from Abraham to tell us about the newly turned up folks of our one Tamil girl. His story was not such that we could let her go to them for Christmas. She took it very well and had a much better time here.

Illness among the women was an ever-present worry and added burden for Ruth and Hattie. Some years were relatively free of serious health problems among the women; others were plagued by almost constant illness. As in all other aspects of the school, Ruth and Hattie took responsibility for the women's care, assisted by the others as need arose.

We have had sickness as never before though not to break into the attendance. Two Karen girls have <u>itch</u>, one very badly and of long standing, had it when she came but didn't tell till it got so bad she couldn't stand it. She is the one who always shuts up the school windows and carries my chair back and forth etc. etc! Miss McAllister has a reputation all through Kemindine for curing itch (!) (a very common trouble) and she gave us salve and directions.

Another has <u>bad eyes</u> and another <u>worms,</u> and worst of all Wednesday one came down with <u>beri-beri,</u> that mysterious, much dreaded, often fatal disease that caused the removal of the Theological Seminary from across the road to Insein. The girl was swollen all over and heavy, and her breathing was difficult. Miss McAllister knows more about beri-beri from practical experience than any doctor and again she prescribed. We felt it was a serious matter, if the girl died or was sick long it would injure the school much, for the natives are afraid of it. The girl however improved at once and seems now to be on the way to recovery, a very plain answer to prayer.

July 22, '05

This has been a queer week; one of the girls had been careless and was taken in the night Monday with a dreadful attack of "gas," was swollen greatly and suffering intensely. We did all we could, and finally sent to the Hospital for something, which enabled her to sleep the rest of the night. We were up most of the time from 10:30 to about 3 A.M. She was as bad as ever in the morning and we sent for the doctor who gave her something to ease the pain, another big dose. At night without our knowing it, the neighbors gave her a dose of powerful Burman medicine and that relieved her. As U Pan Di said, "She is a Burman and needs Burman medicine," and certainly the English medicine did not seem strong enough, though it would have laid out an English person!

As the whole school were up most of the night, and a number were tired out working over her, we found it impossible to have school on Tuesday; we were not sorry on our own account. Three have been out all the week, and one other was out Friday afternoon, having taken cold being up that night. The whole performance served to point a moral, which I took care they should not fail to see, particularly as Ruth took cold too.

June 4, '09

This has been a rather strenuous week; on Tuesday the two Shan girls who came down from Namkhan, came down with fever. One had little fever but extreme exhaustion, the other with high fever. It became evident in the evening that something should be done, as my remedies had little effect, so we called the Hospital Assistant, the native doctor. We found him a nice man, Tamil I think. He examined the girls carefully and sent back by our boy who went with him, medicine for the night. We were up till 11 P.M. and two of the girls watched till 2 A.M., when I went out and sent them to bed, after the doses had been given. All slept till 5 A.M. when I went again and saw to them. They seemed to improve much and the doctor came in the morning and gave different medicine. The servants and we were kept busy cooking proper food for them and going to the Hospital for medicine.

On Thursday night the one who had 104 degrees but had seemed to rally the best was as bad as ever, so the trouble was not gone we saw, and the other one was weak and had no appetite. We, the girls, and the servants were very tired with the extra care and so we decided to send them to the Dufferin Hospital, which we did on Friday noon. It was a great relief; we have no room for the sick and no one to take the responsibility of their care. We cannot teach all day, do the necessary studying and other things, and care for girls who are really sick. It is a great mercy that we are near enough to the Dufferin Hospital to send cases there.

Even in the case of a lengthy illness, Hattie and Ruth saw that their students received all possible care, despite the hardship it placed on them, the other women, and the school.

Nov. 27, '10

One of our Chin girls from Sandoway has been ill all the week, and we have had the native doctor twice for her. He says it is typhoid malaria. Very fortunately for us and the girl, there is a Christian widow, a trained nurse, living across the road from us, whom we have helped considerably, and she had taken in the girl and is caring for her. We send over the milk for her and she is not allowed anything else. It takes a bit of trotting even then, but we trust it will not be a serious case.

Dec. 4, '10

Our sick girl at Ma O Zah's grew worse and when we sent for the Baboo he could not come. The fever went down a little but we had him come the next afternoon, and he advised sending her to the hospital with her nurse, as they had no one there to care for women. This we did, she being carried in a covered litter by coolies. Since then she has steadily improved, and if there is no relapse will be all right. Is allowed nothing but milk yet. The morning after she was removed I saw that the room was thoroughly disinfected and cleaned, so the family could use it again.

Dec. 11, '10

Our sick girl passed the 21st day and was very ill, and the nurse gave out, so that Wednesday I had to rush in to Dufferin Hospital and get a nurse from there to take the case. She is by no means equal to Ma O Zah, being just a young woman with only a year and a half in Dufferin for training. We send one of our girls every night to help her and be a companion. Taking the girls by turns it is not hard for them. When the 28th day comes, Ma O Zah will go for the night, or two nights. All the doctor can say is that she may pull through. Ma O Zah cooks the nurse's food and our pani-wallah takes it to her twice a day.

Dec. 25, '10

Yesterday afternoon I went to see our sick girl. Found her much better and able now to eat a bit of soft rice. But she must stay one week more. Her sickness will cost us over Rs.100, but Mary has given quite a bit toward it, and we shall have help from other sources as well.

Jan. 1, '11

Our sick girl was sent home, as the room was wanted for another patient. She has been kept on a little soft rice and milk all the week, but is beginning on ordinary rice now. Her sickness has left its mark on her very plainly; she does not look like the rest of the school who are all plump.

Jan. 8, '11

The sick girl is now taking her own food, so that is a relief to us.

July 9, '15

We have had a hard week with two girls very sick, so on Wednesday we sent for the native doctor at the Railroad Hospital, where we get medicine for them when what we have in the house does not serve. The trouble proved to be dengue, but we feared something more serious. One had 105 [fever] for a day and night in spite of medicines, and the other was bad with rash and swelling of glands that follows this fever. The fact that we have no separate room for the sick has made us all this sickness, as this fever is contagious. We hope to have a new dormitory next year as Miss Chapman is ready to furnish the cash.

Illness and upsets among the women were not the only factors offsetting any possible monotony engendered by the regularity of school life. Additional excitement was provided on occasion by intruders from outside.

Jan. 8, '11

Last night thieves broke into the pani-wallah's room, took out his box and stole Rs.3. While they were trying to enter cook's room he awoke and drove them off. They took off two fence pickets to get in by. First time we ever had thieves [in Insein].

Aug. 18, '12

The last and most distressing event occurred at 3:30 this morning when I was wakened by the calling of the girls, and found that a thief had, by using an auger, made a hole in their front door, pulled back the bolt, and taken out the first trunk he came to. He must have hit the door for the girls awoke and made a fuss, so he got no more. But it so happened that he got a box of one of the better-off girls, besides all of her clothing, a pair of gold bracelets and one or two small things. I sent in word and the Police Inspector came and took notes and promised to have the pawn shops searched and effort made to find the goods. As rice is very high and the people are poor, there is more thieving than usual. Our servants have been troubled but never the girls before.

Aug. 25, '12

On Tuesday they, or he [the thief] came again. The door had a different fastening, and a jar knocked down a box and woke the girls, who began to talk, get a light etc., but the man tried the window, another door, rapped on the floor, and went off shaking his skirt so they could hear, as much as to say, "I am not afraid of you!!" Now the girls have a bell, which they are to ring lustily, in case of trouble. The Police Supt. said he would send a man to watch the place, but he did not. However, the girls got a good night's sleep, believing he had. We are going to make our house more secure, as an agile man could easily get in.

Sept. 8, '12

We have not had any more thieves, though others have had trouble, the police being just about worthless. Miss Beale told us of a case nearby, when the whole neighborhood was aroused and police whistled for, all up and down the street, without response. The next day someone asked a Burman policeman if he did not hear the fuss, and he said "Yes, but he was afraid to come out"!!! The ladder used by the thief was a police ladder! The barracks are nearby.

Sept. 15, '12

One night the same thief came again and tried his old trick of boring holes in the door, but the girls woke and called to us and he departed. They had the bell right along till that night when the girl who should have taken it over, forgot it.

I wrote the Chief of Police here again and this time he came himself and later sent a young Eurasian policeman, who looked around and about 10:30 came with two native police and spent the night in the girls' cookhouse, watching for the man. They were here again last night, but I do not know how long they will keep it up. We were afraid the thief <u>would</u> come before, now we are afraid he <u>won't</u> — while these men are here!

Sept. 29, '12

After school we went to the headman in the Police, Mr. Hill, living near, and he took my revolver to register, as one is not allowed to use firearms that are not registered. He advised me to fire it off every now and again, so thieves would know we were armed; did not seem to be afraid of my hitting anybody!! He returned it next day with the registration papers.

Thursday after school we went to the Deputy Commissioner's not far off, to get a permit to buy cartridges for my revolver, which he very graciously provided.

The grounds were subject to another kind of intruder who also added excitement to school life.

Aug. 4, '06

There was a great hullabaloo at the dormitory and we heard cries of "snake!" so sent the cook and pani-wallah out to help. After a grand skirmish and much squealing and running on the part of the girls, a snake two yards long was killed and tossed in the creek. The cook said it was poisonous but I doubt it as it had a very sharp-pointed tail.

May 23, '08

Monday while we were at dinner, the pani-wallah suddenly marched through the room with a stick and an air of great caution and determination. I followed and saw a good-sized cobra coming up the front stairs. At the first landing pani-wallah met it with a good blow which sent it hissing down, and at the foot of the flight it was killed. Cook's wife saw it go under the school-rooms and was set to watch, so when she saw it come out in the downstairs lobby she called out. We would have had a fright and likely something worse had it come all the way up. The girls saw a snake in the grass yesterday, so I keep my snake medicine handy.

Aug. 21, '09

As we were in school on Friday a girl suddenly exclaimed "a snake" and we all went out; the cook was called and he chased it, but had only a short hoe so did not dare to hit it and it escaped. It was a cobra and was reared up just under the eaves about sixteen feet from the school door. One of those who saw it said it stood up about three feet, but that might be taken down a third at least. Ruth saw it go across one corner of the baptistery. It was well it ran instead of showing fight as they often do.

At dinner Mrs. Stevens told how she killed a big one with a hatchet, that was under their room when Dr. Stevens was very ill and the servants would not touch it. She fought it till she cut its head off. The doctor told her next day never to do so again; a most dangerous thing, as they attack one, rising up high enough to hit one in the face.

Aug. 8, '14

About our snake scare last Saturday night. Just as we and Miss Putnam had finished dinner, Joseph called me out and whispered that there was a snake in the lobby at the head of the stairs. I looked from a safe distance and so did Miss Putnam. When I urged that they kill it, they said it was a very fast kind and if not killed with one blow, no knowing where it would go. I never knew them to be afraid to tackle one before. So we closed the two doors and waited while he went to call another man. When he came with a big stick we retired to Ruth's bedroom and closed all the doors, but as nothing happened I ventured out to see. The three men were standing around viewing it at a safe distance still, and trying to see it better by holding three lights. Finally the outside man screwed up his courage, took a step forward and brought down his long stick with a resounding whack on the snake in its dim corner. Such a funny look came over his face and then over Joseph's and the pani-wallah's that I ventured near, and behold, the snake had become just Miss Putnam's muddy rubbers!!! To five of us they certainly did look exactly like a snake curled up in a sort of figure eight fashion. Ruth wouldn't look, but as Miss Putnam and I were as much fooled as the men, we all had a good laugh and sat down quite comfortable in our minds. As a cobra did actually come up our front steps once, we were the more easily deceived.

Despite the alarms and excursions provided by recalcitrant girls, heathen influences, illness, thieves and snakes, each year ended in its time. For Hattie this meant facing her annual task of helping the girls prepare their essays — a regular feature of the Bible school graduation exercises.

Sept. 22, '06

My extra work this week has been struggling over the graduating essays, or "sermonettes" of the girls. It has taken alot of time but I think now they will get them into better shape. They have no idea of the logical sequence of thought. Burmans haven't, anyway.

Dec. 15, '07

Graduating essays are on the docket now, and the girls and I are struggling over them. I fancy I shall spend more time over them than they do.

Dec. 25, '10

I have spent a good deal of time on the girls' essays. We discovered to our amazement and amusement that the whole class were combining to write each essay! Or at least the six who did not get theirs done in vacation, and some who did were helping! When taken to task about it, they evidently had not got an idea but that was the proper way to do! It is too late to begin all over again so the class essays will be read by the combined authors!

Vacation periods presented a problem for some of the women. Although most were able to return home to their families, others needed help in making arrangements.

Jan. 18, '14

Miss Fredrickson has very kindly agreed to let our two Shan girls, who cannot go home between terms, stay with her Bible women on that compound, where they will be safe and be acquiring new experiences, not to mention having daily prayers with Miss Fredrickson and her women, and services of the Lanmadaw Church. The arrangements made last year were not altogether satisfactory, and it is a great relief to have them so well provided for.

Jan. 25, '14

Friday morning we had a call from Miss Peck, just back from America, and it was arranged that she should have one of our second year girls between terms. As it is one of the Shan orphans that had to be provided for, we were very glad of the chance of her doing something to support herself and have some practice in practical work as well.

Jan. 3, '15

Saturday we had alot of writing as we always do at this season in connection with getting the girls settled. Our three Chins from Sandoway cannot go for vacation, as boats are not running as formerly, but Mr. Condict will take all, with his own girl, and give them work for the vacation, at which we, and they, are much pleased. How to get our two Shan graduates back to Namkhan, from where they came three years ago, is another question not yet settled. One Burman goes to Miss Ayers, Prome.

Dec. 19, '15

At the end of the year there is always no end of writing around to get the girls settled. Four are still unprovided for owing to lack of funds in the fields to which they belong. The hill people can't work for the Burmans who look down on them, and their own people are too poor to support them as Bible women or teachers.

Graduation exercises were the last great event of the school year and an occasion for public appreciation of the women's accomplishments.

ကိုယ်ဝိညည်ကိုခဲ့းခေါ်တွ၍။

၁
လိုညည့်မို့ ။စွံ့အားထုတ်၍၏။
ကြီးစားဖွဲ့ရွှေးတို့ဧ။
သင်ပြေးရာ၊ကောင်းကင်ထံ့ရောက်လမ်၊
ရရန့်။ရွှသ၇ဉ့။

၂
မိ်ယ်။တိမ်ကဲ့ထို့သက်သေအမှု၊
ပိုင်းရဲ့လျှက်ကြည့်ရှုနေ့၊
ကျွန်ံဖြီး၊ဖြေလွှင်၊ရာ၁ရ့ရင်ထေ၊၊
ရွှေသို့သာတို၊တက်ထေ၊

၃
ဘုရား၊သခင့်ံအဘး၊ေပးသံ၊
ဇလတ်မှ၊ကျ္၊ရရ့ံသည်ံ၊
ဆုလဘ်တော်ကို၊သင်ခြင်းေရန့၊
ရွှလက်တော်ံဆန့်တန့်။၏။

၄
မိုးမင်၊အ၇ရင်၊တိုံ၊မကိုရှ့
ထို့ပွင်း၊ဖျက်ဝီ၊သေ၁၈ံလည်း၊
ထိုဆုလဘ်သည်၊အစည့်တမရိတ်
အ၊ရင်၊တွ့ဉ့၊ေတာက်လိ၍မည်၊

၅
ကယ်တင်ပိုင်ရှင့်၊ေက်ျ၊ရ္ေတာ်ေကျာင့်
ကျွန်ံလ်မ၊ဝင်ဖြီ၊
လမ်းဆုံး၊ေရာက်လော၊ံ၊ေြ၊တော်ရင်လှ၊
ေအာင်ပန်းဆုတ၊ပါမည်၊

Burman Woman's Bible School,

1893—1915.

CLOSING EXERCISES

AT THE

BAPTIST CHAPEL, MINGALADONE ROAD,

INSEIN,

3:45 P.M., January 28th, 1915.

မြန်မာမိန်းမကျမ်းစာသင်ကျောင်း၊

၁၈၉၃ ခု-၁၉၁၅ ခု၊

လွတ်ခြင်းနှင့်ဆိုင်သော အခါလည်ပွဲ၊

အင်းစိန်မြို့၊ ဇန္နဝါရီလ ၂၈ ရက်၊

၃ နာရီ ၄၃ မိနစ်၊

Bible School in charge of Misses Ranney and Phinney.

Programme.

Singing,	"Jesus is a friend of mine."
တီုခြင်း၊ဆိုခြင်း၊	သခင်ေယ၊ရှ္၊ေမိတ်ိ၊ရ္ှတည့်တ၊ကျ္။
Prayer,	Dr. Thomas.
ဆုေတာင်းခြင်း၊	ထ၇ာ၊ေသ၁၊မ၊
Scripture,	Phil. 2:5-11 by the School.
ကျမ်း၊ေ၊ာ၊တ်ခြင်း၊	ဖိ.၂း၅-၁၁ ေကျာင်း၊တို့ဖတ်၊သ၊
Singing,	"Go take your stations."
တီုခြင်း၊ဆိုခြင်း၊	ဆိုင်ရ၊၊လ၊၁ရ၊က်ထို့သွ၊၊ထ၊ေထ၊က္။
A Familiar Question,	Ma E Maing, (Bur.)
ထူး၊ေ၊၊တ်သ၊၁၊ေမး၊ေမ်၊ခြင်း၊	မ၊ရိ၊င်း ေကာ၊ကြီး၊မြို့
God's Calls to Men,	Ma Nan Mo, (Shan).
ေ၁ါ၊ေတ၊ာ်မှ၊ဖြ၊ေ၊၊း၊အ၊ေ၊ာ၊၊၊၊	မနံမို နန့်ခမ်းမြို့
The Meaning of the Jewish Feasts,	Ma Pu (Bur.).
ထုၜပွဲ၊ရ၊၊ေ၊၊ပြ၊သ၊ေ၊ာ၊၊ေ၊၊ာ၊င်း၊အ၊ေ၊၊	မပု ဂလုန့်မြို့
God's Watchcare of His Own,	Ma Dun Hla (Karen).
ဘုရား၊သ၊ေ၊င်၊သ၊ည်၊ အ၊ဆ၊ရ၊ာ၊ဉ့်ပ္ိ၊ပ်ဝ၊င်ေ၊ာ၊င်၊	မဒွ၊က်ြ၊ သ္ု၊လ၊၊င်၊တ၊န့်၊ရ္၊ာ၊၊
	ထိ၊၊န်း၊ေ၊ာ၊၊၊မ္ု၊ခြ၊င်း၊အ၊ေ၊ကြ၊ာ၊င်း၊
The High-priesthood of Christ,	Ma Nan Pwe, (Shan).
၁ါ၊ဘို၊ု၊က်၊ဟ၊ရ်ာ၊ ု၊ေ၊၊ရ္ာ၊။၊၊တိ၊တ်၊မ၊င်း၊ရ၊ေ၊တ၊ာ၊်အ၊ေ၊ကြ၊ာ၊င်း၊	မနံ၊ပွဲ နန့်ခမ်းမြို့
Singing,	"Awake my soul," by the congregation.
တီုခြင်း၊ဆိုခြင်း၊	ဦးေ၊၊ာ၊က်တ္၊ ၊ အ၊သ္၊ာ၊တ္ုံ၊း၊ဆို၊ရ္၊န့်၊
Address,	Miss Dreidrickson.
ဦ၊းေ၊၊ာ၊က်၊စု၊တ်၊	မ၊ဗ၊ေ၊၊ာ၊ရ္၊င်၊
Presentation of Diplomas,	Miss Phinney.
သ၊က်၊ေ၊သ၊၊လ၊က်၊မ၊တ်၊ေ၊ပး၊ခြ၊င်း၊	မ၊ဖိ၊န၊ည်း၊
	God save the King.
	၎င်းဘုရင်၊ဘုန်း၊တော်ကြီး၊
	ကျွန်ဆို၊ုံ၊ေ၊ု၊၊း၊ရ္ု၊ၢ၊၊င်၊သ၊း
	သ၊က်နည်ပါ၊ေ၊ာ၊၊ရ္၊ါ၊း၊
	မ၊ေ၊၊ာ၊ိ၊်၊ပ၊ါ၊
	ေ၊၊ာ၊င်၊ရ္ု၊န့်နှ၊င့်၊ေ၊င်၊လ္ျ၊က်၊
	ဘု၊န်း၊ေ၊၊ာ၊်သ၊၊ရ္္၊ာ၊၊တိ၊တ၊တ်၊
	မိ၊ဖ၊ပ၊ါ၊ေ၊၊ာ၊တ်၊ထ၊တ်၊
	မ၊ေ၊၊ာ၊်မ္ု၊ပ၊ါ၊
	Benediction.
	ေ၊၊ာ၊င်း၊ကြီး၊ေ၊ပ၊း၊ခြ၊င်း၊

1915 Bible School Graduation Program (Top: front and back; bottom: inside).

Bible School Graduates of 1920.

Jan. 12, '08

Monday I took the graduates over to the Chapel and had them practice their essays; also reckoned up their averages, prepared the certificates, and did various last things. Tuesday was the last day of teaching. Wednesday I went over and saw to decorating the platform with two big palm branches and our potted ferns. Our rug and a little table with a red cover made it look very well. The table cover was one Mother sent before I was home last time, a red one with white lace on it.

The exercises passed off very well. Mr. McGuire gave the address and I gave a little report of the school and at the end presented the certificates with some good advice. There were 14 missionaries present and the rest of the room filled with natives.

Jan. 25, '09

That which was to have happened has come to pass. On Monday we had our last session in the forenoon, and after a final rehearsal of songs in the afternoon, I took some of the girls over to the chapel and had it well cleaned and put in order. Some of the young men had trimmed it for Christmas with chains of bright papers, such as children make in Kindergarten, and they had been left for this occasion, so that the room looked very bright and festive. The next morning I saw to having a lot of pots of begonias, bamboo ferns, and crotons arranged around the front of the platform, so the girls' feet were well hidden.

Then we got the house in order and all in readiness and about 11:45 Anna Smith brought Mrs. and Miss Curly and Miss McLaurin. We went downstairs at once and called the girls, who recited and sang for them. Then they each spoke for a few minutes, I translating. After that we gave out the prizes for the highest standing and for the best exercise books, in each class. Two in the third year class got 99% and their books were also the best, so one got one prize and the other the other. Both were Burmans. A Chin stood the highest in the next class and a Shan in the first year. The prizes were fancy tin boxes to keep their tatting in and the books containing John 3:16 in over 400 languages.

Then we came upstairs and had a nice visit with the ladies. After a cup of tea we went over to the Chapel, which was nicely filled. There were 17 missionaries, beside the three other guests, three other English folks, the Seminary students, Mrs. Rose's graduates, and various other Christians. The girls did themselves credit; Mr. Hascall made a good talk and I gave the diplomas with a parting exhortation.

Wednesday morning to Friday afternoon was broken up with seeing off the various groups of girls and having the dormitory put in order and locked up. Miss Fredrickson takes one of the girls, two go to the Mosiers, and later two may go to Dr. Garton.

Jan. 22, '11

A number of girls left that afternoon, more next day but we have ten left to get started this week. They will be scattered over Burma, two to Sandoway, two to Moulmein, two to Tavoy, two to Bhamo, one to Hsipaw, one to Myingyan and the rest will be around in lower Burma.

Jan. 27, '18

The closing went off in good shape before a house literally "filled to the doors" and a few standing. The Karen graduate did splendidly and took the first prize given by U Tha Din's daughter. A lot of Karen Seminary boys and Mrs. Rose's girls were out. Two of the girls spoke their essays without reference to the paper held in hand and it was a great improvement on reading. Dr. McGuire gave a good talk and I am told I did! All but seven left the next morning and I was awake from 4 A.M. and up at 5:30 and "at it" from then on.

Throughout their lives, Hattie and Ruth maintained an active interest in the lives and work of the "old girls" and graduates of the school, and, through visits and correspondence, maintained close ties with many. In many instances, the women married and had families of their own. Those whose husbands were graduates of the Theological Seminary or pastors in local native churches, were able to use their Bible school training in support of their husbands' work, or at least within the Christian community. While Hattie and Ruth expressed satisfaction with all their graduates who remained good Christians, they were particularly gratified by those graduates who went "into the work," becoming Bible women working with a specific missionary in the field.

Apr. 11, '96

We have just heard of the marriage of the fourth one of our graduating class. (The other three are engaged by missionaries in evangelistic work and doing well.) This one has married the school teacher of her village and done well — a good Christian man. We are very thankful.

[From the mimeographed report for 1911]:
With two Shans in Bhamo, two Talains in the Moulmein
district, two Burmans in Tavoy, a Shan in Hsipaw and a Burman in Pegu, we shall have, with former pupils now at work,
25 representatives among seven races. During the year two late
graduates have married, one a lawyer in Zigon, the other a this
year's graduate from the Burman Seminary.

[1913 report]:
Of the nine who graduated before we went to America,
one after working some time, married the ordained pastor in
Maymyo; two married teachers; one is being trained at
Dufferin Hospital; two Shans and a Burman are at work in
Upper Burma; and one Burman in Tavoy, to whom our last
graduate will be a companion.

June 22, '18
One of last year's graduates, a Karen who took the First
Prize — and gave it back, half to this school and half to the
Tharrawady school from which she came — is now working
quite alone in a heathen village, two hours walk from the
nearest Christian. In her last letter to us she wrote "Tho I am
alone in 'Mountain Pool' Village I am not discouraged. When
downhearted I read about Daniel; when anxious I read Ps:121;
when fearful I shall fall I read about Joseph's overcoming
temptation; at opening of my school I use Mark; at closing I
read Luke; for evening prayers Matthew; to reprove and
instruct myself I read Proverbs." She evidently has learned
what the Bible is for. She is the one who when her mother and
sister died of cholera and later her father, read Job and decided
to stay on in school instead of running off as most Karens do.
She has a school of little children, in a place where 10 teachers
have already failed to make good — a hard wicked village of
heathen. One woman (a widow) is very friendly and makes a
home for her.

Taunggyi, Feb. 11, '21
Tuesday our last year's Toungthu graduate who has been
working in the Inle Lake district with a preacher and his wife,
and done well, came to see us, as she had to go home to help

her sick brother living near here. We had a good visit with her. She can work in three languages and is also, now she is at her home village, carrying on a bag-weaving industry.

A summary of the graduates of the school is reported in the *Burma Baptist Chronicle* (1963):

When the two founders of the school retired in 1929 after 44 and 45 years of service, there were 47 of their graduates in evangelistic work in Burmese, and 41 in Shan mission centers.

Hattie Phinney in 1906.

14

Beyond School Walls

1894 to 1928

While Bible school responsibilities and involvement in Insein Baptist community affairs occupied the majority of their time, Hattie and Ruth continued their participation in the activities of the wider mission, when they could, and maintained active social ties with other missionaries. Annual vacations to popular mission "rest spots," in particular, allowed them a chance to catch up on various nonschool projects, socialize, and enjoy a change of scene.

A primary responsibility for Hattie remained her extensive language work for the press; after the Bible school, it represented her greatest effort and contribution to the work of the mission. Her knowledge of Burmese and her familiarity with the press made her an excellent resource for many routine as well as special projects. *The Burman Messenger* in particular benefited from Hattie's skill — as editor for several years, and as contributor and proofreader for many more. Appointed a member of the Christian Literary Publications Committee for the press, Hattie was called upon to read and review manuscripts submitted for publication.

One of Hattie's major chores each year was the preparation of the coming year's Sunday school lesson papers for use in the native Sunday schools. Working from the outline developed by the International Sunday School Society, Hattie translated the lessons into Burmese, which were then printed up by the press and distributed to the Burman missions. Each year during the winter months she worked hard to complete the coming year's lessons before school began again in May.

In addition, Hattie served as a member of the Burmese Language Examining team testing missionaries and Rangoon College staff on

their mastery of the Burmese language, as had been mandated by
the Woman's Board at the 1893 Conference (reported by Hattie
earlier [Oct. 21, '93]).

Hattie's letters over the years reflected the interwoven and
repetitious nature of these responsibilities, and included ongoing
reports on her progress.

Feb. 7, '07

During the week I have finished the preparation of the
copy for the Burman Sunday School papers for the year and
am glad that work is done. I have been at it for three months. I
have also gotten out my first copy of the *Burman Messenger*. It
is just five years since I edited before.

Feb. 16, '08

Work on the Sunday School papers has progressed very
well considering the numerous interruptions, and will be
finished in another week, I hope. The *Burman Messenger* has
also been started. What do you think of a Burman clerk of a
church sending in notices of baptisms and a death in <u>English</u>
for me to put back into Burmese for the *Messenger*!!! I wrote
an epistle to his pastor, Ah Sou's brother, and returned the
notices, which have now come back in Burmese. Young Burma
is getting too smart! One young man sent a notice (in Burmese)
but asked in English to have it put "in my dead news!" I did!

Oct. 10, '08

This has been a busy week, doing up all sorts of odd jobs. I
am on one of the committees to see about the new Burman Hymn
and Tune Book, and Mr. Hascall sent me a lot of material to
consider and approve or disapprove. I have gone through that and
revised and prepared good copies of four hymns of my own to
offer for acceptance or otherwise. One is original, and the others
translations. I have also done my part for the present in getting
ready for the Language examination of missionaries. There are
three to take their second and four to take their first, so we will
have two days of it, Oct. 26, 27. They will come here and Miss
Ranney will give them breakfast and tiffin. The *Burman Messenger*
has been prepared and I have written out a directory of Burman
missionaries and ordained native pastors for it, by request.

Oct. 25, '08

The past has been another strenuous week, and quite a few things have been accomplished. Firstly I have finished what was necessary of the Sunday School papers, so that I will not have to do any more till after we close school again. Have also read the proof of another *Burman Messenger* and finished getting ready for the language examinations which come off tomorrow and next day, the Springs not taking theirs till the Saturday after we have re-opened; so we shall have three days of it! We have also paid off some social debts; had Miss Evans out for the day, and on another day Miss Thompson, Mrs. Rose coming for dinner.

July 4, '09

One day we went to town in the early morning and I attended to the last *Burman Messenger* proof on the way in. The next two days we were at home, and I did some sewing and also put into our new Burmese Hymn and Tune Book over 20 new hymns, translations of my own, Dr. Stevens' and others' which have never been published but the music to which we found in various books. We have a fine book now, which will be very useful as long as it holds together, and as it was bound at the renowned Mission Press of course it will hold together a long time!

Feb. 26, '10

I have had *Burman Messenger* proof to read and am reading a Burmese manuscript as I am on the publishing committee of the Christian Literature Society of Burma. This is a *Life of Paul* compiled by a Christian man living in Insein.

Oct. 22, '10

The *Burman Messenger* has also been read, but the biggest day's work came yesterday when Mr. Parish and Miss Crooks came for their second examination in Burmese. Miss Fredrickson came and helped me and it took from 8:30 A.M. to 5:30 P.M. with time out for breakfast and tiffin. It was a hard day's work, and I shall have two more in November. Both passed, though they did not do so "with credit," Mr. Parish came near it. Ruth got up nice meals for us all and was able to enjoy visiting at meal times with them.

Feb. 15, '14

The most of Thursday was given to the examination of Mr. and Mrs. Safford in Burmese at the McGuires', Ruth going to breakfast. Mrs. Safford passed her second "with credit," being 86%, but Mr. Safford failed utterly on the first, got only 51%. He ought not to have tried it without putting alot more work on it. He had studied off and on for two years and she more for four years.

Sept. 16, '17

I've read a chapter of Dr. McGuire's Vol. II of *Old Testament History* (Burmese) and approved it on behalf of the Committee on Burmese Publication. Both Dr. Cummings and Mr. Rogers said they would leave it to me, as I was nearby.

For three months each year, Hattie and Ruth were able to free themselves of the responsibilities of the school and escape the heat of lower Burma by literally taking to the hills. These vacations did not, however, mean freedom from the other responsibilities that Hattie carried — press work followed her wherever she went. Proofreading, translation, and manuscripts were forwarded to her in whatever rest spot she and Ruth repaired to. Nevertheless, these hot season retreats provided a needed change of routine and the chance to visit with old friends and meet new people.

Over the years Hattie and Ruth visited several of the favorite missionary hot season rest spots in Burma: Maymyo, Than Doung, Taunggyi, and Kalaw. Several seasons were spent in India: in 1907 at Coonoor; in 1914 and 1918 at Ootacamund. Hattie and Ruth's 1920-21 furlough was spent in Coonoor, Ootacamund, and Bangalore (during the cooler weather). A variety of boarding establishments were available to the missionaries, including "Brooklands" in Coonoor and "Willowlea" in Ootacamund ("Ooty" to the initiate).

Ootacamund, Mar. 9, '07

We left by the Madras steamship at 9:35 A.M. We are second class as we could not afford first. It is second class but we can stand it for a few days.

At Madras we got a boat and went ashore quite comfortably. We took the train at 6:15 P.M., booking our trunks through to Coonoor. The wife of the Governor of the Madras Presidency went by the same train coming up to Ootacamund (Lady Lawley) so we had great quiet at all the stations all night instead of the usual hubbub! We enjoyed the ascent of the hills by the cog railroad and arrived about 2:30 P.M. Tuesday.

There were missionaries on both trains and we united with a lady on the last train, when we arrived, in hiring a cart for our trunks and a carriage to come up the hills to the house. We felt the rarified air a good deal at first, and the least exertions set us to panting and our hearts to beating. All were told not to walk much the first week but we have been able to take some very delightful ones nearby. As Jennie says, "it is the most beautiful place we have ever seen." The mountains, forests of all kinds of evergreen and other trees, the great ferns, 30 feet high, calla lilies growing wild, home flowers of all sorts in the gardens, ferns, and most beautiful lichens. We have filled our fireplace and mantle with pine, cedar etc. and lichen on top, till it is a bower of beauty.

We have a double room. The food is simple and good, and the people (all missionaries or ladies carrying on these homes) are very nice indeed.

We have attended four meetings, Bible reading, besides a service down in town at the Union Chapel, a very long way from here. We went and came in the bandy, a covered cart drawn by bulls — slow and sure but better than walking for such a distance. Besides these meetings out of the house, there are long prayers twice a day — very pleasant but altogether we get almost no time for writing. I have taken some sketches, but have not begun on the letters I brought to answer. I have, however, read two batches of proof and have a Sunday School paper proof to read tomorrow.

Friday the household, guests, and helpers took tea up above the house in the woods and tomorrow about 20 go to Lady Cannings Seat, five miles away, where there is a good view for a picnic. These picnics are combined with nice little prayer meetings.

Their 1914 stay in Ootacamund was recommended for reasons of health.

Jan. 13, '14

We must save our pice as the doctor says Ruth ought to
have six months rest, but less in a good climate like Coonoor
or Ooty might be enough. So we are planning to go to Ootacamund for the hot season, and I can write the Sunday School
lesson notes there.

Feb. 15, '14

We took the 8 P.M. train from Madras, changed at
Mettapaeyam at 10:30 A.M. and for four hours were climbing
the mountains in a car all windows so we could see well. The
views were fine. Passed through Coonoor where we were seven
years ago. This is 7,289 feet and that is 6,616 feet altitude and
this is more bracing and better in every way.

The first few days we rested and took short walks and I
took some stitches and crocheted two napkin rings as we
forgot ours. Ruth wrote 13 letters to our girls. This week we
are taking longer walks, and today we walked <u>down</u> to the Post
Office, 15 minutes going <u>down</u> and 30 minutes coming <u>up</u>! We
are 200 feet higher than the railroad station so about 7,500
altitude. The views are very fine and the air delightful but the
sun is <u>powerful</u> as this is quite a bit farther south than
Rangoon. One day we counted the flowers in the garden —
writing out a list — 160 varieties and about 70 species!

This week too I have begun work on my Sunday School
lesson papers. As I have eight months to write, a school
book — outlines of I and II Corinthians to revise and copy, and
a leaflet we put out some time ago to revise, and two dresses
(house frocks) to make, I think I shall not be too idle!

Mar. 4, '14

We celebrated Ruth's birthday by hiring a carriage, which was
perfectly comfortable for four, and all taking a three-hour drive
through the town out to and over the "downs," along a stream
lined with blossoming calla lilies, around the lake, back through
town and called on two ladies from Coonoor, and then back up
the hill home again. There is far more variety of view here than in
Coonoor, we think. The hills are spread out more and the drives
more varied. The climate is more bracing too.

Apr. 9, '14

Yesterday Miss Brown and we had a carriage and went to tea at a very old house where some old ladies live and which is full of very old furniture and no end of tiger heads and skin rugs, deer heads, etc. etc. The ladies are daughters of a Church of England chaplain, and have tea estates, but belong to the "decayed gentility" class. It was very interesting to see the old house, etc. They live in the neighborhood of all the Mysore rajahs, "Niyams," and Baroda Geakwai's palaces!

Vacations spent in Burma's missionary rest spots required less arduous travel, and offered more familiar neighbors and less exotic surroundings. The days were filled in much the same way, however: walks, drives (when available), visiting local sites, attending prayer meetings, Bible readings, and social calls on mission friends. Above all, they provided a much needed break from routine.

For several years, Frank and Jennie spent short vacation periods in Maymyo, where Frank had bought land and built a house (later sold). In 1909, Jennie and Frank were on furlough in America when Hattie and Ruth spent their vacation time there.

Maymyo, Mar. 6, '09

We got in Monday night and are settled now, and at work. Have begun again on the Songs and Solos book (Burmese words and music cut out of books and arranged on blank forms to be bound up later). It has lain untouched since last year for lack of time during school. I have also done some sewing, cut the trail off that gray woolen dress I brought out and so made a useful walking skirt of it. Have plenty more sewing and all sorts of work to do.

We have called on the folks we know about here, — except one place where we go tonight. Have been to bazaar and begun housekeeping in earnest. The first thing there was a social at Miss Slater's for the new soldiers, and others, a new Irish regiment that has just come. The schoolmistress, an Irish lass, very jolly, but an earnest Christian — was there too, and the life of the games played, [including] "My ship has a cargo of A's."

We have also attended Church (the Chapel is just across the street) on Sunday and YPSCE on Thursday evening and Ruth went to a Bible reading at Miss Slater's.

Maymyo, Mar. 13, '09

The week has been a busy one. We have finally finished up the Songs and Solos book as far as can be done here. I have read the Sunday School paper proof and just now prepared copy for the next *Messenger*. Have done quite a bit of sewing for self and Ruth, mostly in the line of repairs. One morning we went to bazaar; twice we have taken long walks up in the woods, something we couldn't do last year because of the distance.

We attended a Bible reading at Miss Slater's and Ruth led the YPSCE meeting on Temperance, and gave a good talk, without getting too much used up over it.

Maymyo, Mar. 20, '09

Ruth has begun to re-write and revise her "Christian Doctrines" (Burmese) which she teaches the third year class — it is a big task. Wednesday she led the Bible reading at Miss Slater's. Besides us four missionaries (American), there were Dr. and Mrs. Duer (English), Miss McClisin (Irish school teacher) and Nurse Breton (Scotch) and Mrs. Denning (English) who is the "second lady" in Burma, her husband being highest up in the Military — a representative gathering, if small!

Maymyo, Apr. 16, '09

This morning we all went up to see "Elephant House," about the finest place in Maymyo; now for sale — furnished — at half its cost. Rs.30000 is asked. The builder Dallarimple Clark, was in the Elephant Dept. of Gov't and made a fortune by cheating. He is now in hiding. It better be called "Clark's Folly."

Maymyo, Apr. 24, '09

Ruth finished her "Christian Doctrines" the day before Mrs. Elliott came and I have finished everything I had to do except to crochet a shawl for the rains. It is well we were so well along in our work, for I foresee we shall do very little now, the visiting, extra time taken in meals, etc. etc. would have left small chance for solid work. Mrs. Elliott is a little Southern lady (from Tennessee) and we enjoy her very much. We never before had any opportunity to become acquainted with her tho she has been at Kemindine School about three years.

Tuesday morning Miss Slater who has the use of a very fine private gharry (Major Duer's, whose wife has just gone home) took us for a drive, which was very delightful. We went to the dairy at the English barracks where she bought not only butter, but cream as well, <u>by the pound</u>! It was first-class. The man in charge gave us a glass of milk free gratis, and it was the best I ever tasted in Burma, tho we have very good milk from the Kulahs. That afternoon Miss Slater had us to tea to meet the Cowasji's and their guests. They are Anglicized Parsees who are always very kind to missionaries. Let Miss Slater use their very fine villa up here for her guests when the Association met here, etc. etc. Thursday evening I led the YPSCE, the subject being "Missionary Heroes of Africa." The Davenports furnished a lot of books, so I spoke on Robert Moffat, Mrs. Davenport on Livingston, Ruth on Mackay, Harrington and Pilkerton, and Mr. Davenport on his own experience of three years as a self-supporting missionary under Bishop Taylor. It was a good meeting but rather long, as Mrs. Davenport went over her time.

Maymyo, May 1, '09

One afternoon we three went to "The Crags" and as the house is empty went up to the top above the house and had <u>such</u> a view of Maymyo, on one side, wooded plateau on the other, and surrounded all around the horizon with ranges of hills and mountains! We had no idea before how pretty the whole situation was. When we went with Frank and Jennie some years ago and did not go to the top we saw nothing to approach it. We took some lemonade and crackers and after disposing of them came back, passing the native barracks just in time to hear the Gurka band play the bag-pipes — quite a treat.

Maymyo, May 7, '09

Tuesday we three and Miss Fredrickson left at 11:30 A.M.
and went up the railroad to Hsipaw, 6:40 P.M., having a chat at
Pyaung-gyaung with Miss Eastman, Mrs. Mix, and Miss Bunn
(and her Bible woman, one of our girls). At Hsipaw, Ruth and I
slept in the railroad station waiting room and the other two on
the train in which we left at 7:30 A.M. for the noted Mansam
Falls. We were dropped off the train at 10 A.M. at the Bungalow built in view of the Falls. There is no station, no inhabit-
ants except the durman and no houses or sign of life aside
from the Bungalow and its outhouse. The Shans are afraid of
the falls.

The Falls are in a tiny valley surrounded closely by high,
wooded hills, sloping right up from the river. Standing on the
veranda you see before you ten most lovely waterfalls, and a
little walking shows you a number of others. In the distance
among the trees are three very high falls, 275 feet, a broken
slope of water and then a plunge straight down into a clear
green pool where the river flows smoothly. Then comes a long
smooth pour over a ledge of rock with two little ones at the
side, another green expanse of quiet water, then five separate
falls over a high precipice with wooded islands between them
on the brink. (Four can be seen from the veranda.) Another
green pool and two big falls nearly as high. Below these out of
sight of the house is another long smooth pour over a ledge of
rock. No two of all the falls are alike, but each is a changing
mass of white foam, and the roar of the falling water is very
considerable. (The sight and sound of it made us so thirsty all
day.) We took two walks and so saw still more. The whole
series of falls is to be seen from the train, in one place. It is the
most lively bit of scenery I ever saw — not grand like the
Alps — but just beautiful and unspoiled by man. We were there
till 4 P.M. when the train picked us up again and we spent the
night as before in Hsipaw, and came back the next day. The
views all along the way, taking in the Gokteik Gorge and the
mountains both sides, and then along the river between
Hsipaw and the Falls with frequent little falls and rapids, were
all very beautiful. We thoroughly enjoyed every minute. We
took food for all the way, but Mr. Cochrane insisted on giving

us dinner the second night at Hsipaw. We are rather tired, but it <u>paid</u> and we are very glad we went. We had missionary concessions on the railroad so the fare up and back was only Rs.10/8 each!! The distance from here is about 113 miles and the time on the train 10 hours. The train from Hsipaw to Lashio and back only runs on three days in the week.

In 1919 Hattie and Ruth spent their vacation in Kalaw, another hot season retreat for the missionary community.

Safford Cottage, Kalaw, Feb. 9, '19 (4,410 ft. altitude)
Thursday we left the house about 3:30 P.M. We arrived at 4:45 P.M. Friday and Mrs. Craig (our Scotch friend in Insein; up here for 6 months) met us and had a friend's trap to bring us to the house — too far to walk. She has the cottage next door and is the only near neighbor. She had had this one cleaned and gave us tea and dinner the first night, so we got settled very comfortably the next day, yesterday. We are in a clearing in the pine woods on a hillside above the railroad station. A valley surrounded by wooded hills is before us.

We hope Frank and Jennie will come while we are here and look over the place as their Maymyo house is sold. We think this is far better than Maymyo in every way for a rest place; also higher and cooler.

Kalaw, Feb. 16, '19
We went to bazaar, a 40 minute rapid walk. Got what we wanted, left cook to finish and came back in a cart — 40 minutes from the railroad station which is minutes this side of the bazaar. Kalaw is a place of magnificent distances, designed for "motor folks." ·

Kalaw, Mar. 23, '19
I did not write last week as Frank and Jennie were arriving and I thought their letter would be sufficient to tell the news. I went and met them, waiting one hour for the train. The week since has passed very quietly, both Sunday mornings we have gone to the site they have taken, quite a little walk from here, on the way, by road to the Railroad Station. The site makes up in view what it lacks in trees!

Frank and Jennie Phinney.

Frank and Jennie's house, "Genesee," Kalaw, circa 1922.

In 1920 Frank and Jennie built a house, "Genesee," on the site in Kalaw. After this, Ruth and Hattie spent their hot season vacations there.

Through the years, Hattie's letters reported her repeated concern over Frank's continual overwork and frail appearance. Neither Frank nor Jennie enjoyed robust health. Both were subject to a variety of illnesses, and several times over the years Hattie was called in to Rangoon to help out in caring for one or the other. Frank and Jennie were twice forced to return to America for medical reasons, once spending five months at Dr. Kellogg's Battle Creek Sanitorium in Michigan in an effort to improve their health.

Three days after Frank's 65th birthday he suffered yet another bout of illness. At first considered a severe but not life-threatening attack of fever accompanied by dysentery, it proved fatal. Frank died on December 15, 1922. As was the custom, the news was cabled to the Rooms in Boston and passed on to the family in Rochester. Hattie's letter supplied the details.

Dec. 16, '22

I can hardly bring myself to write. I had no thought when I wrote last week that this week I should have to tell of Frank's death and funeral.

Wednesday I got back to the Hospital about 6:45. His breathing was most painful and his eyes were open and set. Jennie and I stepped to the door to speak to the doctor a minute; on going back he was perfectly quiet and at 7 A.M. we knew he was gone, but so quietly we couldn't tell just when.

At 7 P.M. we were back from the funeral! So quickly are things done here, but no more or better could have been done if a week had been spent on it. The hearse was <u>beautiful</u>, the Marshalls' car followed with we three and Mr. Marshall and Miss Phillips' car with six ladies who couldn't walk. The rest of the missionaries and English and Americans and natives walked all the way, the hearse going very slowly. The sidewalks were crowded all the way with people who stood and watched. As Frank was on "The Port Trust," the "Charitable Society," the "Board of Trade" and the new University "Council" (not to mention the Press and the

Church and Sunday School) he was known by everybody and was <u>loved</u> and <u>heartily respected</u> by all, and all did all they could to honor him. It would have been a comfort to you, could you have seen and heard it all.

At the cemetery, way had to be made for us through the mass of people to reach the grave, which is just at the head of Dr. Kelley's. It was lined and surrounded with flowers and at the close, all — or many — dropped in flowers till the coffin was covered. The many large flower wreaths were carried aloft after the coffin by natives from the hearse to the grave, like a triumphal procession. There is no road in the cemetery so the hearse had to stop at the gate. The Methodists went to the Horticultural Gardens for a wreath, but the man said he had so many orders for wreaths for Mr. Phinney he doubted if he could supply them.

Frank suffered so much with dysentery and then with the retention of urine, through these two weeks — lacking two days — that we are glad, if he had to go — his suffering was no longer.

Poor Jennie too is very worn but brave through all her grief. I feel as everyone is saying "What will we do without him?" But we sorrow not as those without hope.

There was a note of victory through all that was said; it was the end of a life spent in the truest service for the eternal spiritual benefit of others — not forgetting all manner of temporal help as well. A thoroughly unselfish life. He could truly have said, "I have fought the good fight. I have <u>kept the faith.</u>"

Dec. 24, '22

Last Monday after school I went and met Jennie at the Press and we got out and read Frank's will. As you may know he left his share of 4 Brighton Avenue to be divided equally between Herman and me. Everything else goes to Jennie. Herman and she are executors. It was hard to go to the Press. It seems yet as if he must be there as before.

Jennie has had about a hundred letters and telegrams of sympathy, many of them most beautiful. All expressing a sense of great personal loss, and testifying to his helpfulness in matters great and small, his unfailing patience and

Christian courtesy, many saying, "How can we ever get on without him?" He was a friend of everybody, from the Lieutenant Governor down to the common coolies, who wept bitterly at the grave. His was a life poured forth unstintingly in the service of others, for the sake of his Lord and Master. And it was the outcome of a sound and intelligent faith in the Bible as the Word of God. Without that, he would never have developed the character he did, nor have done the work he did.

Yesterday, Saturday, Miss Phillips brought out Jennie to stay over Christmas with us. She had never been out without him, and we did not want her to come by train. They were out to dinner seven weeks before his death. Mr. Marshall will take or send her in on Tuesday morning. She has been hard at work all the week getting in shape for the Snyders to have all the house but one room. It is a dreadfully sad and lonely Christmas for us all.

Dec. 31, '22

I went in after school Tuesday to see Jennie, and again Saturday morning. She is bravely working along, selling furniture, etc.; is giving us anything we need and selecting things to send you. It is heart-breaking business. I asked her to send Father's crayon portrait for Sedley and his son, since the latter has his great-grandfather's name. We were very glad she was with us over Christmas.

Tuesday morning the Marshalls took Jennie home. It seems more lonesome and we miss Frank more and more as the days go on.

Hattie's concern for Jennie during the days and weeks after Frank's death may have helped sustain her in her own sense of loss. Hattie had hoped that Jennie would stay in Burma with her and Ruth, but Jennie's sister in America was terminally ill and Jennie felt obliged to return to America to be with her. After finishing up Frank's affairs and disposing of their household goods, Jennie sailed from Rangoon in March of 1923. She did not return to Burma; her own health was still poor. In May, 1929 Jennie died after a long period of declining health.

The house that Frank had built in Kalaw was left to Jennie, with the stipulation that Hattie was to have the use of it for her lifetime. After Jennie's death, Hattie and Ruth bought the Kalaw house from her heirs and made it their retirement home.

Frank's death was a serious personal loss to Hattie, and one over which she grieved for some time, but it seems to have had little effect on her work. While there is no doubt that Frank had played an important role in Hattie's decision to come to Burma, and provided support and companionship in her first years, long before the time of his death Hattie had thoroughly established her own unique and independent place in the mission, earned by her determination, hard work, and special skills.

15

The Final Years

1928 to 1938

The 1928 school year was the last under the leadership of Harriet Phinney and Ruth Ranney. What was initially planned as a furlough became in fact their retirement from the school.

In preparation for the projected furlough, no first year class was enrolled and plans were made to find someone to take over the school temporarily in Hattie and Ruth's absence. Miss Phillips, with whom they had worked closely over the years, was their choice to fill the position. The final decision, however, was a different one.

> June 2, '28
>
> Monday we had Miss Phillips out to breakfast and to talk over school matters, as we are hoping she'll take over when we take a rest.

> June 30, '28
>
> The Reference Committee [which handled mission affairs] have voted that Miss Teele succeed us when we take furlough. She'll have to have a native assistant as there is no missionary beside Miss Teele to put here. We'll go to Kalaw and finish the Bible proof. There is no Burmese Bible available, but the tiny <u>fine</u> print (1/-) one.

While many of Hattie's letters home during this period are missing, those that remain reflect the fact that both Hattie and Ruth were subject to more poor health than usual and were not as active in mission affairs as previously.

Hattie and Ruth in 1928.

June 15, '28

I had a bad upset Monday just after school and Dr. Taylor said I must keep still, so I was out of school two days and the other days had my classes upstairs. This made extra work for Ruth and she nearly gave out this week, so as I'm all right I've relieved her of one class for two days and looked after the house more. She has rheumatism pretty badly in one leg and needs to keep it up.

Aug. 2, '28

Monday afternoon Mrs. Marshall called and told us all the news she could think of. As we've only been out once since coming from Kalaw, we don't know what's going on unless she or Mrs. Richardson call and tell us.

Sept. 1, '28

Ruth's gas is affecting the action of her heart and Doctor says she must avoid going up stairs, so she has been having her classes in the house the past two weeks. Thursday after school Mrs. Marshall called and a little later the Chaneys. We asked them to come as we wanted to talk over school affairs before Miss Teele arrives.

We are invited to tea at Mrs. Marshall's to meet some YWCA people. If possible shall try to go, as we've not been out for some time now, four weeks.

Sept. 2. Didn't go as Ruth didn't feel equal to it.

Oct. 7, '28

Well it's some time since I wrote you last but Ruth has kept you informed. A week ago I had a touch of the "flu" I think, with fever all day Saturday, and it's taken my strength.

However, as we had examination the first three days this week I was able to manage that, though I couldn't have taught as I have a bit of a cough, etc. We dismissed Wednesday noon, and by Thursday noon all were gone and quiet reigns.

Sometime between June, when Miss Teele was assigned to take over the school, and the end of the term in October, the decision was made that the planned furlough should become permanent retirement. It is not clear at what point and on what grounds the decision was made that Hattie and Ruth would give up leadership of the Bible school at this time, or even whose decision it was. The pros and cons of continuing their work after the projected one-year furlough were probably spelled out for the "folks at home" in letters that have been lost. It seems likely that age and increasingly numerous bouts of poor health contributed to the decision; it was certainly not due to any lack of pupils or interest in the school on the part of the Burman Baptist community. Enrollment in the years just before 1928 was the highest it had ever been; 30 to 35 pupils attending and others refused admission for lack of space. Money to support the school continued to come in from former pupils and Burman Christians.

Preparations for the move to Kalaw began with the selling off of household goods.

> Dec. 22, '28
>
> Mr. and Mrs. Smith (from the Press) and their two children called. The Smiths will take five more articles, so we've nothing left to sell aside from pictures but my desk and revolving chair, bed and one table! Miss Teele's taking so much makes it much easier for us to get away.

No letters from Hattie are available from January to May 1929, during which time Hattie and Ruth moved from Insein to Kalaw. A later letter from Ruth refers to Hattie's serious illness with flu during the winter months of 1929, after the closing of the school.

By May 1929, when Hattie's letters resume, the permanent move to Kalaw and settling into Frank's house, "Genesee," had been accomplished. Structural changes to make the house more comfortable for year-round living and other adjustments were under way.

> May 18, '29
>
> After two weeks and four days the Chinese carpenters are at last doing the last bit of work — i.e., oiling outside the re-walling — oh no, there is still the eave-boards to be painted. It has been a long, tiresome, noisy, and part of the time smelly job, as the floor is laid in a tar mixture. But it is very nice and

convenient now; a space 10 x 6 feet is added to the dining
room, and that allows the screen to be moved on — to enlarge
the sitting room, and the china (glass) almirah is now moved
into the dining room part. The sitting room has my large
bookcase and a little 2-shelf one that belonged to the house.
The veranda thus taken into the dining room was of no use as
it was on the windy, rainy and sunny corner of the house; the
entrance veranda is sheltered from all, and we've sat out there
a good deal.

On Tuesday our good servants left us to return to their
families. Poonooswami, cook, had been with us for eight years
and the pani-wallah for three years. Their coming up for the
season made our moving and my sickness much easier. Now
we have a Buro-Kulah and his <u>young</u> Burman brother-in-law, as
cook and helper. They belong up here and so will be willing to
stay, "season" or not. They are getting used to our ways and
will do very well, but we miss the old ones!

The garden at Genesee also received extra attention that summer. Over the years, it proved an ongoing source of pleasure and
satisfaction. Hattie reported regularly on its progress.

June 1, '29

We've had to hire an extra mali to help pull the big weeds
that disfigured the place, growing all through the grass outside
of the garden. It is partly done and a great improvement.

Aug. 31, '29

Mrs. Redpath brought us four roots of yucca lilies, same as
they have in California, and mali, who was "tickled to death"
with them, planted two each side of the steps down to the gate,
where when they blossom they will make a fine show.

We've had about 150 fine large chestnuts from one of our
three trees; the other two didn't bear this year. The two walnut
trees didn't bear either — haven't yet at all, but we've had a
big bunch of plantains — (small sweet bananas) enough for
everyone on the compound — two pineapples, and some small
sour peaches. The lime, or rather lemon, trees hang full, and
the one guava tree has a good number on. Roses and dahlias
are in full swing and are very lovely. Asters come next.

"Our plants" in the garden at Kalaw.

Jan. 17, '30

Our one cherry tree is just now coming out, when most of the others are going off. The frost injured the poinsettias that were lower down, near the gate, but not the highest up one. The roses don't suffer, and we have three or four bouquets in the house all the time.

Similarly reported was news of Taffy, their cat, who had made the move from Insein to Kalaw with Hattie and Ruth. She was an important member of the household.

Aug. 3rd, '29

Taffy and her kitten are having a play spell in my lap, not conducive to good writing; a "nursing hour" is now under way and things are quieter, tho somewhat crowded!

Aug. 31, '29

The first day we walked to the gate Taffy as usual went along and the kitten followed, being anxiously watched over by her Ma! The next day they went only part way and Taffy escorted the kitten back to the veranda. Next time the kitten started to follow but Taffy said, "It's too much trouble" and sent her back, and then came all the way to the gate and a piece on the road as far as we went! We found the kitten on top of a veranda chair waiting for us when we returned.

Dec. 26, '31

Thursday morning Taffy presented us with a nice plump yellow and white kitten, the first in a long while, in fact Mrs. Johnson's cat is her only descendant (except her numerous kittens) until this one. I sent [birth] announcement cards, in due form, to Mrs. Johnson and the Tilbes and Mrs. Green here, as they are all very fond of Taffy, and were tickled at the announcement.

Feb. 6, '32

The event of the week was the arrival of the Hannas, on Tuesday. Wednesday afternoon they all came to see us. Stanley is a very nice appearing quiet boy of eleven, and the little three-year-old is a girl, Carol, very dainty and pretty and rather shy but delighted to watch the antics of the kitten and Taffy. Her father brought her up yesterday on purpose to see them.

Mar. 6, '32

Ah Sou came Tuesday morning [and] took the kitten to his daughter to whom it was promised. It <u>was</u> a beautiful one and so full of fun, but it rather troubles Ruth. Poor Ma Taffy has mourned it since!

In many respects, life during the first years of their retirement was not very different from Hattie and Ruth's hot season sojourns in Kalaw. Hattie continued her work on the Sunday school lesson chores as well as proofreading and Bible work for the press.

May 18, '29

The week has been a full one; we've read a form and a half (48 pages) of Bible proof, once with Ruth and once I alone, as no less than <u>four</u> forms arrived on Saturday, all to be read twice.

Mar. 2, '30

Proof, which began again last Saturday, has continued all the week and we have done two forms, which makes 128 pages for me, half aloud.

2nd Sunday morning. Another form of proof came last night, so we must go straight on reading. They really are rushing it.

May 26, '34

During the week I have finished reading the Pocket Dictionary; have only a few pages to o.k. It was begun six and a half months ago. Have finished the August paper and begun the September one.

Sept. 29, '34

Have finished the December Sunday School paper and begun the January 1935 one (being the 42nd year I've done the work except one furlough) and read the November Sunday School paper proof.

Concern over reduced finances was one of the less pleasant aspects of the retirement years. While Ruth had a trust fund and some means of her own, Hattie was dependent on funds from the mission. Miss Chapman, Hattie's original sponsor, had died some time before.

Aug. 31, '29

On March 1st I will be put on the retired list (though I'll not stop working) and my income will be reduced to $500 from $900. I shall have to mind my p's and q's; but I have enough laid aside to "bury me decent." They say that 65 is the age to retire, but it is never enforced and can't be while workers are so scarce and growing scarcer. Dr. Nichols is still touring the jungles at <u>76</u>!

The disruption caused by dacoits, a long-standing problem, caused a stir for the Kalaw community and beyond. Despite decades of British rule, Burma still had its share of political and social upheavals.

June 6, '31

Your [letter] No. 2471 came on Wednesday as usual. But the Monday night mail up from Rangoon was wrecked by dacoits not far from Toungoo, fish plates removed and part of a bridge pier blown up. Three killed and a number injured. More soldiers are being brought over from India, but it is a slow job to clean up. The Buddhist priests do the tattooing to make them invulnerable!! The Burmans are getting tired of it and give information better than formerly, as they suffer tho not so much as Indians, Chinese, and Karens. The dacoits have succeeded in looting a lot of money lately.

July 18, '31

The Burman leaders want all the offenders pardoned and let loose, hardly excepting murderers! Only "<u>serious</u>!! murderers" to be held; also taxes remitted and Gov't aid given to cultivators. Just where Gov't is to get the money for all that, with taxes cut down they don't show, or what the country would be with all the "bad hats" free to do as they please. The other day they — dacoits — thought a woman was not giving up all of her money so they poured kerosene over her and burnt her alive! And some in America think these countries are ready for "full dominion status" and even "absolute independence"!! The Gov't is bringing in more and more soldiers, and the large places are quiet, but the dacoits, led by priests and ex-priests, work in outlying hamlets, and terrorize the farmers so they dare not plow; and then blame everything on the Gov't.

Aug. 1, '31

Things in Burma begin to look more hopeful. The Gov't has brought from India alot of English and Indian soldiers, so the people see they mean business and are able to do something. They have called out, too, alot of Karen irregulars, who know the jungles and can go through them as English or Indians cannot. Moreover, the Burmans themselves begin to have a bit of sense, and alot of Burman sayas have got together and set out to preach good behavior in the worst districts. Gov't has proclaimed an amnesty to all not actual murderers or leaders, and over 1,000 came in, in one month, in Prome District. Gov't. too is helping the farmers.

News from beyond Burma was also noted with interest and often commented upon in Hattie's letters.

Jan. 31, '36

The great event since I wrote has been, of course, the death of King George V and accession of Edward VIII. Tuesday we went over to Miss Craft's at 4 P.M. and heard on her radio the broadcasting of the funeral procession from Westminster to Paddington Station so knew exactly when the Queen and Royal Family was passing. At 8 P.M. those who were there heard the funeral service perfectly. The 4 P.M. was blurred by the sound of moving soldiers etc. That day every school and every shop, from the big English shops to the tiniest stall was closed all day and two minutes silence at 5 P.M. It was the same all over Burma, not to say the Empire.

Dec. 19, '36

We were distressed at the King's [Edward VIII] abdication,
and for the sake of a woman twice divorced! He was so popular,
and the fact that she was a commoner and of another country
<u>could</u> have been gotten along with, but a divorcee for Queen, or a
morganatic marriage was out of the question. So he becomes
"Duke of Windsor" and "King George VI and Queen Elizabeth"
take the throne, and little Princess Elizabeth comes one step
nearer to it. They also are very popular.

During the early years, Hattie and Ruth enjoyed socializing with
various friends and neighbors. Prayer meetings, teas, drives, and casual
visits, as well as formal dinners and holiday celebrations provided
occasions to meet with members of the Baptist community in addition
to Anglo-Indian, Methodist, and Church of England neighbors.

Dec. 29, '29

We had a nice Christmas with a very pleasant midday meal
at the Tilbes' — three Harrises and we three — with them
making eight. A big roast chicken — or rather cock, of their
own raising was as large and as tasty as an ordinary turkey.
Lima beans from their garden were a great treat and also a
fresh apple pie, with celery sweets, etc. We furnished the
soup — "Campbell's tomato." Mrs. Tilbe gave us a flower
holder to put in a bowl, and Mrs. Harris two photos of Helen
in a Karen costume and also six apples from <u>Oregon</u>!! The <u>real
thing</u>! A dealer in Toungoo gets them out; they are not like the
Cabul fruit which <u>smell</u> all right but taste like sawdust. Miss
Fountain gave us each a silk shawl with long fringe. We gave
her a cotton dress pattern just got out from Montgomery Ward
and Co. and a Burmese umbrella, lacquer box, and silver
napkin ring. Another dress pattern went to Mrs. Harris and an
etching of the Mandalay moat to Mrs. Tilbe. We, Ruth and I,
shared the cost of a firescreen and new shades for three windows, which get the full western sun at this season. These were
our gifts to each other. Mrs. Johnson sent us a Chinese embroidered tea cloth and napkins and there were hankies and photos
and lots of cards. Miss Hastings sent a centerpiece of Indian
handmade lace — very fine darned net.

Jan. 17, '30

Tuesday we called on Miss Redpath, sister of the Carstens who keep the only English shop here. Quite a walk down and up but not as far as the Harrises' which is two <u>downs</u> and two <u>ups</u>! Mrs. Tilbe, Mrs. Harris and Mrs. Green have all called and we to Mrs. Tilbe's too one afternoon. The number is limited but we really see more of Americans and Eurasians than we did in Insein.

We had a nice letter from our old girl, Ma Hla Thin, class of 1918, who went to Menthing eight days beyond Bana, both in Yunnan China. The letter took a month to come. She went on a caravan of 30 Lahus, sent down to Lashio by Mr. Buker, and a Karen preacher and his bride, returning to his work (Mr. Buker's). He sent a pony for her to ride and she made the journey all right, though she is a rather frail girl. She has a real <u>call</u> to that work; will have 40 Lahu girls to teach. She was in Bana for some time before a rest in Moulmein. From Lashio it was two days by motor and fourteen by pony.

Occasionally, visitors came from farther afield.

Apr. 4, '31

Friday we had two couples of Burmans to tea. They were Ko Po Lu, the Headmaster of Mr. Dudley's Thazi School, his wife and daughter (19 yrs.) and the preacher there, Ko E Kyu and his wife, Ma Thein Kin is one of our old girls, who never fails to come to the train when we pass through Thazi (the junction for this road and the Rangoon-Mandalay line). They are the ones we had a visit with just now, when we went to Maymyo and Ma Thein Kin brought us 16 eggs in a little Shan woven box. We gave them cake, cookies and tea, and had a nice visit. Ko Po Lu was very much interested in the fireplace and its fire irons. They live in a very hot dry place, and never saw frost even.

May 1, '31

Two of our old girls called on Wednesday from different places — one early and the other late. Today Miss Teele and six Burman young women came by bus from Taunggyi, had a cup of tea and stayed an hour or so. Among them were her two helpers in the Bible school. Mrs. Cummings and Miss Peterson called, and this morning Miss Parish.

The passing years brought important milestones.

Maymyo, Jan. 12, '35

Saturday the 5th was the 50th anniversary of Ruth's arrival in Burma as a missionary. It is almost 78 years since she first arrived in Toungoo. I got up a tea for her — nine of us present, all but Mrs. Hamilton were missionaries. Two Vincents (Wesleyan), Mr. Grigg — now back from Ceylon, Mrs. Elliott, Misses Craft and Johnson and we two. Mrs. Elliott and Miss Craft helped too, and the tea table was all in yellow for the "Golden" anniversary, and also there was a cake with her name and "1885–1935" with a ship on top, sailing from a tiny American flag in one side to a yellow pagoda on the other! You see the point! Mrs. Elliott read some appropriate verses, and each had a card with "Golden Anniversary" and Ruth's name and dates in one side and every one wrote his own name and date of arrival on the other side, for souvenirs.

Maymyo, Jan. 31, '36

Saturday was the 50th anniversary of my arrival in Burma and Ruth gave an "Ebenezer" tea. There were the nine missionaries now living here (including ourselves), two Wesleyans from Mandalay who happened to be here over Sunday and the matron who is staying out the month. Ruth had Mrs. Green of Kalaw make the cake (she needs the work) and it was a very nice chocolate one, and the rest of the tea matched it. After eating, each one told what they were most thankful for and it was a very pleasant and profitable occasion. Among other items (including Ruth herself) I mentioned the privilege of living under the British flag in peace and safety: 18 years under Victoria and all of Edward VII's and George V's reigns. There was applause at that. Ruth told about our being supported so many years by Mrs. Brooks (19 yrs.) and Miss Chapman (36 yrs.).

As time went on, it became apparent that Frank's choice of Kalaw as the place for an up-country home was less than ideal. The Baptist missionary centers were in Maymyo and Taunggyi, and over the years there were fewer and fewer Baptist missionary families living in Kalaw, or even coming up for the hot season. Hattie's letters report news of the illness and death of increasing numbers of friends and co-workers, or their permanent retirement to America. While deaths and departures among the Burma missionaries had always been an all too frequent occurrence, in the past their places were taken by new members of the mission, with whom Hattie soon became acquainted. In the somewhat isolated community of Kalaw, this was no longer the case. Hattie could no longer claim to know all the missionaries working in Burma as she had in earlier years. Unless new workers traveled through Kalaw or Taunggyi, they remained strangers, and the circle of friends grew smaller.

May 11, '35

Last week one day Mr. Dudley took us out and we made five calls across the valley. Had a pleasant time at each, but it was rather strenuous. The next day we took tea at the Dudleys'; that will be the last time as they leave finally next Wednesday, 15th, and sail for home the last of June. As they are retiring, we shall not see them again. We shall miss them.

June 15, '35

On Wednesday Mrs. Weeks came for her last breakfast, and left for Moulmein on the 1 P.M. train. So we are left alone so far as Baptist missionaries are concerned and it is rather lonely.

June 12, '36

Miss Hastings here to conclude the sale of the Safford house... Five of the missionary houses are sold; three are for sale, if a proper price can be had. The Cummings, Case, and ours are all not in the market.

Jan. 1, '37

We thought Mr. Heptonstall was doing fairly well, though Dr. Henderson had been called down and left here Saturday, arriving Sunday morning, but he was not able to rally again, even with blood transfusion as he had before, and died at 5 P.M. Sunday the 27th.

Letters from home also brought sad news. In April of 1934, Ada Phinney died after a long illness. The cable announcing her death reached Hattie before the latter had received the letters concerning Ada's illness.

> Apr. 21, '34
>
> We are both constantly thinking of you and praying for you these very hard days. The cable left New York at 11:45 A.M. the 18th and reached Kalaw at 9:22 and the house an hour later, so I reckon it was about ten hours on the way. I am very thankful you sent it so I knew at once that Ada is free from her weakness and suffering, but you will be terribly lonely and we pray that the "God of all comfort" may comfort and sustain you, and make his presence very real to you.

Herman continued to live alone in the house at 4 Brighton Avenue, running errands for Hattie and Ruth and managing their bank accounts, despite increasing frailty and occasional illness. He had been officially retired from his job as assistant librarian at the University of Rochester in 1930 after 50 years of service, though he retained an office there which he continued to visit.

Eventually, Hattie and Ruth found it more comfortable to spend the cold weather months in the more active Baptist communities. In June of 1937 Hattie and Ruth moved to Taunggyi for the cold season.

> Gray Rock, Taunggyi, June 12, '37
>
> Here we are again all settled in where we were last cold season. The first of last week was spent in selecting and packing and Friday (4th) the Heptonstall car came for us and we left at 8:15, arriving two hours later. The bus with Dooraswami and family and our boxes etc. started an hour earlier and arrived 15 minutes before we did.
>
> We had a number of calls before leaving; several people who had not called before did so, and as the car came for us, Miss Mellinger drove up and made us a call while the car waited. Total callers and visitors during the 83 days at home was _87_! Six of these stayed overnight and quite a few called more than once. While I'm on numbers I'll say the total kinds of flowers was 74. The gladiolus were just beginning but there

was not much else, but mali picked a big basketful for us to bring and we started out here with 8 nice bouquets.

Ruth's health, declining for some time, continued to fluctuate.

Oct. 2, '37

We have decided not to move back to Kalaw for October and November as we usually do, for various and sundry reasons, but we must have our winter clothes, bedding etc. etc. so I am to have Mrs. Heptonstall's car and go on Monday, returning the same day and she or Mrs. Henderson will stay with Ruth. She is so weak in knees and ankles that she must not be left alone, as she cannot get up and down alone, without risk of falling.

Oct. 16, '37

Mrs. Heptonstall came and stayed with Ruth, and let me rent her car for the day, Monday, Oct. 4, and I went to Kalaw and in 1-1/4 hours spent in our house, gathered up our cold season goods and various things we wanted to use here and got back at 3 P.M. — having left at 9:20 A.M. It made a nice change for me, haven't been out otherwise. Ruth is better, but her limbs are still weak and it's not safe for her to try to move about alone, lest she fall. Is dressed and out in the living room every afternoon.

The improvement in Ruth's condition was only temporary. On October 30, 1937, Ruth Ranney died.

Gray Rock, Taunggyi, Nov. 6, '37

Dear Herman,

You may have heard from the Rooms of the Home-going of my mission life-long yoke-fellow, Ruth Ranney.

Friday Oct. 22nd Mrs. Heptonstall took us out in her car — Ruth's first outing since Aug. 12th — and she enjoyed it very much and we hoped to go frequently. But on Sunday 24th at about 2:30 P.M. she became unable to speak so I could understand her. She reclined in the long chair I had gotten her from Rangoon till 6 P.M. when I was able to get Mrs. Heptonstall to help and we got her to bed. Mrs. Heptonstall stayed through the night, though Ruth slept fairly well. Dr. Ah Pon was called and came twice a day, but could do nothing at all. We had two native nurses and I was with her all the days. On Thursday she became paralyzed on the right side. She knew me and Mrs. Heptonstall all day but from that night on was unconscious till she passed away at 8:20 P.M. on Saturday, Oct. 30th.

The funeral was here and at the church (picture in *Watchman-Examiner*) Sunday 4 P.M. but as it rained hard, I decided that the burial would be private and on Monday morning, and it was so. Mr. Varney was here to preach and took the service with Dr. St. John, who returned to Rangoon early Monday, Mr. Varney staying till after the burial.

Mrs. Heptonstall stayed nights and took half the watching with Daw Mi, the wife of Dr. Ah Pon. I am staying on here, taking breakfast with Mrs. Heptonstall and she dining with me — mostly. Everybody is most sympathetic and kind. The three widows know what it means — so do you.

Ruth's death was an overwhelming loss to Hattie, one from which she never fully recovered. While she continued her participation in the activities of the Taunggyi missionary colony, her letters to Herman made constant reference to her loneliness.

Taunggyi, Nov. 20, '37

There is not much to write — the loneliness seems to increase rather than lessen in spite of being asked out to meals and having people here. I won't enlarge on it.

I am going on with my Sunday School lesson work, but have little else to fill the time, with no one to care for or read to.

Dec. 18, '37

Today has been a sadder day than usual for Dooraswami's baby, a month and a half old, died of pneumonia yesterday afternoon and was buried this morning. Mrs. Heptonstall saw to all arrangements and Mrs. Henderson held a little service in their room. The pastor held one at the grave. They lost a six-month-old girl two years ago when we were all in Maymyo.

Another sad thing is that my beloved cat, Taffy, 11 years old, is dying and I shall not have even her to speak to in the house. [Later note]. Pussy has just died.

I've helped Mrs. Heptonstall with her preparations for the school children's Christmas, but the days are long and very lonely.

Dec. 31, '37

Christmas has passed, a very sad and lonely one for me, though everybody did extra things to mark the day. Mrs. Henderson and daughter gave a tea party and tree for Robin and six American or English children on Friday. All the missionaries were there too. Miss Hughes had one for the Rest Haven folks.

On Christmas all 14 of us had dinner, 7 P.M. at Mrs. Heptonstall's.

Feb. 26, '38

Miss Ranney's monument is now finished. It has a marble scroll with name and dates and "Missionary to the Burmans for fifty-three years" and a marble "curb" around the grave.

Genesee, Kalaw, Mar. 12, '38

I have come back alone to our home where I never spent a day or night without Ruth — the emptiness is almost beyond endurance. So many things, but no one to help me use them, such lots of flowers, but no one to help enjoy them!

Mrs. French has been very kind; she sent up a cake and came up to tea on the first day which was a help, and last evening I had her to dinner to help eat a chicken. She is the only one I know this side of the valley. Her car is to take me to her home for tea this afternoon.

During April and May, Mrs. H. K. Smith (from the press) came to Kalaw and stayed with Hattie, relieving some of the loneliness. In June of 1938, Hattie moved back to Taunggyi for the summer. Hattie's letter reporting her arrival was her last.

Gray Rock, Taunggyi, June 4, '38

As you see, I have moved back to the house I was in before. It is a year today since Ruth and I came here together — the last move for her. I seem to miss her more and more.

I came this time in a common (<u>very</u> common) bus, along with the cook and all my things, and all of his — a busful altogether. It was not comfortable like the friends' cars we've always had before, but there was a good bit saved by not having a car, and I arrived at 9 A.M. safely at any rate.

Mee-mee [Taffy's successor] is cavorting all around — not to say over and under me — which is not conducive to good writing. She has developed, in the month I've had her, a gray spot on her shoulders and the rest of her back, which was light grayish white, has become, truth compels me to say — a yellowish, dirty gray, not handsome at all. Her white head and black ears and face are still <u>cute</u>!

The business of having Genesee put in my name alone, was at last accomplished, with Mr. Varney's help; took from March 30th to May 20th. I took tea at the Varneys', with the Vincents of their Mission, whom we were with at the Rest House in Maymyo in '34.

Mrs. Smith is going to send a Red Cross box to the sufferers in Shanghai and I sent down a pah-full, mostly of Ruth's coats, etc.

The very fine and valuable daguerreotypes she had of her parents, Daniel and Mary Bennett Whitaker (Ranney) — Toungoo pioneer missionaries to the Karens; her grandparents the Cephas Bennetts of the Press, and her great-grandparents, the Alfred Bennetts (he was first agent of the original ABFMS); and three paintings on ivory of Mr. Ranney and his first wife, who died in Rangoon, and a miniature of him in a gold frame — I have sent to Judson College Historical Collection. With them I sent a *Life of Alfred Bennett* by Harvey, 1853, and Ruth's *Life of the Cephas Bennetts, a Sketch*, 1892 — a small book, the only copy I know of now. There were a few old letters by Judson, Wade, etc. Dr. Jury was very glad to have all for the Collection and there are no relatives to leave them to. There was a daguerreotype of the class of 1852 from the Rochester Theological Seminary of which A. T. Rose and Dan Whitaker were members — both with their wives came out in 1853 with Mrs. Cephas Bennett (returning to Burma). All (the older ones) were fellow missionaries with Judson, and Mr. Ranney was with him when he died at sea in 1850.

A paisley shawl — very fine — of Ruth's mother's, I sent to Mrs. Emma Smith Marshall, who values it <u>highly</u>, as she, her parents, and grandparents were friends of the Bennetts and of Ruth — the only old-time friend left here. She was six years old in the Smith home when I arrived in Burma.

Reading with hindsight, one can see that many final chores had been completed: Ruth's things disposed of and the house at Kalaw put into Hattie's name. Hattie had returned to the place where Ruth had died and was buried.

The final chapter of Hattie's life is contained in letters from Mrs. Heptenstall, who took on the task of keeping Herman informed of his sister's final days.

Taunggyi, 1st July, 1938
Mrs. C. H. Heptonstall

I am writing for your sister who adds her love.

Harriet thinks it has been a month since she wrote. She came here from Kalaw the 1st June — while I was away in Rangoon and soon afterwards had to go to bed with that most painful disease known as "shingles." She has suffered much, but is now slowly recovering and easier. Has a trained nurse in charge, a good Karen woman who is at night "spelled" by a faithful Christian Burmese woman. Mrs. Henderson helps with the dressing morning and afternoon and Dr. Ah Pon is the Doctor in charge, though Capt. McAdam, the English doctor who was called in consultation at the beginning keeps in touch with the case. Harriet is having good care, and we all go in to see her as much as we can. She can read some herself but cannot write yet, so has asked me to send you this word, accompanied by her love.

Taunggyi, 25th July, 1938 [CHH]

Do you know your sister well enough, after these long years of separation, to be glad that the end of the earthly road is approaching rapidly and that soon for her the Pearly Gates will open and she will see her Master face to face and be united again with her beloved Ruth from whom the parting was difficult beyond telling. During the nine months that have passed since Ruth went Home, Harriet has never ceased to mourn. The days seemed "interminable" she always said and the nights little better.

Ten days ago, a second doctor that we called in, said that there was little or no hope that Harriet would recover; that the "shingles" were but one phase of the breaking up of the earthly tabernacle. That they being cured, other phases would follow and he thought there would be bronchitis and pneumonia.

Neither has appeared yet but she grows weaker rapidly and daily less able to take nourishment. Her mind is wandering now. Yesterday she asked for a pad and pencil saying that she was going to "write to her brother." She was given it but wrote nothing readable, only a series of strokes.

Begun Taunggyi 27th August 1938 — finished
Sept. 2nd, 1938 [CHH]

I am writing at the bedside of your sister on what is apparently to be her last night on this earth and it is 10:30 P.M. There is absolutely nothing I can do but stand by and so I might as well write letters. My last was written here Thursday night and now it is Saturday. She is no longer conscious and is just breathing, but God is answering her prayer that she might "go decently" and "quietly" from earth to Heaven. When we faced facts together some two weeks ago she asked me to pray for that. Up to Thursday night she knew me and expressed herself as being "so glad" I was there. Since then she has not known anything nor anyone — not even opened her eyes. Is slowly sleeping life away and I will not post this letter till I can tell you that for her the Pearly Gates have opened. I can hardly reconcile myself to her going as she seemed to have such a splendid physique and can only account for it in feeling that she could not reconcile herself to living without Ruth. She said when we faced facts together two weeks ago "I want to go." "I have nothing to live for." "My work is done."

And now it is Friday early morning, the 2nd Sept. and your sister Harriet has been in Heaven five days. They have been very busy ones for me. The last breath was drawn at 4:30 A.M. the 28th August, early Sunday morning. The end came most peacefully — not a struggle. The Lord honored her faith by granting it exactly as she wanted it. She was so eager that all should end as Miss Ranney's did and "it was so." Miss Ranney died Saturday night, so did Harriet.

The funeral was on Sunday and we carried out the details exactly the same. There was a service at the house and the flowers were wonderful. They came from Kalaw gardens as well as Taunggyi. At the house it was very simple, we ladies conducted it. I recited John 14. Mrs. Henderson prayed. Loving hands placed the casket (patterned exactly as for Ruth) on the same private motor car that took Ruth's.

At the Church the service, at the request of the Burman Christians, was partly in Burmese and partly English and the church was filled. Mr. Varney from Kalaw was in charge of the English, assisted by our own Mr. Young and the Scripture read by Mr. Chartrand. Mr. Varney outlined her life for which I had given him the outline. Mr. Young prayed. A double Quartette sang beautifully, "Lead Me Gently Home, Father," the congregation sang, "How Firm a Foundation" in English and Burmese. It lasted an hour and as rain was coming down at the end we followed Harriet's desire as carried out with Miss Ranney and left the casket in the church till early morning when we took it to its last resting place. All the missionaries and all the leading Native Christians followed and gathered around the grave while Mr. Varney made the commitment, assisted by Mr. Young. From first to last it was all very beautiful and orderly. Mrs. Henderson has written it up for the *News* and you will read it there later.

Pinned to my copy of the Will was a half sheet note paper giving the outstanding features of her long and useful life. By which I realized that she anticipated that I might be writing up her life for the *News* which I have done. I am executor to the Will "for personal effects etc." The Mission Treasurer "for Real Estate and money." Before another week I will make and send you a copy. It seems a very wise one in line with her life. She gives her house to be sold for the benefit of printing Bibles and Scripture portions in any language at the disposal of the ABM Press. Her books and bookcases to the Memorial Rest House at Maymyo. Her linens and cutlery, curtains, cushions, etc. to the Guest House at Rangoon. Her personal effects including hand-painted china and odd bits of crockery to me and at my disposal. Any money in the Monroe Bank at Home to you — Frank's picture to be hung in the Field Secretary's House.

I cannot take time for more in this line but if you think of anything you would like sent home to you please tell me and I will do my best to carry out. I have already put wheels in motion for her monument, the counterpart of Miss Ranney's, a marble slab and when it is all in place some month's hence, you shall have a picture. It will cost over Rs500/- but there is money for it. I have already made some distribution of personal effects here — Her fountain pen to Dr. Ah Pon who was so attentive to her. Her Burmese Bible to a preacher's wife in

Kengtung, Ma Hla Thin, an old pupil of whom she was very fond, a small handbag to her faithful nurse who wanted it to carry instruments. Her clock — an ordinary small "Big Ben" that she carried about with her to Dooraswami.

And now I must stop or miss the Post. With deep sympathy and a great appreciation of your Sister, congratulating you that the Phinney family gave two such valuable workers to the missionary cause as Frank and Harriet.

The September 1938 edition of *Burma News* carried the following obituary notices of Hattie's death.

MISS HARRIET PHINNEY 1861-1938

Harriet Phinney was born in Gerard, Pa., 18th April, 1861. The family later moving to Rochester, N.Y., she was baptized by Dr. Henry L. Morehouse on the 22nd of February 1874, joining the East Avenue Baptist Church of Rochester. She was appointed a missionary of the W.A.B.F.M.S. in September 1885, and sailed in November, arriving in Rangoon, January 26th, 1886. Her brother Frank D. Phinney had already been Superintendent of the Mission Press for several years and for the first few months she lived with him at Kemindine with Dr. Maria Douglass. Later she was appointed to work with Mr. and Mrs. Hascall at Henzada going with them to open a new Station in Sagaing, May 1887, where she remained a little over a year.

By this time Miss Phinney had acquired such an accurate knowledge of the Burmese language that it became necessary to call her to Rangoon to undertake proofreading for the new edition of the Burmese Bible, a task in which Dr. Eveleth was employed and had to lay down on account of ill health obliging his return to America. In the *News* of September, 1888, we find this chronicled:

"At a meeting of all the Rangoon missionaries September 3, called to consider this matter, after considerable discussion it was resolved that we approve of Mr. Eveleth's plan for his Bible work, that Dr. Jameson be asked to come to Rangoon for three months to take charge of the work and that Miss Phinney be asked to assist him and to take charge of the work at the end of that time."

In the December *News* of the same year Miss Phinney announced that she had been appointed to edit the *Burman*

Messenger and called for items of interest. She continued this during a period of some twenty-five years.

Miss Phinney's first furlough ran from March '91 to December '92 and during it she and Miss Ranney together interested two ladies of some means in the need for a Bible School for Women in Burma and the two ladies undertaking the support of these two missionaries, they were set for the work. Returning to Burma thus designated, they opened the Burman Woman's Bible School in Rangoon, May 1893, in which they continued until retirement in 1929.

After the second furlough 1902-03, the Bible school was removed to Insein on the invitation of Burman Christians who gave the land on which the necessary buildings were erected.

Miss Phinney's accurate knowledge of Burmese made her always a valuable proofreader and in addition to her other work she did a great deal of it, including that for the 1930 edition of Judson's Bible as well as a large part of the Burmese Concordance.

At her brother's request she wrote "Beautiful Burma," a hymn composed specially for the Judson Centennial of 1913 and also composed forty other hymns and songs which Miss Ranney had published under the title "Hymns of the Heavenly Way," and which is used in Woman's Societies. Many fine translations of old hymns in the Burmese Hymn Book much valued by the Burmans, are the product of her pen.

Miss Phinney wrote the Burmese notes on the International Sunday School Lessons, beginning in 1893 and continuing to the date of her decease. If my information is accurate the Sunday School paper for this month is the last of her work. She served on the Burman Manuscript Committee for more years than I can name and the Committee for Language Examination most of her missionary life. In her death on 28th August the mission has lost a talented member. Few know how much of the artist was in her make up, but visitors to their Kalaw home must have seen a good deal of beautiful hand-painted china, pictures, and knickknacks that are the product of her paint brush.

My personal acquaintance with Miss Phinney dates back to 1886 when I was sent to Rangoon for dentistry and stayed with Mrs. Eveleth at the old Mission House on the present site of the A.B.M. Press where Miss Phinney called to visit. I remember her saying that she was thirteen years old when I was born. In later years our paths seldom crossed and I felt that I did not really know her till the two ladies began coming to Taunggyi to spend the months of the Rainy Season, beginning in 1934, though our friendship grew rapidly when they retired to Kalaw and visiting there, we had many a happy meal at their house. The cords grew tighter when after Miss Ranney's death, we exchanged meals and I had my dinner and, taking my work with me, spent my evenings with her while she came up and ate breakfasts with me, staying as long afterwards as it pleased her to do. I have counted it a privilege that it fell to me to watch beside her during her last night on earth and to close her eyes on this world at early dawn on Sunday morning, and I am left with a deep sense of grief and personal loss that I had not known existed.

Others will write of her last illness and of the fitting services that marked her funeral in which the Burmese Christians showed their appreciation of her life.

Elizabeth M. Heptonstall

Miss Phinney passed gently from this world to the next on August 28, at half past four o'clock in the morning, after more than two and a half months of suffering from a very painful disease called "Shingles." Her bodily resistance was not equal to overcoming the condition.

The whole atmosphere of the funeral was uplifting as it was conducted in both Burmese and English and brought before us the outstanding features of her service in Burma, and our Church was well filled with those who wished to honor her memory. The women of the church supplied beautiful floral tributes and the choir sang tenderly, "Lead Me Gently Home." The weather conditions were so similar to those on the day of Miss Ranney's funeral that we followed the plan she approved then, and had the interment at the cemetery early next morning when the day was bright and a group of her closest friends met for the simple burial service led by Mr. Varney of Kalaw, whom she had asked to officiate, while she was in Kalaw during the hot season.

During the latter years of Miss Phinney's life, we of Taunggyi have had many opportunities to know her and her devoted colleague intimately. One year when they were my next door neighbors, Miss Ranney was spiritually depressed because of physical weakness and could hardly believe, some days, she was worthy to inherit the great promises of Christ Jesus. One morning when I made my first call earlier than usual, Miss Ranney said, "I'm so glad that you've come early, for I am faint hearted to-day. Hattie is so sure of every promise in Scripture, <u>always so sure,</u> that she finds it difficult to be patient with me when I am not equally sure. Do talk the matter over with me and help me to get back my confidence." That illustrates Miss Phinney's attitude of absolute dependence upon God's Word and of course Miss Ranney was just as firm in her faith, when she was her real self. I thought when that grand old hymn, "How Firm a Foundation" was sung so heartily by a large congregation at her funeral, how fittingly it expressed her confidence in God's Word.

Both Miss Phinney and Miss Ranney for years entertained the lively hope that like Simeon of old they might live to see the living presence of the Lord Christ on earth and follow him into the next life, without physical death. But neither expressed any bitterness of spirit because that desire was not granted.

Miss Phinney's habit of Bible study was a strong one. During her illness she often had her Bible and devotional books placed on her tray table, and putting on her glasses would try to read. When she found she could not, one of us would read aloud to her and help her grasp a thought to comfort her in her need of help to bear her affliction. What a blessing it would be if all who fear to trust God's promises, lest they merely become "wishful thinking" would take to heart Christ's assurances as Miss Phinney did! This wishful thinking has led to the doing of the greatest things in this world, cooperating with God, in faith.

With all her faith in God's love, the latter months of her life were lonely ones without her life companion, who knew so well how to adapt herself to Miss Phinney's deafness and found such loving ways to bring outside conversation and mutual friends into her daily life. Her literary work on the Sunday School lessons in Burmese she felt was the <u>one</u> thing left for her to do, and she often said, "I can't make that fill the day."

She greatly enjoyed writing the hymn book in Burmese, each hymn being based on some Scripture text and this will be a lasting memorial — an extra effort to use helpfully her knowledge of Scripture and the Burmese language. Hers was a helpful, capable service given to the Burma Mission and we can rejoice in its influence for good in all its out reaching through teaching in the Bible school and through religious literature and other avenues that reached the lives of the people in Burma.

Cora M. Henderson

Recently I have been reading a most interesting book. It is the history of our Burman Woman's Bible School from the time when it was only an idea in the minds of Miss Ranney and Miss Phinney, through the days of its beginning, and through the thirty-six years of which they wrote such careful reports, until the time of their retirement in 1929. So Miss Phinney has been much in my mind of late.

On Monday, August 29, we received a telegram telling of her home-going and bringing a request from the Burman Women of Taunggyi that we close the school for one day. We closed school on the next day, and held a memorial service here at one o'clock. We invited as many of the former pupils of the school as we could reach, and there were perhaps twenty who joined with us in the meeting. Daw Oh Za, Daw Hnin Ein, and Daw Bwint each spoke briefly of the inspiration she had received from Miss Ranney and Miss Phinney in her Bible school days.

It is difficult to speak of one of these ladies without mentioning the other also. They contributed much to the spreading of the Gospel in Burma, both in direct evangelistic effort, and in literary work. But the Bible school is their monument. As long as the Bible school lasts they will be remembered in Burma. And they will continue to inspire both the Burman women and the superintendents of the school.

The school had its ups and downs as all institutions have. But many times through their yearly reports I read, "This has been the best year yet." I feel sure that they are now saying, "This is the best year yet."

Beatrice A. Pond

Author's Epilogue

Even before I undertook the task of sorting, reading through, and transcribing the family letters, the spell of the "Burma connection" had led me to look into the possibility of visiting the country myself. For many years, however, foreigners' visits were limited by the Burmese government to a single day, and Burma was not included in the itinerary of tour groups. My plans had to be deferred for several years.

By 1986 restrictions were eased, and in January of that year — exactly 100 years from Hattie's first arrival in Rangoon — my husband and I were able to travel with a tour that included a seven-day visit to Burma. By then I had begun the transcription of the letters, but had not become thoroughly familiar with their details; I had only a general idea of the sites that had played an important role in Frank and Hattie's lives. Any opportunity for seeking out even these places was limited, however, by the carefully prescribed tour schedule.

It was impressed on us at the time that Burma was under military control and that we would need to follow the approved travel plan without attempting any independent excursions or deviations. This itinerary consisted of an overnight stay in Rangoon; a flight north to the Shan hills near Kalaw to spend one night in Taunggyi and visit the Inle Lakes region; another flight to Mandalay, with two nights spent in this capital of the last Burmese king; another flight to Pagan, the site of hundreds of temples and pagodas; and back to Rangoon for a visit to the Shwedagon Pagoda, the Reclining Buddha, and other approved sightseeing attractions.

Despite the restrictions, it was a highly rewarding visit and introduced us to a Burma not essentially different from the one Frank and Hattie knew a century before. We were able to drop in on a pwe, a ceremony held by a farmer to celebrate his good fortune (and to propitiate the nats responsible for good or poor fortunes); to travel on the Irrawaddy River in a boat similar to those in which Hattie and Ruth traveled on their trips upriver; and to attend a major festival to which hundreds of native families traveled from miles around in oxcarts like those in which Hattie and Ruth had jolted through the jungle. The dusty streets of the villages, the mat and teak houses, the broad streets of Rangoon, the open markets, were not very different from the pictures and descriptions of life in Burma sent by Frank and Hattie to the family at home in Rochester.

It was a fascinating and frustrating experience; fascinating in bringing to life the exotic land I had dreamed of visiting so long; frustrating in the little opportunity it provided to look for the places that were most closely associated with Frank and Hattie.

In October 1987, my husband and I arranged to visit Burma for another seven-day stay. By that time, I had read all the Burma letters, and was familiar with many more of the places and activities that had made up Hattie's world. I also had contacted the American Baptist Mission headquarters in Valley Forge, Pennsylvania, and had been given the name and address of the head of the Baptist Convention in Rangoon. This time we arranged for an independent tour to spend the seven days entirely in Rangoon, being assigned a tour guide and driver from Tourist Burma, the state-controlled tourist agency.

We were fortunate in our guide, not only because she was charming, articulate, and knowledgeable, but also because, as she herself pointed out, she was a Christian, and supportive of my interest in visiting Baptist, rather than Buddhist, religious sites. She was a tremendous help in locating people and places relevant to our visit and explaining its purpose.

Another striking (and appreciated) feature of this trip was the fact that once we made contact with the officials within the Baptist community, an itinerary was mapped out for us based on what was known of Hattie and Ruth's connections. It was not necessary for me to spell out the people or places that I would like to visit, or which had significance for me: our Baptist hosts made the arrangements and called together the people whom they felt were relevant.

By the end of our stay, we had been able to visit the building that had housed the old Baptist College where Hattie had taught for Mrs. Packer when she first arrived in Burma; the Kemindine

School where Hattie and Frank lived at that time; the site of the first building built for the Bible school in Insein; the present Woman's Bible School, now part of the Myanmar (Burmese) Institute of Theology in Insein. We attended church services in Burmese at the Kemindine Church and in English at Immanuel Baptist Church, and visited the Lanmadaw Church, which Hattie and Ruth attended when in Rangoon, and where Po Min became the minister in his later years.

We were invited to meet with members of the Burman Baptist Woman's Missionary Society, which Hattie and Ruth had initiated so long ago, and where they were remembered as its founders. I was presented with a copy of a book (in Burmese) commemorating the Society, which contains pictures of Hattie and Ruth, as well as U Pan Di and Daw Oo, their benefactors. One of the members present at the meeting, now 88 years old, had been a pupil at the Bible school under Hattie and Ruth; she had a copy of the photograph of Hattie and Ruth in their Kalaw garden, and we discussed the family likeness.

The meeting was held in Ahlone, in what may have been the Russell Place house; the house next door was identified as the Bennett House. There we were introduced to a very old and bedridden woman who had helped run the Bible school after Hattie and Ruth retired. When we attended the English Church, I was approached by a middle-aged woman who identified herself as someone whom Hattie and Ruth had befriended when she was a young girl, and she spoke enthusiastically of their garden at Kalaw and their kindness to her. It was clear that word had spread quickly through the community as to our identity.

In both churches we attended there were no other Westerners present. Missionaries had been expelled from Burma by the government many years earlier; the continuation of the Baptist work was entirely a matter of the native church members (with support from the American Baptists). All of the people we met were native Burmese.

At his invitation, we dined at the home of the director of the Myanmar Institute of Theology, U Tha Din, and I was presented with a xeroxed copy of the *History of the Burman Woman's Bible School*, in Hattie's handwriting, as well as a copy of a picture of Wahklu Lodge, the first site of the Bible school.

There could be no doubt that Hattie and Ruth were remembered, and that their work was still a part of the Baptist community. We were shown a copy of a Burmese Baptist Hymn Book that contained hymns attributed to Hattie. Mention was also made of the trust fund that Hattie had set up in her will, and we were told that they are still receiving funds from it.

It was harder to find remembrances of Frank's role in Rangoon. The Baptists still own the Mission Press building, we were told, but they no longer maintain a press. The Japanese during their occupation of Rangoon (1942-1945) removed all the press machinery, and it has not been replaced. The Baptists receive rent moneys from the building, but that is all.

In 1996, my husband and I made our third trip to Burma. The ten years since our first visit had brought about many visible signs of change in the handling of the foreign visitor to the country. Tourists now were guided through the customs process with signs and courteous airport personnel. Downtown Rangoon sported freshly painted buildings, new construction was under way all around, and several modern hotels were available. The old Strand Hotel, a Victorian relic of the British Raj, was in the process of being modernized to world-class standards. A trip to Shwedagon Pagoda revealed a waiting room for tourists with a special place to wash one's pagoda-soiled feet.

Our itinerary this time was a six-day boat trip on the Irrawaddy River, the famous "Road to Mandalay," that had played such an important role in Hattie's early years in Burma. A shallow-bottomed river boat from Germany had been imported to provide luxury cruise accommodations for the tour — a far cry from the river steamers that Hattie and Ruth traveled in. The river traffic, however, was much the same: teak logs tied together into mammoth rafts, piloted by a family living in a canvas tent on the logs; river steamers crowded with people traveling to other villages; fishing boats, their nets spreading out behind them; and small boys in dugouts paddling out from shore. Recognizable, also, were the high river banks, raw mud and sand, which matched Hattie's descriptions of disembarking by narrow plank from river boats at low tide.

The surrounding countryside, too, was unchanged from those earlier days. Men drove their oxcarts down to the river's edge, scooping up the muddy, brown water to fill their water tanks. Our boat, shallow bottomed as it was and equipped with the latest in depth sounding devices, ran aground on a sand bar and had to be dislodged by a river police team. The only evidence of the tourist makeover was in Pagan, where the crumbling stupas and pagodas of our previous visit were being painted and restored as historic treasures. Overall, however, life for the Burmese people seemed little changed.

Looking back, I realize how well these trips, especially in combination, offered a real glimpse into Hattie's Burma. The first "official" itinerary incorporated the major geographic regions that figured prominently in her life: Rangoon, where she lived and worked so many years; Kalaw and Taunggyi, where she and Ruth spent their retirement and where both are buried; and Mandalay and Pagan in Upper Burma, the region where Hattie lived and worked with the Hascalls.

Our second visit, centered around the Baptist community in Rangoon, attested to the enduring value of Hattie and Ruth's career-long efforts to work with and educate Burmese women in their own language. Long after the expulsion of westerners, the organizations and institutions on whose behalf Hattie, Ruth, and their colleagues labored so tirelessly, are thriving and carrying on the work.

Finally, our days on the Irrawaddy provided a window into a world both antique and modern, inescapably attuned to seasonal climate, the rise and fall of the river, the monsoon and dry seasons. Life here on the river, especially, must be today very much as Hattie experienced it.

About the Author

Joan W. Swift was born in New York City, where she grew up. She attended Swarthmore College and received a doctorate in psychology from the University of Iowa. She worked as a research psychologist for many years and later as a community college administrator. She and her husband Hewson, Professor Emeritus of Cell Biology at the University of Chicago, live in Chicago and have two daughters.

About the Editor

Barbara Swift Brauer began her career in book publishing in 1975. In 1984, she and her husband Laurence founded Wordsworth, a small business providing writing, editing, and pre-press production. They live in San Geronimo, California, and have one son.

Printed in the United States
1138800001B/358-396